CLASS, CONFLICT AND PROTEST IN THE ENGLISH COUNTRYSIDE, 1700–1880

Class, Conflict and Protest in the English Countryside, 1700–1880

Edited by

Mick Reed and Roger Wells

FRANK CASS

First published in 1990 in Great Britain by
FRANK CASS AND COMPANY LIMITED
Gainsborough House, 11 Gainsborough Road,
London E11 1RS

and in the United States of America by
FRANK CASS
Rowman & Littlefield Publishers, Inc.,
8705 Bollman Place,
Savage, MD 20763

British Library Cataloguing in Publication Data

Class, conflict and protest in the English countryside,
1700–1800.
1. England. Rural regions. Social conflict, history
I. Reed, Mick *1942 May 15–*   II. Wells, Roger A.E. (Roger
Anthony Edward *1947–*
303.6'0942

ISBN 0-7146-3343-7

Library of Congress Cataloging-in-Publication Data

Class, conflict, and protest in the English countryside, 1700–1880 /
edited by Mick Reed and Roger Wells.
    p.   cm.
    ISBN 0-7146-3343-7
    1. England—Social conditions—18th century. 2. England—Social
conditions—19th century. 3. England—Rural conditions. 4. Social
conflict—England—History—18th century. 5. Social conflict—
England—History—19th century. I. Reed, Mick, 1942–
II. Wells, Roger A.E.
HN398.E5C55   1990
306'.0942'09033—dc20   89–70799
                                                              CIP

Printed in Great Britain by
Antony Rowe Ltd, Chippenham

Contents

Editors' Note:

The problem of cross-referencing the original references in each article to the pages in the present volume has been met by leaving each original reference as it is but to add to it after a stroke (solidus), the relevant page number(s) in this volume, hence: [*Wells*, 1979: 201] might become [*Wells*, 1979: 201/110] where 110 is the page number in this volume.

The first and final two articles in this volume are published here for the first time. The remaining contributions have previously appeared in *The Journal of Peasant Studies* as follows:

Article 2 appeared in Vol. 6, No. 2 (1979)
Article 3 appeared in Vol. 8, No. 1 (1980)
Article 4 appeared in Vol. 8, No. 4 (1981)
Article 5 appeared in Vol. 9, No. 4 (1982)
Article 6 appeared in Vol. 10, No. 4 (1983)
Article 7 appeared in Vol. 12, No. 1 (1984)
Article 8 appeared in Vol. 15, No. 3 (1988)

Acknowledgements

In all historical research and writing, there will be many to whom authors are indebted, most of whom are never named, or sometimes not even remembered. In our case we must, however, single out two people. First, no researcher on the left who works on English history since the seventeenth century, can fail to be indebted to the work of E.P. Thompson. Secondly and in our case much more directly, the editor of *The Journal of Peasant Studies*, Terry Byres, not only encouraged us independently to address the 'Peasants' seminar convened by him at the Institute of Commonwealth Studies, University of London, but subsequently convinced us that our findings would interest readers of the journal.

Those who picked up the cudgels and developed the debate through their own contributions – namely, John Archer, Andrew Charlesworth, Dennis Mills and Brian Short – must be thanked for granting permission for their essays to be reproduced in this volume. Each also gave advice on where they felt the debate had led, and thus influenced us in constructting the essays we wrote expressly for this book.

Both editors and the other contributors to the debate are indebted to Terry Byres and his co-editor of the journal – Charles Curwen, and later Henry Bernstein – for having given space to us to explore our ideas in what were often clearly provisional findings.

Roger Wells wishes to extend grateful thanks to Malcolm Chase, John Rule as well as Professors Gwyn Williams and George Rudé for extended and invariably rewarding discussions on many of the topics embraced in this volume. Mick Reed would like to acknowledge the influence of Ian Carter's work upon much of his approach to the problems of rural history.

Mick Reed and Roger Wells

Class and Conflict in Rural England: Some Reflections on a Debate

Mick Reed

Rural history in England is not in good health. This is especially true of the history written about the period covered by this volume. For too long the most prominent historians of the English countryside have been obsessed with 'ploughs and cows'. Rural history has been synonymous with agricultural history. The case against 'agricultural history' and especially against its present profoundly ossified state as exemplified by the *Agricultural History Review,* has been put extremely fluently by Keith Snell [personal communication] who rails against

> Its narrowly defined conception of the subject, and its reluctance to make any progress into topics which ... ought to be central to a properly considered definition of our discipline and academic concerns. 'Agricultural history' has been so narrowly conceived for such a long time that it is almost hard to imagine that it could be otherwise. We believe that there is now widespread disillusion within the relevant scholarly community with the general unimaginative and reactionary tone of 'plough and cow' agricultural history, and with the ways in which so-called 'established views are perpetuated in an increasingly pedestrian style, which often lacks the support of fresh research and more original thinking.

Economic agricultural history is of course a vital part of any study of rural England. The problem is precisely as Snell points out, that there is virtually no original thinking. All too often, hackneyed neo-classical concepts are applied to the study of many very different societies without any questioning as to whether the concepts have any applicability to those societies. Indeed the fact that these concepts are actually neo-classical is so seldom hinted at that one suspects such authors are unaware that they are actually using theoretical concepts at all. So much of the work within the discipline is – superficially at least – based on a naive empiricism. One could be almost excused, whilst reading many works on agricultural history, for failing to realise that agriculture is not simply something that happens autonomously, or at the simple behest of a wealthy farmer or landowner, but is in fact a product of political economy – by which I mean of people in production relationships, of authority and subordination, indeed in relations of class.

Of course not all rural history is of this traditional kind. There are numerous social historians working within the subject area, as well as historical geographers and scholars from other disciplines. For many of these however, the 'orthodoxy' has been already created from within the barren premises of 'agricultural history'. After all, the standard textbook on rural England in the eighteenth and nineteenth centuries is still *The Agricultural Revolution* by Chambers and Mingay [1966]. Despite its strengths – and there are many – this book encapsulates much of the failure of 'agricultural history' to engage with the crucial issues of rural history. A broader brush has been applied to the canvas by Pamela Horn in a series of books [1980; 1984; 1987] that already feature heavily on undergraduate reading lists for the period. Horn though is of this same school. Her work is detailed and copiously researched, yet it tells us little about the life and motivations of rural people. The categories she addresses are unimpeachably orthodox, and without an iota of real analytical value. Her work remains entrenched within Snell's 'unimaginative and reactionary' category and the views it presents are firmly those of the 'establishment'. Regretfully, a new book on the farm worker by Alan Armstrong [1988] remains 'old fashioned in approach' [*Reay*: 1988] and fails in any significant way to advance our understanding of the rural world.

It is of course easy to criticise and it remains the case that, apart from the Hammond's superb work, *The Village Labourer*, first published in 1911, the only overviews of rural English history during the period have been written by representatives of the 'establishment'. No major synthesis has yet been produced by those who are so critical of the 'orthodoxy'. To an extent this is no doubt because the lacunae in research carried out to date are so great that simple re-interpretation of existing work is likely to be quite inadequate for the task. A massive amount of original research at local, regional and national level is needed before the obvious shortcomings of agricultural history and its derivatives can be fully exposed. That these shortcomings are real and significant is evident from the recent work of a number historians who have begun to move away from the old sterotypes thereby providing a glimpse of other possibilities [e.g. *Snell*, 1985; *Howkins*, 1985; *Bushaway*, 1982; *Samuel*, 1975; *Searle*, 1983; *Winter*, 1984; 1985].

It was as part of this move towards reinterpretation that Roger Wells made a contribution to an unfamiliar journal for historians of rural England. This appeared in *The Journal of Peasant Studies* in 1979, and gave rise to a wide-ranging and prolonged debate in the pages of that journal over several years. The various contributions form the major part of this book and demonstrate some of the shortcomings as well as the possibilities facing rural historians. Perhaps one of the most fruitful aspects of the debate is that, as John Archer commented in his contribution [1982: 282/87], it 'has underlined our ignorance'. Our nescience about life in the English countryside during the eighteenth and nineteenth centuries became increasingly apparent to several contributors during the course of debate. In the penultimate piece in this volume, Wells highlights some of the hiatuses in our knowledge as they appear to him. In so doing he has clearly been influenced by other contributors to the debate and several of the gaps identified by them are expressly addressed by Wells in his essay.

Thus the debate contributed to the learning process of at least some of the contributors, and it is this that perhaps best justifies the separate publication of the articles within a single volume. I first came across Wells' original contribution soon after finishing my undergraduate career, and I followed subsequent interventions with fascination as I crystallised my interests and developed a post-graduate research programme. Finally, I made my own intervention as the often ragged pieces by various historians, stimulated my thought processes. It was the fact that the pieces were often so ragged that was their strength. Here were scholars of experience engaging in polemic that opened up possibilities rather than closing them down. So much academic work has been characterised by a desire to tie up loose ends and by attempts to produce the 'definitive' text on a topic. By such methods has the orthodoxy retained its position of eminence for so long. In this debate though, punches were not pulled. The flavour of the discussion at some of the best research seminars comes through in a way that is seldom encountered in the British rural history journals. Deference and feigned politeness were thrown where they belong – to one side – and a vibrancy that should be part of all historical learning came to the fore. Whatever the shortcomings of each contribution, the interested student could hardly fail to be excited at the avenues suggested for further research. Perhaps it is as a teaching aid, and a catalyst for future researchers, that the debate's greatest strengths lie.

The ignorance about the rural past that the debate revealed, is of two kinds. One is empirical. There is so much about which we know so little. Wells addresses many of these empirical lacunae in Chapter 9 in this volume and readers may well identify more. The other massive shortcoming of both the debate and of rural history in general is theoretical. The failure of most historians of rural England to develop clear concepts and models firmly located within a body of theory, is perhaps the most significant deficency of rural history. The development of suitable concepts can occur only through the inter-relationship of empirical research and a recognition of the underlying premises that inform historians' practice. The remainder of this essay is devoted to a preliminary exploration of some of the necessary conceptual developments which should be a prominent part of rural history.

Roger Wells' interest at the start of the debate, was with the development of characteristic forms of protest by the rural proletariat during the eighteenth and early-nineteenth centuries. This concern dominated subsequent contributions by Andrew Charlesworth, John Archer, and indeed by Wells himself. Charlesworth introduced [1980: 102/55] an additional dimension of differential development in 'open' and 'close' parishes, which although not explicitly stated, introduced a relational element into the discussion. The proletariat was best understood within the context of variable relationships with capital. Within the 'close' parish, labour confronted capital directly and face-to-face, yet owing to the personal nature of this relationship and the power of capital within the 'close' parish, labour was apparently reduced to an acquiescent role with little opportunity to 'make its own history'. Conversely, the 'open' parish was characterised by a social structure with no dominant individual capitalist presence. Capital was fragmented between many landowners and farmers on the one hand, and labour on the other. Crucially there were likely to be substantial numbers of small farmers and tradespeople who could not be fitted easily into the capital/labour schema. In this situation, capital was unable to exercise the oppressive control over labour characteristic of the 'close' parish. Despite Wells' objections to Charlesworth's arguments, the case was developed by Dennis Mills and Brian Short [1983] and later countered in my own contribution [*Reed*, 1984a], with a final riposte by Mills [1988]. The important point to be made at the moment, is that the debate moved inexorably, from the relative narrowness of Wells' original interest in the proletariat and protest, to a discussion of how best to conceptualise rural society as a whole, and the role of conflict and protest within it. Implicit at first, the debate moved towards a discussion of class within rural society.

Orthodox views of the class structure of the English countryside have been criticised elsewhere [*Reed*, 1984b; 1986] but it is necessary to summarise that argument here. Most historians have argued that by the end of the eighteenth century, England was 'a country of mainly large landlords, cultivated by tenant farmers, working the land with hired labourers' [*Hobsbawm*, 1969: 98]. This triadic structure has been reiterated by Pamela Horn [1984: 10] and many others. The corollary of this was that there was, for practical purposes, no peasantry in England by 1800 [*Wells*, 1979: 115; *Chivers*, 1983: 33; *Crossick*, 1984: 62; *Hobsbawm and Rudé*, 1973: 3]. It is true that the *term* 'peasant' has been used by a few historians of the period, and it was of course used by contemporaries. The latter saw the 'peasantry' as synonymous with the agricultural workforce, or sometimes more generally with the 'poor'. It was in other words roughly identical with the proletariat in Wells' original article. This identification with the rural proletariat, and the often pejorative usage of the word 'peasant' in English, does raise difficulties for academics who may wish to use the word to describe individuals or groups within the English countryside, assuming that groups existed, or exist, to which the term could be plausibly applied. These problems led John Beckett [1984: 113–23] to suggest that to use the term to describe people other than the rural proletariat in post-medieval England is to use it unhistorically. Nevertheless, historians have used the term to describe non-proletarians though there has been little agreement as to definition, and usage has been descriptive rather than analytical. Joan Thirsk [1975: 5, 7] believed that a looseness of usage was necessary in English conditions, and she argued that a peasant was 'an occupier of land for agricultural purposes who does not claim the title of Gentleman, or rank as landlord .... A peasant economy involves all classes of land cultivators, except gentry/landlords'.

Generally though, historians have defined 'peasant' holdings by unit size, usually as those smaller than 100 acres [*Hoskins*, 1957: 215; *Thompson*, 1976: 312; *Hill*, 1942: 93]. Dennis Mills, one of the very few historians to use the term specifically in the context of the nineteenth century, included in his 'peasantry' 'all kinds of small entrepreneurs, tradesmen, craftsmen and perhaps small factory owners' [*Mills*, 1974: 201]. In an earlier article [*Reed*, 1984b], I used the terms to identify virtually the same groups as Mills, although the conceptual bases of our definitions were far apart, a point I will return to.

Nevertheless, whatever our differences, both Mills and myself have identified the existence of a very large group within the nineteenth-century countryside which cannot be subsumed in a straightforward way – if at all – into the conventional triadic class structure of historiographical orthodoxy. In a series of essays, Mills has elucidated his argument for the existence of a peasantry in many parts of England [*Mills*, 1974; 1980; 1984; *Mills and Short*, 1983], while my own presentation of a similar case is contained in two articles [*Reed*, 1984b: 54–59; 1986: 80–88]. Of course, we were not alone in being aware of the existence of such people. B.A. Holderness [1981: 228] has observed that 'the small family farmer [and] the ability of his kind to survive both the mania for amalgamation and improvement and the new regime of "low farming" after 1875 was demonstrated repeatedly during the century'. Similarly Chambers and Mingay [1966: 88–96, 133, 172–4] argued that 'in nineteenth-century England small farms and small holdings remained everywhere a common feature of the agrarian structure' and that even in the arable districts 'there were numerous small farms and even many small holdings' [1966: 133]. Such views were often acknowledged [*Mingay*, 1963: 96, 184; *Horn*: 1982: 5; *Howkins*: 1985: 4–5], but seldom afforded any significance. In contrast, both Mills and myself attempted to elevate the existence of 'peasant' groups to the centre of the historical stage, along with capital and labour.

Beyond this however, we differ greatly in the underlying premises of our arguments. In presenting my case, I found myself at greatest odds with those historians with whom I have the most ideological sympathy, arguing [*Reed*, 1986: 91] that 'it is amongst Marxists and other left-wing historians ... that [the] neglect [of 'peasant' production] is probably most pronounced and least excusable'. Marxists had been among the most vigorous critics of the highlighting of small, family based production by Chambers and Mingay, and Marxists had most neglected family farmers [*Thompson*, 1967: 118; *Saville*: 1969: 258; *Hobsbawm*, 1969: 258; *Hobsbawm and Rudé*, 1973: 3–4; *Obelkevitch*, 1976: 47,49]. I now realise that the implications of my findings – and indeed those of Mills – is that a reassessment of that central problematic of Marxist political economy – *the agrarian question* – is long overdue within the one context in which it has been considered to have been satisfactorily resolved – the context of rural England. Regional studies of Cumbria by Charles Searle [1983], and of the west country by Michael Winter [1984; 1986] confirmed my view of the need for this, as did implicitly the work of Ian Carter [1979] on northeast Scotland.

The agrarian question is concerned with 'the complex and varied means whereby capitalism became the dominant mode of production in agriculture' [*Byres*, 1977: 258]. The history of Marxist concern with the agrarian question is itself fascinating and has recently been summarised by Terry Byres [1986: 6–19]. A key aspect of this problematic is that of the 'agrarian transition', or as Byres puts it 'those changes in the countryside necessary to the overall development of capitalism ... and to the ultimate dominance of ... [this] mode of production in a particular national social formation [*Byres*, 1986: 4]. A successful agrarian transformation is one in which capitalism does indeed become the dominant mode of production, though it need not necessarily be on the basis of a class polarisation between capital and labour.

The case for a polarisation of the classes between capital and labour is central to much of the orthodoxy regarding the agrarian transition. A central feature of the transition has generally reckoned to have been enclosure. From Marx [1973: 877–95] to the Hammonds [1911: 43–96], enclosure was seen as a device for the expropriation of the English peasantry, and their transformation into proletarians. Those apologists for agrarian capitalism, Chambers and Mingay [1966: *passim*] managed to establish, to their own satisfaction at least, a more benign version of events, in which, as Edward Thompson pointed out [1967: 118], 'they manage to have it both ways: to present English agriculture as a successful capitalist growth industry, while at the same time suggesting that this was accomplished with minimal deleterious social consequences upon the status of labour or of small farmers'. Recently, the profound and deleterious effects upon labour have been convincingly demonstrated by Keith Snell [1985: 138–227], but the effects upon 'small farmers' is less clear. As Wells discusses in the final essay of this volume [1988:] relatively little parliamentary enclosure occurred in the South-east, though where it did there was widespread if apparently low-key resistance. There needs to be a huge amount of research before we can ascertain fairly precisely the effects of enclosure upon household producers. A recent article suggests substantial reductions in the numbers of these producers in the Feldon of Warwickshire as a result of enclosure, and the author argues 'that village traders and craftsmen formed a major source of recruitment for the rural proletariat of the nineteenth century' [*Martin*, 1984: 180]. What he *does not* claim is that enclosure led to the *extinction* of these producers. Martin is convincing about changes in the nature of craft activity between 1750 and 1850 [1984: 180–181], but is less so when he argues for an overall reduction in numbers [1984: 187]. To be sure, the small producers in his study declined in relative terms, but his claim for absolute decline derived from a comparison of the 1851 census returns with estimates for earlier periods is possibly flawed. Since he has no accurate figures for earlier populations, his estimated percentages are no guidance to the actual numbers of producers in any parish. Moreover, the census returns seldom give evidence of dual occupations, so that for example, an individual returned as a small 'farmer', or even 'labourer' might have been involved in trade or craft [*Reed*, 1982: 41–2; 1984b: 57]. Neither is Martin's demonstration of loss of land ownership rights and of selling up as a result of enclosure, conclusive either in a specific or more general sense. I have shown elsewhere [*Reed*, 1982: 33–42] that access to the land was achieved in many ways: through ownership, tenancy, sub-tenancy, and so on. Many former owners simply continued their activities as tenants. Moreover, recent work has suggested that, in some areas at least, enclosure provided opportunities for household producers to develop additional strategies to cope with pressures from capital and from the market [*Searle*, 1987]. We should examine more closely this hypothesis.

Clearly though there were enormous local and regional variations in the degree of changes in class structure. Moreover the trajectory of change was similar in principle in parishes affected by parliamentary enclosure, and those enclosed very much earlier. Nevertheless it seems reasonable to suggest that an absolute reduction in the numbers of household producers in most areas is an unlikely hypothesis [*Reed*, 1986]. What we need to know is how household production *changed* as a result of these trends, not how it was extinguished. Indeed, an argument for a considerable augmentation in the numbers of 'small masters' or household producers is posited by E. A. Wrigley [1986: 202–3]. The old certainties are dissolving, but there is much to do before they can be finally dispatched.

Despite these complexities however, by 1800 it is quite certain that there had been a successful agrarian transformation in England. Capital was dominant both in agriculture and in industry. This transition had been the one studied by Marx in *Capital* and following his work, Marxist historians have concluded that English agriculture was characterised by the familiar 'triple division into landlords, tenant-farmers and hired labourers' [*Hobsbawm and Rudé*, 1973: 6]. But this division masked as much as it revealed, since it virtually required historians to either ignore the existance of a 'peasantry', or to deny its significance. The work of Mills, Searle, Winter and myself suggests strongly that, however the agrarian question was resolved in England, it was not by the elimination of the 'peasantry'.

The extensive and vigorous existence throughout the eighteenth and nineteenth centuries of groups of people who *might* be considered as a 'peasantry' now needs no further demonstration. What is needed is research into how these groups created and reproduced themselves within the massive changes constituting the English agrarian transition. This is a large-scale and long-term project and is incapable of resolution on the basis of current knowledge. More immediately perhaps, we need to be able to assess the economic, social, cultural and political significance of these groups in the period that is covered by this book. A first step might be to construct a model or models that can incorporate something of the real complexity of class structures in the countryside. Even this is a significant undertaking, and is only at a preliminary stage.

Despite the adherence of most historians – Marxist and non-Marxist to the familiar triadic structure of landlords, tenant-farmers, and hired labourers, this schema does not in itself constitute a class model. Within our period, it includes landlords and workers, but only those farmers who relied on hired labour, and who, by extension, extracted surplus value from that labour force. We are talking here about two fractions of capital, each with specific material interests, but with basically common interests in relation to labour [*Poulantzas*, 1978: 92]. The triadic structure is really a dual but complex structure of capital and labour. The debate started by Wells remained firmly anchored, albeit implicitly, to this model. The proletariat referred to by Wells and Charlesworth was just that. A landless class with nothing to sell but their labour power. Indeed Wells, with some hyperbole suggested that the agricultural workers and their families comprised 'the only real Marxian proletariat that England ever had' [1979: 115/29]. At the start of debate, there was little sense of any fundamental problematic relating to protest and conflict. Workers it was argued protested, overtly or covertly, against the predations of agrarian capital, which in its turn, sought vigorously to force labour into the new working practices, and new forms of social behaviour necessary for maximisation of returns on capital. Charlesworth [1980: 104–5/57–8] it is true, was aware that interests between the two capitalist fractions were not always identical, and that labour might on occasion appeal over the heads of their employers, directly to the landowning bourgeoisie.[1] However, we have moved on, and are now aware of new complexities, though I will argue below that these complexities have sometimes been forced into the Procrustean bed of the old orthodoxy.

So far as the debate was concerned, the first introduction of this new and necessary complication, came from Mills and Short [1983: 254/91] who somewhat hesitantly, introduced the 'peasantry' into the equation. Their lack of confidence is suggested by their desire 'to give it a more neutral label, that body of small rural entrepreneurs, which included agriculturalists, non-agriculturalists and dual occupationists'. Given the later cautions of John Beckett, perhaps their hesitation was justified. The use of the term 'peasant' is problematic in the English context, partly due to its historical usage, and partly due to the unfamiliarity of English historians working on the period with the debates over definition that have occurred primarily amongst scholars working on contemporary poor countries [e.g. *Littlejohn*, 1977; *Durrenberger*, 1982; *Ennew, Hirst and Tribe*, 1977; *Shanin*, 1979; *Friedmann*, 1980; *Bernstein*, 1979; *Leeds*, 1977; *Franklin*, 1965; *Mintz*, 1973]. It is for these reasons that I have moved away from my earlier reliance on the term [*Reed*, 1984b: 69–71], preferring now the term 'household producer'. Nevertheless, names are merely labels unless they have specific conceptual content. 'Peasant' and 'household producer' are not class terms and have no analytical value on their own.

Dennis Mills and myself have used the term 'peasant' to identify a broadly similiar group of people with a substantial and significant presence in the rural English social formation until the Great War. Despite my subsequent adoption of a different term, we continue to refer to the same kinds of people. Since Mills is not a Marxist historian, it is inappropriate to criticise his failure to identify his 'peasantry' in Marxist class terms. However, since he has vigorously defended his use of the term against my earlier criticisms [*Mills*, 1988: 395–7] – and indeed against criticisms that I have not even made – it may be useful to discuss the matter further, and such discussion is necessary in any event if household producers are to be located within a class model of rural England. The point of my earlier comments [*Reed*, 1984b: 70; 1986: 79] was to reveal the central characteristic of Mills' 'peasantry' and contrast that with the central characteristic of my own definition.

Mills most recent definition of a 'peasant' is as follows:

> A peasant is regarded as any self-employed man below the rank of the large tenant farmers and the yeomen .... Unlike the labourer, he did not rely entirely on wages and, unlike the higher groups, he did not rely mainly on directing the work of others. His living was obtained by virtue of a combination of a modest amount of capital with family labour and, in some instances, hired help. The typical ... peasant was a dual-occupationist ... [*Mills*, 1984: 481].

As it stands, this is as good a *description* of a nineteenth-century household producer as any, although the presumption that all 'peasants' were male needs sustaining. However, Mills has an additional dimension to his definition. His 'peasants' are also 'rural entrepreneurs' [*Mills*, 1974: 201; 1984: 481; *Mills and Short*, 1983: 254/91] Indeed, Mills went further in insisting 'that the most important point is not the use of the term "peasant", but the distinction between the large entrepreneurs who were part of the estate system, and the small ones who stood outside it within an independent socio-economic system' [*Mills*, 1980: 43]. It was this that led me to suggest that the central feature of Mills' peasantry, was one of scale. His entrepreneurs were, ultimately, distinguished from other entrepreneurs, only by the scale of their enterprise. I argued that this position was analytically the same as that whereby 'peasants' were defined by the size of their holdings. 'The *scale* of the undertaking rather than the way it is organised and worked – the social relations of the unit of production – [is] the key definitional characteristic' [*Reed*, 1986: 79]. From this I deduced that reliance upon family labour was one of several features of secondary importance to Mills. For me on the other hand, reliance upon family labour was central for the reasons I discuss below.

Mills goes on to describe household producers as 'capitalist in the

sense that the bulk of their production ... was destined for the market'
[*Mills*, 1988: 397]. This, along with Mills' other points just described,
demonstrates what I consider to be an inadequacy of his formulation and
indeed of that of Roger Wells, who adheres to a similar model [*Wells*,
forthcoming]. I will return to the question of entrepreneurial activity
and market orientation, but for the moment will discuss the alleged
capitalist nature of household producers. Within Marxist analyses,
producers that do not hire labour, or who do not appropriate surplus
value from hired labour are not capitalist, regardless of the destination
of the product. Household producers are qualitatively different kinds
of producer to capitalist producers appropriating surplus value from
a hired labour force. They constitute a different class – or conceivably
classes. Precisely what kind of producer they are, and what class position
they hold is a matter of debate within Marxism, and of course must
depend upon the precise nature of their productive relationships, and
the destination of their product [see for example: *Friedmann*, 1978a;
1978b; 1980; 1981; *Chevalier*, 1982; 1983; *Smith*, 1983, 1984a; 1984b;
1984c; *Cook*, 1984a; 1984b; 1984c; *Gibbon and Neocosmos*, 1985; *Scott*,
1986; *Llambi*, 1988]. For the moment it is sufficent to stress that they
were not capitalist, and Mills [and Wells] confuses matters by insisting
that they were. On the other hand, neither were they proletarian since
they did not rely on selling their labour power, or at least not entirely
nor predominantly [*Reed*, 1986: 92]. Unlike capitalist producers, who
sought to obtain a return on capital invested, household producers
primary concern was to obtain a living and to maintain the household
autonomy and equilibrium. For the former, hired labour was an integral
element in the pursuit of profit; for the latter, resort to hired labour
was merely a transient element, in the maintenance of the household's
viability as a production and consumption unit. Of course many households would seek to maximise income to better their standard of living, but
'whether they attain simple reproduction or extended reproduction (leading to capital accumulation) is contingent on their different forms of
insertion within capitalist commodity circuits at any given time' [*Llambi*,
1988: 354].

Although we can now see the general distinctiveness of these groups in
class terms, it may be worthwhile taking a short diversion to construct an
outline for more precise delineation of the characteristics of these kinds of
producer. For the purposes of class analysis, the type of production
undertaken by a particular individual probably matters little, although
this would be of great importance for all other purposes. Household producers were it is very clear, extremely heterogeneous, and it is necessary
to subdivide the category so as to bring the concept closer to reality. The
schema developed by Lenin [1966: 153f] still has great value in this regard.
He divided the peasantry into four categories: semi-proletarians, small or
poor peasants, middle peasants and rich peasants. While within the
English context it might be preferable to change the label, the basic

strategy holds good, and individuals that fall into one or other category are frequently recognised by the researcher. An adaptation of Lenin's categories follows:

> Semi-proletarians engaged in very small-scale agricultural and/or craft/trade production, which provided only part of the household's necessary income. The remainder was earned by wage-labour in capitalist agricultural or non-agricultural enterprises.
>
> Small household producers were agricultural and/or craft/trade producers who neither hired out their labour, nor hired in labour.
>
> Middle household producers engaged in agricultural and/or trade/craft production which was sufficent to provide as a rule, a meagre living and on occasion a surplus that might be converted into capital. Labour might also be hired in accordance with the family life-cycle and at seasonal or other peaks.
>
> Rich peasants for Lenin were capitalist entrepreneurs who as a rule employ several hired labourers, and are connected to the peasantry only by their similar cultural level, habits of life, and by the fact that they also were heavily engaged in manual labour on their own farms.

A model on these lines was used to great effect by Ian Carter in his study of north-east Scotland [*Carter*, 1979], and has equal relevance in the English context. Of course, the allocation of individuals to these categories from the historical record will not be straightforward and will be have to be based on specific local and regional research. Nevertheless, the rewards are likely to be great so long as an awareness of the conceptual and methodological difficulties exists. Fortunately much work has been done on non-English contexts, that will provide limitless inspiration [e.g. *Athreya et al.*, 1987; *Crummett*, 1987].

Returning from this diversion, it should be made clear that my comments do not fundamentally disprove Mills' case about the 'capitalist peasantry' since he does not operate within a marxist framework. I would suggest though, that even within a neo-classical framework, his definition of capitalist is suspect, but let us move on to another important feature of his model, and one that is also adhered to by Wells [1989: 121]. Both insist that these groups were entrepreneurial, yet neither define what they mean by this, nor produce a scrap of evidence to demonstrate that 'peasants' or 'petty entrepreneurs' actually behaved in accordance with any definition of any sort. As featured in our contemporary thought, the entrepreneur is an impeccably neo-classical creature. Leaving aside the specific Schumpeterian features of the innovating entrepreneur, there is agreement about certain key characteristics of the entrepreneur. Central to any definition, is the fact that entrepreneurs *take risks*, and seek to *maximise returns* on capital. Of course, there may have been individuals among household producers, particularly amongst the wealthier 'middle' household producers who did fulfill these characteristics, but in the absence of specific research into motivations and practice, it is unwise to generalise from this to posit the notion that all were entrepreneurial. On the contrary, I would argue that few were. The behaviour of the great majority was precisely the opposite to entrepreneurial, in that most producers of this kind actively sought to *avoid* risk, and were concerned primarily with obtaining a living, rather than maximising profit. In a word they were concerned, whether producing for direct consumption or for exchange, mainly with *subsistence*.

I have discussed this question briefly elsewhere [*Reed*, 1984: 61–3; 1987] but will give provide more detail here. Central to my argument is the claim that different *values* prevailed among household producers during the period, than those prevailing amongst capitalist producers. That capitalist producers were 'market-orientated', is a truism. 'Market-orientation' and profit-maximisation, is often taken as an indicator of 'modernity' opposed to 'self-sufficency' or subsistence production which is seen as an indicator of some kind of 'traditional' society, although I would dispute this view. In the orthodox view, 'market-orientation' was universal during the nineteenth century, indeed it could hardly be otherwise in a society where

> ... markets are ubiquitous, dominant, integrating all production nationally: that is interlocking markets in a national purchase and sale network at money price, organised on an economy-wide basis, a market network essential to all industrial and agricultural lines of production ... Practically all farm output was sold for cash. All factors of production, land, labour, tools, transport, artificial fertilisers, were available on national markets for purchase at money price .... Here we have total market dependence, for livelihood and the ubiquitous use of cash ... [*Dalton*, 1974: 241]

Given these kinds of statements it is unsurprising that Mills and Wells hold the views they do in this regard. The problem for them is of course, that such statements are simply not true. I am not suggesting that large numbers of producers were 'self-sufficent' in that direct-subsistence production them with all their needs. Indeed, the simple distinction between 'self-sufficent' and 'market-orientation' fails to do justice to the varying strategies of production and exchange followed by household producers during the period. 'Self-sufficency' and 'market-orientation' were instead, the two poles of a continuum upon which producers took up varying positions according to circumstances [*Clark*, 1987: 2]. These could be family circumstances, trade circumstances, and local patterns of practise and behaviour. It is clear that the market became increasingly significant during the period, but even this model ignores the existence of a sphere of exchange between the levels of household and market. This sphere was of great importance in influencing economic behaviour and is probably best characterised as 'local' or 'neighbourhood' exchange [*Clark*, 1987: 2–3], and will be discussed later.

Unlike capitalist producers who sought to maximise the return on capital invested, household producers conducted production and exchange more with family than with individual concerns in mind, and concerned themselves more with family needs and neighbourhood obligations than with profits from trade.

Few if any producers were fully self-sufficient at any time in the nineteenth century. In order to provide all of the goods and services needed by even the poorest households, some division of labour between households was necessary. It follows therefore that producers who were not market-orientated would generally have needed to have been non-specialised, and it is indeed clear that most household producers throughout most of the nineteenth century, were engaged in a variety of productive and/or service undertakings [*Reed*, 1984: 56–9; 1986: 86–8; *Mills*, 1984: 499–506]. Production of a range of agricultural produce would be carried on alongside various trade, craft, or service activity. Thus the distinction between 'small farmers' and rural trades/craftspeople may be a false one in the majority of cases.

For many of these producers, a part of their subsistence was obtained directly from their holding [*Reed*, 1984b: 55] but few, in any obtained their entire subsistence from their own production. It follows therefore, that exchange was always necessary and production had to be directed to this end to some degree. A great deal of production was destined for what, following Chris Clark [1987: 6], I call 'neighbourhood' exchange, but commercial exchange was increasingly engaged in. For some producers, close to urban markets, market gardening, or livestock/dairy production enabled specialisation to be a viable strategy from the eighteenth century and earlier, and this option increased throughout the period. For the majority though, production for the market was merely a part – though an increasingly important part – of their productive activity. Butter, milk, poultry, and vegetable production, features more and more, on smaller holdings, frequently as the preserve of the female members of the family. But the aim was still only to make a living, rather than accumulation. Frank Kemsley's father was a horsedealer, and farmer of 30 acres around 1900. 'He'd never dreamed of having a 200 acre farm. He told me I was mad when I took 60 .... [He] got a living, that's all that mattered ...'.[2]

Virtually the only detailed comments about exchange between small rural producers in the nineteenth century are to be found in Walter Rose's book *Good Neighbours*, in which the author described aspects of his childhood in Buckinghamshire during the 1870s and 1880s.

A large part of the trade within the village was carried on by a system called *gnawing it out* – a method something like the primitive trade by barter in days before coin came into general use. ...

The butcher, having had his cart repaired by the wheelwright, rather than part with ready cash, expected the wheelwright to run up a bill for meat in settlement. The system worked both ways, the wheelwright often being of like mind and motive. It was more or less the same in almost all the other trades; each individual thus secured to himself an assured amount of custom and the whole village kept its trade to its own circle [*Rose*, 1942: 54].

Another writer recalling the late nineteenth century, this time on the edge of Dartmoor, was bewildered by these kinds of exchange.

Within the last twenty years I have seen an account set out between a blacksmith and a farmer without any reference at all to money. On one side there were horseshoes, ploughshares, etc., and on the other side, pork, butter, geese, etc. And both parties reckoned the items up, and saw that the totals balanced. They seemed to have some weights and measures in their mind that are not found in books, say, 4 horseshoes make 1 duck [*Torr*, 1979: II, 11].

Usually however, money amounts do appear in the account books kept by household producers, but in other respects accounts like this one are not uncommon and they provide the basis of what follows.

Exchange could be entirely in goods. Thomas Taylor, a beer and spirits seller of Cranbrook in Kent was also a shoemaker, and from his account book it is clear that he also was involved in agriculture to some degree. On 27 October 1832, he 'sold' two 'runt cows' to William Oliver of High Halden, some eight miles away, for the sum of £16.0.0. This 'debt' was cleared as follows. On 10 January 1833 he received from Oliver two quarters of beans at 30/– per quarter. He then received another quarter, value 30/–, and on the 20 February he received four quarters of oats worth in all £3.8.0. A year later on 10 March 1834, he received 120 bundles of straw worth £2.18.4 and on 1 July the same year, more straw valued at £3.3.0. All of this adds up to £13.19.4 and Taylor sent Oliver a bill for the balance of £2.0.8.[3]

Not all account books are as detailed as this. A butcher from the Chart Sutton area of Kent (possibly William Watts) supplied meat to a Mrs. Bellingham for some eighteen months during 1824 and 1825. All was 'paid for' by unspecified goods. A person named Link had meat from this butcher to the value of £6.8.6¾ over a six–month period at this time, and this bill was also paid for by unspecified goods to the same amount.[4]

William Osmer of Smarden in Kent was a baker and grocer who also kept and 'broke' dogs for a variety of customers. Many of his creditors paid with goods. John Shadget paid with horse and cow hides, William Watson with grouse, and various people gave him dogs.[5] It was more common for accounts to be balanced in a variety of ways rather than a simple exchange of goods. Bills would be paid by a combination of goods, services, work and cash. Phillip Rapson's dealings with Henry Ede provide an example. Rapson was a sawyer of Lodsworth in western Sussex. In addition he had about an acre of land and two or three cottages in the village, as well as rights to common land in the parish. He sold livestock, cider, apple trees, candles and many other items. In the autumn of 1837, Ede owed Rapson 14/6. He then brought from the latter two buckets, a washtub, and a pork tub, for which 'credit' was given. He then worked for Rapson for 13 days at 1/8 a day, reducing his debt to 7/–, which remained outstanding for a year when Ede brought another bucket on credit for 2/3. He then did a little work for Rapson, wheeling dung and opening a ditch, for which he was credited. He bought two pigs from Rapson for 17/6 in November 1838, leaving a final debt of £1/4/3. No cash changed hands in all this time though it began to now, but it was mid-summer of 1840 before the debt was cleared.[6]

Jonathon Baker, a Gloucestershire shoemaker, who not only made and repaired shoes, but was also an agriculturist. He sold butter, seeds, plants, peas, cider, cheese, potatoes, wheat, as well as quires of paper, button thread, nails, mutton, bread, veal, flour and so on. His dealings with William Ranels are typical. In 1786, Baker repaired shoes for Ranels and his family to the amount of 3/3. This debt was cleared by Ranels doing four days work in February 1787 at 1/– per day, leaving Baker ninepence in his debt. Baker settled a Mrs Cadel's bill for schooling his children by providing her with cider.[7]

Transactions could be of great complexity. Phillip Rapson had accounts with several people including his son James. The two sides of the account include all the features already described. Goods were exchanged in both directions. Cash passed in both directions. Services and loans passed in both directions, and so did work. Phillip sometimes worked for his son, and James sometimes worked for his father. It is impossible in cases like this to determine just who was buyer and who was seller. These exchanges would appear to be between equals.

To sum up thus far. Exchange between household producers might be in kind, in services, by work or by cash, or most likely by a combination of some or all four. And of course the two elements of exchange were usually widely separated in time. However direct – albeit delayed – reciprocal exchanges of this kind were not the only type of relationship. John Bourne a carpenter from the Tenterden area of Kent owned several cottages during the 1830s. One of these was let to a Mr Alcock at 2/3 a week. The rent due for the week of 14 March 1836 was paid on time in cash. That for the following week was paid for by work. That for the next week was however paid 'by Austens Bill'. The rent due from 4 April mounted up until on 15 October 38/3 was paid in cash. Apart from 1/9, no more was paid until 20 February of the following year when 21/– was paid again 'by Austens Bill'. In this instance, Austen owed Alcock money. By issuing a bill on Austen to the amount that Alcock owed Bourne in rent, and then by giving that bill to Bourne, Alcock was able to bring two of his accounts closer to balance. Austen now owed Bourne rather than Alcock, and Alcock was out of debt with Bourne.[8]

The raw materials for production were often provided by the recipients of the finished product. William Leggatt provided the apples from which his father-in-law, Phillip Rapson brewed cider for Leggatt, on a typical occasion, making a labour charge of 6/– for brewing 72 gallons. Similarly John Burgess, a fellmonger and glover of Ditchling during the 1780s obtained much of the raw materials for his trade from his customers. On November 29 1785, Burgess took eight sheep skins from a Mr. Marten of Stantons at Plumpton. These were made up into breeches that were delivered to Marten some eight days later [*Burgess*, 1982: 13].[9] Now these accounts were not simply left to carry on endlessly – or rather not usually. Every so often accounts were 'settled'. This took place at irregular intervals and was frequently a social occasion. John Burgess' and Thomas Turner's diaries abound with references to 'settling-up' over dinner or a drink. The latter was often followed in Turner's case by a hangover and profound remorse [*Burgess*, 1982: *passim*; *Vaizey*, 1984: *passim*]. Settlement dates and presumably, pressure to settle, varied considerably. Some accounts show fairly regular settlements, monthly, six-monthly, annually, and so on, but others were quite irregular, and others were often years in the waiting. John Payne, a blacksmith and small farmer-shopkeeper-innkeeper of Kirdford in western Sussex, noted on 14 Febuary 1825:

> Mrs Cobby and I settled all Accounts Up to Christmas 1822 and she left to Pay a Bill for 1823 and 1824 and I owed Her out of them Bills for old Iron and Oats and Pease to said amount £7–3–0.[10]

Delays of this sort were not unusual. According to Walter Rose, one settlement was reached after 14 years by the toss of a sovereign [*Rose*, 1942: 55].

Transactions were not invariably conducted in conditions of sweetness and light. Walter Rose, who was admittedly hostile to this kind of dealing, describes how he believed the system worked during his childhood in the 1870s or 1880s, and in doing so highlighted the difference between the values of the would-be commercial operator and those of the older kind of household producer.

> The boy at the village school was taught that the debtor was servant to the creditor. But on leaving school, if he should happen eventually to take up trade in the village, he found the principle reversed. He learned that coin was a cherished commodity, highly prized and far from plentiful, and that many who were known to have it were as likely as those who had none to plead inability to pay the amount they owed him. Having rendered his account for work done or goods supplied, he found it next to impossible to get the money. In despair he had at last to fall into line with the time-honoured method of taking, instead of money, the particular commodity that the debtor was able to supply. Nor would it be long before he discovered that by rendering his own account he had placed himself at the debtor's mercy: once the debtor knew exactly the amount he owed he was

certain to hold his own contra statement back at least until that debt was cleared; or even worse, when the long-deferred settlement did at last take place, the creditor might find that instead of taking some money he had some to pay [*Rose*, 1942: 54].

This somewhat jaundiced view demonstrates the potential conflict between the ethics of commercial exchange and those of neighbourhood exchange. But it also shows that integrity and trust were central features of the latter. He makes it clear – and many surviving account books support this – that few producers knew the state of their accounts with their neighbours.

To draw the balance at settlement was the studied ambition of many. As, however, everyone could not do this, those who knew the amount of their own indebtedness were at an advantage. This was easy enough when trading with one like my father, who always rendered his accounts quarterly and, if they were not paid, sent the 'account rendered' at the appointed times. I am quite sure that the cute ones were amused at his simple straightforwardness, and that ... they were glad to know just what they owed him; it was a simple matter then to compare the amount with the total standing against him in their own ledgers, biding the time when it should be more than their own debt. ...

The matter was very different when both parties were of the same disposition, acting with the same motive, and knowing the dodge to the last letter. Then it was 'diamond cut diamond' indeed, fruitless attempts on each side to get a bill from the other; each determined not to be the first to declare, because each knew for certain that the other would straightway make his to a larger sum. And so these contra transactions often went on for years without any account being rendered ... [*Rose*, 1942: 54–5].

Tension was probably a fairly common feature of these kinds of relationship, and disagreements could occur. On 18 Febuary 1834, John Bourne a Brenchley carpenter wrote to Mr Hards,

Sir, I am disatied [sic] with your Bill I wish to have it look over by to memen you to git one and I a one and his Settl it for I wish to pay what is Right.[11]

Referees appointed in this way would examine the books and agree between them what the extent of debt between the two parties was. In the account book of Henry Tolhurst, a wheelwright of Debtling in Kent, there is a slip with the following upon it.[12]

Agreement made 13 Feb 1818 between John Whyman of Boughton and John Masters of Debtling To settle the 2 Bills between Henry Tolhurst & John Green both of Debtling

Henry Tolhurst Bill	£18–5–4
John Greens Bill	£15–2–6
Due to H.Tolhurst	£3–2–10

Henry Tolhurst Dr. to John Green for journeys to Maidstone for timber	£2–2–0

By Balance of Accounts & debt due to Henry Tolhurst	£2–8–4

If arbitration of this kind failed, then a case could be resolved in court. In 1826, Richard Puttock, a shopkeeper and farmer of Tillington in western Sussex ordered a waggon from Luke Wadey a wheelwright of Billingshurst, as a present for his son. According to the solicitor's brief for Wadey when the case went to the summer Assizes in 1832[13]

> Richard Puttock also occasionally employed Pl[ain]t[iff Wadey] to do his work and Pl[ain]t[iff] was in the habit of having Shop Goods of him to the amount and sometimes to more than the amount of the work so done and the Def[endan]t himself has also allowed the Pl[ain]t[iff] to have at different times in part liquidation of the debt Money and Goods which amount to about £29 and which may be enumerated as follows

By Bill and Cash of Richard Puttock	£8–0–0
Bill for shop goods had of do.	£11–4–4¾
Of Plt. 1 fat pig 15 stone @ 3/10	£2–17–6
By cash	£5–0–0
By 2 sacks of Peas	£2–0–0
	£29–1–10¾

These transactions were the norm for much of the period. Cash transactions occurred of course, but whether paid immediately or after a period, they were limited generally to transactions with 'outsiders'. That is, people who were not themselves small producers, gentry, clergy, labourers perhaps and so on. People from outside the locality were also frequently excluded from these kinds of transaction. These kinds of relationships seem generally to be between certain kinds of small producer, between neighbours and kin, and in the case of John Burgess of Ditchling between members of the same dissenting denomination as himself but in this case, spread over a fairly wide geographical area. I have found few instances where full-blown capitalist producers exchanged in this way at all, and in the very few exceptions, such transactions were occasional only. What is clear though is that cash transactions became more frequent as the nineteenth century progressed with the further development of the market. But even into this century the ethics of neighbourhood exchange continued. As grocer's son E. A. Stanger recalled, 'mostly our stuff we brought in ourselves from our own customers. we wouldn't take eggs and that unless we badly wanted them from anyone who wasn't a customer'.[14]

So what are we to make of this? Because, within the English context, these kinds of exchange relationships have largely escaped historians' notice, it is necessary to start virtually from scratch and I would argue that these are *not* standard commercial relationships. Household producers are usually considered to be petty capitalist, petty-bourgeois, and so on, and as Mills and Wells show, are generally considered to have acted in conventional entrepreneurial ways. But it is clear that the maximisation of returns on capital was not always pursued, indeed a case could be made that it would seldom have been so. The arrangements just described inhibited maximisation to a very large degree, since they forced varying degrees of reciprocal obligation and commitment on the parties involved. Small farmers in the Surrey Weald around 1800 had 'so little of the impartial spirit of commerce, that they prefer selling their grain to an old customer at a lower price, to deserting him and accepting a higher offer from one with whom they have not been in the habit of dealing' [*Stevenson*, 1813: 88]. John Burgess of Ditchling in the 1780s would pass up the chance of selling a pig at the local market, but would let it go to a neighbour within a day or two for substantially less [*Burgess*, 1982: 48].

To suggest that these relationships were not really commercial is likely to provoke a discussion of the similarities between these kinds of exchange and more familiar commodity relationships. The fact that items are normally given money values in the account books might indicate that goods were exchanged according to conventional market criteria. In fact these sums were merely book-values, assigned to help keep track of transactions between different people. The shortage of cash that is well documented in rural areas after 1815 and the general rural depression, has been suggested as a cause for these people being 'reduced to barter' [*Wells*, 1985b]. The problem for this hypothesis is that the system operated as previously indicated certainly during the later-eighteenth century, and doubtless earlier. Cash shortage may have been a factor, but the system went deeper than that. It was a product not just of necessity, and people often preferred dealing with a member of the network than with outsiders, even if less was obtained during a transaction. Walter Rose's comments already alluded to clearly indicate that these arrangements were preferred rather than merely tolerated. An advert in the *Sussex Agricultural Express* demonstrates that arrangements like these were actively sought after.

To Respectable Tradesmen
Reciprocal Advantage

> Mr. and Mrs. Arkoll, of Cliffe Academy, Lewes, Sussex, will be happy to receive the Sons or Daughters of either Butcher, Grocer, Miller, Baker, Linen Draper, or Stationer, upon the plan of reciprocal dealing ....[15]

Cash was not universally sought after. As Chris Clark has argued in an American context [1982: 73]

> Money was seen as having specific uses in the local economy and its dealings with the wider world, but among farmers it was not widely regarded either as a universal equivalent for other values ... nor as a necessary means of accumulation for its own sake. The means of exchange rested in the true use-values of the goods and services being transacted. In many instances this recognition of use-value is evident in the records ....

Indeed it could be argued that cash itself was seen in many cases not as wealth or even as a universal equivalent, but rather as a particular kind of use-value.

> Neighbourhood exchange conformed in its practices with aspects of the commercial economy, but participants viewed their transactions in non-commercial ways. It can be argued, for example, that the system of accumulating book accounts or of passing notes in payment, either directly or via third parties, was an effective system of credit, similar to that of the commercial [economy] [*Clark*, 1982: 76].

And so it was up to a point. It was enforceable at law as already described, but there were important contrasts with commercial credit.

> To many farmers and craftsmen, it was not a 'credit' system as such because it was part of the fabric of rural society, and of the need to balance out demands between neighbours and across the seasons of the year. Above all it needed to be flexible; it could not be pursued with the rigour and discipline that commercial relationships often demanded [*Clark*, 1982: 76–77].

The tangle of indebtedness frequently eluded solutions and reclamation by executors upon the death of a rural producer. 'Credit' in the countryside has received little attention from historians apart from a recognition – usually derived from the study of probate inventories – that it was widespread. B.A. Holderness in one of the few studies of rural credit [1975], itself based on probate inventories, is unable to distinguish between debts reflecting genuine credit, loans, mortgages, and so on, and those derived from the exchange relationships previously discussed. Indeed it does not really occur to him to do so, though he does observe 'that rural communities generally financed their own needs for all purposes except the sale of commodities outside the region' [1975: 106].

Moreover, unlike conventional credit, there was seldom any interest charged. The system of running accounts inhibited this in any event. For instance, a settlement would have to be made to establish a principle.

So, far from being merely a disguised form of commercial transaction, exchange of this kind

> rested on neighbourhood and kinship ties, on reciprocity and on a degree of mutual respect and integrity. This is revealed in the flexibility with which the system appears to have worked and the extent to which parties to transactions were apparently willing to make allowances for each others interests and concerns. The ritual which surrounded the actual settling of accounts to some degree reflects this [*Clark*, 1982: 82].

This reliance on integrity can be deduced from the actual way many people kept their books. Not all producers kept books that showed both sides of an account as Walter Rose's comments already given make clear. Many, perhaps a majority, only indicate the items and services supplied by them to others. The settlement entry usually makes it clear that exchange was based on the principles I described, but the goods and services received are not detailed. It is clear that the other party to the transaction kept his/ her own book and that memory and trust were depended upon to ensure that no deliberate or accidental errors were entered.

Although opportunities to produce for the market gave household producers a wider range of strategies for obtaining a living, it had its price. Once enmeshed in the market, the laws of the market held sway. Bankruptcies became relatively common. Not all producers were able to sustain themselves once the ties of neighbourhood exchange weakened. Market production increasingly placed household producers under the influence of buyers of their produce and the suppliers of raw materials. Moreover the depression of the later nineteenth century, led many capitalist farmers into direct competition with household producers, although it also encouraged an increase of household production within agriculture. The market became dominant in the lives of most rural household producers, but it did not – for most – alter their priorities of earning a living rather than accumulating capital.

This lengthy diversion, by providing evidence of the exchange practices of rural household producers during the nineteenth century, provides the basis for an alternative assessment of motivations. The system clearly mitigated against systematic maximisation of profit, thus negating one of the twin pillars of the argument for their classification as entrepreneurs. Moreover, it also inhibited risk-taking. Producers were so bound up with obligations to their neighbours, that it was both difficult economically, and probably contravened social and cultural mores, to attempt the risky undertakings so necessary for the entrepreneur. There is no space to describe the sophisticated local exchange networks that existed well into the second half of the nineteenth century, but these networks were 'not a "market" in any meaningful sense, but a system of reciprocal personal obligations' [*Clark*, 1987: 3]. These kinds of relationship were identical with those in the north-eastern United States during the same period which have been the subject of a fascinating and essential debate in that country [*Merrill*, 1977; 1979–80; 1985; *Clark*, 1978; 1979; 1982; 1987; *Henretta*, 1978; 1980; *Wessman*, 1979–80; *Pruitt*, 1984; *Karsky*, 1983; *Lemon*, 1980; *Shammas*, 1982; *Rotenberg*, 1981; *Bellesiles*, 1986].

Not only is much more research needed before we can even begin to chart fully, the extent of these kinds of exchange networks, and the ways in which exchange of the kinds described were intermingled with what are for us, more conventional kinds of exchange relationship, in which cash and the market feature explicitly, but a great deal of theoretical work also needs to be done. It seems that much of this exchange was not commodity exchange, from which it follows that the rural English economy was not fully commoditised even by the later nineteenth century. Indeed in a fully commoditised economy, there would be no household producers. There would be only capitalist production units, and all labour would be wage labour [i.e. labour in commodity form]. A household production unit 'is by definition only partially commoditised, at least some labour and probably also some means of production are "non-commodities"' [*Athreya et al.*, 1987: 160]. In rural England, at least part of the product was in 'non-commodity' form well into the industrial era. In this respect, the rural economy of England resembled that of North America during the same period [*Merrill*, 1977].

Household producers in rural England then, produced for direct consumption; for exchange within neighbourhood networks; and for exchange through the market. The precise combination of these elements varied enormously geographically, chronologically, and according to the nature of a particular enterprise. Even household producers who exchanged the whole of their product through the market would not be capitalist. The concept of petty commodity production is essential for our understanding of the dynamics of these kinds of production units, and the ways in which they interact with other classes. Once again endless inspiration is available from the work of numerous scholars working on these problems in non-English contexts.[16]

What we have then is a group of people who held class positions distinct from both capital and labour, and who – as Marxism would lead us to expect – behaved, economically at least, in equally distinctive ways. The precise delineation of their class positions needs further theoretical elaboration, and detailed empirical research at local and regional levels as indicated earlier. Moreover we need research into the ways in which class position created other manifestations of class. In his concluding essay in this book, Wells [1988:   ] examines the development of class consciousness amongst rural workers. Drawing on E.P. Thompson's thesis of class formation [*Thompson*, 1971; 1974; 1978], he seeks to broaden the application of Thompson's argument, into a rural context. Readers will make their own assessments of Wells' case, but despite the excellence of the research, and his highlighting of previously neglected aspects of rural political thought and action Wells, 1985], it is clear, as he would surely agree, that much remains to be done, including consideration of what class actually means.

Class is about opposition and antagonism – and of course, power. But there are no simple lines of cleavage that can seperate classes into opposing and antagonistic camps.

> Rather, the alliances and oppositions must shift, and break, and shift again, each time re-forming in a new way. ... This means that social and historical processes within a class – as people reach out for, or turn away from, a range of potential alliances and oppositions, and as issues become understood and acted upon in ways that include and exclude in new combinations – are as crucial to defining what happens as are the struggles *between* classes [*Sider*, 1986: 8]

Initially, the authors of the debate reproduced here made a hesitant beginning to the understanding of some of these processes. As I pointed out in my own contribution [1984: 121], Charlesworth, Mills and Short, through their reliance on the 'open/close' model, hint at the possibility of shifting alliances in 'open' parishes. The model itself is fundamentally flawed as I will argue below, but for such hints we should be grateful. Wells' early work seemed to deny such a possibility [*Reed*, 1984a: 121], and even in his new contribution to this volume, he moves away from this position a little reluctantly. The great strength of Wells' early contributions was to demonstrate some of the crucial developments *within* the rural proletariat, and he has built on this impressively in this collection.

Wells' interest in, and demonstration of class consciousness [1988], is of supreme importance in this debate. Nevertheless, much more is needed. The familiar Marxist formula of 'class-in-itself' and 'class-for-itself', lies at the root of this interest. Class position of the kind discussed here, enables us to identify 'class-in-itself', but there are many Marxists who would insist that a class can only really be defined by the presence of class consciousness – 'class-for-itself'. Consciousness though is only one of many events that occur within classes. Rather, class is defined

> by its internal dynamic as well as by its interclass confrontations and collusions. Further, the shifting and transient alliances and opposi- tions in a system of classes implies that the composition and internal structure of any particular class are fluid and dynamic – due not only to changes in the material basis and productive activities of the class but also to changing political and ideological claims, assertions, and practices [*Sider*, 1986: 8–9].

E.P. Thompson's seminal work, *The Making of the English Working Class* [1968], embodied implicitly these points of Gerald Sider's. So too does Wells' final essay in this volume. Thompson demonstrated the for- mation of a working class in the urban and industrialising areas of England during the classic phase of the industrial revolution. Many others have since contributed to this thesis, and Wells has now demonstrated that, for a while at least, there existed in the villages of the English countryside, a class-conscious working class. Yet what was this working class? What indeed was Thompson's? Apart from the proletarians, both the urban and rural working class included very many small masters – in fact, household producers [*Thompson*, 1968: *passim*; *Behagg*, 1979; *Wells*, 1988b]. The essential and unanswered question is why should household producers with their distinctive class positions, have identified themselves so closely with the proletariat prior to mid-century, that they adopted a consciousness of themselves as 'working class'? What happened seems to have been that two 'classes-in-themselves' entered into an 'alliance' and became, for a few years, a single 'class-for-itself'. Why and how it happened, needs explaining.

The view is cloudy, but not irretrievably so. Real life does not fit neatly into any model, and an awareness of the complexities that a model must deal with is vital. But the foregoing suggests the outlines of a viable class model for the study of rural England during the period. The undoubtedly capitalist social formation of rural England featured at least two capitalist fractions – landlords and capitalist tenant farmers – and proletarians employed in agricultural or other forms of enterprise; and a large extremely heterogeneous group of household producers whose relationships with each other, and with other groups in the social formation needs substantial research before overall assessments can be made. What is clear is that the agrarian transition did not proceed in the simplistic way suggested in the past, and that the complexities of rural society were enormous.

Such a model has significant implications for our debate. Mills objects to my criticism of his [with Short] use of a model 'that dictates the questions asked and the answers obtained' [*Mills*, 1988: 397]. A calmer reading of my comments would have revealed the suggestion that this was true of all models and for all historians [*Reed*, 1984a: 110/101], and it is therefore true of the model proposed here. It becomes a question of what gives the greatest payoff. For the study of conflict, the 'open/close' model as developed and enhanced primarily by Mills, cannot give the same insights into human behaviour in class contexts as does a class model in which conflict is central. At most, the 'open/close' model provides a descriptive shorthand of *landownership patterns*. As Sarah Banks [1988: 57] has suggested, Mills sometimes appears to believe that the model is an explanatory theory. Despite Mills' protests [1988: 398] that he has addressed the problems of measurement in his earlier work [1980: Ch. 4], it remains true that the amount of detailed local and regional research to ascertain details of landownership spatially *and over time*, is simply vast. Despite so many years of study, only two English counties have been at all reasonably studied in this regard – Leicestershire [*Mills*, 1963; 1980] and parts of Lincolnshire [*Mills*, 1980; *Obelkevich*, 1976]. The 'open/close' model was first introduced into the present debate by Charlesworth [1980: 102/56] who pointed to differing social characteristics and therefore of capital/labour relationships in the two types of parish. Following Wells' rejection [1981: 516/67] of Charlesworth's use of the model, Mills and Short [1983] brought the specific version of the model as developed by Mills, to bear on the debate. It should be realised that there is no agreement as to the criteria for defining parishes as either 'open' or 'close'.[17]

B.A.Holderness appears to define 'open' and 'close' parishes on the basis of labour supply, although as Sarah Banks has indicated [1988: 54] his position is more complex than this and not entirely consistent. For Mills on the other hand, the chief definitional criterion is landownership, and he posits the model not as a polarisation, but as a continuum – 'from wide open … to firmly shut' [*Mills and Short*, 1983: 254/91]. The most detailed exposition of the model is to be found in his book *Lord and Peasant* [1980]. Although Mills identifies a 'closed' parish as one where over 50 per cent of the land is owned by a single individual, he prefers to identify at least two types of 'open' and two types of 'closed' parish rather than a simple dichotomy. He further argues that 'for many purposes it is desirable to go further and to work with a continuum measured by the concentration of landownership …' [*Mills*, 1988: 398]. At the risk of parody, it is possible to interpret this as an argument for producing a classification by which the acreage of a parish is divided by the numbers of owners. One could end up with a continuum with almost countless points thereon. The characteristic gloss given the model by Mills however, is that of *predictive power*. From this single premise, a critic suggests, 'the presence or absence of a dominant estate in any one settlement – [he] then combines bundles of characteristics such as population size, class structure, occupational diversity, degrees of poverty, quality of housing, varying tendencies towards order or disorder, and religious propensities' [*Phythian-Adams*, 1987: 8]. Whereas one can concede that the model may have some value as a *descriptive* device of landownership patterns, it is difficult to allow it any scope for prediction on this scale. The exceptions to the rule even at the most basic level, are too numerous to ignore. For example a village that appears to have been a classic example of an open village in social, economic and cultural terms – Corsley in Wiltshire [*Davies*, 1909], turns out on investigation, to have had 85 per cent of its area owned by Lord Bath – a Millsian 'closed' parish indeed [*Short and Reed*, 1987: 95]. A most detailed and convincing critique of Mills use of the model has recently been produced by Banks, in which she suggests that historians have been duped into turning 'a nineteenth-century scandal into a twentieth-century model' [1988: 71], and demonstrates the inadequacy of such a model for predictive purposes.

Within the context of the debate, the demonstration by Mills and Short [1983] of variable relationships of class in different parishes, has been of considerable importance. All that is in dispute is the claim that these variations and their ramifications, can be predicted from landownership patterns. Conflict was to be found in all social contexts [*Reed*, 1984a: 110–115/101–6], and not simply in so-called 'open' parishes. Forms of conflict vary, not only over time, but also according to specific class relationships. The 'open/close' model is prescriptive in a normative sense, and therefore restricts the search for prescribed phenomena to those contexts determined by the model. Hence the claim by Mills and Short [1983: 254/91] that 'we should not expect to find conflict in closed villages', which in fact translates as "we need not search for conflict in closed villages because the totality of control precludes it".

For social historians working within or influenced by Marxism, the model is simply irrelevant. There can be no short cut to the establishing of local social, economic, and cultural structures and associated phenomena. Models though, are crucial to the *understanding* of these structures once they have been established by empirical research. Models aid explanation, they cannot be a substitute for the hard graft of historical – or any other – research.

In a sense of course a model based upon some definition of class has underlain the debate from its inception. The concept of class embodies the concept of conflict and conflict between the classes – or more accurately, between capital and labour – has been the focus of every contribution. At the start of the debate, the definition of conflict was too narrowly defined being restricted to a category called 'protest', and I suggested that it required broadening to include at least conflict in the labour process and in employment relationships [*Reed*, 1984a]. This too, has incurred Mills' displeasure, and he suggests that I am 'diluting the focus of debate unacceptably'. He prefers the unelaborated 'concept' of 'friction' to describe – but not explain – 'mild' expressions of opposing interest [*Mills*, 1988: 398–399/118–19].

Everyone is entitled to use and develop whatever concepts they find useful, but the corollary of this is that everyone should expect their concepts and their usage to be subjected to scrutiny. In one sense of course, conflict in employment relationships for example, is much more easily identified as 'friction'. Mills' paternal grandfather might well not have seen his actions as manifestations of conflict [*Mills*, 1988: 399/119]. Perhaps one response could be 'So what?' It is true that the kinds of action I described [*Reed*, 1984: 111–115/102–6] were usually directed by individual or groups of workers against individual employers, and very probably were not seen as political action against an entire class, or against the capitalist system. But of course, the same would be true of most arson attacks, most strikes, and most other manifestations of 'protest'. The important point is that in situations where similar employment relationships exist, and within similar social, political and cultural contexts, the responses of workers and others to exploitation are likely to be broadly the same. Faced with similar strategies by members of a class or classes, members of the opposing class[es], are likely to adopt more or less uniform strategies in response.

Class is about power, and the power of subordinate classes is limited, varying with specific class contexts. Subordinate classes are by definition weak, but their weakness is at some times greater than at others. In positions of weakness, members of a subordinate class must adopt appropriate weapons. These 'weapons of the weak' [*Scott*, 1985] include the kinds of actions previously described by myself [1984a] and many others. Along with the more spectacular manifestations of 'protest' that featured in much of the debate, they provide a physical demonstration of the fundamental differences of interest between classes. Research is needed to establish the myriad forms adopted by members of different classes to protect or assert their interests. Of course differences of interest during the nineteenth century are 'a given fact' [*Mills*, 1988: 399/119]. What are not given are the ways in which these differences were expressed, the forces that moulded the ways they were expressed, nor the ways in which their expression led to social and economic change. Much research is needed before proper assessments of these problems can be made, but a recognition of the need is at least, a start.

One can only speculate how the debate might have been different had some of the ideas put forward here been present. A far greater sensitivity to the nuances of class relationships as well as to varying responses to the many pressures faced by members of the different classes could be expected. The crude bludgeon of social control criticised earlier [*Reed*, 1984a: 111/102] as a feature of previous contributions, would have necessarily been developed into a more delicate instrument. Much greater emphasis upon the *detail* of productive, social and cultural relationships, and indeed, perhaps an increased concern with culture as something that matters in any study of class, may have emerged. My earlier comments about non-market exchange relationships rely upon the fact that the development of the market was uneven – between classes and between areas. Increasing but variable exposure to the market was a crucial feature of eighteenth- and nineteenth-century life and a recognition of the uneveness of this would have led to increased concentration upon the market as a factor in conditioning people's responses and even consciousness. It is quite possible that the impact of the market upon the neighbourhood exchange networks, were an important determinant of household producers consciousness as 'working class'. Whatever else may have emerged, there would have been much greater emphasis upon complexity, and Wells' [1981: 514] plea for a greater emphasis upon everyday life rather than historical landmarks, would have been unnecessary. Nevertheless things are beginning to move as the massive amount of fine detail presented by Wells in this volume demonstrates so well. The fact of our ignorance is increasingly recognised. The opportunities for imaginative thinking backed up by innovative research methods [e.g. *Snell*, 1985] are beginning to suggest that there is a future for rural history in which 'ploughs and cows' will no longer be all-embracing. The problems confronting historians are mainly conceptual and not empirical nor evidential.

At the start of these reflections, I commented on the poor health of English rural history, and despite welcome steps in the right direction [e.g. *Samuel*, 1975; *Bushaway*, 1982; *Snell*, 1985], the comment holds good. That diagnosis may be quite easy, but the remedy is less so, and is controversial. No single approach can claim to provide all of the answers, and few approaches are incapable of providing something of value. There are exciting developments afoot, but it is clear is that the simple accumulation of empirical detail will not on its own, provide an iota of explanation. Explanation can only be achieved by the development of concepts that are a product of empirical research informed by appropriate theoretical questions. Historians of the English countryside need to become less parochial by recognising that similar problems to their own are being encountered by historians and other social scientists across the world. The concepts the latter have developed may often be of value for the study of rural England. Few historians of these islands have embarked upon such a course. The few that have suggest the pay-off could be great indeed [*Carter*, 1979; *Searle*, 1983; *Winter*, 1984; 1986].

NOTES

1. 'It is a strain on one's semantic patience to imagine a class of bourgeois scattered across a countryside and dwelling on their estates, and it is easier to see in mercantile capital "the only truly bourgeois kernal of the revolution." But if we forget the associations with the French model which the term introduces, and think rather of the capitalist mode of production, then clearly we must follow Marx in seeing the landowners and farmers as a very powerful and authentic capitalist nexus' [*Thompson*, 1978b: 40].
2. University of Kent Oral History Project. Frank Kemsley, pp. 12 and 28.
3. Kent Archive Office [KAO] Q/CI 212/4.
4. KAO Q/CI 36.
5. KAO Q/CI 317/2.
6. WSRO Add.Ms.22650.
7. Univ. of London, Goldsmiths Ms. 527.
8. KAO Q/CI 301.
9. I am grateful to Douglas Burgess for granting access to the diary of John Burgess, and to Leonard Maguire for the gift of privately published edition [*Burgess*, 1982].
10. John Payne's memo book. I am indebted to Reg Thompson for allowing me access to this document.
11. KAO Q/CI 301.
12. KAO Q/CI 69/1.
13. HMC 648.
14. University of Kent Oral History Project, E.A. Stanger, p.18.
15. *Sussex Agricultural Express* 4 February 1837.
16. A useful and up-to-date discussion of petty commodity production has been edited by Alison M. Scott [1986] and includes contributions from many of the most important contributors to this debate.
17. It should be noted that whereas most adherents and critics of the model prefer the term 'close', Mills uses 'closed'.

The Development of the English Rural Proletariat and Social Protest, 1700-1850

Roger A.E. Wells*

This paper suggests that covert social protest, including theft, the sending of anonymous threatening letters, and arson, was the most enduring mode of protest in the English countryside after the 1790s. Developments in this exceptional decade were responsible for increasing the scale of covert protest. Inflation, under and unemployment, with standards of living falling beneath subsistence levels, necessitated a massive increase in poor relief. Its administration required an unprecedented extension of authority over the lives of working people. This generated class conflict, but the establishment successfully suppressed overt protest, demonstrations, 'food riots' and strikes. Protest was driven underground, and in spite of two important semi-covert movements in 1816 and 1830-1, protest remained essentially covert until after 1850.

I

If by peasant we mean a subsistence, or neo-subsistence farmer, England had relatively few peasants in 1700 and virtually none by 1800. This is an elementary fact in English agricultural history, though in establishing the point we have to sweep away the romantic assumptions of Victorian urban man, and his latter-day equivalents. The vast bulk of the inhabitants of the English countryside since the mid-eighteenth century were landless agricultural labourers and their families, who have been described — with some economic justification — as 'the only real Marxian proletariat that England ever had'. [*Dunbadin, 1974, p.248*].

Socio-economic developments in England prior to 1800 created this proletariat; the component parts of this transition conditioned most proletarian reactions. This conditioning was of crucial importance. It ensured that what can be called the labourers' struggle had extremely conservative objectives, and this very conservatism was responsible for the failure of the struggle prior to 1850. The 1790s were a crucial decade in this conditioning process. Firstly those developments which created the proletariat accelerated during the nineties and were irreversible by the end of the decade. Secondly the extraordinary features of the inflationary nineties led to the start of the labourers' disjointed struggle to resist those factors which made his life an unmitigated misery. Thirdly, and most importantly, the forms of resistance, which evolved in the nineties,

* Brighton Polytechnic. I should like to thank Terry Byres and the members of the Peasants seminar at the Centre of International and Area Studies at the University of London for their kind invitation to present an earlier version of this paper, and for their helpful criticism of it.

became the countryman's main weapons during the first half of the nineteenth century. In advancing these claims I am not unaware that the last great labourers' revolt, the Captain Swing risings, came in 1830-31. I am contending that the main features of that rightfully famous episode in English rural history, conformed with the precedents set thirty to forty years previously. For it was the intensity and the scale which made the Swing revolt the greatest rural rebellion in England since the sixteenth and certainly since the seventeenth century, not the nature of the protest.

II

Any attempt to analyse social protest necessitates an understanding of economic conditions, and their historical causation. Here we are dealing with a landless class. What were its origins? The most emotive economic development is obviously enclosure, the process whereby the entire structure of land ownership and tenantry was transformed over much of the country from its communal to its individual basis. Socialist historians, notably the Hammonds, have always maintained that eighteenth-century enclosure with its heavy capital outlay in obtaining an Act of Parliament, and then in drainage and fencing of fields apportioned to individuals from the huge open fields, in accordance with the Act, was expensive. The costs were well within the means of the greater landlords, and the more substantial owner-occupiers, but posed severe financial problems for small-holders. Such historians also insist that enclosure regularly deprived those with common rights (of grazing, fuel collection), as opposed to outright ownership, of their heritage. While these rights were normally recognised by the enclosure commissioners, their recognition in the form of small allotments, again placed a heavy financial burden, which the majority of proprietors were unable to meet. Thus the pecuniary obligations attendant upon enclosure embarrassed small-owners and right-holders, who had little alternative to sell out to their more substantial neighbours, and join the ranks of the landless. [*Hammonds, 1911, passion. Peacock, 1965, chs. 1-4. Thompson, 1963, ch. 7. Hobsbawn and Rudé, 1969, ch. 1*].

This interpretation of the social impact of enclosure has been severely criticised. Detailed work on the costs of enclosure has suggested that these have been exaggerated, and that they were not automatically beyond the resources of small owners. [*Tate, 1952, esp. p. 265*]. It has also been stressed that rising prices for agricultural produce after 1750, and especially during the French wars (1793-1815) guaranteed the economic viability of small holders, well into the nineteenth century. [*John, 1967, p. 45. Mingay, 1968, pp. 14-15*]. Further research on the effect of enclosure on the *numbers* of landowners has indicated that enclosure did not inevitably produce a rapid and pronounced reduction. [*Chambers, 1940, p. 126*]. But this revisionist picture is itself undergoing revision. The costs of enclosure have been found to vary greatly from area to area: in places costs were a severe obstacle for the survival of small farmers. [*Martin, 1967, pp. 126-51. Turner, 1973, pp. 35-47*]. Precise attention to the history of individual proprietors, as opposed to numbers, has revealed that if the numbers of owners did not invariably decline greatly at the time of enclosure, the owners themselves changed. Small owners did sell out, not necessarily to richer neighbours, but to urban-based speculators anxious to invest money in land. [*Turner, 1975, pp. 566-9, 573-4. Cf. Hoskins, 1957, pp. 167, 249-51*]. Where large numbers of small farmers survived, the proprietors were commonly part-time farmers, their agricultural interests being an adjunct of their industrial interests [*Wordie, 1974, pp. 601-2*] or — in other areas — small farms survived through specialisation, especially in market gardening. [*Beavington, 1975, pp. 23-31*]. Intensive farming, even of small acreages, required considerable capital; near towns rents were also very high. [*Laurence, 1731, p. 55. Fussell, 1968, p. 303. MacMahon, 1964, p. 20*]. Clearly only a minority of small farmers could have survived enclosure by such means.

The evidence strongly suggests that the size of farms in the main cornlands (with which this study is primarily concerned[1]) increased quite markedly during the eighteenth century. This phenomenon is consistent with the view that enclosure played a part, but it does not mean that enclosure was solely responsible for the decline in small proprietors. For landlords (rentiers) owned the bulk (perhaps 80 per cent) of farming land in England, and, of course, their letting policies are vital. The so-called agricultural depression of 1730-50, a period of low corn prices, resulted in many bankruptcies, particularly among less substantial tenant farmers. Major landlords responded by preferring to increase the size of farms, reducing the numbers of tenants, thus favouring those with greater capital. [*Mingay, 1956, pp. 309-26. Mingay, 1968, p. 13*] The depression appears to have stimulated a marked trend in landlord preference for substantial farmers. [*Mingay, 1963, chs. 2-4*] Certainly eighteenth-century complaints are too numerous and too consistent at this 'engrossing of farms' to be dismissed. The decline of middle sized farms, say from 50 to 150 acres, is quite marked on some estates, as is a concomitant increase in farms over 150 acres. [*Mingay, 1961-2, pp. 480-4. Wordie, 1974, pp. 597-8*]

There is little doubt that changes in landownership, and new patterns of tenantry during the eighteenth century, reduced the numbers of farmers. Farms, whether those of owner-occupiers or tenants, became larger, and their proprietors deployed ever increasing capitals. Rising prices for their products in the later eighteenth century, accelerated the development of a highly-capitalised farming industry. Higher profits led to significant capital accumulation in the agricultural sector of the economy, some of which was invested in further enclosure, drainage, farm buildings, and in experimentation with the more scientific methods, which were increasingly popularised.

Increasing capitalisation of the industry was consolidated by the almost universal adherence to primogeniture[2] to produce a farming élite in the countryside. Owner-occupiers passed their farms to eldest sons; so too were leases. Thus the accumulation of capital, like land, was not reversed by divisible inheritance practised in so many peasant societies. [*Perkin, 1969, pp. 60-1*] While there was some movement both in and out of the farming community, moving in required considerable capital, both fixed and working, and was clearly beyond those who were not born into the landed classes, or who had not made money in the commercial and industrial spheres. The bulk of the rural population could entertain no such aspirations. The dice were loaded against the survival of the small proprietors: there were few opportunities for entry at the bottom of the farming hierarchy. The majority were clearly divorced from proprietorship and its possibility. [*Collins, 1967, p. 93*] Labourers became a hereditary race.[3]

The low price epoch of the earlier eighteenth century, notably the years 1730-50, is traditionally seen as the golden age of the labourer. The quality of the gold need not concern us; suffice to say that standards of living in the countryside were higher before 1750 than after. It is ironical that the golden age produced the phenomenon which of all was to be the most disastrous for the labourer during the classic period of the industrial revolution. Demographers are fairly unanimous that higher living standards before 1750 were responsible for the initial trigger to the eighteenth-century population explosion. A cumulative effect was caused once the birth rate consistently rose above the death rate. The death rate was also held down by the decline in epidemic disease, the spectacular victory over smallpox as a killer, and the end of subsistence crises of medieval, Tudor and continental severity.[4]

Population increase was primarily responsible for the supply of rural labour outstripping demand. Demand was, of course, seasonal; greatest in the spring and early autumn, and lowest over the winter. The peaks in demand were among several factors which helped to keep the rural population relatively immobile, in spite of the fact that structural underemployment became a norm in those agricultural regions at the greatest remove from urban and industrial locations. While it is true that large towns, above all London, took some of the excess population, [*George, 1925, ch. 3. Wrigley, 1967, pp. 46ff.*] and the developing industrial regions of the Midlands and the North provided employment for much of the extra population in counties north of the Trent, [*Deane and Cole, 1962, ch. 3, part ii*] the failure of industries to develop in the South and the East [*Jones, E. 1974. Cf. Chambers, 1953, pp. 94-127*] meant that with a few very partial exceptions in these areas[5], there was no alternative to agricultural employment. In fact, the decline of Southern and Eastern industries with medieval and Tudor origins seems to have aggravated the growing problem of unemployment from 1780 throughout the first half of the nineteenth century. [*Jones, D., 1976, p. 26*]

The development and survival of structural underemployment owed not a little to the unique English system of statutory poor relief.[6] The Poor Law compelled every parish to maintain — in or out of workhouses — all those, who for reasons of age, health, or unemployment, were unable to provide for themselves and for their families. The Settlement Laws[7] which decreed that a parish need relieve only its own poor, militated against, though they did not prohibit, migration. Relief was certain for an individual in his home parish; he was less likely to receive assistance elsewhere. In the event of not obtaining work he ran the risk of being removed to his original village. [8] The social security system therefore encouraged workers in the South and East to remain put and become part of the growing pool of underused labour. Here underemployment and periodic unemployment began to assume serious proportions in the late 1760s and 1770s. The cost of relief to the ratepayers started to cause grave concern. The roles of the overseers of the poor[9] became more important, as they grappled with an ever increasing number of claimants. Various improvisations were made to ameliorate the problem. The most infamous, the Roundsman System, whereby unemployed men were distributed round the parish farmers, was widely, though not universally established in many southern and eastern counties by 1790. Some areas, notably in East Anglia, adopted the provisions of Gilbert's Act (1782) to amalgamate for the purposes of administering a workhouse, to try to recoup some of the cost of relief by putting the poor to work. But the bulk of residents were the aged, orphans, and the unemployable. The able-bodied, the victims of seasonal unemployment, who required periodic as opposed to permanent assistance, received doles of cash, food and clothing, while living in their own homes. By 1790 periodic dependence on Poor Law provisions was a fact of life for many agricultural workers and their families.

The difficulties with which Poor Law authorities struggled were aggravated, even partially caused by the response of the farmers, as employers, to the abundant supply of labour. Certain of a supply, farmers began to reduce their permanent workforce, and the custom of hiring labour by the year began to decline. So too did the practice of farmers providing board and lodgings for their workers. Farmers could employ fewer men all the year round yet rely on the pool of labour to supply sufficient workers in times of maximum demand. The numbers of casual workers increased markedly; hiring and firing at will became a commonplace. Most importantly, wage rates began to fall; living standards slid inexorably from around 1750. By the mid-1780s most agricultural labourers, according to a reliable contemporary investigator, could 'scarcely with their utmost exertions supply his family with daily bread'. Budgeting was so tight that they 'reckon cheese the dearest article they can use'. Few could afford more than the odd pound of bacon per week. [*Davies, 1795, pp. 8-13, 19, 28-36*] The majority in the South and East were forced to subsist, to some degree of totality, on wheaten bread, which was 'nearer to being a complete food' than any alternative cereal.[10]

The corollary of the labourer's divorce from the land, his dependence on cash wages and supplements from the parish, was his reliance on retail distributors for his food. His ability to augment his income by producing some food himself was eroded by the enclosure of wastes and commons; these sources of a remnant of independence were not replaced by the provision of allotments. The allotment movement was very much a nineteenth-century development, and even then very limited in scale. [*Barnett, 1967, pp. 162-83*] The eighteenth-century growth in rural retailing establishments was very marked. Contemporary complaints that the more opulent farmers especially, refused to be bothered with small sales of foodstuffs to their working neighbours, and their employees, are both numerous and constant.[11] Instead workers relied on village shops and itinerant bakers. 'Scarce a village consisting of a dozen houses is without a shop' was a typical observation.[12] In Hertfordshire 'deemed the first corn county in the Kingdom Yorkshire bacon, generally of the worst sort, is retailed to the poor from little chandlers shops, at an advanced price; bread is retailed to them in the same way.' [*Walker, 1795, pp. 9, 70*] Itinerant bakers are commonly found on daily rounds of twenty miles serving several villages.[13] Workers who lived in the vicinity of the many market towns scattered throughout the South and East purchased much of their subsistence here on weekly visits. [*Bourne, 1912, pp. 30-1, 88-9*] One staggering feature of this transformation in the countryside was the complete absence of anything which could be called a protest movement. Indeed Edward Thompson, never one to minimise either the strength nor incidence of popular reactions against change, speaks of the 'fatalism of the cottagers' and the 'seeming passivity of the victims' of enclosure. Few enclosures — especially of moors and wastes — went ahead without some overt or covert protest. Crowds commonly, if briefly, obstructed the proceedings of enclosure commissioners, and threw down the new fences; the initiators of enclosures were regularly addressed by pseudonymists. [*Thompson, 1963, pp. 240-1; 1975, pp. 275-6, 313-4. Hammonds, 1911, pp. 73-4, 87-91*] But viewed nationally enclosure was a piecemeal process whatever the amount of land involved in aggregate; enclosure actually took place at village, not regional levels. The cause of protest in one village was not present in the next, and this factor, reinforced by the insular structure of rural England, militated against the development of a cohesive movement. The demographic revolution, however momentous, was nevertheless slow, with the supply of labour only gradually outstripping demand. The remedies, the vast extension in the role of poor relief, were implemented equally slowly, perhaps imperceptibly to the recipients, however apparent they became when overseers made decennial calculations of the cost. The evolutionary nature of the multi-dimensional British agrarian revolution served to secure mass acquiescence: change was too slow for the genesis of a past 'golden age' notion in workers' minds. They were generally 'reconciled to the fact that for the duration of their lives' those in power, employers, clergymen and magistrates, were 'likely to remain their masters'. [*Thompson, 1975, p. 307*] By 1800 few English agricultural labourers, unlike their Irish counterparts and Irish peasants, had any concept of ever having owned land, whatever sentiments romantic radicals would have liked to instil in the nineteenth century. The English agricultural worker accepted his position in society, because the vast majority alive in 1800 had been born into that station. Their expectations were in perfect accord with their situation. They wanted work; they sought a living wage; while they expected their local rulers to provide both, they had also been taught in lieu to accept occasional assistance from the rates. Those rulers might periodically have to be reminded of their duties, but essentially the English agricultural labourers had few aspirations, and these were conservative, based on an acquiescence with their occupancy of the bottom rung in a hierarchial, paternalist society, with social relations based on deference.

By 1790 the rural labourer was the most depressed sector of the English working classes. In contemporary jargon the word 'poor' became synonymous with agricultural labourer. The cohesion, indeed the stability of rural society, however fragile, ultimately depended on the operation of the Poor Law. The delicate equilibrium of rural society was already strained by structural unemployment; working families were on the verge of falling below subsistence levels. The final push came in the 1790s. One immediate product was the first widespread signs of class conflict.

III

The British war effort during the first phase of the fearsome struggle with revolutionary France (1793-1801) was financed by inflationary measures taken by the Pitt ministry. All price series rose inexorably. Of still greater importance were the two grain crises of December 1794 — August 1796, and November 1799 — September 1801, which commenced with poor harvests in 1794 and 1799, and were prolonged by subsequent substandard crops in 1795 and 1800. Grain production was only just adequate to demand in normal years; twenty per cent harvest deficiencies were serious and prices rose disproportionately to the degree of deficiency. Wheat, which had averaged 43/- per quarter in 1792, averaged 75/- in 1795, 79/- in 1796, and 114/- in 1800 before attaining the astonishing price of 120/- in 1801. [*Mitchell, 1962, pp. 488-9*]

The severity of these bland figures becomes apparent when they are reworked to show subsistence costs.[14] In September 1794 the wheat component *alone* of the diet of a family with two children cost 4/5 per week.[15] By May 1795 it had risen to 6/-, and it topped 8/- in August. After an ephemeral fall the cost climbed to a peak of 10/5 in March 1796, and had declined only to 6/10 in August. In the second crisis the cost rose speedily after the wet harvest period in 1799 led to immediate expectations of a damaged crop; the cost was 8/- in November; it had rocketed to nearly 15/- in June 1800. Prices fell during the gloriously hot summer, reflecting popular anticipation of a bumper yield, but such hopes were decimated by another soggy harvest period. Our family's weekly cost had nearly reached 12/- in October, and went on to a peak of 17/- in March 1801. The wheat component was still costing well over 10/- weekly at the end of August.

The full horrors of deprivation are revealed, however, only when we balance prices with known wage-rates to show the 'surplus' or 'deficit' after our nominal family had purchased a subsistence level wheat-based diet. During the entire season from September 1794 to August 1795 a 'surplus' (of 2d per week) was recorded for one quarter only. The average weekly 'deficit' was 1/9. During the 1795-6 season wage increases — in Sussex at least — appear to have reduced the average weekly 'deficit' to about 4d. But worse was to follow: weekly 'deficits' averaged 3/10 during the 1799-1800 season, and 6/10 during the 1800-1801 season. For some of the first crisis, and for the entire twenty-four months of the second, agricultural labourers' wages (assuming full employment) were inadequate to purchase even the wheat component of a wheat-based diet. Then the cost of cereal swallowed a family's entire earnings with nothing remaining for other articles of diet, fuel, clothing and rent.[16]

While their labourers hovered on the verge of starvation, and succumbed to famine conditions, the farmers as a class benefitted handsomely from these disproportionately-inflated prices. Increased investment in agriculture led to the final major phase of enclosure, with *marginal* land, waste and commons coming under the plough. [*John, 1967. Huckel, 1976, pp. 334-45*] But clearly something had to be done, and indeed was done to alleviate the plight of the labourers, or England would have experienced demographic crises of fourteenth-century dimensions. Broadly speaking, the farmers left the relief of their employees to the parochial Poor Law authorities rather than augment wages to levels commensurate with living costs.[17]

Two reasons may be advanced for this. Firstly, the crises were expected to be temporary, with prices quickly returning to pre-famine levels after the harvest. The traditional eighteenth-century maxim held that any form of relief was preferable to increased wages 'by those who knew the difficulty of reducing them again'. Secondly, the Poor Law placed the burden of relief on the community, the parish, not the employer. The ability of the farmer to pay more was largely irrelevant. The relief of distress was the community's statutory obligation.

It is therefore ironic that the most famous emergency relief-scheme which was adopted in one region, commenced with a determined attempt by the Berkshire County Bench to make farmers pay a living wage. The Bench provided a sliding scale of minimum wages, based on the size of employees' families and the price of bread. The same levels were also ordered to be paid to the unemployed, the disabled and ill, by Poor Law authorities. The Bench failed. Firstly, the issue of increasing wages was a political one, and was being advocated by the Parliamentary Opposition. Secondly, wage levels partially dependent on the size of an employee's family, meant that those with large families would require much more than single men, and therefore employers would be encouraged to employ bachelors to the exclusion of family men. Thirdly, an ambiguously phrased directive from the Bench, failed to demarcate clearly between the Bench's instructions to employers and to Poor Law officials. It seemed to order overseers to subsidise the wages of family men who were paid less than the subsistence levels calculated by the magistrates. This mix-up was eagerly seized by the farmers, who now appeared to have magisterial authority absolving them from any responsibility to pay wages commensurate with subsistence costs.[18]

This system of wage subsidies from the rates became known as the Speenhamland system after the place at which the Bench convened. The system met the problem almost perfectly, because the subsidies rose or fell with prices, and guaranteed subsistence incomes. For this reason it was phenomenally expensive, and was not universally implemented even in Berkshire in spite of the Bench's directive. [*Newman, 1972, pp. 85-127*] The most common alternative was the provision of *static* as opposed to variable wage supplements which did not rise with prices, and did not guarantee a living income to recipients. Static supplements were cheaper, and in an age which was becoming hysterical about the escalating cost of poor relief, and equally unsure of the morality inherent in the provision of universal relief and its social effects, obviously preferable on many counts.[19]

A whole range of other relief schemes was adopted during the crises. Many parishes entered the wholesale market, and bought food stocks which were sold cheaply to claimants. Public bakehouses and soup kitchens were established in many villages. Such schemes cut out distributors' and retailers' profits and reduced the ratepayers' bill. Thousands of rural charities were created, funds being expended on food, clothing and fuel. In many parishes the number of different schemes run by committees or philanthropic individuals as adjuncts to the Poor Law presents a bewildering picture.[20] But one aspect is common to them all. A high proportion of the rural population, in many locations the entire workforce, depended ultimately for their survival, not on their employers, but on either the Poor Law authorities, or the charitable, and very often on both. While the degree of servility dependent on these arrangements provoked some contemporary criticism,[21] the new dependence was seized on as a form of social control which assumed an unprecedented significance.

The employing and the affluent classes administered both the Poor Law and the charities. Assistance from either necessitated the potential recipient subjecting himself to a searching enquiry into his personal means. It was normally assumed that relief must 'be proportioned to . . . merit and distress'. The Woodford (Essex) vestry typically decreed that relief would follow 'minute enquiry into' applicants' 'respective circumstances'. In Suffolk the Sandford Union compiled lists of the ages of claimants' children to facilitate the payment of differential rates.[22]

Although the reason most commonly advanced in support of 'minute enquiry' was the need to guard against fraud,[23] this knowledge was increasingly deployed to administer relief in accordance with the growing conviction that the 'idle' should not be treated equally with the 'industrious poor'.[24] Oxfordshire 'Gentlemen and Yeomen' were asked to inform authority of 'the persons they observe to be idle, disorderly, or frequent public houses'. 'Those who are industrious, orderly and frugal ought to be better taken care of than those who are of an opposite character . . . even with respect to subsistence', determined the Old Windsor vestry. Overseers were to examine all claimants' 'circumstances as to age and health and behaviour' and relieve accordingly. The Kingston Lisle (Berkshire) authorities decided that relief levels should be calculated on the basis of what the best worker could earn, not what the average worker actually received. Bingfield vestrymen insisted that 'only such as shall have been orderly and industriously employed during the preceding week, unless prevented by indisposition' were eligible to make cut-price purchases at the new village shop.[25]

Rigorous scrutiny and discrimination against supposed idlers were facilitated by numerous innovations. Huish Episcopi (Somerset) overseers lost their discretionary powers of relief: instead relief was to be ordered by a full vestry, whose numbers would have a greater collective knowledge of the workers. The church commonly assumed a new significance. Relief at Great Parndon (Essex) was granted 'each Sunday at Church in provisions'; presumably non-churchgoers were placed in a dilemma. They certainly were at Greenford in rural Middlesex; here a shop selling cheap food was opened to the poor who collected their tickets after the service, but 'if by the absence of any ticket, it appears that the owner (*sic*) was absent from church', he was 'deprived of the advantages of the shop for the ensuing week'. The vicar blatantly admitted that 'the congregation is greatly increased' and asserted that the poor's previous 'habit of indolence . . . would be overcome, and an improvement in the morals of my customers may be reasonably expected'.[26]

An integral part of this increased surveillance, and in the long term perhaps the most significant result of this overall extension of public authority over great sectors of the working population, occurred with the implementation of the universal demand that *all* those assisted should work. The South Weald (Essex) vestry was particularly concerned to find a way 'of bringing up the children in some habits of work thereby preparing them for service'. As it was commonly assumed that children over the age of ten or twelve could earn their keep, this initiative involved the very young too. 'Or else they must have been relieved without doing any Thing' recorded the horrified vestrymen of Heathersett in Norfolk.[27] The cost of relief could be curtailed and 'habits of industry' instilled at a stroke if, as the Hertfordshire Bench put it, 'the children of all parents . . . not able to keep and maintain their children' were 'set to work' by and in every parish. [*Le Hardy, 1935, pp. 450-2*] Increasingly during the nineties, and especially in the second grain crisis, parish after parish, and county after county, put these ideas into practice. The work most commonly organised — spinning — was appropriate for the wives and children of working men who relied on wage supplements. Where this was organised, whole families who were normally independent through the wage of their heads, were placed under the daily supervision of local authority. At South Weald the vicar supervised spinning with an open brief 'to draw up such regulation as may be necessary'. He subsequently anounced that wool would be supplied 'according to the number in their families under 10 years of age'. Work was handed in weekly to 'be weighed and reeled again to detect waste or false reeling'. Payment was governed by the price of bread but 'to encourage good spinning' poorer work was penalised. Another expedient often adopted on a grand scale in the cause of education for labour was to distribute claimants' children among the farmers: the parish paid nominal wages.[28]

This major extension of public authority over claimant families was consolidated by many minor regulations to govern behaviour. Although many were merely irksome, they symbolised the increased control over daily lives. One of the most common, the adoption of which amounted to a craze, was to stop relief to those who persisted in keeping a dog.[29] The Terling (Essex) vestry 'having always in view of the goodness of the industrious and orderly poor', turned their benevolent eyes on traditional customs, and introduced stringent regulations over gleaning. Single persons, except widows, were stopped from gleaning altogether. Those still eligible had to give farmers notice of intent; if they failed to inform on illicit gleaning, what was now their privilege instead of a time-honoured right, was withdrawn.[30]

Examples of especially hard treatment meted out to those unlucky enough to require parish aid can be found in any period of Poor Law history. The dearths were no exception. We might mention the Suffolk day labourer who was forced to pay for his new spade, provided by the vestry, out of his meal allowance.[31] In spite of the vast increase in the numbers assisted, relief was conditional on deference. The degree of subservience demanded can be gauged from the case of a Hampshire overseer who 'took offence' at a claimant 'stepping into the vestry without being sent for . . . and turned him out', and the magistrate who imprisoned the pauper for a refusal to apologise. The attitude enshrined in a letter from an estate steward to his employer speaks for itself:

> You will have a very serious loss and disappointment in your Bacon this year . . . the largest Hogs . . . mostly bad . . . and . . . a very small part of them is now eatable; but none of those parts fit to eat in your House . . . the Poor People would . . . pick and eat part of it . . . would you have me . . . give it away to the Poor?[32]

The subservient poor were to take what was offered, and acquiesce in the decisions of their affluent neighbours.

In order to survive the crises, the government advocated that the wheat deficiency could be partially overcome by the substitution of poorer cereals and other foodstuffs for wheat. [*Wells, unpublished, chs. 12-14*] Recipients hated all types of substitute, but such food was literally rammed down their throats by magistrates and overseers. Sir Christopher Sykes 'had such persons who will live on Barley bread alone . . . supplied by the overseer . . . but those who will not must buy as they can'. Chigwell vestrymen represented hundreds of others who simply turned their back on claimants who would not submit to dietary expedients.[33]

Such then, in brief, was the character of the new social control through poor relief. Two other major aspects must be stressed. Firstly, there is not a shred of evidence to suggest that relief was adequate: all the evidence indicates a fall in the real value of relief by 1801 [*Wells, unpublished, ch. 21 part iii*] Secondly, in the countryside the vestries were dominated by squire, parson and farmer. The owners of property and the employers of labour combined to exploit the terrible conditions of the nineties by cementing their control over the working population. The result was a polarisation of class and expressions of class antagonisms. For hundreds of bones of contention were inherent in the new system of control. The evidence contains many fruitful insights.

The contempt exuded towards their charges by many officials can be seen in the case of the overseer who beat a recalcitrant pauper with a flail.[34] But the coercion of the poor was never absolute. Mutual hatred became the order of the day. A handbill threatening arson in Essex complained that the author, who had a wife and six children, was 'all most starved', yet the overseers only 'allow me 4 and 6 a week'.[35] Resisting an overseer who came to incarcerate him in the workhouse, Thomas Kitchener exclaimed 'I now know my Friends from my Foes and Vengeances shall take place sooner or later'[36]. Such altercations became common. In Devon a group who had been denied relief looted the parish potato-store; in West Sussex another group of claimants 'with violent Oaths and Imprecations did demand . . . an increase in their weekly pay'. John West of Petworth was just one of hundreds imprisoned for threatening local officials.[37] With the law on their side, authority clearly had the upper hand in these face-to-face situations.

IV

This transformation in rural social relationships should not be seen in isolation. Rocketing food prices and plummeting living standards invariably provoked hostile comment and serious unrest. In every eighteenth-century dearth, popular opinion accused farmers, dealers and retailers of profiteering through charging excessively, withholding stocks from market to inflate prices, and sending stocks to take advantage of higher prices in distant markets. The common remedy was the 'food riot', which saw the crowd using its numerical supremacy to redress these grievances. The crowd blocked the roads and canals to stop food shipments, and imposed maximum prices.[38]

The first rapid acceleration of prices in the spring of 1795 provoked numerous disturbances throughout the country. No region was entirely free. But almost every incident occurred in an urban location, even if many of these were in the market towns in broadly agricultural regions. The evidence, while often imprecise, strongly suggests the involvement of rural workers in such disturbances.[39] Purely rural food disturbances are rarely recorded in the sources, which suggests that while the record may be defective, such disturbances were very minor.[40] The vast majority of disturbances were the product of that critical eighteenth-century conflict of interests, between the increasingly urbanised industrial consumer and the increasingly capitalist producer, the farmer and his 'agents' the wholesalers and retailers of food.[41] Moreover, as the nineties advanced, the geography of 'food riots' exhibited a pronounced shift away from the agricultural South and East, to the industrial and urban Midlands and North. Here they also became inextricably intermixed with industrial conflicts, and also with popular radical political movements which began to engulf urban societies in the Midlands and North. [*Wells, 1977b pp. 24–9, 38–46. Booth, 1977*]

Food disturbances in the South and East mainly occurred in the spring and summer of 1795. Their intensity was not repeated in spite of the greater prices current in 1799-1801. The new control through poor relief was partially responsible, but the 1795 outbreaks, while productive of greater relief, were also suppressed rigorously, if rarely brutally by both regular and volunteer soldiers. The role of the latter is crucial. The Volunteer Movement, a deliberate creation of an armed patriot party by the government to act as a reserve in case of invasion, but also as a police force, was predominantly, though not exclusively, a rural movement. The landowning and farming classes played a role out of all proportion to their numbers. [*Western, 1956*] Keeping the peace gave these enthusiasts the chance to show their mettle; they had little sympathy with the price-fixing objectives of their social subordinates.

Similarly, the yeomanry and magistracy were not prepared to tolerate trade unionist tactics aimed at increasing wages. Many apparently isolated attempts at strike action by workers in the countryside led to the imprisonment of their instigators.[42] There is some evidence of a mass movement in certain localities. In the autumn of 1795 an attempt by Norfolk farm labourers to co-ordinate demands for increased wages flickered briefly.[43] In 1800, identical moves in Essex and Berkshire led to violence. The Berkshire labourers were dispersed by the Volunteers. The leaders in Essex were indicted at the Assizes, where no less a personage than Lord Chief Justice Kenyon announced that the offence 'bordered on High Treason'. *The Times*' reporter was so incensed that he advocated the widest possible publication of the prison sentences to show to farm workers 'what would be the consequence of combining to distress their employers'.[44]

These failures to win redress of grievances by the traditional demonstration-cum-disturbance or by the much newer mode of strike action were serious. They deprived the rural worker of overt means of seeking to protect himself. The farmers as a class — aided and abetted by the clergy and the gentry — became the oppressors of the poor on four counts. As employers they provided little job-security, while paying inadequate wages. As armed patriots they used the sword to suppress open protest. As village worthies they controlled poor relief, and through it, they supervised and governed the lives of the poor.

V

The repressive agencies were fully adequate to the suppression of disturbance in the countryside. Overt protest was virtually impossible: it would clearly endanger a man's claim to relief. The rural workers' alternative was crime, and ultimately arson and the threatening letter.

Crime, principally the theft, and notably the poaching of food, was endemic in the eighteenth century countryside; but it 'was almost entirely economic — a defence against hunger'. [*Hobsbawn and Rude, 1969, p. 54*] Although fellow workers were commonly the victims of theft[45], the real losers were the propertied. Rural, as opposed to urban, crime rates (inasmuch as they can be measured) invariably rose in direct correlation with prices [*Beattie, 1974*] There can be little doubt that theft attained unprecedented levels in the countryside during the nineties, particularly during the famines. The press teemed with anguished but menacing announcements by landowners of their intention to prosecute offenders.[46] The Stockland (Devon) vestry minute is representative of countless others: 'Whereas several Gardens, cultivated lands and orchards . . . have been frequently robbed and plundered of Cabbages, Carrots, Potatoes, Turnips . . . and many sheep have been also lately stolen . . .' the principal inhabitants agreed to subscribe to a fund to launch a legal offensive.[47] The Parliamentary Opposition, in the person of the Duke of Bedford, even made political capital of a country full of 'miserable wretches, whose poverty left them no other resource but depredation' and suggested that empirical evidence was available if fellow peers 'repaired to the fields or the woods'.[48] Whether Bedford himself skulked in Woburn ditches is an interesting speculation, but what is certain is the development of the poor's own moral justification for

TABLE 1

The Incidence of Arson 1794-6, 1799-1801

a) The South-east (Surrey, Sussex and Kent)

Date	Location	County	Target
6.12.1794	Heyshot	Sussex	Barn
29.4.1795	Carshalton	Surrey	Barn
2.6.1795	Worth	Sussex	Barn
19.1.1796	Hastings	Sussex	Wheat rick
7.12.1799	East Greenwich	Kent	Barn
Dec. 1799	Not given	Sussex	Several corn stacks
7.3.1800	Friston	Sussex	Stack unthreshed wheat
5.4.1800	East Dean	Sussex	Wheat rick
12.4.1800	Beeding	Sussex	Wheat rick
4.5.1800	Worthing	Sussex	Stack of faggots
5.12.1800	Rochester	Kent	Wheat stack
26.12.1800	Ninfield	Sussex	Wheat stack

b) The West (Berkshire, Hampshire, Somerset, Wiltshire and Gloucestershire)

Date	Location	County	Target
30.1.1795	Peasemore	Berkshire	Barn
25.2.1795	Boxford	Berkshire	Farmhouse
9.4.1795	Wilton	Wiltshire	Barn
10.7.1795	Wokingham	Berkshire	Baker's store
11.7.1795	East Garston	Berkshire	Farmhouse and stable
8.3.1796	East Perrot	Somerset	Tithe barn
12.2.1800	Whiteparish	Wiltshire	Barn
28.2.1800	Odiham	Hampshire	Barn
7.3.1800	Bath	Somerset	Brewery store
13.3.1800	Kingsweaton	Somerset	Several hay stacks
10.6.1800	Wimborne	Dorset	Two barns
21.6.1800	Minehead	Somerset	Farmhouse and barns
24.8.1800	Cleewell	Gloucestershire	Magistrate's barn
28.8.1800	Speen	Berkshire	Barn newly-housed wheat
15.11.1800	Stoke Green	Berkshire	Wheat ricks and barns
17.2.1801	East Quanstockhead	Somerset	Wheat ricks
8.3.1801	Painswick	Gloucestershire	Hayrick

c) The Midlands and the North

Date	Location	County	Target
5.1.1795	Liverpool	Lancashire	Merchant's house, Warehouse
13.2.1796	Swinefleet	West Riding	Barn
14.2.1796	Swinefleet	West Riding	Barn
17.2.1800	Longer	Shropshire	Oat stack
27.4.1800	Shrewsbury	Shropshire	Wheat stacks
27.4.1800	Sutton	Shropshire	Wheat stacks
12.10.1800	Twyford	Derbyshire	Wheat stacks
19.10.1800	Market Bosworth	Leicestershire	Wheat stacks
27.10.1800	Sawley	Derbyshire	Mill owner's barn
1.11.1800	Not given	Derbyshire	Rick
17.11.1800	King's Newton	Derbyshire	Farm buildings
18.11.1800	Nr Nottingham	Nottinghamshire	Hayrick
1.12.1800	Keighley	West Riding	Corn mill
17.4.1801	Burford	Shropshire	Wheat rick
26.10.1801	Elsdon	Northumberland	Seven corn and one hay stack

d) East Anglia (Essex, Hertfordshire, Cambridgeshire, Huntingdonshire, Suffolk and Norfolk).

10.1.1795	Eye	Suffolk	Straw sacks
11.1.1795	Eye	Suffolk	Barn
30.11.1795	Blo' Norton	Norfolk	Barley stack
30.12.1795	Diss area	Norfolk	Several fires, no detail
14.1.1796	Ware	Hertfordshire	Hay stacks
11.2.1800	Watford	Hertfordshire	Wheat stack
April 1800	Trinley	Suffolk	Barn
April 1800	Harleychurch	Suffolk	Barn
29.4.1800	Harlow	Essex	Barns
23.6.1800	Blackmore	Essex	Stables and piggery
15.7.1800	Essendon	Hertfordshire	Barn
5.8.1800	Bickham	Essex	Wood piles
24.9.1800	Little Swaffham	Suffolk	Barn
16.10.1800	Braintree	Essex	No detail but third fire
18.10.1800	Clare	Suffolk	No detail but third fire
20.10.1800	Dunstable	Bedfordshire	Barley rick
26.10.1800	Clare	Suffolk	Overseer's corn stack
29.10.1800	Linsell	Essex	Barn
5.11.1800	Chatteris	Cambridgeshire	Farmhouse and barn
22.11.1800	Braintree	Essex	Malt office and store
22.11.1800	Brocking	Essex	Straw ricks
22.11.1800	Bracken	Essex	Stable
24.12.1800	Southwold	Suffolk	Barn
25.12.1800	Holt	Norfolk	Several corn ricks
July 1801	Walham	Hertfordshire	Barn

theft. 'Tom Nottage', exclaimed an Essex labourer, 'is a damn Rogue . . . you sink (his prices) for we have Rob your Mill seaval Times and we will rob it again'.[49]

Arson and threatening anonymous letters, which invariably threatened arson, were interrelated forms of protest, and both had a long history as modes of exacting private vengeance. [*Radzinowicz, 1948-68, I, p.9. Thompson, 1975*] The upsurge in the use of arson and threatening letters in the nineties is very marked. Equally noticeable is their deployment to express *public* protest rather than exact private vengeance. Victims were selected from the locally infamous members of the ruling class. Farmers, the authors of the subsistence problem in popular opinion, low-paying employers and overseers predominated, but the clergy and the magistracy were not exempt. 'And if the Farmer (w) ont give us more money a good Fier s(h)all be without . . . Delay . . . within 10 days . . . your ricks bournd to the Ground'. The 'Ruler of the Parish' of Eastbourne, Edward Augur, was told that incendiaries 'shall begin first with sonthing be longing to you'. £500 damages by fire were inflicted on a Sussex farmer who 'had stupidly said he would not thrash' and sell 'until wheat was £40 per load'. Bewildered local authorities hoped that incendiaries would limit their offensive to the especially unpopular.[50] Sir St. John Mildmay hopefully confided that Hampshire fires 'arose from some obnoxious proceedings on the part of the Farmer, respecting his conduct to the Poor'. He was speedily disappointed. Within two days he reported that 'the Premises of the most opulent and most considerable Farmers have been threatened with immediate destruction'. Similar threats were made in Sussex against 'every Stack of Corn', and in Wiltshire 'all the farmers' were menaced by incendiaries. Clearly these were expressions of something approaching class war; the farmers and their supporters, the gentry, were identified as the enemy. But arson never reached these proportions, not least because of the poor's discrimination. Odiham (Hampshire) labourers announced that '*we know* Every Stack of Corn about this Country and Every Barn that have Corn concealed . . . the poore in Every place is very willing to tell us the Farmers that ask the most money (for corn) and Likewise the Millers that Bid the most'.[51] Fourteen separate cases of arson have been found during 1794-6.[52] Berkshire fared worst with four cases, Sussex second with three, and Suffolk and Norfolk joint third with two each. These statistics relate to incidents which were definitely believed to be arson by local authorities. The figures may understate the extent of arson, because before definite cases assumed unmistakeable proportions, investigators possibly believed that fires were accidental. While the incidence of arson does not permit a sophisticated analysis, these four counties, together with Essex, Somerset, Wiltshire, and Hertfordshire (which had only one incident in 1794-6[53]) were to experience more numerous instances in the later dearth.

The incidence of arson during 1799-1801 may be roughly divided into two main periods, the spring and summer of 1800. Several distinct outbreaks can be traced. The South-East, notably Sussex, was seriously affected by threatening letters and incendiarism when prices rose rapidly from November 1799. The fires were accompanied by waves of anonymous missives; a Lewes journalist vainly warned the 'writers of the many threatening and inflammatory papers almost daily dropped and posted in different parts . . . of the heavy punishment which await their discovery'. His warning was greeted by another fire at Worthing. East Anglia experienced an identical protest movement in the spring.[54]

Popular indignation at the failure of prices to fall after the 1800 harvest reached its zenith in the autumn in both urban and rural areas. While arson was scattered in most regions, East Anglia experienced its worst outbreak with at least seventeen fires. The intensity of the outbreaks saw three insurance companies combining to publish handbills to stress that they, and not the farmers, suffered the loss. In Suffolk nightly patrols by special constables drawn from the farmers were established. The tenor of the press reports illustrates the universal alarm.[55]

All bar one of the fires in 1800 were started under cover of darkness, very often in the evening. The Marquis of Buckingham explained that they started 'at the same hour of the evening, viz. at eight o'clock (which) sufficiently shews that they have been produced by the labouring poor who at that hour are going home'. Virtually no incendiaries were caught.[56] But whoever they were, and Buckingham's opinion, that they came from amongst 'the poor of . . . very hard pressed parishes' is certainly plausible'[57] they could surely take satisfaction that their protest registered. The threat of arson alone provoked prodigous fears, as every letter to the Home Office on the subject testifies. Landowners, magistrates and farmers regularly asked for troops to patrol affected areas.[58] The threatening letter and arson played a similar role to the urban food riot; it forced the ruling classes to examine the complaints of the poor, and stimulated greater relief measures. For the army was not the only answer; the rulers of the countryside responded by digging deeper into their pockets.

VI

The condition of the rural workforce declined further during the first half of the nineteenth century. The labour market was swollen intolerably by discharged soldiers and sailors after the end of the war in 1815. Demand for labour was deflated by the introduction of threshing machines. The Poor Law's significance for the labourer grew inexorably. The post-war agricultural depression hit farmers' profits, giving some justification to their constant assertion of inability to increase pay. This threw the levels of rent and tithe into a new perspective, and the farmers were able to pass on some of the odium for the state of rural society to the landowners and clergy. Two major protest movements, in East Anglia in 1816, and the much more widespread Swing movement in 1830-1 were the almost inevitable product of the worsening of the labourers' situation. But as landmarks in the history of social protest these spectacular outbreaks may have assumed a disproportionate importance. While the Swing revolt produced some curious social permutations — with farmers joining labourers against the clergy — these outbreaks were expressions of class war. They are the most famous *overt* expressions. But were covert expressions in fact more significant?

Arson was not Captain Swing's major weapon: it was one of several but not the most important [*Hobsbawm and Rudé, 1969*] Yet arson became a continuous form of rural protest in nineteenth-century England, even it its intensity varied.[59] So too did that other form of covert social protest, theft, as any history of the game laws shows. Covert social protest was certainly more enduring than any other sort, and it was essentially conservative. The labourers wanted what they conceived to be a comfortable standard of living; above all they wanted adequate food. Farmers, landowners, magistrates and clergymen were increasingly identified as the enemy, because they were considered responsible for the non-realisation of limited expectations. These classes were the victims of rural theft; they were the recipients of anonymous letters; their property was fired. But these poachers, pseudonymists and incendiaries certainly did not envisage any major structural changes in society; incendiarism is not synonymous with political 'radicalism' even through the incendiaries articulated sentiments pertinent to class war in their anonymous warnings. Covert protest was not replaced until the later nineteenth century when, through their faltering adoption of trade unionism, the labourers readopted an overt mode of protest. The origins and intensification of covert protest are to be found in the repression, and the development of the new control, in which the 1790s assume a paramount importance.

And as we can't have a Riot
We'll do things more quiet
As provisions get higher
The greater the Fire.[60]

APPENDIX A

Specimen Family Budgets, Agricultural Labourers

(*Source:* D. Davies, *The Case of the Labourers in Husbandry*, (1795), pp. 8-13, 138-41, 146-7. Evidence collected 1787-9.)

Families 1 to 3. Wheat-eating, domiciled in Berkshire.

Family 1.

Man, wife, 5 children, aged 1 to 8. Total income, 8/6 per week. Cost of food, 8/11¼.

7½ gallons wheaten flour.
1 lb bacon.
½ lb butter.
¾ lb sugar.
1 oz tea.

Family 2.

Man, wife, 3 children, aged 1 to 5. Total income, 8/8 per week. Cost of food, 6/11¼.

3 gallons wheaten flour.
2½ lb bacon.
½ lb cheese.
½ lb butter.

Family 3.

Man, wife, 1 child, aged 10. Total income, 7/5 per week. Cost of food, 7/-.

4 gallons wheaten flour.
1½ lbs bacon.
½ lb butter.
½ lb sugar.
2 ozs tea.

APPENDIX B

Wholesale price of wheat at Chichester in shillings. The cost of the wheat component of a family with two children can be roughly obtained by dividing the wholesale price by ten.

NS = No Sales
NR = No Return
Source: PRO. Ministry of Agriculture and Fisheries, 10/279-285

Date		Date		Date	
6.9.1794	44	27.9.1794	48	18.10.1794	48
13.9.1794	44	4.10.1794	48	25.10.1794	50
20.9.1794	48	11.10.1794	48	1.11.1794	50

Date		Date		Date	
8.11.1794	50	21.11.1795	92	7.12.1799	98
15.11.1794	52	28.11.1795	96	14.12.1799	88
22.11.1794	52	5.12.1795	96	21.12.1799	80
29.11.1794	52	12.12.1795	84	28.12.1799	82
6.12.1794	52	19.12.1795	84	4.1.1800	92
13.12.1794	52	26.12.1795	84	11.1.1800	98
20.12.1794	54	2.1.1796	84	18.1.1800	99
27.12.1794	54	9.1.1796	96	25.1.1800	100
3.1.1795	54	16.1.1796	96	1.2.1800	102
10.1.1795	54	23.1.1796	100	8.2.1800	108
17.1.1795	54	30.1.1796	100	15.2.1800	112
24.1.1795	54	6.2.1796	100	22.2.1800	120
31.1.1795	54	13.2.1796	100	1.3.1800	122
7.2.1795	56	20.2.1796	100	8.3.1800	120
14.2.1795	56	27.2.1796	100	15.3.1800	112
21.2.1795	56	5.3.1796	104	22.3.1800	112
28.2.1795	56	12.3.1796	104	29.3.1800	118
7.3.1795	58	19.3.1796	104	5.4.1800	120
14.3.1795	58	26.3.1796	100	12.4.1800	121
21.3.1795	60	2.4.1796	96	19.4.1800	120
28.3.1795	60	9.4.1796	76	26.4.1800	124
4.4.1795	64	16.4.1796	NS	3.5.1800	124
11.4.1795	64	23.4.1796	NS	10.5.1800	130
18.4.1795	64	30.4.1796	72	17.5.1800	128
25.4.1795	60	7.5.1796	NS	24.5.1800	120
2.5.1795	60	14.5.1796	66	31.5.1800	120
9.5.1795	60	21.5.1796	66	7.6.1800	132
16.5.1795	60	28.5.1796	70	14.6.1800	136
23.5.1795	60	4.6.1796	70	21.6.1800	136
30.5.1795	66	11.6.1796	76	28.6.1800	148
6.6.1795	68	18.6.1796	76	5.7.1800	148
13.6.1795	66	25.6.1796	76	12.7.1800	148
20.6.1795	66	2.7.1796	80	19.7.1800	148
27.6.1795	66	9.7.1796	72	26.7.1800	144
4.7.1795	66	16.7.1796	72	2.8.1800	116
11.7.1795	72	23.7.1796	72	9.8.1800	72
18.7.1795	80	30.7.1796	72	16.8.1800	NS
25.7.1795	89	6.8.1796	72	23.8.1800	80
1.8.1795	98	13.8.1796	72	30.8.1800	84
8.8.1795	100	20.8.1796	72	6.9.1800	100
15.8.1795	100	27.8.1796	NS	13.9.1800	112
22.8.1795	100	7.9.1799	NR	20.9.1800	101
29.8.1795	100	14.9.1799	NS	27.9.1800	82
5.9.1795	80	21.9.1799	73	4.10.1800	80
12.9.1795	76	28.9.1799	74	11.10.1800	84
19.9.1795	76	5.10.1799	72	18.10.1800	96
26.9.1795	72	12.10.1799	78	25.10.1800	108
3.10.1795	76	19.10.1799	78	1.11.1800	120
10.10.1795	76	26.10.1799	80	8.11.1800	124
17.10.1795	80	2.11.1799	80	15.11.1800	120
24.10.1795	80	9.11.1799	80	22.11.1800	122
31.10.1795	84	16.11.1799	84	29.11.1800	128
7.11.1795	84	23.11.1799	94	6.12.1800	124
14.11.1795	92	30.11.1799	100	13.12.1800	130

Date		Date		Date	
20.12.1800	144	21.3.1801	168	13.6.1801	142
27.12.1800	148	28.3.1801	164	20.6.1801	142
3.1.1801	148	4.4.1801	168	27.6.1801	140
10.1.1801	148	11.4.1801	168	4.7.1801	136
17.1.1801	136	18.4.1801	164	11.7.1801	141
24.1.1801	152	25.4.1801	158	18.7.1801	160
31.1.1801	160	2.5.1801	148	25.7.1801	162
7.2.1801	160	9.5.1801	120	1.8.1801	140
14.2.1801	160	16.5.1801	100	8.8.1801	136
21.2.1801	164	23.5.1801	102	15.8.1801	110
28.2.1801	158	30.5.1801	124	22.8.1801	120
7.3.1801	158	6.6.1801	140	29.8.1801	NS
14.3.1801	170				

NOTES

1. South and east of a line drawn roughly from Scarborough in Yorkshire to Weymouth in Dorset

2. For exceptions see [*Mingay, 1968, p. 27*]

3. There is no reason to believe that the picture in parts of Suffolk in 1837-51 was very new: then 89 per cent of labourers were the sons of labourers, and 78.6 per cent of labourers married the daughters of labourers. [*Jones, D. 1976, p. 7*]

4. For a recent survey of the complex issue of population growth, see Flinn [*1970.*] Cf. Deane and Cole, [*1962, ch. 3*] and Razzell, [*1978*]

5. Spenceley [*1973, pp. 81-93*] relates how the pillow lace industry's growth in some South Midland counties, was of importance for a rural 'population which . . . was anxious to find suitable means of adding to family incomes' derived from agricultural labouring.

6. Recent literature on the Poor Law is well covered in Marshall [*1968*] and Oxley [*1974*]. For a short outline see Martin [*1972*].

7. An individual normally obtained a settlement by birth, or by working for a year in a parish.

8. Until 1795 a migrant could be forcibly removed from any parish to which he tried to move: after 1795, parochial authorities could not remove migrants until they applied for relief. The 1795 legislation gave statutory backing to what seems to have been a common and well established practice in many regions.

9. Full-time overseers were rare. Usually farmers and others from the more affluent strata of the community undertook the task of supervising the poor, and implementing decisions taken by parish vestries, on a rotating basis.

10. [*Burnett, 1966, pp. 61-2*] See Appendix A for typical diets, which are based on the evidence, largely collected in the 1780's, by Davies [*1795, pp. 8-13, 138-41, 146-7*].

11. E.G. Claridge, [*1793, pp. 24-5*]. Vicar of Richmond, harvest return, P(ublic) R(ecord) O(ffice), H(ome) O(ffice), 42/54.

12. Cheshire window surveyor's harvest return, 1800. PRO. Chatham papers, 30/8/291, f. 73.

13. Prosecutor's brief re. trial of Mary Killingbeck for riot, Essex Michaelmas Quarter Sessions, 1795, E(ssex) C(ounty) R(ecord) O(ffice). Q/SBb/361; 362/84. [*Sherborne Mercury,*] 20 July 1795. [*Mackie, 1901, I, p. 223*]

14. For the methodology see Wells, [unpublished, Tables 14-17, Appendices 1-5]

15. See Appendix B. The series here is based on Chichester wholesale prices. The major price trends were national, and series calculated on wholesale prices elsewhere in the country are similar.

16. Quarterly 'surpluses' and 'deficits' for both crises are given in Appendix C.

17. Wages in general rose during the nineties, but although some increases were clearly a direct product of the crises, prices still rose out of all proportion to incomes. Gilboy, [*1934, p. 179*] an early investigator of wage rates, was obviously flabbergasted by the size of the disparity.

18. The best-known account of the origins of the Speenhamland decision is given by the Hammonds [*1911, ch. VI*]. For more recent accounts see Poynter [*1969, pp. 76-81*] and Neuman [*1972, pp. 86-91*], and for an alternative interpretation, Wells, [unpublished, ch. 21, part i]

19. The arguments that sliding-scale supplements guaranteed the same income irrespective of how much effort workers applied to their job, and rendered overtime pointless, were increasingly heard. Static payments meant that employees would receive more if they worked harder and for longer hours.

20. At Hayes in Kent in 1800-1, 'Some bread' purchased from Communion funds 'was given to the poorest every Sunday after Church'. Free clothes were given to 'The large families and very poor persons . . . in the course of each Year'. Each autumn 'Every Family' was supplied with a stock of potatoes 'at half prime cost'. 'Most of the poor' had skimmed milk, 'some of it gratis, some at 1d per Quart'. 'Additional Relief when Bread is very dear' included a pint of soup for all, coal at low and constant prices, and various meats at low prices. Agricultural wages were maintained at the higher summer rates throughout the year, and women and children were given work. These benefits were partially paid for by the parish, and partly by affluent individuals, like the coal merchant who made no profit on the poor's fuel supply. Mss. entitled 'Hayes in Kent', 1801, D(evon) C(ounty) R(ecord) O(ffice), Sidmouth Papers, D152M/corr.1801.

21. 'What was the state of a country which first compelled every man to dependence and then reduced him to servitude?' asked Charles James Fox, the leader of the Opposition. T.B. Barnard, a leading philanthropist, articulated his concern at the social effects of the workers being encouraged to 'look up to the rich, for daily alms of food': 'the distinction between independence and poverty' was undermined by universal receipt of poor relief. *Debrett's Parliamentary Debates*, 2nd ser. vol. 43, pp. 247-8, 649-50. *Reports of the Society for Bettering the Conditions of the Poor*, vol. III, (1802), pp. 26-8, 157-8.

22. *Sussex Weekly Advertiser*, 3 February 1795. Woodford vestry minute, 1 December 1800, ECRO DP.167, 8/3. Sandford Union Committee minute, 14 July 1795, I(pswich) and E(ast) S(uffolk) R(ecord) O(ffice) ADA7, ABI/2.

23. e.g. Huntingdonshire County Meeting handbill, 30 July 1795, British Museum Additional MSS. 35462, ff. 123-4, to guard against 'Collusion between the Poor and the Bakers'.

24. One overseer, William Fawcett, typically alleged that he had, 'Complaints come before me almost every day . . . from the Poor . . . and I am sorry that I have little to say in their favour, as they are most of 'em, an idle, indolent set of people who do not use their best endeavours to earn their bread, so long as they can be maintain'd in idleness.' Fawcett to R. Howard, 6 March 1800 N(orfolk) and N(orwich) R(ecord) O(ffice), How. 758/29. 349X.

25. *Reading Mercury*, 6 July 1795. Bingfield vestry minutes, Kingston Lisle overseers' accounts, and Quarter Session minute book, B(erkshire) C(ounty) R(ecord) O(ffice). DP. 18, 8/1; 115B, 12/4. Q/SO/9, ff. 36-8.

26. Vestry minutes, Great Parnden, 22 July 1795, ECRO. DP.184, 8/2; Huish Episcopi. 27 March 1801, Somerset County Record Office, DP.h.ep. 9/1/4 *Reports of the Society for Bettering the Condition of the Poor*, vol. III, (1802) pp. 60-5.

50   *Class, Conflict and Protest in the English Countryside, 1700–1880*

27. *Reports of the Society for Bettering the Condition of the Poor*, vol. III (1802), pp. 192-9. Vestry minutes. ECRO. DP. 128, 8/4; NNRO. PO.41/32.

28. Vestry minutes, South Weald, 14 June and 4 August, Moreton, 30 December 1800, ECRO DP.128, 8/4; 72. 8/1.

29. The press reported many such decisions; e.g. *Hull Advertiser*, 20 March 1795. *Derby Mercury*, 23 July 1795.

30. Terling vestry minutes, 6 July and 12 August 1795, ECRO DP. 299, 8/2.

31. Werlingworth vestry minute, 11 January 1796, IESRO. FC.94. A1/2.

32. *The Iris*, 7 August 1800. J. Howson to W. Spencer-Stanhope, 9 April 1796, Sheffield City Library, Spencer-Stanhope MSS. 60586/10.

33. Sykes to William Wilberforce, 27 January 1796, Humberside County Record Office, DD.SY 101/54. Chigwell vestry minute, 24 January 1796, ECRO. DP. 168, 8/9.

34. And afterwards imprisoned him without blankets in 'a cold noisome and unwholesome Room . . . By means whereof the Feet . . . were mortified'. Indictment of W. Wright, H(ampshire) C(ounty) R(ecord) O(ffice), Quarter Session File, Easter 1795.

35. Lord Braybrook to the Essex Clerk of the Peace, with enclosures, 18 July 1800, ECRO. Q/SBb, 380/66/1-4.

36. Indictment of Kitchener, HCRO, Quarter Sessions File, Easter 1799.

37. Prosecutor's brief against six inhabitants of Winkleigh, PRO Treasury solicitor, 11/914. Indictment of N. Hopkins and others of Cocking, December 1794, and Committal of West, December 1800, W(est) S(ussex) C(ounty) R(ecord) O(ffice), QR/W 608, W632.

38. For a superb analysis of this phenomenon, the popular imposition of the 'moral economy' to overthrow the laissez-faire market economy, see Thompson (1971).

39. For example, a riot at Cambridge forced the Mayor to subsidise the town workers' bread. Subsequently there were fears 'of a battle between the Country People and those of the Town', because the Mayor's generosity was not to be extended to villagers who had played a part in the initial disturbance. *Bath Chronicle*, 22 July 1795.

40. An example of a minor rural 'food riot' which occurred during the short hyper-crisis in the midsummer of 1795, involved the North Yorkshire villagers of Bridforth, who stopped a cart laden with flour; one of the two leaders admitted that 'she was unhappily concerned in obstructing Mr. Cleaver's waggon . . . which she is sorry for.' North Yorkshire Record Office. QSB. Michaelmas 1795.

41. Cf. Wells [*1977a*] and review by Thompson [*1974, pp. 480-4*] of Shelton [*1973*] in which Shelton's assumption that agricultural workers were the main instigators of disturbance in the 1760's is criticised.

42. e.g. Imprisonment of four Funtingdon labourers, 1795, WSCRO, W.608 f.58 Appeal against conviction by twelve workers, Kent Michaelmas Quarter Sessions, 1801. E. Melling (ed) *Kentish Sources: Crime and Punishment*, (Maidstone, 1969) p. 152. Case against five Botley men, HCRO Quarter Sessions File, Michaelmas, 1800.

43. *Norfolk Chronicle*, 14 November 1795. See also MPs Hume and Baker to the Home Secretary, both 6 July 1795, claiming that such manifestations were encouraged by supporters of the Opposition's minimum wage bill. PRO. HO. 42/35 Nottingham University Library, Portland dep. PWF.233.

44. Essex: *The Times*, 14 June, 9 and 13 August. *Chelmsford Chronicle*, 13 June *Morning Chronicle*, 26 June. Indictments, PRO Assizes, 31/8. Berkshire: Newbury JPs to Secretary of War, 10 June, PRO. War Office, 40/17. *Reading Mercury*, 16 June 1800.

45. e.g. cases against Hannah Moore, singlewoman, and John Muggeridge, labourer for stealing 'part' of loaves of bread from other labourers at Petworth and Fittleworth respectively. West Sussex Michaelmas 1801 Quarter Sessions, WSCRO QR/632.

46. e.g. *Sussex Weekly Advertiser.*

47. Vestry minutes, 2 July 1801, DCRO. D121SA/PO.3.

48. Debrett's Parliamentary Debates, 3rd ser. vol. 10, p. 234.

49. Threatening letter, 18 June, enclosed by T. Hall, Essex, to the Home Secretary, 14 July 1800, PRO.HO.42/50.

50. Bill posted on East Hangbourne church door, *Reading Mercury,* 30 March 1795. Lord Sheffield to William Pitt, 18 December 1799, PRO Chatham papers 30/8/177, ff. 233-5. *London Gazette,* March 1800.

51. G.Y. Fort to W. Hussey, 19 February. Mildmay to Lord Hawkesbury, 2 and 4 March, PRO.HO.42/49. *London Gazette,* March 1800.

52. See Table 1.

53. Evidence compiled from local press, letters to the Home Office and notices of rewards offered for information in the *London Gazette.*

54. Sheffield to Pitt, 18 December, PRO Chatham papers, 30/8/177, ff. 233-5. *London Gazette,* 23 December 1799, 1 March, 10 May, 12 and 19 July, and 16 August. *Sussex Weekly Advertiser,* March–May. Letters to the Home Secretary from H. Shelley and W. Green, Lewes, 31 March, H.T. Shadwell, with enclosures, 17 April, M. Burgoyne, 2 May, T. Ruggles, 24 June and 6 July, and T. Hall, PRO.HO. 42/49-50. Letters to Essex Clerk of the Peace, July, ECRO. Q/SBb/380/66/1-4. *Chelmsford Chronicle,* 27 June, *Gentleman's Magazine,* August 1800, p. 784.

55. Letters to the Home Office from J. Spude and R.C. Barnard, 24 and 26 October and Mr. Watts, Sun Fire Office, 1 November, PRO.HO. 42/51-5. *London Gazette,* and *Norfolk Chronicle,* October–December 1800.

56. Several persons were locked up, and even tried for threatening arson. See cases against Jane Bungay of Berkhampton and Hannah Bye, HCRO Quarter Sessions Files Midsummer 1800 and Easter 1801. Others were acquitted by juries. Cases against Richard Drewe of Cullompton and Edward Jeans of Essex, PRO. Assizes, 25/3/1; 31/19, p.3. Ironically the only reported guilty verdict was obtained against a Hertfordshire labourer whose crime was clearly the product of private vengeance. *Derby Mercury,* 30 July 1801.

57. Buckingham to the Home Secretary, 2 November 1800, PRO.HO. 42/53.

58. e.g. letters to the Home Office from G. Greathead, 2 May, and Burgoyne, 19 June 1800, PRO.HO. 42/50.

59. Especially in East Anglia, as the work of Jones, D. 4(*1976*] and Peacock [*1974*] has shown. Further regional research is needed to complete the picture.

60. Anonymous doggerel, printed in the *London Gazette,* 22 March 1800.

REFERENCES

Barnett, D.C. 1961, 'Allotments and the Problem of Rural Poverty, 1780-1840', in G.E. Mingay and E.L. Jones (eds.) *Land, Labour and Population in the Industrial Revolution.*

Beattie, J.M. 1974, 'The Pattern of Crime in England, 1660-1800', *Past and Present*, 62.

Beavington, F. 1975, 'The Development of Market Gardening in Bedfordshire', *Agricultural History Review*, 23.

Booth, A. 1977, 'Food Riots in the North-west of England, 1790-1801', *Past and Present*, 77.

Burnett, J. 1966, 'Trends in Bread Consumption', in T.L. Barker, J.L. Mackenzie and J. Yudkin, (eds.) *Our Changing Fare.*

Chambers, J.D. 1940, 'Enclosure and the Small Landowner', *Economic History Review*, 1st ser X.

Chambers, J.D. 1953, 'Enclosure and the Labour Supply in the Industrial Revolution', in E.L. Jones (ed.), *Agriculture and Economic Growth 1650-1815*, (1967).

Claridge, R. 1793, *A General View of the Agriculture of the County of Dorset.*

Collins, K. 1967, 'Marx on the English Agricultural Revolution', *History and Theory*, VI

Davies, D. 1795, *The Case of the Labourer in Husbandry.*

Deane, P. and Cole, W.A. 1962, *British Economic Growth, 1688-1959.*

Dunbadin, J.P.D. 1974, *Rural Discontent in Nineteenth-Century Britain.*

Flinn, M.W. 1970, *British Population Growth, 1700-1850.*

Fussell, G.E. 1968, *The Dairy Farmer, 1500-1900.*

George, M.D. 1925, *London Life in the Eighteenth Century.*

Gilboy, E.W. 1934, *Wages in Eighteenth Century England.*

Hammond, J.L. and B. 1911, *The Village Labourer.*

Hardy, le, W. (ed.) 1935, *Hertfordshire County Records: Calendar to the Quarter Sessions Minute Books, 1752-1798.*

Hobsbawn, E.J., and Rudé, G. 1969, *Captain Swing* (References to 1973 edition).

Hoskins, W.G. 1957, *The Midland Peasant.*

Huckel, G. 1976, 'English Farming Profits during the Napoleonic Wars, 1793-1815', *Explorations in Economic History*, 13.

John, A.H. 1967, 'Farming in Wartime, 1793-1815', in G.E. Mingay and E.L. Jones, (eds.) *Land, Labour and Population in the Industrial Revolution.*

Jones, D. 1976, 'Thomas Campbell Foster and the Rural Labourer: Incendiarism in East Anglia in the 1840's', *Social History*, I.

Jones, E.L. 1975, 'The Constraints on Economic Growth in Southern England', *Third International Conference of Economic History.*

Laurence, E. 1731, *The Duty and Office of a Land Steward* (2nd edition).

Mackie, C. 1901, *Norfolk Annals*, 2 vols.

MacMahon, K.A. 1964, 'Roads and Turnpike Trusts in the East Riding of Yorkshire', *East Yorkshire Local History Series*, no. 18.

Marshall, J.D. 1968, *The Old Poor Law, 1795-1834.*

Martin, E.W. 1972, 'From Parish to Union: Poor Law Administration, 1601-1834' in E.W. Martin (ed.), *Comparative Development in Social Welfare.*

Martin, J.M. 1964, 'The Cost of Parliamentary Enclosure in Warwickshire', in E.L. Jones (ed.), *Agriculture and Economic Growth in England, 1660-1815*, (1967).

Mingay, G.E. 1956, 'The Agricultural Depression 1730-50', in E.M. Carus-Wilson (ed.), *Essays in Economic History*, 3 vols. (1954-62), II.

Mingay, G.E. 1961-62, 'The Size of Farms in the Eighteenth Century', *Economic History Review*, 2nd ser. XIV.

Mingay, G.E. 1964, *English Landed Society in the Eighteenth Century*.

Mingay, G.E. 1968, *Enclosure and the Small Farmer in the Age of the Industrial Revolution*.

Mitchell, B.R. 1962, *Abstract of British Historical Statistics*.

Neuman, M. 1972, 'Speenhamland in Berkshire', in E.W. Martin (ed.), *Comparative Development in Social Welfare*.

Oxley, G.W. 1974, *Poor Relief in England and Wales, 1601-1834*.

Peacock, A.J. 1965, *Bread or Blood: the Agrarian Riots in East Anglia, 1816*.

Peacock, A.J. 1974, 'Village Radicalism in East Anglia, 1800-50' in J.P. Dunbadin (1974).

Perkin, H. 1969, *The Origins of Modern English Society, 1780-1880*.

Poynter, J.R. 1969, *Society and Pauperism. English Ideas on Poor Relief, 1795-1834*.

Radzinowicz, L. 1948-68, *History of English Criminal Law*, 4 vols.

Razzell, P. 1978, *The Conquest of Smallpox*.

Shelton, W.J. 1973, *English Hunger and Industrial Disorders*.

Tate, W.E. 1952, 'The Cost of Parliamentary Enclosure in England', *Economic History Review*, 2nd ser. V.

Thompson, E.P. 1963, *The Making of the English Working Class* (References to 1968 edition).

Thompson, E.P. 1971, 'The "moral economy" of the English Crowd in the Eighteenth Century', *Past and Present*, 50.

Thompson, E.P. 1974, Review of Shelton (1973) in *Economic History Review*, 2nd ser. XXVII.

Thompson, E.P. 1975, 'The Crime of Anonymity', in D. Hay, P. Linebaugh and E.P. Thompson (eds.), *Albion's Fatal Tree*.

Turner, M.E. 1973, 'The Cost of Parliamentary Enclosure in Buckinghamshire', *Agricultural History Review*, 21.

Turner, M.E. 1975, 'The Parliamentary Enclosure and Landownership Changes in Buckinghamshire', *Economic History Review*, 2nd. ser. XXVIII.

Walker, D. 1795, *A General View of the Agriculture of the County of Hertford*.

Wells, R.A.E. Unpublished. 'The Grain Crises in England 1794-96, 1799-1801', (D.Phil. thesis, University of York).

Wells, R.A.E. 1977a, 'The Revolt of the South-west 1800-1; a Study in English Popular Protest', *Social History*, 6.

Wells, R.A.E. 1977b, 'Dearth and Distress in Yorkshire, 1793-1802', *Borthwick Papers*, 52.

Western, J.R. 1956, 'The Volunteer Movement as an Anti-Revolutionary Force, 1793-1801', *English Historical Review*, LXXI.

Wrigley, E.A. 1967, A Simple Model of London's Importance in changing English Society and Economy, 1650-1750', *Past and Present*, 37.

Wordie, J.R. 1974, 'Social Change on the Leveson-Gower Estates, 1714-1832', *Economic History Review*, 2nd. ser. XXVII.

The Development of the English Rural Proletariat and Social Protest, 1700–1850: A Comment[1]

Andrew Charlesworth*

Dr. Wells is to be congratulated on his attempt to delineate the main features of the development of the English rural proletariat and of the associated onset of protests by agricultural labourers during the period 1790–1815 [*Wells 1979*]. Too often accounts of the agricultural labourers and their defence of their living standards commence with the events in East Anglia in 1816. I find however that there are, on the one hand, omissions in Wells' arguments that weaken his case whilst, on the other hand, there are misinterpretations that seriously undermine his main thesis.

There are four main strands in Wells' arguments. In the first place, he explores the origins and the process of becoming of the English rural proletariat. Wells draws together evidence for the steady pauperisation of the agricultural labourers and the swelling of their numbers as the structures of capitalist agriculture and industry unfolded and expanded between 1700 and 1850. He then goes on to explain why that process of becoming a proletariat was not, before 1790, accompanied by serious unrest on the part of the agricultural labourers. The third and fourth, and the major, parts of his thesis are devoted to what happened in contrast between 1790 and 1815. By 1790 Wells sees the rural labourers as the most depressed sector of the English working classes. In his view the subsistence crises of the 1790s and the 1800s were the final push that broke the delicate equilibrium of rural society and led to the first widespread signs of class conflict between agricultural labourers and their masters. The form of that conflict, covert protest, was shaped by the efficacy of the social controls that were either inherent in the nature of capitalist agriculture or a product of the measures taken by the ruling classes to meet either the crises themselves or the wartime emergency. In particular, Wells accords a crucial role to the massive extension of the poor relief system. This led to a much greater degree of control over the lives of agricultural labourers. 'Overt protest was virtually impossible: it would clearly endanger a man's claim to relief' [*Wells 1979: 127/41*]. The potential strength of the labourers was thus checked. The protests of 1816 and 1822 in East Anglia and of 1829–31 throughout Southern and Eastern England are then to be viewed as sporadic outbursts of direct collective action in the endemic and

* *University of Liverpool. I would like to thank Roger Wells for his forebearance and help, without which this commentary on his article could not have been written.*

more important covert struggle waged by labourers with the weapons of theft, threatening letters and arson. Indeed, the culmination of Wells' case rests on the evidence of the use of such weapons.

Although I can accept the tenor of Wells' interpretation of the development of the rural proletariat, I still feel that he has neglected the social component of that process: the changes in the daily lives of the agricultural labourers that emphasised for them their new condition as a proletariat, as a group separate from their employers. The larger workforces more irregularly employed and more regularly to be found on poor relief, and the decline in the number of living-in servants, made the farmer a more remote figure with whom the men had less day-to-day contact. Farmers were seen to want a different lifestyle from their labourers by banishing them from their tables and farms. The growing segregation between the two classes was further compounded in the latter half of the eighteenth century by the clearer emergence of 'open' and 'close' parishes. In 'close' parishes the number of labouring families living there was rigidly controlled by landlords and ratepayers so as to limit the number of such families gaining settlements, and hence being eligible for poor relief. Many labourers employed by farmers in the 'close' parish were then forced to live in the neighbouring 'open' parishes [*Holderness 1972: 126–39; Samuel 1975; 14–16; Digby 1978: 89–97*]. Thus there began to develop in many villages, but in particular in the more populous, 'open' villages, a separate community of labourers all suffering the common experience of exploitation and increasingly antipathetic to their masters.[2]

At the same time the processes of social and spatial segregation meant that labourers were increasingly freed from the patriarchal web of control of the farmhouse and the 'close' village [*Samuel 1975: 16*]. Moreover, with the growth in size of the labouring community, specific institutions centred on the labourer developed, both formally and informally: meeting houses, chapels, pubs, friendly societies and benefit clubs, poaching gangs, football teams, drinking parties. These were complementary to the daily groupings of men that labourers were perforce to take part in: agricultural workteams, and when on poor relief, road gangs, quarrying parties and parish gangs for general farmwork [*Peacock 1965: chs. 2 and 3; Hobsbawm and Rudé 1973: chs. 3 and 10; Hasbach 1908: ch. 3*]. Thus the labourers had the freedom and the opportunities to discuss together their grievances and hence to identify common points of antagonistic interest between themselves and their employers. Contemporaries reached similar conclusions but were more flamboyant in their language. Beershops, for example, were described in 1834 as places 'where the dissolute may meet unperceived', 'with facilities for union and combination', but the attributes could have been just as well ascribed to the labourers' pub or the drinking party at the village shoemaker's in earlier days. Similarly, road gangs were looked on as an opportunity for men to 'corrupt one another' and to listen 'to every bad advice', there being no one 'to look after them'.[3]

It was thus from these separate communities, relatively *free* from social *control*, and with the necessary groupings of men for mobilising for collective action, that the protests of the agricultural labourers sprang [*Peacock 1965: ch. 3; Hobsbawm and Rudé 1973: chs. 9 and 10; Huzel 1976: 31*]. In contrast, in the earlier part of the eighteenth century, when the web of social control in agricultural villages was tighter and there was no separate community of agricultural labourers, enclosure, as Wells indicates, went ahead with little clamour [*Wells 1979: 120/34*]. The quiescence in agricultural villages is high-lighted if one remembers that at the same time there were serious protests against enclosure, but these occurred in villages that had substantial numbers of industrial workers, a separate group with a solidarity of interest and the strength to mobilise [*Wearmouth 1945: ch. 1; Neeson 1977: ch. 7*].

By ignoring these elements, Wells' account moves too quickly from the development of the rural proletariat and the grievances of that class to the outbreak of social protest. That approach smacks too much of the discredited hardship model of social protest.[4] Granted that, in the short run, hardship can sometimes explain the timing of a particular outbreak of protest, in the long run, it is the solidarity of communities and interest groups that is the mainspring of collective action.

In his account of the wartime period of 1793–1815, Wells focuses most of his attention on the subsistence crises and the extension of the poor relief system to cope with those emergencies. Yet the wartime boom with its attendant inflation was more than this. It was a period of conjunctural change that brought into fruition many of the underlying structural changes that had been taking place in rural society from 1750 onwards. The increased prices led to increased profits for the farmers, a 'hectic scramble to enclose and . . . to expand cultivation' and 'a widened enthusiasm for improved methods of farming' [*Chambers and Mingay 1966: 108–18; John 1967*]. They also increased the farmers' desire to cut labour costs. Consequently machinery, especially threshing machines, was introduced for the first time on a wide scale, and there was a marked acceleration in the decline of living-in servants [*Jones 1965: 324–5; Kussmaul 1978: ch. 7*]. There was a 'reinforcement of the natural periodicity of arable farming', an increase in piece work, and an upsurge in temporary work associated with 'reshaping the physical capital of farming' [*Jones 1965: 325, 323; Richardson 1977: 70*]. In the farmhouse, now more of a private dwelling, the opulent stockjobber culture was more easily afforded and rapidly adopted by the farmer and his family [*Chambers and Mingay 1966: 112*]. The social distance between farmer and labourer decidedly widened between 1790 and 1815.

Moreover, it was the rapidity of these changes precipitated by the wartime conditions which was all important in shaping the labourers' consciousness of their new position in the social order. So rapid had been the 'forcing' of the changes in the conditions of employment and in the levels of wages, prices and profits under the hothouse climate of the war, that the labourers could look back on the 1770s and 1780s with a genuine sense of loss, sentiments that Cobbett echoed throughout his 'Rural Rides' [*Cobbett 1853: passim*]. This was in marked contrast to the earlier part of the eighteenth century when, as Wells rightly notes, the evolutionary nature of agrarian change did not allow 'The genesis of a past "golden age" notion in workers' minds' [*Wells 1979: 120/34*]. By 1815 the agricultural labourers did have a golden age against which to measure their present lot, and one not only in terms of their standard of living but also in terms of their relationship with their masters.

Thus far I have presented evidence to strengthen Wells' case for the interrelationships between the development of the English rural proletariat, the changes wrought in rural society between 1793 and 1815 by the effects of the war, and the commencement of agricultural labourers' protests during that period. It is with his arguments concerning the draconian controls implicit in the extension of the poor relief system, and concerning the dominance of covert protests in the labourers' struggles to defend their living standards, that I find myself in serious disagreement.

The basis of Wells' argument for the efficacy of the new social controls on claimant families rests on his view that the administration of the Old Poor Law had come to be dominated at all levels by a like-minded class alliance of squire, parson and farmer. With one accord they 'combined to exploit the terrible conditions of the nineties by cementing their control over the working population' [*Wells 1979: 125/39*]. Wells arrives at this conclusion because his evidence is focused on the village worthies and the parish vestries, which were dominated by the farmers. He thus tends to ignore the gentry and the clergy, with their very different attitudes to the poor. As Neuman and Digby have clearly shown for the counties of Berkshire and Norfolk, however, in the early nineteenth century these men were still most concerned to fulfil a paternalistic duty towards the poor [*Neuman 1972; Digby 1978: ch. 11*].

The gentry and clergy as magistrates were actively involved in the social administration of Petty and Quarter Sessions. They had general supervisory oversight over the Poor Law at the parochial level, the ordering of statutory relief being perhaps their most significant role. Even so, looking at the failure of the Speenhamland resolutions and recommendations to gain ground even in its own home county, Berkshire, one may feel that the actions of magistrates counted for little if they were so disregarded at the parish level [*Neuman 1972*]. This would be the wrong conclusion to draw on two counts, one particular to East Anglia and one more general. In East Anglia this division between the gentry and the clergy and the more local officials did not exist. There the former were actively involved in the administration of relief through their activities as Poor Law guardians and directors in the local unions and incorporations [*Digby 1978: 105, 201*]. More generally, the gentry and the clergy were the traditional leaders of rural society. What they recommended and resolved as magistrates may have been disliked and ignored by the more cost-conscious parish vestries but, as in Berkshire, the growing number of clashes between the gentry and the ratepayers and farmers reverberated throughout that wider society. The justices at Speenhamland in 1795 failed to set rates of wages for day labourers but they still urged farmers to raise their labourers' wages. Farmers may have ignored the justices but the latter's words would not have fallen on deaf ears amongst the labourers. The continuing presence and steadfastness of men such as Charles Dundas, the archetypal paternalistic magistrate, chairman of the Speenhamland meeting in 1795 and still the defender of the labourer's rights thirty-five years later, meant that the labourers were not faced with the closed ranks of a like-minded alliance of squire, parson and farmer. The labourers understood the moral economy of paternalism. They knew it gave them a third party to which to appeal whenever they came into conflict with the farmers, as they increasingly did from 1790 onwards. At the very moment when developments in agrarian capitalism should have torn down the veil of paternalism, the persistence of the gentry and the clergy in upholding their time-honoured roles as guardians of the poor gave the needed legitimation to any defence the labourers might attempt of their traditional rights under that code.

This is why we find in the protests of 1816 and 1830 numerous meetings with and mobbings of magistrates [*Peacock, 1965: chs. 6–10; Hobsbawm and Rudé 1973: chs. 6–8*]. The appeal made by the labourers' spokesman at Boughton Monchelsea in Kent in 1830 was typical at such encounters. He harangued the assembled gentry to 'do that which as Men, as Englishmen, as Magistrates, and as Christians, ye are bound to do – to protect the liberties and promote the interest of the poor, industrious labourer' [*quoted in Dutt 1966: 155–6*]. Similarly, the men of Tolpuddle had in 1832 attended in all good faith a meeting between themselves and the local farmers under the auspices of the county magistrates, in the hope of resolving their wage dispute with their masters [*Marlow, 1971: 39*]. The fact that at these meetings the labourers appeared in full view of the magistrates shows the trust they had in these 'Men'. Indeed, there is a good deal of evidence right up to and during the Swing riots of 1830–31 to show that this trust was not misplaced. We have already mentioned Charles Dundas, the influential chairman of the Berkshire Quarter Sessions in 1830 [*Neuman 1972: 126*]. Similarly sympathetic to the labourers' cause, though abhorring their actions, was the magistracy of Norfolk, for which pains they were severely censured by Lord Melbourne, the Home Secretary [*Hobsbawm and Rudé 1973: 124, 199–200*].

The three strands of openness and trust on the part of the labourers, and the sympathetic attitude of the gentry to the labourers' grievances, were clearly brought out in the early months of the Swing protests in Kent in 1830. One of the turning points in the movement was the lenient sentences passed on the first machine-breakers by Sir Edward Knatchbull, the presiding magistrate at the East Kent quarter sessions. By his action he appeared both to condone the men's actions and to express his distaste of the new order of capitalist rural society. After this, not only did the number of collective protests increase, but they began to occur in broad daylight for the first time [*Hobsbawm and Rudé 1973: 75–6; Charlesworth 1979: 8–10*]. It is often overlooked how dissimilar, from this point in time, was the Luddism of Captain Swing from the guerrilla tactics of its earlier, northern counterpart.

This is all very different from Wells' account. The rural society he describes would have been one where protests on the scale of 1816, 1822 and particularly of 1829–31 would have been unimaginable. That this can be said with such certainty is because such a society did emerge in rural England in the late 1830s, with the expected results for the labourer. As Digby has pointed out for Norfolk, the disturbances of 1816, 1822 and 1830–31 gave a fatal blow to the traditional, paternalistic order of rural society. The poor had not responded with the dependent loyalty expected of them by the propertied classes. The gentry and the clergy thus gradually withdrew themselves from active involvement in village life, particularly involvement with what they now regarded as the 'undeserving poor'. The gentry now turned all their attention to tending their 'close' villages [*Digby 1978: ch. 11*]. With the old paternalistic framework from which the labourers' collective actions had drawn their legitimation dismantled, but with the labourers still clinging to the now archaic values of that society, they were left 'in a state of general demoralisation and confusion' [*Harber 1972: 54*]. With the tight controls of the new Poor Law, now administered by the farmers as Poor Law guardians, and with a more closely supervised system of charitable doles, victimisation of the troublesome labourer could easily be achieved. Under such circumstances all the labourers could manage by way of protest were arson attacks, and at times spates of threatening letters [*Harber 1972: pts. II and V*]. Not until the 1860s when the labourers had learnt the rules of capitalist social relations, did they begin again to fight effectively and openly for their share of prosperity, and then it was with weapons better fitted for the struggle [*Obelkevitch 1976: 71–102*].

Where does this leave Wells' evidence on threatening letters and arson attacks? Given the arguments he presents, one would expect the threatening letters to have been received and the arson attacks to have taken place predominantly in agricultural parishes. Yet this is not the case. An analysis was undertaken not only of the evidence Wells presents on the incidence of arson in southern and eastern England[5] but also of the evidence of threatening letters specifically concerned with issues of food prices or the marketing and supply of food, for the same region for the years 1799–1801.[6] For the four areas considered, in all of them half or more of the incidents occurred in 'non-agricultural' and 'mixed' parishes [*Table 1a*].[7] Many of them in fact happened in market towns; this is particularly noticeable in the case of the threatening letters [*Table 1b*]. The incidents therefore occurred in the same type of localities that were the locus of food rioting and were thus likely to be the work of the social groups at the centre of those disturbances.

As Wells and others have shown, food riots were the direct collective actions of industrial workers, artisans and at times the Volunteers and the militia, but not agricultural labourers [*Wells 1977; Bohstedt 1972: passim; Stevenson 1974: 46–9*]. Agricultural workers rarely participated in such disturbances, for they had more direct access to food, either supplied by farmers at lower prices – a custom revived during the grain crisis of 1795–6 [*Stevenson 1974: 48*] – or simply by taking grain without payment, either as a

TABLE 1

THE INCIDENCE OF ARSON, 1794-96 AND 1799-1801, AND THREATENING LETTERS, 1799-1801

(a) Proportion of incidents in non-agricultural and mixed parishes[a]

	ARSON		*THREATENING LETTERS*	
	percentage	*(total)*	*percentage*	*(total)*
Eastern England[c]	75	(18)	50	(14)
South-east England[d]	64	(11)	100	(3)
Central Southern England[e]	50	(10)	92	(13)
West Country[f]	50	(8)	71	(7)

(b) Proportion of incidents in market towns[b]

	ARSON		*THREATENING LETTERS*	
	percentage	*(total)*	*percentage*	*(total)*
Eastern England[c]	50	(18)	29	(14)
South-east England[d]	19	(11)	66	(3)
Central Southern England[e]	30	(10)	69	(13)
West Country[f]	38	(8)	71	(7)

a: For classification see note 6.
b: Market towns as designated in the 1792 list contained in the Report of the Royal Commission on market rights and tolls (1888) Appendix XXI.
c: Cambridgeshire, Essex, Hertfordshire, Norfolk, Suffolk.
d: Kent, Surrey, Sussex.
e: Berkshire, Hampshire, Wiltshire.
f: Gloucestershire, Somerset.

'perk' of the job or as simple pilferage [*Bohstedt 1972: 161*]. In market towns and rural industrial communities there were men with greater grievances against farmers, dealers and millers over food prices and food supply than agricultural labourers. Those men were the most likely arsonists and authors of threatening letters. They meant them to be adjuncts to the food riots: underlining the point of a demonstration in the same settlement or reminding the authorities of disturbances elsewhere.

Further evidence of the non-agricultural origin of some of the covert protests is provided by their appearance in certain areas at a critical juncture in the industrial evolution of those regions. This is particularly evident in the textile regions of Essex, where the cloth industry had been in decline during the whole of the second half of the eighteenth century and where the decline turned into a dramatic collapse in the 1790s [*Brown 1969: ch. 1*]. The industry's fortunes were mirrored in the changing nature of protests over the issue of food. Thus, one moves from extensive food rioting in 1772, to a more limited outbreak in 1793–6, to the fires and threatening letters in 1800–01 [Fig. 1].[8]   The ability of workers from textile communities to intervene collectively in the marketing of food was related to the strength of solidarity in those communities. When that ability was cut short by the dramatic collapse of their industry, all that workers in those moribund communities could deploy against their old protagonists – the millers, the dealers, the

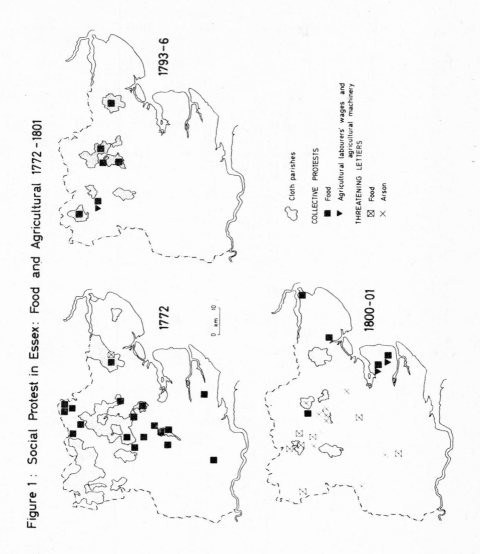

Figure 1 : Social Protest in Essex: Food and Agricultural 1772–1801

1793–6

1772

1800–01

0 km 10

Cloth parishes

COLLECTIVE PROTESTS

■ Food

▼ Agricultural labourers' wages and
   agricultural machinery

THREATENING LETTERS

⊠ Food

✕ Arson

farmers – were threatening letters and arson. In contrast, when the agricultural labourers did launch their first major resistance to the new forms of capitalist agriculture in East Anglia in 1815–16, their protests sprang from their newly emergent communities and were overt, direct collective actions. The arson attacks were peripheral to the main movement and threatening letters were few and far between [*Peacock 1965: chs. 5–10; Amos 1971: ch. 3; Charlesworth, forthcoming*].

It would seem, therefore, that in the period 1794–1801 threatening letters and arson were not primarily a weapon of the agricultural labourer. If this was so, then our attention is drawn back to the scattering of collective protests by agricultural labourers over the issue of wages that occurred throughout southern and eastern England between 1793 and 1805 [*Amos 1971: 18; Hobsbawm and Rudé 1973: 58; Emsley 1979: 31; Wells 1979: 127/42*]. Unlike the spatial distribution of covert protests for the same period, they occurred in regions of predominantly capitalist arable farming [*Charlesworth, forthcoming*]. These overt protests were one of the first signs of the growing strength of the agricultural proletariat, whose potential was to be fully realised for the first time in East Anglia in 1815–16 after the sudden removal of the wartime employment conditions. Other signs of labourers' collective action during the period of relative labour shortage that held from 1793 to 1814, were the successful attempts at collective bargaining by threat of either moving on or absenteeism, particularly at the critical times of hay and harvest [*Jones 1965: 324; Brown 1969: 131*]. It was the experience of these early overt struggles that was finally to cement the solidarity of the labouring community, and thus help to sustain the labourers' resolve to protest openly against the changed conditions of the period 1815–31. Thus the forms of resistance, which evolved in the 1790s, did become the countryman's weapons in the first forty years of the nineteenth century. The principal form of resistance was not, however, covert, as Wells maintains, but overt, direct collective action.

NOTES

1. A reply by Roger Wells was published.

2. The antipathy between master and men is noted in many of the answers to questions 38 and 53 of the Rural Queries of the 1834 Poor Law Report [*P. P. Reports of the Commissioners of Poor Laws*; 1834 (9), XXVII *Appendices*, vols. B.4 and 5].

3. *P. P. 'Poor Laws' op. cit.* vol. B.5 question 53, Sussex: Isfield, Ticehurst, Brede, Slaugham; Berkshire: Bradfield.

4. For a critique of the hardship model applied to food rioting, see Thompson [*1971*]; Bohstedt [*1972: passim*]; Williams [*1976*]; Wells [*1977*]. For evidence that stresses the importance of occupational groupings and social networks in the initiation and propagation of food riots, see Bohstedt [*op. cit.: 177 ff.*] and Wells [*op. cit.: 720–44*].

5. I have excluded the arson incidents in the Midlands and the North that Dr. Wells presents in his table, so as to concentrate our attention on the main regions of agricultural labourers' overt protests between 1790–1831.

6. Notices of threatening letters placed in the *London Gazette*. In the crisis of 1795–96 the government thought it prudent not to gazette the bulk of threatening letters about which it received information. This is why I have excluded from the analysis the six threatening letters for those years that mention a grievance about food prices or its marketing and supply. I would like to thank Mr. Edward Thompson for making available to me the material from the *London Gazette* that formed the basis of my analysis for 1799–1801.

7. The classification of parishes as non-agricultural, mixed and agricultural was similar to that used by Dr. D. A. Baugh [*1975: 58*]. Where the number of families in agriculture was less than 60 per cent, the parish was classified as agricultural; where the number was under 40 per cent, non-agricultural. The residual parishes were put into a mixed category. The *Census Abstract* of 1811 was used as the earliest reliable indicator of the occupational structure of a parish. As Baugh notes, 'The 1801 occupational data dealt in individuals rather than families, and was known to the census takers to be useless almost as soon as it came in' [*ibid*].

8. The map was prepared from the following: Brown [*1969: ch. 1 (cloth parishes) and 131–2 (protests)*]; Amos [*1971: ch. 2*]; Stevenson [*1974: 36*]; *London Gazette* 1772–1801. Again my thanks to Mr. Edward Thompson for the latter material.

REFERENCES

Amos, S. W., 1971, 'Social Discontent and Agrarian Disturbances in Essex 1795–1850', University of Durham, unpublished M. A. thesis.

Baugh, D. A. 1975, 'The Cost of Poor Relief in South-East England 1790–1834', *Economic History Review* 28.

Bohstedt, J. H., 1972, 'Riots in England: 1790–1810, with Special Reference to Devonshire', Harvard University, unpublished Ph.D. thesis.

Brown, A. J., 1969, *Essex at Work 1700–1815*, Chelmsford.

Chambers, J. D. & Mingay, G. E., 1966, *The Agricultural Revolution 1750–1880*, London.

Charlesworth, A., 1979, *Social Protest in a Rural Society. The Spatial Diffusion of the Captain Swing Disturbances of 1830–31*, Norwich.

Charlesworth, A. (ed.), forthcoming, *An Atlas of Agrarian Protest in Britain 1549–1900*.

Cobbett, W., 1853, *Rural Rides*, London.

Digby, A., 1978, *Pauper Palaces*, London.

Dutt, M., 1966, 'The Agricultural Labourers' Revolt of 1830 in Kent, Surrey and Sussex', London University, unpublished Ph.D. thesis.

Emsley, C., 1979, *British Society and the French Wars 1793–1815*, London.

Harber, J., 1972, 'Rural Incendiarism in Suffolk, 1840–1845', University of Warwick, unpublished M. A. thesis.

Hasbach, W., 1908, *A History of the English Agricultural Labourer*, London.

Hobsbawm, E. J. and Rudé, G., 1973, *Captain Swing* (revised Penguin edition).

Holderness, B. A., 1972, '"Open" and "Close" Parishes in England in the Eighteenth and Nineteenth Centuries', *Agricultural History Review* 20.

Huzel, J. P., 1976, 'A quantitative approach to the agricultural labourers' riots of 1830 in Kent' (abstract), *Peasant Studies* 5.

John, A. J., 1967, 'Farming in Wartime, 1793–1815', in G. E. Mingay and E. L. Jones (eds.) *Land, Labour and Population in the Industrial Revolution*, London.

Jones, E. L., 1965, 'The Agricultural Labour Market in England, 1793–1872', *Economic History Review* 17.

Kussmaul, A., 1978, 'Servants in Husbandry in Early Modern England', University of Toronto, unpublished Ph.D. thesis.

Marlow, J., 1973, *The Tolpuddle Martyrs*, London.

Neeson, J. M., 1977, 'Common Right and Enclosure. Northamptonshire 1700–1800', University of Warwick, unpublished Ph.D. thesis.

Neuman, M., 1972, 'Speenhamland in Berkshire', in E. W. Martin (eds.), *Comparative Development in Social Welfare*, London.

Obelkevitch, J., 1976, *Religion and Rural Society. South Lindsey 1825–1875*, Oxford.

Peacock, A. J., 1965, *Bread or Blood. The Agrarian Riots in East Anglia, 1816*, London.

Richardson, T. L., 1977, 'The Standard of Living Controversy 1790–1840 with Special Reference to Agricultural Labourers in Seven English Counties', University of Hull, unpublished Ph.D. thesis.

Samuel, R., 1975, 'Village Labour', in R. Samuel (ed.), *Village Life and Labour*, London.

Stevenson, J., 1974, 'Food Riots in England, 1792–1818' in J. Stevenson and R. Quinault (eds.), *Popular Protest and Public Order*, London.

Thompson, E. P., 1971, 'The "Moral Economy" of the English Crowd in the Eighteenth Century', *Past and Present* 50.

Wearmouth, R. F., 1945, *Methodism and the Common People of the Eighteenth Century*, London.

Wells, R. A. E., 1977, 'The Revolt of the South-West, 1800–1801. A Study in English Popular Protest', *Social History* 6.

Wells, R. A. E., 1979, 'The Development of the English Rural Proletariat and Social Protest, 1700–1850', *Journal of Peasant Studies* 6.

Williams, D. E., 1976, 'Were "Hunger" Rioters Really Hungry? Some Demographic Evidence', *Past and Present* 71.

Social Conflict and Protest in the English Countryside in the early Nineteenth Century: A Rejoinder

Roger A.E. Wells*

In response to Charlesworth's critique (Journal of Peasant Studies, vol. 8, no. 1 October, 1980) of his 1979 Journal of Peasant Studies article, (vol. 6, no. 2, January) Wells adduces further evidence in support of his argument that covert rather than overt protest was more significant in the English countryside in the early nineteenth century. Implicit in Wells' original postulating of the enduring nature of covert protest was a plea for a study of everyday life rather than concentration on so-called historical landmarks. Here he offers some preliminary findings concerning Burwash, a large, 'open' village in the East Sussex Weald. He finishes by stressing that the identical experiences of counties like Essex, Suffolk and Sussex, with important differences between their rural economies, prove the significance of covert protest in general and arson in particular.

I

Mr Charlesworth suggests that my outline account of the proletarianisation of the English agricultural labour force is weakened by omissions. [*Wells, 1979*] [*Charlesworth, 1980*]. With characteristic scholarly philanthropy, Charlesworth fills several paragraphs with empirical data, and congratulates himself for fortifying my thesis. Having established this benign basis for a critique, he proceeds to overturn — to his own satisfaction — the central tenet of my argument, namely that covert rather than overt protest was more significant in the countryside in this period. 'The principal form of resistance', to under- and unemployment, plummeting real wages, and ever-increasing dependence on hard-faced and tight fisted poor-law officials, writes Charlesworth, 'was not. . . covert, as Wells maintains, but direct collective action'.

Mr Charlesworth is the author of an inspiring, if initial attempt to reinterpret the nature of the Captain Swing revolt of 1830-1, the major episode of overt popular protest in southern and eastern rural England [*Charlesworth, 1979*]. He has, therefore, a vested interest in overt protest; his critique emphasises Swing's more localised precedent, the wave of disturbances in East Anglia in 1815-6.

* *Brighton Polytechnic*

Surprisingly, other important examples of open rural resistance are ignored; his omissions deserve repayment in kind. The implementation of the Poor Law Amendment Act[1] generated considerable overt opposition in southern and eastern districts in 1835-7; physical attacks on the administrators of the reformed system and their properties were coupled with more on the hated central facet of the new organisation — the penal workhouses erected in the interests of 'less eligibility' literally to deter claimants [*Lowerson, 1977.*] [*Digby, 1978, ch. 12*]. The principal authority on the opposition to the New Poor Law, Edsall [*1971*], certainly underestimated the degree and intensity of rural violence, and more local and regional research is required to complete the picture. The impression remains that this bout of public protest ended essentially, like Swing, in failure. Open resistance to the Act did not stop its implementation, and, as in 1815-6 and 1830-1, many protesters ended up with at least custodial sentences.

Another under-researched aspect of rural proletarian life in the 1830s also largely eludes Charlesworth. Comment on trade unionism in the countryside is usually limited to the harsh legal offensive mounted in Dorset, ending with the transportation of the celebrated Tolpuddle Martyrs. Yet rural unionism was not confined to Dorset; signs of vigorous campaigning have been detected in Kent and Sussex. [*Lowerson, 1977*] and again one must argue for parallel investigations into other areas. The primary reason for historians' ignorance of the phenomenon was the movement's collapse with little trace. Its revival in the 1870s — when its potential was greatly enhanced by an incipient labour shortage caused by rural depopulation — has attracted much attention. As events in the 1870s proved, trade unionism necessitates the adoption of overt tactics; covert organisation was unequal to the realisation of objectives. The known history of rural unionism emphasises that overt protest was limited to remarkably few years, a tiny minority in the first half of the nineteenth century. The uniqueness of the Swing revolt is a major characteristic; if it is lost on Charlesworth, it did not escape a contemporary composer of a commemorative ballad:

> The mob such a mob
> You never did see before,
> And if you live a hundred years
> You never will no more.[2]

Mr Charlesworth's myopic devotion to the significance of these uncharacteristic explosions of overt protest is aggravated by his stubborn refusal to explore the ramifications of their defeat, just as his critique ignores the effects of their predecessors' defeats in the critical evolutionary decade, the 1790s. He interprets the East Anglian protests of 1815 as 'the first signs of the growing strength of the agricultural proletariat'. Subsequent signs presumably include the more momentous defeat of Swing. One is reduced to sheer despair at Charlesworth's notion of 'full realisation' of strength. One must protest, of course; personally I would feel weak and defeated in the event of a number of my friends, relatives, neighbours and workmates, making an ignominious exit on the public gallows, or a less spectacular but similarly awesome departure on a convict ship to Van Dieman's Land. But, perhaps I'm faint-hearted.

However, Charlesworth interestingly observes the 'social component' of proletarianisation, and some of the mechanics of evolving class-consciousness. He emphasises — as I did not — the value of comparison between 'open' and 'closed' parishes. Land in the latter was owned by no more than three men, who exercised patriarchal control, notably by restricting new labourer settlement, either through rigorous application of the poor law, or by non-provision of additional housing, or both. Such operations slowed the escalation of the poverty problem, and simultaneously forced the resident labouring community to observe the minute rules of deference. Conversely, 'open' parishes had no one, or tiny group of dominant landowners, but a multitude of mostly small owners. Such parishes lacked the means of social control operated in one- and two-landlord villages; the result was heavy new settlement, facilitated by the jerry-building activities of a host of petty entrepreneurs, anxious to exploit plebeian necessities. Such parishes were, according to orthodox contemporary views, notoriously badly administered; pauperism burgeoned as the supply of labour outstripped demand. Charlesworth adopts and extends this view; 'open' parishes permitted the development of 'separate communities' of employers and labourers. The latter, we are informed, were 'relatively *free* from social control' and able — unhindered by some autocratic resident magnate — to create their own 'specific institutions', including 'meeting houses, pubs, friendly societies and benefit clubs, poaching gangs, football teams, drinking parties'. The socio-economic situation obtaining was perfect for the genesis of the 'necessary groupings of men mobilising for collective action', and 'the protests of the agricultural labourer sprang' from such places. Charlesworth states that 'in the long run . . . the solidarity of communities and interest groups . . . is the mainspring of collective action', and inevitably this entire part of his critique is servile to an explanatory causal analysis of the distribution of overt protest in those odd years when there was any [*Charlesworth, 1980*].

II

Mr Charlesworth's orientation of his material is essentially unhelpful. Implicit in my argument of the enduring nature of covert protest, and therefore its detailed analysis, was a plea for the study of everyday life, rather than concentration on so-called historical landmarks. In this connection I wish to offer some preliminary findings respecting Burwash, a large and typical 'open' village in the East Sussex Weald.[3] Population rose from 1,524 in 1801 to 1,966 in 1831. Landownership and tenancy exhibited a complex variety of copyhold and freehold, small and large owner-occupiers and tenants, but there was no one major landlord. In addition to the farmers the parish was home to many craftsmen, artisans and shopkeepers; the social structure accommodates Dr Mills' recent emphasis on the significance of the large entrepreneurial class common in 'open' villages [*Mills, 1980: 43*] Arable farming predominated, and as in neighbouring communities, hop-growing was important. Burwash was badly hit by the post-war depression in agriculture in general, and in the 1820s in particular by the debilitating combination of low hop prices and high hop duties. Heavy under- and unemployment increasingly strained the social fabric. The main agent of control was the village's select vestry, dominated by a handful of the greater farmers and the largest resident landowner.

Only a small, and probably decreasing percentage of the labouring force was able to secure stable employment on the traditional annual basis. The remainder were fully employed only during the harvest and hop-picking seasons in the late summer and autumn. The relief of unemployment and inadequate wages by periodic provision of public employment, weekly doles, allowances-in-aid-of-wages, and family supplements, had a long history, but pauperism attained an unprecedented intensity in the post-1815 period. The vestry sought to extend and regularise its modes of relief, and exploit the supervisory potential of the poor law machinery to preserve its own authority and with it a semblance of social equilibrium. The majority of the village's proletarian population required some public aid; some of the regularly employed, notably those with large families, needed wage supplements. The dependence on authority for those in irregular work was greater, indeed virtually unremitting. No wonder that the very language was permeated by the phraseology of dependence; 'Dole Beef' speaks for itself; 'steady relief' was a euphemism for family supplements. 'He was out of employ and being a pauper . . . he was sent . . . for work', explained an overseer to an examining magistrate: 'the paupers . . . that receive relief' emphasises the synonymity of the terms labourer and pauper.[4]

> A great number of Labourers belonging to and solely maintained by Burwash Parish on account of their being unable to get employment are become very much depraved and have contracted habits of extreme Idleness.

This uncompromising statement made in March 1822 announced the vestry's determination to grasp the nettle. The 'remedy' advocated hinged on the creation of a norm, whereby farmers were expected to employ one man or two youths full time for each £15 of rentals. Compliance permitted farmers to draw on the pool of parish-paid labourers or Roundsmen, without restriction, for whom they paid a nominal sum. As a minimum wage was expressly ruled out, farmers were free to pay pittances to their quotas of regularly-employed men — whose incomes had to be supplemented from public funds — and benefit from parish labour too. This blatant manipulation of a serious situation by the largest employers caused a revolt by lesser ratepayers, and after an altercation — obscured by the formal minutes — a minimum daily wage of 1s 6d (12½n.p.) was introduced; farmers who did not comply were henceforth ineligible for Roundsmen. In addition farmers were limited to one Roundsman for every £15 of rentals.[5]

The system lasted well into the 1830s. The labour pool, designated the 'Surplus Hands', was never absorbed completely; numbers totalled over ninety in 1829. This residual labour force was employed directly by the parish, either on Bough Farm — rented specifically to create public employment — or on the roads. As farmers selected their own Roundsmen, those who ended up on Bough Farm or the roads were the least able and/or the more truculent workers, and automatic stigmatisation was aggravated by lower wages. Nevertheless, the introduction of rules to be observed by these labourers suggests some compensation in the form of less supervision. Rules established the working day from 6.30 a.m. to 6 p.m. Men not present at these hours lost a whole day's pay, the same penalty accruing to workers failing to dig ten loads of stone daily during the six day week. Strict instructions governed the route taken by these workers, especially when quarrying on private land. Men 'caught bringing home wood, or committing other depredations', or trespassing, were sacked. Roundsmen were under the direct supervision of their employers, but the vestry nonetheless fixed the length of the working day, and publicly called on every 'respectable Person' to report 'all Persons employed by the Parish seen loitering and idling their time during the hours they ought to be at work': 'such time' would 'be deducted from their Wages' by the vestry.[6]

The vestry also registered all pauper children in order to ensure that everyone over the age of nine worked, but this was not achieved without resistance as recourse had to be had to the baptismal register. Annual contracts were the ideal, the vestry fitting out such children with a complete set of clothes and paying premiums. The distribution of children was organised at annual meetings, at which mothers were ordered to attend. But the parish was never able to place all eligible children; unplaced girls and younger boys were commonly sent to the workhouse: older boys joined the men on the roads or Bough Farm.[7]

The sources do not reveal the percentage of the population in receipt of relief in the decade before Swing; 1822 in Burwash, as in much of rural England, clearly witnessed the depth of the depression. Then 'nearly half' an estimated population of 1,900 'are receiving relief to a great extent': between eighty and a hundred and twenty men, with between three and four hundred dependents were totally out of work. Hence the need for the mass registration of children and other surveys, including one in 1821 involving the printing of '1000 Bills . . . to give to each Labourer to ascertain what each family earns', and another the following year to employers, who were to list their full-time workers.[8]

Vestry organisation and supervision of work was complemented by considerable control over housing. Pressure on the housing stock inflated rents, and many workers — including some in full-time employment — were forced to solicit at least part of their rent from parochial funds. Cottages occupied by labouring families were owned by many individuals, including landowners, farmers, tradesmen and shopkeepers. Others were owned by the parish, together with additional accommodation in almshouses and the workhouse. Many cottages were occupied by more than one family: for example the families of shoemaker Thomas Chandler and labourer Henry Pettit each had a bedroom, 'but the Kitchen and Washhouse are used in common'.[9] The parish used the housing stock under its direct superintendance, including cottages not owned but for which rent was paid, as convenience dictated, and also punitively. The vestry minutes contain many orders for people to move house, and in 1819 a thorough rationalisation of occupancy commenced with an application to the Bench for warrants 'to give possession of all Houses hired by, or belonging to paupers'. Rooms in Jesse Relf's house, for example, had a succession of other occupants, including the Blackwood family, moved from the workhouse in 1827. Resistance to enforced transfers was regularly terminated by warrants, and inability to pay rents was commonly penalised. Stephen Haseldon was just one victimised defaulter; if he 'does not pay his own Rent for the future', decreed the vestry, 'another family [will] but put in with him', and many workers found their accommodation stretched by the designated sharing of limited facilities. Nor would the parish tolerate cohabitation or *ad hoc* private lettings. Samuel Shorter's dole was stopped when he put up Benjamin Russell. James French was threatened with the same penalty if he continued to 'harbour James Hinds about his House'. Chandler's contract to mend paupers' shoes was withdrawn 'whilst Hanah Russell is living with him'.[10]

The vestry's control of work and housing facilitated social control. 'Resolved, as it appears . . . that the Single Men run about at night and commit depredations they be . . . taken into the workhouse', ran one typical blanket injunction affecting considerable numbers, which also epitomises the penal role of the workhouse. John Etherington and James Langridge — both widowers with reputations for dishonesy and truculence — were ordered into the workhouse for misbehaviour. Pauper resistance to their children being put out by the parish often ended with the children's incarceration in the house. A typical decision was recorded against Charles Weston; his '2 Oldest Girls to go into the House and nothing granted till they do'. The venomous reaction to pauper obstinacy is evinced by the language; 'if Thos Braban do not get rid of his daughter he will not be employed'. Vestrymen assumed that workhouse accommodation was cheaper. One victim, the recently-widowed Mrs Copper, was informed that if she 'cannot live on 3s 6d [18 n.p.]p. week she must go into the Poorhouse'. The additional stipulation that she must also 'wear a Parish Dress' suggests that Mrs Copper had an intolerable degree of vanity in vestrymen's eyes.[11]

The vestry could bite as well as bark. Messrs S. Langridge, T. Pennell and T. Collins lost their parish employment 'for not attending to their work as they ought'. Nor was Roundsman status an automatic right, as Messrs T. Kemp, T. Sweetman senior, W. Budd junior, and S. Leaney discovered on the vestry's ruling that they 'are not to be employed by the Parish in consequence of their being out of employ by their own misconduct'. Pauperisation precipitated entire families into a predicament where deference was the only defence against power exercised by an affluent, arbitrary minority. For Burwash vestrymen were unfamiliar with biblical rhetoric, 'and if the father eateth the sour grape are the children's teeth set on edge?' Rulings included: J. Pennell's 'allowance to be taken off in consequence of his Sons behaviour in the Street'; Richard Kemp's weekly flour supply 'stop'd next week through his wife's misconduct'; Thomas Clifton's 'discharge from Parish work for his abuse to' the vain, vigorous and despotic churchwarden Richard Button; and Stephen Langridge's identical punishment 'for abusing Wm Evans (Beadle)'. Reinstatement was conditional on a humiliating admission of guilt as the following minute, signed by the seven vestrymen present, proves: 'Ordered that Underdown having made his appearance to the Vestry and admitted the impropriety of his having been insolent to the Overseer, and evincing considerable contrition, that he therefore be allowed his request' for relief.[12]

Sundays, as a day of rest, slightly threatened the omnipresence of vestry control. Village boys and youths congregated in gangs, played in the churchyard, and behaved anti-socially. In 1826 the vestry responded by ordering parents to send all children over six 'to Church or some other place of Worship on Sundays'; the usual penalty of loss of benefits was inflicted on the obdurate. Months later the rule and the penalty were extended to 'all Young Men & boys who work for the parish'.[13] Every form of independence was resisted. Claimants who 'follow smoaking' had doles reduced by a shilling. One doubts if this Draconian regulation was enforceable, but the vestry consistently tried to apply its 'no dogs' rule. The struggle generated is obvious; in force in 1819, the rule was reissued in 1822, 1824 and 1829. Early victims included Stephen Haseldon and Charles Weston whose relief was witheld in 1821 'till they part with their Dogs'. But dog-owning claimants evaded the order 'by sending their Dogs to a neighbour for a time'; in 1824 the vestry undertook a test case to establish a precedent when widow Eastwood was deemed not to have 'fairly parted with' her canine companion, now housed by an independent neighbour, John Ellis, recently sacked from the parish surveyorship. Eastwood and Ellis were hauled before the Bench, the vestry resolving 'that in future poor persons shall not be consider'd to have parted with their Dogs fairly unless they prove to the satisfaction of the Magistrate that the Dogs are actually kill'd or sent out of the Parish or . . . sold or given away'.[14]

The vestry unremittingly waged war on paupers drinking: in July 1819 the unpaid amateur constables were 'desired to visit the Public Houses and to report the names of paupers found there that receive relief'. Not satisfied with the bankruptcy of one publican, the vestry extended its policy nine months later with the introduction of printed lists of 'Paupers receiving relief . . . delivered to each Inkeeper' for 'conspicuous' display. The onus for enforcement was put on luckless licensees who were 'not to permit any Person named . . . tippling or drinking'. The creation of a full-time, publicly-funded, two-man police force in 1822, relaxed the pressure on the publicans, as the beadles' first formal duty was to 'daily supervise' the pubs and to report pauper customers to the vestry. The campaign against alcohol also led to the further debasement of the much stigmatised pauper funeral; beer allowances for pall-bearers were stopped.[15]

The documentation exudes an increasing aura of oppression; naturally, with so many subjected to the whims of an affluent minority, the poor law system and its vestry-room administration proved to be volatile flash points. An unsigned, but literate letter articulated the frustrations felt by claimants. Four men approached overseer Westover for relief; he refused, referring the four to another vestryman, who, in turn, referred the group to the vicar; he was not at home. The men returned to Westover, who adhered to his refusal summoning a constable to his assistance. The policeman adopted a more conciliatory line, agreeing to provide 'something to eat' on condition of the labourers going home. Authority reneged on this deal, and after two days the four reapplied to Westover who allegedly said 'he did not Cair', and 'sent for some of the Gentlemen of the parish', namely landowner Haviland and major farmer Cruttenden, who supported the overseer. The group refused to leave 'except that they would give our familis something for they was all starving'. Outraged the 'Gentlemen . . .

began to strike away and we still kept Beging for relief but we maid no resistance at all for that they Cripled one of us'. Massive protests erupted on two occasions. In 1819 five characters were prosecuted after a crowd disturbed the 'principal Inhabitants' while comfortably ensconced in the Rose and Crown legislating for the village, in an incident in which an unpaid constable 'and his assistants' were assaulted. In 1820 four men were jailed for assaulting an overseer and two vestrymen.[16]

Similar incidents were common in Sussex in the early 1820s; they provoked a widespread movement for the appointment of full-time beadles, permanent special constables, and other repressive measures, including increasing the frequency of Petty Sessions for the speedy punishment of miscreants.[17] Burwash participated, erecting a small jail in 1821, significantly appointing two men 'to watch the Cage during the Night while building'; five shilling bonuses were added to the high daily wage of two shillings (20 n.p.) 'for each . . . conviction for wilfully pulling down or injuring' the structure. Within months the first permanent police force was created, to which was added a full-time night watch. Affidavits were sworn before the Bench outlining the necessity for additional police powers through enrolling important inhabitants as special constables. The odd overt protest has left its mark in the source materials, but the initiation of a night watch emphasises the potential and fear of covert, nocturnal, anti-establishment activity. The latter, rather than the mass explosions of open protest, occupied much of a petition drafted by Burwash for parliamentary consumption in 1822. The petition stated that the farmers were

> unable to employ the labouring Class, who are . . . experiencing great inconvenience, which has caused them to become very dissatisfied . . . disrespectful and insolent to their superiors, riotous and turbulent in their dispositions and behaviour . . . ready for extreme acts of depredation; premises and property have been set fire to and otherwise destroyed, anonymous letters dropt. . . threatening the lives of individuals.[18]

Employment problems and poor law administration clearly generated fierce antagonisms between vestry personnel and the workers. Vestries in 'open' parishes like Burwash were the regular targets of early nineteenth-century anti-poor law enthusiasts on the grounds that relief was haphazardly granted, with no demarcation between deserving and undeserving claimants; alternatively, the same school of thought singled out irresolute magistrates who failed to support discerning vestries, and who indiscriminately used their powers to over-rule punitive vestry decisions against the profilgate poor. Charlesworth's emphasis on magisterial attempts to maintain the paternalist society against cost-conscious vestries accords with this view, as does his rejection of my identification of an alliance between farmers in the vestry and magistrates on the Bench. Charlesworth takes a similarly benign view of the clergy, many of whom were also JPs; they too aimed to re-inforce paternalism [*Charlesworth, 1980*]. The question of clerical magistrates is irrelevant in Sussex, for an idiosyncratic succession of Lord Lieutenants perceived the conflict inherent in the conjunction of the two roles, and refused to elevate vicars to the Bench. In most counties the percentage of clerical justices increased markedly after 1750, and Dr Evans has singled out their judicial role as a major contributory factor to the development of pronounced anti-clericalism in the same period [*Evans, 1975*]. Burwash vestrymen might have capitulated to the prevailing social tension and sought safety in lax poor law administration; but the reverse is the case, as we have seen, and moreover, the vestry expected the Bench to uphold its decisions, regularly seeking formal endorsements of punitive actions, or the imposition of severer punishments beyond the vestry's prerogative. The confidence of a minute respecting Stephen Sands — that his 'Wife & family be stopt from going to the Poorhouse' for their meals 'and that he support them or be sent to Prison' is obvious.[19]

Many cases demonstrate the support given to the Burwash vestry by the County Bench. John Langridge was summoned 'for his abusive language to the Vestry'; Thomas Adams' Roundsman's pay was withheld 'until he has been before a Majestrate to shew cause why he left Mr Jos. Hylands work'. Hannah Sand's appearance before their worships resulted in a summary conviction for absenting herself from the workhouse for fourteen hours, and Thomas Kemp, another Roundsman, went to the treadmill in Lewes jail after he dug land to a depth of 'only about four or five Inches' instead of the 'fifteen Inches' commanded by the farmer. Some paupers caused concern by appeals against the vestry to the Bench, but the former fought back by suggesting an additional deterrence, the payment of 'the customary fee of a shilling' to the justices' clerk when appeals were rejected.[20]

The contemporary and historical view that 'open' parishes were a haven for the footloose and displaced poor seeking a home finds little support from Burwash. One of the first duties of the newly-appointed beadles was to eject migrants; wanderers who persisted in transgressing the boundaries went before the Bench who could — and did — imprison summarily. As a further deterrence overseers were prohibited from assisting 'any travelling people on the roads'. The parish also stopped occupants of parish houses from taking 'any persons . . . as Lodgers that does not belong to the Parish'. The vestry could be ruthless when resorting to the Settlement Acts. Richard Waterhouse's newly-acquired stepson was not permitted to join his mother in the home of her second husband, but packed off to his place of settlement. Other migrants were peremptorily expelled; 'if Rebecca Cottington does not leave Burwash in a few days proper means will be taken to remove her'. The problem for vestries after 1795 hinged on their inability to implement the Settlement Laws until an inhabitant — newly arrived or not — actually applied for relief. When this occurred Burwash was quick to exploit any possibility under the law. Relief to widow Etherington and her son was witheld till they gave 'a true account of their Settlement'. Many investigations were mounted, and legal opinion obtained in complex cases; Burwash regularly contested cases with other parishes in the courts. When paupers were ejected, further arguments were avoided with the registration of summary removal orders at the Quarter Sessions. The parish did, it is true, receive paupers moved back from elsewhere under the law, but in the 1820s, at least, the law's operation reveals a net loss of paupers.[21]

The fact that the Settlement Acts led to the expulsion of relatives of workers settled in the village suggests that this was another source of conflict. Yet conflict was not the simple product of the relationships between the ratepayers and the rest. As early as 1823 Burwash owed over a thousand pounds, and the liquidity problem was so great that the vestry issued tickets exchangeable for goods at the shops to claimants. Retailers certainly exploited the situation; baker Honeysett's conviction for adding alum to bread did not compromise his contract to supply the workshouse, not least because he was owed £300.[22] The monotonous regularity of blanket threats to defaulting ratepayers is a prominent feature among the vestry minutes; typical entries record that in December 1828 all defaulters were to be 'spoken to'; the following February the vestry announced the immediate collection of outstanding sums, and in July distress warrants were sought against all remaining non-payers.[23] Soaring rates encouraged people to contest their valuations. One year resistance came from 'several persons': 'to prevent litigation and expense', the vestry ordered a complete revaluation, which provoked a new round of dissent when some valuations were increased and others reduced. 'To preserve peace in the parish' required the waiving of half the extra demands on those revalued upwards.[24]

Escalating rates posed problems for smaller payers, and the vestry came under pressure to waive demands on petty entrepreneurs, pressure which was resisted with the resolution 'that all the Master Tradesmen be charged with the Poor Tax ... and if the Parish should think proper to take it off afterwards they will... do it'. This placed independent men in the same client relationship to the big boys of the select vestry as the paupers, a predicament militating strongly against harmony. The case histories of two appellants illustrate the process. John Chandler was ordered to present his case to the vicar, who would represent it to the vestry. Henry Haviland, the landowner, would do the same for Richard Waterhouse. His slate was wiped clean, but Chandler ended up with a distress warrant.[25] Legal actions meant further traumas and expense. Thomas Ellis was just one resident who suffered the indignity of the seizure and auction of his goods, followed by an order for the reimbursement of the vestry's legal costs. William Russell — a dealer of sorts — was told that his rate demand would be waived if he stopped trading, but full and immediate payment was required if he kept going.[26] Quite serious altercations occasionally erupted between ratepayers over parish policy. The annual general meeting in March 1824 was abruptly adjourned due to 'the turbulent and improper conduct of a number of the lower Class of Tax payers (urged forward by one or two ill judging Shopkeepers and small Tradesmen many of whom have not a legal right to be present)'. Several hours later 'the disorderly persons' safely dispersed, the self-proclaimed 'principal Inhabitants' reconvened, only to be confronted by Richard Waddle and John Shoesmith, whose presence was legally admissable. Their affluent neighbours recorded the dissenting voices, adding, with obvious satisfaction that the objectors' 'rating together amounts to £57 16s 0d but neither of whom have paid up their Rates'.[27] So much for the entrepreneurial hegemony and harmony postulated by Mills [*1980, p.46 but cf. p.52*]: the reduction of social analysis to mathematically-based diagrammatics may look sophisticated, but it ignores conflict, and is thus blind to the fact that the dictatorship by the affluent was such as to place pauper, artisan and small shopkeeper in the same powerless predicament.

This picture of multidimensional conflict is at once reinforced and complicated by reference to the criminal records. According to one estate sale notice, Burwash 'abounds with game'.[28] The villagers, and not just plebeians, had a reputation for poaching. One gamekeeper, Henry Cheal, alone successfully prosecuted an average of two men a year in the 1820s.[29] In later years there is irrefutable evidence of a poachers' mutual aid club, whose funds were used to pay the heavy fines inflicted under the notorious Game Laws.[30] Its existence cannot be proved before the Swing era, but hardly any Burwash folk appear to have been imprisoned in default of paying fines, though occasionally convicts spent a few days in jail while fines were paid: clear suggestions that poachers helped each other, or that black marketeers with whom they dealt advanced the cash. One well-known poacher apparently paid a fifty pound fine for the possession of ten items of game in 1825, and shelled out a further five pounds on a subsequent conviction within a year.[31] The black marketeers are an elusive bunch, not least because they combined legitimate dealing in poultry with illegal trading in game. The Bell Inn appears so regularly in criminal documentation that it was undoubtedly a centre of illegitimate activity. Gamekeeper Coppard was openly challenged in the pub by Frederick, a member of the notorious Siggs family, who blandly announced 'that he had got two Wires in his Pocket and defied' Coppard 'to take them away'; threatened by John Buss, from an equally deviant family, Coppard decamped hurriedly, but was felled by a housebrick and savagely beaten.[32]

The conflicts between paupers and vestrymen, and between poachers and gamekeepers, were not the sole causes of violence. Robberies were not uncommon, and the records reveal that Burwash's criminal fraternity preferred to operate under the cover of darkness. One victim, carpenter Axel from nearby Dallington, was found unconscious 'without his small clothes and shoes' near the church at 2 a.m.; his fate might have been worse, but for a publican who 'seeing his condition, and knowing the danger of the road, had taken his money out of his pocket' before Axel left the bar. John Hayward, a poultry-dealer and probable black marketeer, spent six hours in the Rose and Crown on 22 August 1831, getting 'somewhat in liquor'; he moved to the Bell Inn where 'he had some Brandy and water some Rum and Water and a Bottle of Wine', and 'he treated several [un-named] persons'. He later explained that he left 'sometime in the middle of the night' and had 'no recollection of what became of him', till between three and four in the morning when 'he found himself alone near the Church . . . he then went down to James Pilbeam who sells Beer by retail . . . and had some Beer', during which unorthodox sobering up period he discovered that he had been robbed of 'Several Sovereigns' and a bank note. Two well-known villains were charged after a lengthy investigation which spotlighted the activities of several notorious nocturnal depredators.[33]

However, theft — much of it petty — was the major concern of property-owners in Burwash. These records reveal a deep division in plebeian circles, between the habitually criminal and those accustomed to subservience, a division articulated by a labourer elsewhere who identified the 'lawless, drinking and worthless part of the community' from whom he totally disassociated himself [*Digby, 1978: 220*]. George Pope's first experience of the dock occurred at the age of fifteen when he was acquitted at the Assizes on a charge of housebreaking; fined for poaching in 1825 and 1826, in 1827 he received three months' hard labour for assaulting a constable, together with members of three other criminal families, William Relf, John Buss and Thomas Vidler. Thereafter Pope was a marked though a resourceful man. Two farmer vigilantes waging constant war against thieves deposed that they 'frequently found' Pope's 'footprints about the land'. Within seven months of his release from jail in 1827, Pope was arrested for stealing butter. He escaped conviction, probably due to a sister filching the key prosecution exhibit from the waggon taking her brother to a magistrate. Within a fortnight of this acquittal, Pope was fined another £5 for shooting a pheasant.[34] Pope's mate, and occasional partner in crime, John Buss, had an even more distinguished record; at the age of twelve in 1823 he was implicated in the theft of a sack, and fined for wilful damage. In 1826 he was fined again, for stealing apples, and for poaching, and received his first taste of prison for assaulting the police. His second term of imprisonment came in 1829, again for assault, and he was fined for poaching within six months of his release. In August 1831 he was transported for seven years for his part in the robbery of poultry-dealer Maynard.[35] Buss's accomplice on that occasion, and fellow transportee, was another labourer, the younger Richard Siggs; implicated, but not charged with the theft of a silver spoon at the age of nineteen in 1828, Siggs was also before the court on indictment for thieving hay at the same Sessions which determined on exile to Australia. Siggs's brother Frederick had also been in prison for assault. Their father received poor relief during the 1820s.[36]

Members of notoriously delinquent families like the Pope's, Siggs's and Buss's, and others including the Cliftons and the Collins, with unimportant exceptions,[37] never gave evidence against other plebeians. Only a handful of labourers with criminal records are found in the witness box, and those from families with records were reluctant informers. For example, William Eastwood was an unhelpful witness to an incident in which a gang of labourers looted the parish faggot store to keep the bonfire going on Guy Fawkes' Night in 1821; Eastwood would not 'say who the Men were as he did not speak to them nor they to him nor had he any suspicion of their having stolen the Faggots'.[38] The contrast between Eastwood's reticence, and the dexterity of other labourers in detecting criminals, reinforces the view that the workers who gave evidence belonged to a separate plebeian stratum from their actively criminal neighbours. Joseph Debley and John Langley immediately followed fresh footprints on discovering a break-in at their employer's barn, an exercise which led to the vicinity of William Pope's house; Pope was later seen 'driving a wheelbarrow' by Longley — on watch — who:

> took notice of the Prints made by his . . . boots and perceived that they were like the prints traced from the . . . Barn and in particular one of the . . . boots had thirteen nails in the Heel with the appearance of one nail broken out.[39]

Edward Pankhurst belonged to that disappearing category, the farm servant who still lived under his employer's roof, in his case sleeping in the bedroom of farmer Hicks' two sons; woken in the dead of night by goose thieves, all three went in pursuit, and overtook two suspects, one of whom, Richard Wickham was armed with a 'large Club' and threatened to use it. A bloody affray was avoided because Pankhurst 'knew both the . . . Men', whose arrest was safely deferred till the following day.[40]

Most labourers who acted in defence of property are not recorded in receipt of poor relief, a fact which supports the contention that the minority who obtained regular employ helped to preserve their reputations and jobs through active opposition to the criminal fraternity; but if this enhanced job security it was not without danger. Pankhurst was assaulted in the following year by members of the Eastwood and Leaney families.[41] Early in 1824 'fifteen young Men . . . labourers and others', waylaid two other labourers after church and 'made a great Noise and halloed them through the Town calling them informers', after which they were punched.[42] The younger Nicholas Crowhurst was no saint, but his refusal to divulge what he knew about a theft because the suspect 'Clifton would damn near kill him', no doubt typified the grounds for the repeatedly-evinced reluctance of workers to testify against each other.[43]

Clearly the major property owners could not expect help from many proletarians. The provision of funds for a police force, despite the dire state of parochial finance, and nearly twenty years before the first permissory legislation to create a rural police, is an eloquent testimony to the insecurity of persons and property. But this was not enough; the propertied had to look to themselves. While the activities of many farmers and others are recorded in preventive policing and detective work, two men, churchwarden Richard Button and 'respectable' butcher John Vigor, deserve special mention. Button was invariably first to be informed of criminal incidents; he commonly directed the legal counter-offensive, and Vigor was regularly among the first summoned to assist. A typical series of events followed the discovery of a concealed sack of stolen wheat. Button, 'having received the Information . . . went in Company with . . . Vigor and others . . . in the Evening to watch if any Persons came to fetch away the . . . Sack'. An all-night vigil resulted in the arrest of two suspects, whereupon Vigor and Button skilfully collated the evidence into an impressive prosecution case. Vigor's vigilance was rewarded with the presentation of a 'quart Silver Cup' by grateful 'neighbours and others' for his 'Courage in the cause of Justice'. The intrepid Button showed his metal in 1830, when at the height of the Swing disturbances the long-serving overseer of the poor, Edward Freeman resigned; Button immediately deputised and daily directed relief measures in those troubled times.[44]

III

These provisional findings suggest that devotion to the orthodox categories of 'open' and 'closed' parishes obscures more than it reveals [*Cf. Mills, 1980: ch.4*]. So, too, does concentration on the famous but unrepresentative outbreaks of overt rural protest; that approach misses many of the fundamental facets of day-to-day life in the countryside, which are revealed only by painstaking analysis of ample documentation on a local and regional basis. The developing debate on 'social crime" [*Rudé, 1978*] [*Rule, 1979*], [*Thompson, 1978*] will hopefully encourage substantive micro-studies. My present investigation into post-1815 protest in Sussex confirms my original identification of the virility of covert protest. Sufferers from malicious damage include: farmer Catt of Westfield, after 'some evil disposed person opened' doors allowing three horses to kill themselves by eating vast quantities of wheat; Sir William Geary, three of whose 'valuable riding horses' were maimed by a nocturnal visitor; farmer Wood some of whose beasts were injured by 'poisoned beans', and farmer Kingsnorth whose standing corn was 'wantonly trampled' by 'several young men' — the latter practice 'became so serious' that a legal offensive was mounted.[45] It is of interest that Burwash folk prosecuted for minor offences involving malicious damage were unable to pay fines and commonly went to prison, whereas poachers mainly paid up.[46] In Sussex arson emerged as a common and lethal form of protest in the 1790s; it remained so after 1815, with for example at least three reported instances in each year between 1821 and 1825.[47] Malcolm Chase has also drawn my attention to the regularity of arson in Essex in the 1815-20 period;[48] here resort to arson in the 1790s created a tradition, which is reflected in its serious recurrence in — among other years — 1829, twelve months before the county was engulfed by the Swing movement [*Richardson, 1977: 221-2*]. Suffolk pseudonymists announced that they would 'burn and plunder' in 1819, leaving General Hammond in no doubt of a resurgence of a popular campaign, only lately quiescent.[49]

Charlesworth questions my evidence emanating from Essex in the 1790s on the grounds that the arsonists may have been textile workers, severely hit by the rapid contraction of the local cloth industry in the last decades of the eighteenth century [*Charlesworth, 1980*]. The inability of authority to catch incendiaries preempts a definitive conclusion; suffice to say that redundant textile workers were forced to either migrate, or to look for work in agriculture, the only other source of local employment; those who remained — possibly the majority — and their families quickly swelled the ranks of the agricultural proletariat. In 1817 the premises of Essex farmers who used threshing machines were fired; anonymous bills and messages chalked on walls threatened to extend the campaign to all those who persisted in reducing winter employment by mechanical devices. Similarly, high bread prices in the same year provoked a 'Bread or Blood' notice: 'If an alteration is not made in the bread for the better beware of fires in your barns and stacks'.[50]

The identical experiences of counties like Essex, Suffolk and Sussex, with important differences between their rural economies, prove the significance of covert protest in general, and arson in particular. Charlesworth's claim that arson reached appreciable proportions only *after* the Swing episode is flatly confuted by the known facts, let alone those which will emerge from further research. So too is his bland assumption that rural labourers, unlike their urban counterparts, could steal enough food to ameliorate effectively their dreadful predicament. Certainly theft was endemic in the countryside, and for the minority of successful and resourceful poachers, it may have been the route to a modicum of comfort. But rural criminals engaged in battle with property; the comcomitant expressions of class war were no substitute for victory and ultimately property had — through the law — the upper hand, except as the legal records show with respect to arson, the most undetectable of all crimes: that point was not lost on the rural poor.

NOTES

1. Ostensibly the Act illegalised the payment of relief to people living in their own homes; henceforth only paupers who entered the disciplinarian workhouses were eligible for relief. The ancient parochial administration of relief, a system permitting local autonomy, was swept away; large unions of parishes, presided over by relatively remote committees of Guardians, were created and made responsible to an unelected, central executive authority, operating from London.

2. I owe this reference to Mr Alun Howkins of the University of Sussex.

3. My thanks are due to my colleague, Shirley Fereday, who is completing a study of 'Crime and the Creation of the Rural Police in East Sussex 1820-60' for providing some source materials.

4. East Sussex County Record Office, Par.284/12/1, Burwash select vestry minute book, (henceforth SV), 3 July 1819, 10 Dec. 1825, 16 June 1826. East Sussex County Record Office, Quarter Sessions Rolls (henceforth QRIE) 782, deposition of T. Vigor, 14 Dec. 1825.

5. SV. 2 Mar. and 9 Dec. 1822, 30 Apr. 1823.

6. SV. 2 June and 18 Aug. 1823, 1 Nov. and 13 Dec. 1827, 21 Feb. and 6 Mar. 1828, 22 Jan. 1829.

7. SV. 8 Apr. 1820, 7 Apr. 1821, 5 Apr. 1823, 21 Feb. 1824, 6 Apr. 1827.

8. SV. 3 June 1821, 29 Nov. 1822. *Sussex Advertiser*, 3 June 1822.

9. QRIE. 782, deposition of T. Chandler, 14 Dec. 1824.

10. SV. 30 Oct. and 18 Dec. 1819, 31 Mar. 1821, 10 Dec. 1825, 6 Apr. and 15 June 1827, 28 July 1828, 17 Apr. 1830.

11. SV. 22 Dec. 1821, 2 Nov. 1822, 28 Dec. 1827, 26 Feb., 17 May and 12 July 1828, 7 Feb. 1829.

12. SV. 8 Jan. 1820, 8 Dec. 1821, 6 Apr. 1822, 5 Feb. 1825, 17 May and 15 Nov. 1828, 31 Oct. 1829.

13. SV. 11 Aug. and 15 Dec. 1826.

14. SV. 3 Nov. 1821, 2 Mar. and 7 Dec. 1822, 5 June and 19 Aug 1824, 26 Dec. 1829.

15. SV. 3 July and 18 Sept. 1819, 22 Apr. 1820, 4 Jan. 1822.

16. SV. 3 July 1819. QRIE. 763, undated letter, and indictment of J. Sellings senior, and others.

17. *Sussex Advertiser*, 21 Dec. 1821, 13 and 27 May 1822, 6 Oct. 1823. QRIE. 770, indictment of ten Hellingly labourers.

18. SV. 18 Aug. and 8 Dec. 1821, 4 Jan and 16 Feb. 1822. *Sussex Advertiser*, 3 June 1822.

19. SV. 7 May 1825.

20. SV. 23 Feb., 29 Nov. and 13 Dec. 1827. QRIE. 779, 780, summary convictions.

21. Based on QRIE. 762-805. SV. 5 Jan. and 6 Apr. 1822, 28 Dec. 1827, 24 Jan. 1828, 27 June and 12 Dec. 1829.

22. SV. 19 Apr. 1823, 15 and 29 May 1830. *Sussex Advertiser*, 18 June 1821. QRIE. 783, Honeysett, summary conviction.

23. SV. 27 Dec. 1828, 7 Feb. and 11 July 1829.

24. QRIE. 779, statement by Philcox and Son, n.d., but 1823-4.

25. SV. 20 July 1822, 12 and 26 Jan., and 9 Mar. 1827.

26. SV. 21 Sept. 1827, 20 Feb. 1830.

27. SV. 25 Mar. 1824.

28. *Sussex Advertiser*, 20 Aug. 1821.

29. QRIE computed from summary returns.

30. Allen, 1979, pp. 60-70. Cf. *Sussex Express*, 11 May 1867, 5 Dec. 1868, 20 Jan. 1880.

31. QRIE. 786, 790, summary convictions.

32. QRIE. 800, deposition of J. Coppard, 18 May 1829.

33. *Sussex Advertiser*, 20 Aug. 1821. QRIE. 809, deposition of T. Hayward, 24 Aug. 1831.

34. *Sussex Advertiser*, 18 Nov. 1822. QRIE. 786, 790, 794, 795.

35. QRIE. 776, 790, 800, 803, 808.

36. QRIE. 794, 800, 808, SV. 17 Nov. 1821, 6 Mar. 1824, 24 July 1830.

37. Two cases in which female members of these families in regular employ gave evidence against fellow domestic servants.

38. QRIE. 770, deposition of W. Eastwood, 7 Nov. 1821.

39. QRIE. 769, depositions of Debley and Longley, 5 Oct. 1821.

40. QRIE. 782, depositions of Pankhurst, W. and T. Hicks, 2 Oct. 1824.

41. QRIE. 785.

42. QRIE. 779, deposition of T. Hicks, 27 Jan. 1824.

43. QRIE. 777, deposition of T. Weeks, 8 Oct. 1823.

44. QRIE. 786, depositions of Button, Vigor, and others, 5 Nov. 1825. *Sussex Advertiser*, 18 Nov. 1822. SV. 23 Dec. 1830.

45. *Sussex Advertiser*, 12 Nov. 1821, 21 July and 3 Nov. 1823.

46. East Sussex County-Record Office, QDB/2/E1, Battle House of Correction, Register of Committals, 1822-32.

47. Computed from the *Sussex Advertiser*, 1821-25.

48. I wish to thank Mr Malcolm Chase of the University of Sussex for several references to the Home Office papers used in notes 49 and 50.

49. Public Record Office, Home Office, 42/188, Hammond to the Home Office, 2 June 1819.

50. Public Record Office, Home Office, 42/166, 168, Vicar of Thaxted, and Dr. Scott, to the Home Office, 14 June and 11 July 1817.

REFERENCES

Charlesworth, A, 1979, *Social Protest in a Rural Society. The Spatial Diffusion of the Captain Swing Disturbances 1830-31.*

Charlesworth, A, 1980, 'The Development of the English Rural Proletariat and Social Protest: A Comment', *Journal of Peasant Studies*, Volume 8, No. 1, October.

Digby, A, 1978, *Pauper Palaces.*

Edsall, N.C., 1971, *The Anti-Poor Law Movement.*

Evans, E.J. 1975, 'Some reasons for the growth of English rural anti-clericalism', *Past and Present*, 66.

Lowerson, J.R., 1977 (unpublished), 'The aftermath of Swing: anti-poor law movements and rural trades unions in the south-east'. My thanks are due to Mr Lowerson for permitting me to read this paper.

Mills, D.R., 1980, *Lord and Peasant in Nineteenth Century Britain.*

Richardson, J.L. 1977 (unpublished). 'The standard of living controversy, 1790-1850, with specific reference to agricultural labourers in seven English counties', (Ph.D. thesis, University of Hull).

Rudé, G, 1978, *Protest and Punishment.*

Rule, J.G., 1979, 'Social crime in the rural south in the eighteenth and nineteenth centuries', *Southern History*, 1.

Thompson, E.P., 1978, review of Rudé, 1978, *New Society*, 14 December.

Wells, R.A.E., 1979, 'The development of the English rural proletariat and social protest,   1700-1850', *Journal of Peasant Studies*, Volume 6, No. 2, January.

The Wells – Charlesworth Debate: A Personal Comment on Arson in Norfolk and Suffolk

J.E. Archer*

In this brief comment Archer responds to the debate between Wells, (Journal of Peasant Studies, Vol. 6, No. 2, January, 1979 and Vol. 8, No. 4, July, 1981) and Charlesworth (Journal of Peasant Studies, Vol. 8, No. 1, October, 1980). He identifies a lack of communication between the two protagonists and also suggests that, in the case of Norfolk and Suffolk, incendiarism only became endemic after 1830. He also notes that covert and overt collective protest occurred simultaneously after 1830. In his conclusion Archer believes the arguments put forward by Wells and Charlesworth are overemphatic and premature because research on the 1800-30 period is still far from complete.

The interesting and vigorous debate between Wells and Charlesworth [*Wells*, 1979, 1981; and *Charlesworth*, 1980] has produced a large measure of agreement on the important issue of the proletarianisation of English farm labourers, but it has also generated a fierce disagreement on the crucial topic of rural social protest between 1790 and 1850. The point at issue, to state it simply, is concerned with the question of what the characteristic methods of protest were during the first half of the nineteenth century. Wells has argued that covert protest was the significant and enduring feature of social unrest in the English countryside. Charlesworth, who is accused of having a vested interest in overt protest, has argued that arson attacks were peripheral to the mainstream of the protest movement in East Anglia, which, until 1830, was characterised by collective unrest. Their difference of opinion has been exaggerated still further by Wells. In his emphatic rejoinder he wrote:

> Charlesworth's claim that arson reached appreciable proportions only after the Swing episode is flatly confuted by the known facts, let alone those which will emerge from further research [*Wells, 1981: 527/78*].

I will return to the 'known facts' in due course, but before I do so I feel a number of general observations need to be made.

Let me make it clear from the outset that I have no vested interest in overt protest, nor do I possess shares in Bryant and May matches. My one piece of research has been concerned with rural unrest in Norfolk and Suffolk, 1830-1870, and this had led me to consider arson, poaching, animal maiming and almost every conceivable form of collective overt protest.[1] I, in common with Wells, feel a sense of unease about the academic preference for the historical landmarks – Swing [*Hobsbawn and Rudé, 1973*], Tolpuddle [*Marlow, 1974*] and Arch [*Horn, 1971*] to name but three – which

J.E. Archer is a history lecturer at Edge Hill College of Higher Education, Ormskirk, Lancashire.

pervade the study of the development of English farm labourers. Similarly, I also share in common with Wells a belief in the study of everyday life, although I have not been able to construct the detail he presents of Burwash [*Wells, '81: 516-26/61-77*]. However, I do believe that Well's charge against Charlesworth, namely that of 'myopic devotion', should be treated with considerable care, for cannot a similar devotion to a single parish produce even more serious ophthalmic defects?

Having considered the three articles in question, I was struck by the apparent lack of communication between the two protagonists. First, are Wells and Charlesworth actually in agreement as to what constitutes an act of covert social protest? There is certainly a consensus on incendiarism, animal maiming and threatening letter-writing But I cannot help thinking that Wells' conception of social protest is somewhat broader than Charlesworth's. This not only creates misunderstanding but, in fact, makes further debate between them pointless until they both set out their terms of reference more fully. There appears to be a second area of misunderstanding which is also fundamental but as yet has not been recognised in any explicit way. The key to it came in Wells' conclusion:

> In Sussex arson emerged as a common and lethal (sic) form of protest in the 1790s: it remained so after 1815, with for example at least three reported instances in each year between 1821–25 [*Wells, 1981: 527/78*].

While I cannot actually speak for Charlesworth I suggest he does not regard three as implying 'common', and, if the debate continues, I would imagine there will be a disagreement concerning the emphasis placed on the frequency of incendiary activity. I, for one, regard three as an insignificant number. Also, by way of explanation to non-specialists of agrarian protest, Well's description of arson as being 'lethal' in its consequences is a metaphorical figure of speech. Incendiary fires aimed to destroy property, not life. From my own research I have discovered one death, and it was accidental. The unfortunate victim was a fireman who was struck by a collapsing beam. In no other case did anyone sustain serious injury, let alone death, through the premeditated actions of the incendiaries.[2]

Leaving aside these rather basic points, I want to make some specific remarks on the subject of arson which could well provide arguments in favour of both Wells's and Charlesworth's cases. This may sound contradictory, but it is hoped that the argument will become clearer as I proceed. Acts of covert protest in East Anglia did become frequent enough to disturb the equanimity of major landowners in the late eighteenth century, as Wells has suggested. The very fact that Associations for the Prosecution of Felons were established at this time suggests as much. These associations continued to be formed as and when landowners felt their property to be endangered by acts of covert protest: for example, the North Elmham Association was established in 1789, whereas the Foulsham Association was formed much later, in 1817.[3] Although such associations existed, it does not necessarily follow that all acts of social protest became 'common'; nor does it follow that all acts of covert protest can be simply grouped under the generic heading of social-protest crimes. There was, and is, a world of difference between turnip stealing and arson. It is a question of degree, and the latter was considered by landowner, farmer and labourer as being 'a crime second only to murder'. Theft and misdemeanours may have increased after 1790, but this does not mean that incendiarism increased in the same proportion or became 'common'. Indeed, contemporary observers found arson sufficiently novel in 1816 for them to pass comment. J.H. Kent regarded 1816 as the year when 'the first race of incendiaries' became active [*Kent, 1844*]. One farm labourer, whose life spanned the entire nineteenth century, thought arson only assumed serious proportions as late as 1832-34, when he wrote in his autobiography that 'a maliciousness of a kind not previously known was painfully manifest'. [*Glyde, 1894*].[4] Furthermore, in Suffolk a hitherto dormant clause of the Black Act was resurrected in 1815. This allowed victims of incendiarism to claim compensation from the hundred in which they resided. Hobsbawn and Rudé also remind us that the use of this Act was described as 'unprecedented' in 1823 when Wrench claimed £140 damages from the inhabitants of Holt, Norfolk [*Hobsbawn and Rudé, 1973: 56*]. The government saw fit to take this Act off the statue books in 1827. We must assume that by this time the law was a potential liability if not an actual liability to ratepayers. However, the point which really needs emphasising is that it was not repealed until 1827. Had incendiarism been frequent the Act would have been repealed earlier.

There are other indications which suggest that incendiarism was not a major cause for concern before 1830. First, the total number of commitments for arson in England and Wales show that, with the exception of 1822, the number of cases was low: 33 cases in 1816 and 37 in 1829, or to put it another way, less than one commitment a year per county [*Hobsbawn and Rudé, 1973: 56*]. The Norwich Union Fire Insurance Company minute books show a similar picture for England as a whole.[5]

Incendiary Fires on Property Insured with the Norwich Union

Year	Fires	Year	Fires
1821	1	1826	5
1822	18	1827	7
1823	7	1828	8
1824	5	1829	9
1825	9		

From such evidence it is possible to conclude, albeit tentatively, that in no year before 1830, not even 1822 when there were 60 fires in East Anglia, did the number of fires attain the level and frequency of the post-1830 period. There are a number of explanations for this, although space allows me to deal with only a few.

First, let us consider how fires were ignited, a simple point overlooked by Wells and Charlesworth. (This surely must be an 'everyday life' question.) There were a number of techniques; hot coals or cinders, fireballs, tinder box and flint, pipe and 'lucifer' matches. Any self-respecting incendiary would choose a box of matches. They were light, portable, concealable, cheap and effective, in fact, superior in every respect to all other methods. The point I really want to emphasise is that 'lucifer' matches, as sold in every village shop, only came onto the market in 1830.[6] This proved an absolute boon to would-be incendiaries. Their practical, almost liberating, effect can be seen in the example of Christopher Birch who started eight fires in South Norfolk in 1850 as he staggered home from the public house.[7] In 1825 Birch would have been faced with a practical problem – it conjures up the unlikely picture of a drunken man wielding a brazier. Similarly a tinder box and flint was not a particularly effective method of starting a fire in high winds or heavy rain. The essence of a successful incendiary was his speed and stealth, and the 'lucifer' match with its effective ignition allowed him to strike the match and then escape quickly across the fields. The 'lucifer' thus opened up a whole new vista for the angry labourer.

The next point for consideration concerns the people known to have started the fires, in other words, the convicted. Admittedly the convicted formed the minority before 1851: the majority were never detected.[8] However, what we do know may provide us with some clues about the mysterious identity of the incendiary. From my own research the convicted incendiary was male, and young, up to seven years younger than the Swing rioter; he was single and often knew his victim. Such a general and brief description gives credence to the observation that the most active were often the most discontented [*Hobsbawn and Rudé, 1973: 41; Jones, D., 1976*].

The plight of young single farm labourers in East Anglia intensified only after 1815 when the decline of 'living-in' gathered momentum. From the available evidence it seems that 'living-in' continued longer in Suffolk than in Norfolk. In the former county it was still very much the normal practice in the early 1820s and only probably declined in the late 1820s and early 1830s.[9] This decline had profound repercussions on the crime rates, the state of social relations and the level of incendiarism in East Anglia. The position of the young workers deteriorated still further after the implementation of the new Poor Law in 1835-36.[10] After that date they became the rural rebels 'par excellence'. When they began to leave the region in large numbers after 1851 incendiarism not only decreased in frequency, it also changed in character.[11] Incendiarism was the young labourers' response to their appalling plight, and for that reason high-level incendiary activity has a specific time location between 1830 and 1851. Incendiarism before and after this period never achieved such an intensity.

I now come to a problem of semantics. What is meant by the word 'common'? Perhaps I have become hardened, even blasé, on the matter of endemic incendiarism. I have found over 1700 fires between 1830 and 1870 in Norfolk and Suffolk.[12] It should be clear to Wells why I am rather dismissive about his reference to three fires a year. As a keen collector of incendiary fire examples I am disappointed if I cannot find a total of around 25 fires a year in Norfolk and Suffolk. In fact the annual occurence fell below 25 in only ten of the 41 years before 1870. As Wells so rightly points out, arson was an enduring feature of rural protest in the first half of the nineteenth century, and, what is more, it continued well after 1850. I have dwelt on the phenomenon of post-1830 incendiarism at some length, but I think it is important to know what the scale of the intensity was and this should aid any comparative studies in the future. As for the timing of this sudden surge of activity, the number of fires in Norfolk does appear to have increased as a direct result of the failure and repression of the Swing riots. In the case of Suffolk the picture is less clear:

Number of Incendiary Fires in Norfolk and Suffolk 1830-34[13]

Year	Norfolk Fires	Suffolk Fires
1830	28	19
1831	53	11
1832	52	12
1833	58	14
1834	33	17

However, by the 1840s no such doubts remain; incendiarism reached spectacular proportions [*Jones, 1976; Harber, 1975*]. In Norfolk and Suffolk there were 302 fires in 1843 and 1844 and in the country as a whole the number undoubtedly exceeded 600 for these two years.[14]

I will turn to the dichotomy between overt and covert protest which so troubles Wells and Charlesworth. Their arguments appear to become exaggerated during the course of the debate. Wells, who probably quite rightly and very sensibly argued that arson evolved in the 1790s and became the labourers' main weapon during the first half of the nineteenth century, altered his stance in his spirited rejoinder. Fires no longer evolved in the 1790s as he originally argued, they had now become common. My views on commonality have already been stated but I would not question his original thesis that arson evolved during that decade. Similarly, I think Charlesworth's defence of overt protest has much to commend it when placed in the context of Norfolk and Suffolk. (He cites 1816, 1822 and 1830-31 as examples of overt displays of collective protest.) Charlesworth could have mentioned the 37 strikes and demonstrations which took place between 1831-34 and the 25 demonstrations and riots in 1835-36 to give his case further strength.[15] These additonal examples of overt protest took the forms of riots, demonstrations, strikes, marches and even in one case a 'sit-in'. The sheer wealth of examples seems to suggest that these traditional methods, so commonly associated with hierarchical paternalist communities, were far from being extinguished. Rural workers in East Anglia do not appear to have discovered that overt means to protecting themselves had failed in the 1790s as Wells suggested. Furthermore Wells's contention that the Swing Riots were unique displays a scant disregard both for the facts and the definition of the word unique. The Swing Revolt of 1830 may well have been unique when placed in a national context but when it is viewed in an East Anglian context it represented a phase of a rebellion which had been waged for over a decade [*Peacock, 1965; Hobsbawn and Rudé, 1973*].

Did arson simply replace collective overt protest? Such an assumption needs to be examined more clearly. Wells suggested that arson increased in the 1790s in response to the high price of corn and a decline in living standards; in short, a general subsistence crisis of very serious proportions brought about the increase [*Wells, 1979; 121/35*].Incendiarism after 1830 rarely coincided with high wheat prices.[16] It is possible therefore, to conclude that incendiarism did not replace the food riot in any straight-forward manner. Why this should be so would require a complete article on its own. The next point worthy of note is the continuance or survival of overt methods such as strikes, demonstrations, enclosure riots and charity disputes, all of which increase again after 1850 and exist alongside incendiarism. Labourers and rural working-class communities appear to have been quite selective in their choice of tactics when furthering a dispute. For example, disputes over charity rights and enclosures usually produced mass meetings and demonstrations in the full light of day and in full view of the police. Three examples, in particular, show how overt protest existed alongside covert unrest. In 1844, a year renowned for incendiarism, the village of Snettisham (Norfolk) experienced a serious enclosure dispute. Arson was not employed by the protesters, but instead, they took to felling a large number of trees on the disputed land despite the presence of a large body of heavily armed police. In another enclosure dispute at Burwell (Cambridge) in 1851 the villagers demonstrated, rioted, struck in the full view of police, magistrates and eventually the army, which seems to suggest they were not completely overawed by the strength of the law-enforcement agencies. In nearby Fordham (Cambs) strikes, threatening letters, marches and fires all appeared simultaneously during a dispute.[17] Overt and covert protest could and did exist alongside one another and from this I infer that the tactics chosen by the protesters is a good deal more complex than those suggested by Wells or Charlesworth.

Finally, arson gave the labouring community the opportunity to transform an individual act of covert protest into a collective and overt display of hatred against the farmers. As a tactical weapon incendiarism was ideally suited since perfectly legal, and some not so legal, displays of collective joy were possible. Examples of singing, dancing, cheering, booing, card playing, 'frolicking' and determined refusals to lend assistance by the large numbers of spectators are too numerous to mention [*Jones, 1976: 16*]. The authorities were powerless and could do little but condemn such 'unfeeling behaviour'. The dichotomy between overt and covert protest, therefore, may not be so great when one separates the act of starting a fire from the subsequent reaction the fire engendered. However, these points are not meant to deny the replacement role of arson. After the defeat of Swing fires were directed at the very targets which had come under attack during the riots, threshing machines were burnt and clergymen's property was destroyed.[18] But we should not forget that fires provided outlets for displays of collective strength and unity.

In conclusion I would like to make a few broad observations concerning the debate which could, if we are not careful, become an obscure argument on the manufacture of matches or the plight of individual families in Burwash. The one enduring feature of this debate which has struck me is how little we know about the plight and response of farm labourers between the 1790s and 1830. The published literature covering this period is scandalously sparse; the Hammonds still remain one of the authorities and their work was published in 1911 [*Hammonds, 1911; Peacock, 1965*]. We are not in a position as yet to start generalising about which method of protest became or did not become the hallmark of the period. The 'known facts' to which Wells referred are sparse and his emphatic concluding remarks premature. He may well be right in the long term but I suspect that the overall picture which finally emerges will lie somewhere between the extremes of Charlesworth and Wells. In time we should be able to construct a clearer picture county by county and from this it will become plain how varied were employment customs, how different were landowners' attitudes towards their paternalistic duties, how in one area the 'unholy alliance' of landowner, farmer and parson was a reality by 1815-20, yet not so in another region, and how one form of protest was superseded by another. But until we are in a position to understand such developments we must pose more pertinent questions and then seek the answers. This debate, useful and interesting though it is, has underlined our ignorance and for that reason alone we should be grateful. What, I would like to ask, do we really know about the labourers and their families during the Napoleonic wars? Wells conveniently ignores the 1801-1815 period, but he is not alone since we are all in the same unfortunate position. We need to examine this period carefully and we should try, if possible, to determine the farm labourers' contribution to the war effort. How many of them went off to join the army? Also, what was their reaction when they returned home to find rural society in the process of rapid change? One would expect their initial protests to be of a collective and overt nature; they had, after all, been in a large organised group when in the ranks of the British Army.

Similarly, not enough is know about the role and importance of rural industries in such backwaters as East Anglia. I, for one, do not subscribe to the view expressed by Wells that, 'with a few very partial exceptions' there was no alternative to agricultural employment. In East Anglia the flax industry, weaving, herring fishing and brick-making had not all failed or declined to insignificant proportions before 1830. The operation of the Poor Law, too, would repay close scrutiny for it is almost impossible to generalise on this subject. In Norfolk, for instance, the 1830 rioters never directly mentioned the Poor Law or its inequities. However, after 1830 and before the implementation of the new Act it is possible to detect a hardening of the Poor Law authorities' attitudes which in turn contributed to the rise of incendiarism. And finally we need to examine the different groups of workers who are normally labelled generically as farm labourers. It is my opinion that an examination of the plight of the young single men will yield valuable clues on the development of protest. Broadly speaking, the young casual labourers started the fires, shepherds stole sheep, horse-keepers maimed horses and the community as a whole joined together collectively to halt the erosion of rights. The arsenal of weapons at the disposal of farm labourers was enormous but their choice and use of such weapons in the class war against landowners, farmers, clergymen and the Poor Law authorities are incompletely understood by historians at the present time.

NOTES

1. 'Rural Protest in Norfolk and Suffolk, 1830-1870', unpublished Ph.D. thesis, University of East Anglia, 1982.

2. *Norfolk Chronicle,* 25 May 1834 at North Walsham (Norfolk).

3. These associations were established to combat theft, fence breaking, sheep stealing and poaching in the first instance. Only later were associations formed with the specific purpose of protecting property holders from incendiarism and animal maiming. See *Norfolk Chronicle* 8 Nov. and 29 Nov. 1834 for the establishment of the Fakenham (Norfolk) Association concerned with animal maiming; and *East Anglian*, 15 Nov. 1831 and 29 Nov. 1831 on incendiarism.

4. J.H. Kent, *Remarks on the Injuriousness of the Consolidation of Small Farms and the Benefit of Small Occupations and Allotments; with some Observations on the Past and Present State of the Agricultural Labourer. On the Physical and Moral Condition of the Agricultural Labourer* p. 81, Bury St Edmunds, 1844.

    Kent constructed a table of protest in Britain as a whole. It ran as follows:-

    | 1795 | '1st bread and wage riots'. |
    | 1799-1801 | '2nd bread riots'. |
    | 1809-10 | '3rd bread and wage riots'. |
    | 1812-13 | '4th bread and wage riots'. |
    | 1816-17 | '5th bread and wage riots and 1st fires'. |
    | 1822 | 'Riots and 2nd fires'. |
    | 1830-32 | 'Riots (1830) and 3rd fires'. |
    | 1835 | 'Riots and 4th fires'. |
    | 1838-39 | '5th fires' (East Anglia was completely free of incendiarism) |
    | 1843-44 | '6th fires'. |

5. I am indebted to Roger Ryan for supplying me with these figures. The Norwich Union was the second largest insurance company in the country in the 1820s.

6. *Everyman's Encyclopedia,* Vol. 8, p. 121, London, 6th edn, 1978.

7. *Norfolk Chronicle,* 29 June and 3 August 1850.

8. After 1850 one person was convicted for every four fires which had taken place; between 1830-39 the ratio was 1:21.

9. For Snettisham, see *Norwich Mercury* 16 March, 25 May and 12 Dec 1844; for Burwell, 142-143: Glyde, J. The Autobiography of a Suffolk Farm Labourer, *Suffolk Mercury,* 1894, p. 14; *Times,* 10 June 1844.

10. *Morning Chronicle*, 8 Dec 1849; *Times*, 10 June 1844.

11. After 1851 convicted incendiaries were frequently young children and vagrants. Bainbridge A. and Jones, D.J.V., have noted the high proportion of tramps among the convicted in the second half of the nineteenth century in Wales. *Crime in Nineteenth Century Wales*, SSRC Report (1975), pp. 304-46.

12. Archer, J.E., op.cit., pp. 163-4.

13. Ibid.

14. At present I have collected examples of 575 incendiary fires in 1843-44 in Britain and I have yet to study the local newspapers county by county.

15. Archer, op.cit.

16.
Year	Wheat prices/Qtr.	Fires in Norfolk and Suffolk
1838	64s. 7d.	8
1839	70s. 8d.	5
1840	66s. 4d.	13
1843	50s. 1d.	84
1844	51s. 3d.	218
1849	44s. 3d.	78
1850	40s. 3d.	75
1851	38s. 6d.	75

17. For Snettisham, see *Norwich Mercury* 16 March, 25 May and 12 Dec 1844; for Burwell, *Cambridge Chronicle*, February and March editions, 1851; for Fordham, *Bury and Norwich Post*, 6 March 1850.

18. *East Anglian*, 18 Dec. 1832; *Bury and Norwich Post* 19 Dec. and 26 Dec. 1832

REFERENCES

Archer, J.E., 1982, *Rural Protest in Norfolk and Suffolk 1830-1870,* unpublished Ph.D. thesis, University of East Anglia.

Bacon, R.N., 1844, *Report on the Agriculture of Norfolk*, Norwich.

Bainbridge, A. and Jones, D.J.V., 1975, *Crime in Nineteenth Century Wales*, S.S.R.C. Report.

Charlesworth, A., 1980, 'The Development of the English Rural Proletariat and Social Protest, 1700-1850: A Comment', *Journal of Peasant Studies*, Vol. 8, No.1, October.

Glyde, J., ed., 1894, 'The Autobiography of a Suffolk Farm Labourer, in *Suffolk Mercury*, Ipswich and East Suffolk Record Office.

Glyde, J., 1856, *Suffolk in the Nineteenth Century*, London.

Hammond, J.L. and B., 1911, *The Village Labourer 1760-1832*, London.

Harber, J., 1975, *Incendiarism in Suffolk 1840-45*, unpublished M.A. Thesis, Essex University.

Hobsbawn, E. and Rudé, G., 1973, *Captain Swing*, Harmondsworth.

Horn, P., 1971, *Joseph Arch 1826-1919, The Farm Worker's Leader*, Kineton.

Jones, D.J.V., 1976, 'Thomas Campbell Foster and the Rural Labourers: Incendiarism in East Anglia in the 1840's, *Social History*, No. 1.

Kent, J.H. 1844, *Remarks on the Injuriousness of the Consolidation of Small Farms and the Benefit of Small Occupations and Allotments; with some Observations on the Past and the Present State of the Agricultural Labourer. On the Physical and Moral Condition of the Agricultural Labourer.* Bury St. Edmunds.

Marlow, J., 1974, The Tolpuddle Martyrs, London.

Wells, R.A.E., 1979, 'The Development of the English Rural Proletariat and Social Protest, 1700-1850', *Journal of Peasant Studies*, Vol. 6, No. 2, January.

Wells, R.A.E., 1981, 'Social Conflict and Protest in the English Countryside in the Early Nineteenth Century: A Rejoinder', *Journal of Peasant Studies, Vol. 8, No. 4, July.*

Social Change and Social Conflict in Nineteenth-Century England: the use of the open–closed village model

Dennis R. Mills* and Brian M. Short†

Following earlier articles on social change and conflict in rural England 1780-1850, we assert the relevance of the open–closed model of social structure, particularly to the study of Burwash by Wells [1981]. This paper demonstrates that no parish was insulated from economic and other influences exerted in and by neighbouring parishes. More especially, although open parishes challenged the upper Establishment, they were not devoid of internal strife, since different interests were not subject to the overriding influence of the large landowners who dominated the populations of closed parishes.

The open–closed model of rural social structure has no claim to explain every aspect of village life in the nineteenth century. To begin with it is basically a static model. It is, therefore, quite efficient in explaining a period picture and is particularly relevant for dates between about 1780 and 1850 when population was growing so rapidly. When we turn to social *change*, as opposed to conditions of life at a specific period, it is less useful, but it cannot be ignored, since the study of change implies comparison between conditions in one period and those obtaining in a subsequent period. Therefore, it is important to use all available means of static and comparative static social analyses, before passing on to dynamic analysis. As to social conflict, it is not entirely a straightforward matter to decide whether we should see it as a manifestation of change, or as a built-in feature of the social environment. For example, conflict over the enclosure of a common can best be regarded as part of the process of economic and social change, but the trade-union type of activities by farm labourers cannot be wholly associated with marked changes and particular events since they were and are a continuing feature of a capital-oriented system of farming. Therefore, a static model like the open–closed model cannot be comprehensively explanatory, but will have some significant relevance to the study of social conflict.

Before progressing further, it will be useful to consider a few points about the actual nature of the open–closed model. As first conceived by the eighteenth-century poor law writers, it attempts to explain behaviour on the basis of the differential distribution of power within different types of village social structures and this premise has continued to hold its place in the model over a period of two centuries. However, the early users of the model, to whom we owe the name, can easily be shown to have oversimplified the circumstances. While the basic distinction between

* *The Open University*   † *University of Sussex*
We should like to acknowledge the helpful discussions we have had with Mr A. Charlesworth and Mr R. Grover, while retaining responsibility for the opinions offered.

villages of many owners and villages of few or one remains important, a much more sophisticated understanding of rural society can be achieved by thinking in terms of a continuum (from wide open – Headington Quarry – to firmly shut – Cotesbach),[1] or at least in terms of a sub-division of each of the two main categories. By adopting either of these strategies (or both, since they are not mutually exclusive), the researcher can get much nearer to historical reality without being overwhelmed by parochial detail.

However, it will be convenient here to concentrate attention on the polar types within the continuum or the fourfold classification, partly for reasons of space, but also because in so doing we might begin to resolve the complexities of the debate between Wells [1979: 1981] and Charlesworth [1980]. In stressing covert (under-cover) social protest Wells has adopted a deferential model of rural society, with clergy and gentry supporting the repressive activities of the farmers. This is essentially the model of those villages which were dominated by resident landlords, where power descended from the top of the pyramid, the lower orders responding with at least outward deference.

Charlesworth has challenged this view to the extent that he believes that there were situations in which this did not work, situations in which the labourers felt they could appeal to the clergy and gentry over the heads of the farmers. They therefore dared to indulge in overt protest, i.e., trade-union activities, daylight meetings, and rioting, rather than arson, theft, and anonymous letters. Not only does this imply less than total agreement between farmers and the ruling classes [*Charlesworth*, 1980: 104], it also hints at the significance of moral support for labourers from the peasantry or, to give it a more neutral label, that body of small rural entrepreneurs, which included agriculturalists, non-agriculturalists and dual occupationists [e.g., *Charlesworth*, 1979: 12]. This 'peasantry' was to be found in open villages, especially those in the sub-division where property was divided between many owners, say over forty per village. We should also note some evidence of sympathy between farmers and labourers at Burwash itself during the Swing Riots [BPP, 1834: 495e].

Wells's confusion over the use of the open–closed model (and possibly any form of explicit modelling of society) is best illustrated in his response to Charlesworth [*Wells*, 1981]. After briefly reasserting the validity of his earlier argument, he uses most of the article to describe social conflict in one very strife-torn parish (Burwash, Sussex) and appears to believe that by demonstrating conflict in an open village he has disposed of the open–closed village model altogether. Needless to say, it needs more than one contrary example to dispose of a concept which had its origins in the eighteenth century. Models do not anyway endeavour to explain *all* reality, but to set out basic structures of everyday experience. There is no inherent conflict between the use of such a general concept as the open–closed parish dichotomy and the 'study of everyday life' [*Wells*, 1981: 516], since the former rests firmly, though not mechanically, on the latter.

More importantly, the case of Burwash, as reported by Wells, appears to confirm, rather than to dispose of the open–closed model. Wells's surprise at finding strife in an open village, seems to be due to a misunderstanding of the model. We should not expect to find conflict in *closed* villages, especially those with resident gentry (estate villages), such as neighbouring Ashburnham. There the dice was too heavily loaded against the labourers, who were in any case better off materially than their fellows in open villages. Employment was more likely to be continuous, wages were marginally higher for the skilled men who were selected to reside close to their work and cottage accommodation was cheaper and of higher quality, often with larger gardens than in open villages. For example, Lord Ashburnham, a resident landowner a few miles south of Burwash, took great pains to exclude potential tenants from his estate who threatened local employment by bringing large households with them. He even had single men's accommodation, which survives, purposely built on the estate [*Short*, 1976: 157]. Moreover, it is likely that the few labourers who were in need of poor relief got more generous individual treatment than those in hard-pressed open villages [*Mills*, 1963: 205-6].

On the other side of the equation, the totality of estate control can also be used to explain why revolt was less likely than in open villages. The labourers were less numerous, therefore better supervised. There was more control over licensed premises, and attendance at church and Sunday school was monitored. Non-conformist chapels, meeting houses, and beer shops were unusual in estate villages and could, therefore, not act as foci of dissatisfaction with the rural establishment generally. Most basic of all, as we have already seen, is the estate-controlled cottage accommodation, not only the amount, but also who occupied it and whether or not they kept lodgers. It would not be surprising, therefore, to find that estate owners did not have to resort very often to ejecting paupers or potential paupers. For example, Lord Ashburnham faced no protests in 1830-31, unlike Lord Gage and Lord Sheffield in more unruly parts of the Weald [*Short*, 1976: 170].

Turning from one polar situation to look at the other, let us consider if Charlesworth, Hobsbawm, and Rudé, and ourselves are correct in expecting to find evidence of protest in the open villages with large numbers of owners [*Hobsbawm and Rudé*, 1973; *Charlesworth*, 1979; *Mills*, 1980]. One fundamental point to notice is that being open villages they had become the gathering ground for some of the surplus of labourers who undoubtedly existed in most corn-growing non-industrial parts of the countryside from about 1780 until rural population began to subside. More than that, they had to accommodate many of the irregularly employed day labourers who worked, when they could, on farms in neighbouring closed parishes.

As an amplification to this general point, we should note that although the parish was generally a meaningful unit of analysis to the Victorians, its size could sometimes cause the need for qualifications. In the Midlands and the North many parishes contained a number of separate *townships* and these were the effective unit of poor law administration. Even where parish and township were co-terminous, the large area involved and the settlement pattern prevailing require us to look separately at different parts of the parish. For example, Flora Thompson noted the distinction in north Oxfordshire, between the hamlet and the village in the same parish [*Thompson*, 1945: Ch. 1], while in Sussex, Hartfield and Withyham were closed villages surrounded by otherwise 'open' areas in the same parishes [*Short*, 1979]. A final example comes from the Lincolnshire Wolds, where Olney [1975: 12] has described Binbrook as an open village surrounded by substantial outlying areas within the boundaries of large (i.e., 'closed') farms belonging to nearby estates.

Individual parishes or townships cannot be studied in isolation from their neighbours. Wells should have explored the area around Burwash for evidence as to journeys to work, since it seems possible that some of the protest was indirectly related to the conditions of employment on neighbouring estates, such as Brightling, Ashburnham, Wadhurst, and Shoyswell Manor in Etchingham parish.

The results of a very elementary exercise of this kind are shown in Table 1, which summarizes data for places within a five-mile radius of Burwash – walking distance for farm labourers commuting daily to work. In this instance there seems to have been little scope for Burwash labourers to have walked to work in nearby closed

TABLE 1

DATA RELATING TO PARISHES WITHIN A FIVE-MILE RADIUS OF THE CENTRE OF BURWASH PARISH, SUSSEX (EXCLUDING THE TOWN OF BATTLE)

Parish		Area 1851 mls^2	Popn 1851	Density 1851 PP ml^2	Popn 1801	Growth 1801-51 per cent	Imperial Gazetteer** designation
Ashburnham		5.70	865	151.7	473	82.88	–
Brightling		7.21	812	112.6	507	60.16	Subdivided
Burwash		11.43	2,227	194.8	1,524	46.13	Much subdivided
Dallington	(R)	4.49	664	147.9	401	65.59*	Divided among a few
Etchingham		5.86	950	162.1*	414	129.47	Much subdivided
Heathfield		12.45	2,208	177.3	1,226	80.10	Subdivided
Mayfield	(R)	21.25	3,055	143.8	1,849	65.22	Subdivided
Mountfield		6.00	769	128.2	564	36.35	
Penhurst		2.28	120	52.6	67	79.10	One estate
Salehurst	(R)	10.13	2,191	216.3	1,611	36.00	Much subdivided
Ticehurst	(R)	12.81	2,362	184.4	1,436	64.48	–
Wadhurst	(R)	15.85	2,802	176.8	1,677	67.08	Subdivided
Warbleton	(R)	9.00*	1,509*	167.7	908*	66.19	–

Note: the areas were only approximate measures, but comparison with later maps suggest that the errors in these figures were minimal, with the exception of Dallington and Mayfield where the estimates may have been of the order of one third too low. The median figure in each column is shown by an asterisk.

R = Swing incidents of any kind [*Hobsbawm and Rudé*, 1973: Appendix III]

**J. M. Wilson, *The Imperial Gazetteer of England and Wales*, [London 6 vols., 1870 or two volume edition 1875].

Source: 1851 Census of England and Wales

parishes, since columns 4 and 7 reveal relatively narrow differences in population density between parishes and few great contrasts in landownership structure. The chief exception seems to have been Penhurst parish, where the population density was less than a third of the median figure for the thirteen parishes in 1851. However, Penhurst was part of the Ashburnham estate, where Lord Ashburnham erected barracks for single labourers near New Buildings Farm.

A further point to notice is the very large size of the parishes: Warbleton, the median parish contained 5,763 acres, an area which would be counted large in many parts of champion England. However, this Wealden area of Sussex was a land of hamlets, rather than true villages, and of wood pasture, rather than common field. Such areas appear to have been more favourable to the growth of open communities, rather than to the sharply contrasting open and closed pattern of common-field England [*Mills*, 1980: 98-106, 117-19]. Insofar as this is part of the acknowledged open–closed model, these observations in the Burwash area support the model. It is also relevant to quote similar observations in nearby Kent, where a preponderance of Wealden and Forest parishes were 'much subdivided' and the 'much subdivided parishes' in Kent as a whole were over twice as extensive as those 'in a few hands' [*Everitt*, 1972; 87-8].

Regional analysis of the Imperial Gazetteer confirms this picture for Kent, Surrey, and Sussex. Over two-thirds of the designated parishes in the High and Low Weald were classified as open, a figure matched only by the relatively small Bagshot Sands area (Table 2). Relatively high proportions of closed parishes were to be found in the

TABLE 2

THE REGIONAL PATTERN OF LANDOWNERSHIP IN KENT, SURREY, SUSSEX c. 1870

	High Weald		Low Weald		Scarpfoot zone		Romney/ Pevensey Marshes		North Downs		South Downs		Sussex Coastal Plain		North Kent		Bagshot Sands		London Basin		Totals	
	No.	%	No.	%	No.	%	No.	%	No.	%	No.	%	No.	%	No.	%	No.	%	No.	%	No.	%
Essentially closed parishes	13	25.5	23	31.6	57	62.7	15	48.3	77	61.2	33	84.5	19	63.3	26	59.1	2	18.2	11	37.9	276	52.6
Essentially open parishes	38	74.5	50	68.5	34	37.4	16	51.6	49	38.9	6	15.4	11	36.7	18	40.9	9	81.9	18	62.0	249	47.4
Not represented	23		20		68		13		66		21		29		25		4		30		299	
Total parishes	74		93		159		44		192		60		59		69		15		59		824	

Where:

'Essentially closed' is Wilson's 'Most or all land in one estate' *and* 'Not much divided' *and* 'divided among a few'
and

'Essentially open' is Wilson's 'Subdivided' *and* 'much subdivided'.

Source: J.M. Wilson, *The Imperial Gazetteer of England and Wales*, 1870

Scarpfoot zone, the North and South Downs, the Sussex coastal plain, and North Kent. However, no one region is a complete collection of any one polar type. Finer distinctions can be drawn than is possible from Wilson's generalized survey, by the analysis of land tax assessments, which are extant until 1832 and sometimes beyond. Communities which contained very large numbers of agricultural labourers might indeed have existed, but they would have been scattered among other parishes, some dominated by relatively few landowners. There were no areas in Kent, Surrey, and Sussex which did not contain some mixture of the two polar types.

Returning to the Burwash area, there were several parishes which contained markedly lower densities than the average; Penhurst, Brightling, and Mountfield in particular. The range of densities in 1851 ran from 52.6 persons per square mile up to 216.3, a ratio of about 1:4 and quite enough for us to suspect an imbalance of farm labourers which required daily commuting. Burwash at 194.8 ppsm was at the top end of the range, a fact which helps to put Wells's findings into perspective. A fuller study would, of course, look at alternative forms of employment, the effect of the decline in iron-working [*Ashworth*, 1970: 61-4; *Tomlinson*, 1976: 389] and the actual social distribution of landownership. It would also take into account the effects of agricultural depression which appear to have been very marked in Sussex [*Baugh*, 1975: 54-7, 60, 66].

A final point to notice is that population growth was not necessarily the greatest in the most heavily populated parishes of 1801. Indeed a comparison of the fourth and sixth columns of Table 1 gives a Spearman's correlation coefficient of −0.166, suggesting that there was very little relationship between density and growth. Again this is an interesting point which, if explored further, might be seen to be related to closed parishes gaining population on top of a very low base in 1801 through a policy of estate cottage building and to a decline in rural industry in open parishes. Enough has to be done to show the importance of studying any parish, including Burwash, within its local context.

Another quite basic factor, which not surprisingly causes confusion, is that the bulk of the land even in open parishes with numerous owners was farmed in large units, just as it was on the estates. But that is not the same as saying that most of the *employers* were large farmers.[2] Nevertheless, those large farmers who worked land in open parishes would presumably be just as anxious as their fellows elsewhere to keep down the cost of their labour in order to maintain their competitive position. This appears to be what was happening in Burwash.

Furthermore, the tradesmen and craftsmen class and the small farmers (and those who combined both callings), who were numerous in open parishes and for the most part significant ratepayers, would also have had good reason for keeping down the rates. Their situation, however, was different from that of the farmers. Their labour demands were fairly constant through the year and it is by no means clear whether they were involved in the roundsman systems in use in some parishes. Moreover, the small entrepreneurs included many who had a vested interest in keeping up the population of their villages, publicans and shopkeepers in search of trade, and more especially that species who specialized in building and/or letting the jerry-built cottage properties in which the unfortunate labourers lived. Rents were generally acknowledged to be higher in open than closed villages, for poorer accommodation, and were more or less guaranteed by the system of outdoor relief. Thus for some rate payers, increases in rates could be offset by direct financial gain from their enterprises accruing from population increases.

So if we look at the open parishes purely from the point of view of rates, there was plenty of scope for conflicts of interest to develop. While Burwash was probably an extreme case it nevertheless illustrates this general principle and other examples can be found, such as Enderby in Leicestershire. Here rival factions, one led by the Loraine Smiths of Enderby Hall and the other by the parson, fell out over the principles of re-assessment to the poor rate.[3] It is interesting to note that the principal owner in 1830 paid £49 out of a total land tax of £134, the remaining £85 being shared between sixty-seven other proprietors, including many small ones with whom the vicar took sides.[4] The resident of Enderby Hall was powerful enough to exert pressure on the Vestry, but not powerful enough to have avoided open conflict or to win every vote. Where the squire was all powerful, argument would be unusual, but where some sort of democracy prevailed we can expect argument and conflict as part of the democratic process. Nevertheless, some forms of social control could be exercised in open parishes, such as Burwash, by powerful groups, rather than through the dominance of a single estate owner.

Disputes might also arise over church rates, with the parson, large farmers, and large owners ranged on the side of the Anglican right to levy rates on those who attended any place of worship or none. Here the cause célèbre appeared to be religious, but was in fact socio-structural. Most nonconformists, particularly their leaders, belonged to the ranks of the small owner-occupying farmers, craftsmen, and tradesmen, who could exercise some independence from the Establishment. Insofar as they bothered themselves with such matters, it is likely that the labourers took sides and chose their religion according to personal advantage, which would usually come down to not offending employers.[5]

Returning to Wells's point [1981: 516] that Charlesworth is wrong to assume social solidarity in open villages, it may now seem that he has won the argument handsomely, since it was not only Burwash which saw one group set against another. Yet if we are talking in Marxist class terms, with the owners of capital ranged against the providers of labour, estate villages showed the sharpest distinction but few signs of protest. By contrast open villages had a more subtle 'class' structure but there was widespread opposition to the establishment of Church and Land. Hobsbawm and Rudé referred to such communities being independent of squire, parson, and large farmer in economic, social, and ideological terms [1973: 158] and Charlesworth [1979: 51] claimed that the Captain Swing riots spread in a way which indicated 'the work of local men of *independence* and political enquiry mobilizing their neighbours to take collective action during a period of political crisis' (our emphasis).

Inter-marriage between the peasantry and the labourers and various forms of common interest, such as young men of peasant families working as labourers until their fathers' land passed down to them, would give the anti-Establishment groups some kind of unity. It would not be proof against all developments, but to be on the same side of the major class divide to whose development during the eighteenth century Wells has rightly drawn attention, would have counted for a great deal when a Malthusian pressure of population was made worse by what can only be regarded as the callousness of the most selfish of the large farmers.

Since we have shown that the open–closed model can be related to differential developments in village class structure, its relevance to the understanding of social protest has also been demonstrated. But when we come to analyse a chain of rioting and other disturbances, such as those which took place in the period of Captain Swing, the model is only part of the necessary framework of analysis. It can be seen as an appropriate starting point, but because it is a static model, it must be supplemented by other dynamic approaches.

Hobsbawm and Rudé accepted the validity of the open–closed model as a supplement to the hardship model, since hardship was a necessary but not a sufficient condition of rioting, a point emphasized by Charlesworth [1979: 31]. They also took into account the reaction of the authorities [1973: chap. 13] and employed a simple contagion model to explain the spread of rioting [1973: 159].

To this array of models and factors, Charlesworth has recently added the significance of the London highways and the role of linkmen who moved up and down those highways. Thus he has replaced the simple contagion model with a much more complex model of diffusion, in which, however, one can see a potential role for the open village. This is because the large highway village with inns and other facilities for travellers is more than likely to have been an open village, although Charlesworth has not directly explored this angle. Charlesworth has also done more to explore the radical political context in which the Captain Swing riots took place. This brings to the fore two particular aspects of radicalism: (a) the timing which can be related to other events such as revolution in Belgium and France and Wellington's refusal to consider electoral reform; and (b) the distribution of radicalism, which again stresses the role of independent men living in open villages.

To conclude, it has been shown that the open–closed model is helpful in the context, not only of general social conditions in early nineteenth-century rural England, but also of social protest and social change. It can subsume a deferential model of rural society, without denying a role for more complex models of class relationships of a less deferential kind. On the basis of this interpretation of the static social geography of the period, one can then go on to explain a range of political events and social change (temporal aspects of rural life) in such a way that the open–closed model helps to predict their distribution. Like the hardship model, there are contexts in which the open–closed model provides an understanding of the necessary, if not sufficient conditions for social and political protest. Historians and social scientists could perhaps usefully move on to other waves of protest, such as those over church rates, and analyse them in a comparable manner.

Finally, it is worth noting that there is less disagreement between Wells and Charlesworth than their papers might lead us to believe. In his first paper, Wells, as a historian, accumulated evidence to show that covert protest was more important in the first half of the nineteenth century than later. We agree with this basic distinction between the two periods. Charlesworth's work, on the other hand, is spatial in orientation. Both approaches are legitimate and complement each other. Our objection has been to Wells's second paper which attacks the spatial analysis of Charlesworth without using the appropriate spatial concepts.

NOTES

1. Headington Quarry, a squatter settlement near Oxford, is well described by Samuel [1975]. A contemporary description of Cotesbach, Leics., in 1791, appears in Mills [1980: 27]. The latter reference is the fullest discussion so far of the open–closed model.

2. The answer to Rural Query No. 3 shows that at Burwash there were some farms of 200-400 acres, though the majority were 50-100 acres each [*BPP*, 1834: 95a]. Query 3 was: 'Are there many or few landowners in this Parish, and are the farms large or small? The Burwash respondent chose to ignore the first half of the question.

3. Enderby Vestry Minutes, October 5th, 8th and 12th, 1826.

4. From the land tax assessments in Leicestershire Record Office.

5. For the Melbourn (Cambs.) church rate dispute see Mills [1979].

REFERENCES

Ashworth, G. J., 1970, 'A note on the decline of the Wealden iron industry', *Surrey Archaeological Collections*, vol. 67, pp. 61-4.

Baugh, D. A., 1973, 'The cost of poor relief in South East England, 1790-1834', *Economic History Review*, 2nd series, vol. 28, pp. 50-68.

British Parliamentary Papers (BPP 1834-44), *Report of HM Commissioners on the Operation of the Poor Laws*, Appendices B.1 (pts I–V), Answers to Rural Queries, vols XXX–XXXIV, answers for Burwash, Sussex on pp. 495 a-e. [Irish University Press Edition, vols Poor Law 10-14]..

Charlesworth, A., 1979, *Social protest in a rural society: the spatial diffusion of the Captain Swing disturbances of 1830-1831*, Historical Geography Research Group, order from Geo Abstracts Ltd, University of East Anglia.

Charlesworth, A., 1980, 'The development of the English rural proletariat and social protest, 1700-1850: a comment', *Journal of Peasant Studies*, vol. 8, pp. 101-11.

Everitt, A., 1972, *The pattern of rural dissent: the nineteenth century*, Leicester University Press, Occasional Paper, Department of Local History, Second Series, No. 4.

Hobsbawm, E. J. and Rudé, G., 1969, *Captain Swing*, revised edition, Harmondsworth: Penguin, 1973.

Mills, D. R., 1963, *Landownership and rural population with special reference to Leicestershire in the mid-19th century*, unpublished Ph.D. thesis, University of Leicester.

Mills, D. R., 1979, 'The Court of Arches and church rates disputes as sources of social history', *Bulletin of Local History: East Midland Region*, vol. 14, pp. 1-11.

Mills, D. R., 1980, *Lord and peasant in nineteenth century Britain*, Croom Helm.

Olney, R. J. (ed.), 1975, *Labouring life in the Lincolnshire Wolds: a study of Binbrook in the mid-nineteenth century*, Society for Lincolnshire History and Archaeology, (47 Newland, Lincoln), Occasional Paper no. 2.

Rudé, G., 1981, 'Review of Charlesworth 1979', *Journal of Historical Geography*, vol. 7, pp. 188-9.

Samuel, R. (ed.), 1975, *Village life and labour*, London: Routledge and Kegan Paul.

Short, B. M., 1976, 'The turnover of tenants on the Ashburnham Estate, 1830-1850', *Sussex Archaeological Collections*, vol. 113, pp. 157-74.

Short, B. M., 1979, 'Landownership in relation to demographic and agricultural change in the eighteenth and nineteenth century Weald', in Wanklyn, M. D. G. (ed.), *Landownership and power in the regions*, Wolverhampton, pp. 43-57.

Thompson, F., 1945, *Lark Rise to Candleford*, Oxford: Oxford University Press (Later edn., Penguin, 1973).

Tomlinson, H. C., 1976, 'Wealden gunfounding: an analysis of its demise in the eighteenth century', *Economic History Review*, 2nd series, vol. 29, pp. 383-93.

Wells, R. A. E., 1979, 'The development of the English rural proletariat and social protest, 1700-1850', *Journal of Peasant Studies*, vol. 6, pp. 115-39.

Wells, R. A. E., 1981, 'Social conflict and protest in the English countryside in the early nineteenth century: a rejoinder', *ibid.* vol. 8, pp. 514-30.

Wilson, J. M., 1870, *The Imperial Gazetteer of England and Wales*.

Social Change and Social Conflict in Nineteenth Century England: A Comment

Contributions to the debate over social change and conflict in nineteenth-century England, despite differences, have much common ground. Particularly, they have a conception of conflict that limits it to a category called 'protest'. In addition, they subscribe to social control models, to a greater or lesser extent, with detriment to our understanding of rural society. The so-called 'open/closed' dichotomy which has become a major dimension in the debate, assumes that conflict is absent from the 'closed' parish. This paper argues that conflict extends beyond protest, and was a phenomenon of both 'closed' and 'open' parishes. It further argues, particularly against Wells, that Swing and the opposition to the New Poor Law, did not end in unmitigated failure. A brief examination of the implications for the 'open/closed' model is made, with a suggestion that models of class conflict are more appropriate for the study of rural society.

On hearing two women shouting insults at one another from windows on opposite sides of the street, Sydney Smith is said to have remarked, 'They will never agree, for they argue from different premises' [*Boston*, 1974: 70–1]. With less wit, Durrenberger and Tannenbaum [1979: 49] commented that 'one consequence of two people operating under different paradigms or sets of assumptions, is their failure to understand each other.' The debate between Roger Wells [1979; 1981] and Andrew Charlesworth [1980] has been joined by John Archer [1982] and now by Dennis Mills and Brian Short [1983]. Agreement among such different approaches to the problems of rural conflict and change seems unlikely.

Yet, despite the different models advocated by the contributors, there exists between them certain common ground that severely limits the

* *University of Sussex, Falmer, Brighton, Sussex, BN1 9QN; and Portsmouth Polytechnic, Kings Rooms, Bellevue Terrace, Southsea, PO5 3AT.*

potential of any for the study of conflict and the processes of change in the English countryside. This paper will examine this common ground and its shortcomings, while proposing an approach that may transcend the constraints that the participants in the debate have placed upon themselves. The implications of this critique for the 'open/closed' model will then be discussed. Like several previous contributions, the paper draws largely upon evidence from the southeast of England, especially Sussex.

I

All the papers published so far in the debate have been concerned with conflict, and they have exhibited unanimity on one thing at least: on what constitutes conflict in the countryside. This has been effectively confined to a category called 'protest', with profound implications for the arguments presented. In addition, all the authors have accepted a model of social control, and of deference. Wells [1979; 1981] has gone furthest in this respect, and he sees little difference in the repressiveness and degree of control in both 'open' and 'closed' villages. This repression, with rare exceptions, forced protest underground and restricted it to arson, poaching and the like. Failure to conform would result in unemployment, eviction, or loss of relief [*Wells*, 1981: 519–26]. Wells [1981: 526] implicitly goes further, so that whenever we find labourers in regular work, we can be fairly sure that they are 'class collaborators' of one kind or another. Charlesworth [1980] and Mills and Short [1983] see social control as universal in the 'closed' village, though less so in the 'open' parish. Charlesworth [1980: 102] writes of 'the patriarchal web of control of the farmhouse and the "close" village' where the numbers of labouring families were 'rigidly controlled'.[1] Mills and Short [1983: 255] point to 'the totality of estate control' in the 'closed' village, and they also [1983: 259] accept that 'some forms of social control could be exercised in open parishes ... by powerful groups, rather than through the dominance of a single estate owner'. This 'totality' of control means that 'we should not expect to find conflict in *closed* villages, especially those with resident gentry' [*Mills and Short*, 1983: 254].

The acceptance of these paradigms, for such they are, limits the insights to be derived from research. Although paradigms and models are both vital and inescapable tools of historical research, they 'define the ranges of questions to be asked of a subject, the methods to be used for answering them, and the criteria of assessing an answer' [*Durrenberger and Tannenbaum*, 1979: 49].

Although all the contributors accept the notion of conflict, Mills and Short [1983: 253] are unclear as to how it 'fits' into the social environment. They are certainly [1983: 259] uncomfortable with Marxist definitions of class and concepts of class conflict, pointing out that 'estate villages showed the sharpest [class] distinctions but few signs of protest.' They contrast this situation with that of the 'open' village which 'had a more subtle "class" structure but [with] widespread opposition to the establishment of Church and Land.' It is, of course, their view of conflict that leads them into this comparison, as well as their schematic approach to Marxism. Since they use 'conflict' and 'protest' as synonyms, they are unable to find conflict in the 'closed' village. They are, possibly, right to argue that protest is unlikely in the 'closed' village, but quite wrong to assume that conflict is absent. Their view is reinforced by their adherence to a social control model. If one really believes in the 'totality' of control by landowners over other human beings in 'closed' villages, then it becomes superfluous even to look for conflict. Their paradigm has defined the range of questions they ask. Wells ultimately accepts the same paradigm though he believes that social control is prevalent in all social situations, and he, therefore, cannot believe that there may be mediation of class relations, or that conflict – again synonymous with protest – can be anything other than covert. His assumptions also ensure that protest will always end in complete failure, a point we will return to. This control or the 'dictatorship by the affluent was such as to place pauper, artisan and small shopkeeper in the same powerless predicament [*Wells*, 1981: 524/75]. He may, of course, be right about Burwash, though I doubt it, but I do not think the model would work in similar Sussex villages.

Let us return to conflict. Firstly, let us identify forms of conflict that seldom feature in studies of rural England, and that certainly would not fall into the category of 'protest' as usually defined, but which would definitely be recognised by Marxists as a fundamental conflict, and which ought to be present in both 'open' and 'closed' villages. I mean conflict between employer and worker – conflict in the labour process and in relations of employment. Rural historians have tended to ignore these kinds of conflict, since they tend to be looking for institutional forms that conform both to those developed by urban workers, and also to their own preconceptions of what forms are appropriate to workers in capitalist social formations. Usually they concentrate on the trade union [*Wells*, 1981: 515/66], and in so doing fail to notice other less familiar forms of institution, and also conflicts that occur outside of any institutional form. Alun Howkins [1977: 226–7] has demonstrated how rural workers developed institutions like the 'teaman' or the 'lord' to give maximum bargaining power at those seasonal moments when labour was in great demand.

Indoor servants in the southeast, throughout our period, seem to have acted to protect themselves against undue treatment by their employers. Historians have accepted uncritically the decline of indoor service from the beginning of the nineteenth century [*Hobsbawm and Rude*, 1973: 23–4]; *Wells*, '79: 119/31; *Charlesworth*, '80: 102/55; *Kussmaul*, 1981]. To generalise from the experience of only a relatively small area of the country from East Anglia to Dorset is, however, to miss the great variety of social relations that actually existed. In most of the southeast, there seems to have been little decline in absolute terms before the 1850s [*Reed*, 1982: 25–31; *Short*, 1982] and living-in was still common in Kent and Sussex as late as the 1920s [*Lemaitre*, 1931: 379–80; *Winstanley*, 1978: 34; *Reed*, 1982: 26]. Farm servants exercised their strength by their mobility, but there were important differences in rates of mobility between 'open' and 'closed' parishes. Kussmaul [1978: 108] found that between the seventeenth and the nineteenth centuries in eastern and east midland counties, 76 per cent of indoor servants remained with one employer for a maximum of one year, while only 9 per cent stayed for longer than two years. It is probable that her main source, settlement examinations, led her to exaggerate the degree of mobility, since the population subjected to settlement examination was, by definition, the most mobile. Nevertheless, her figures are closely paralleled on farms in 'closed' parishes on the South Downs. On a large unidentified farm on the Sussex/Hampshire border, 72 out of 93 (77 per cent) of male indoor servants employed between 1799 and 1818 stayed for a maximum of one year, and only ten (10.7 per cent) remained for longer than two years. At Chilgrove, in western Sussex, there was a similar trend. In 'open' parishes things were different. At an unidentified farm near Pulborough, between 1813 and 1839, only 49 per cent left during or at the end of the first year, and 19 per cent stayed for longer than two years. At a farm in Lodsworth and Easebourne, in the western Weald, the farmer, George Mullens, hired 40 male servants between 1805 and 1831, of whom only 17 (43 per cent) failed to work a second year, while 11 (28 per cent) remained for more than two years.[2]

We seem to be seeing here two different strategies by farm servants to assert themselves. Kussmaul [1978: 113] has argued that 'frequent mobility ensured that the master was a stranger. Servants might have hoped that their bargaining position might be stronger with a master ignorant of the last wage they had received.' She goes on: 'Servants preferred hiring in the open market. It was there, removed from the obscurity of the household, that they could be powerful collectively' [*Kussmaul*, 1978: 131]. This latter statement is correct, though collective power at the hiring fair arose precisely because the employer was *not* a stranger, or rather, because he was not an unknown quantity. The fair, by bringing all local farmers and servants together, provided unequalled opportunities for checking each other out [*Carter*, 1979: 144–52; *Caunce*, 1975: 50; *Kebbel*, 1907: 94]. The hiring fair is supposed to have been almost nonexistent in the southeast by the early nineteenth century [*Hobsbawm and Rude*, 1973: 23], but this is something of an overstatement. Petworth and Angmering fairs seem to have operated as hiring fairs well into the nineteenth century[3] [*Harris*, 1912: 32] and the 'Jack and Joan' fair at Canterbury, said to be 'vestigial' in 1799 [*Hobsbawm and Rude*, 1973: 22] was still functioning as such in 1914 [*Winstanley*, 1978: 37]. Most servants, though, were probably hired on the doorstep. This, however, would in no way diminish their ability to confer with each other about prospective employers. Frequent mobility ensured that servants could exercise collective power at least annually, and those farmers who did not provide wages and conditions considered as adequate by the workforce, could have difficulty in finding sufficient labour. In the 'closed' parish, servants may well have been isolated on the farm, some distance from a pub or other meeting place with potential allies. Distance from a pub could be a crucial bar to social life, since the servant might 'like all the Fellows and Boys to go to bed by 9 o'clock at night.'[4] Hence mobility on an annual basis or less gave the servant some opportunity to retain some control over his or her conditions of work.

The second strategy may be discerned in those farms in 'open' parishes where mobility was much lower than in the 'closed' parish. To be sure, mobility was probably used in the same way by the 40 to 50 per cent of servants who did change jobs annually, but another pattern is to be seen in these farms. Frequently, the records show *all* the indoor servants leaving at the same time, a pattern that *never* occurs in the 'closed' parishes studied. George Mullens at Lodsworth experienced complete turnovers in 1808, 1811 and 1824. On the Pulborough farm referred to above, complete turnovers of servants took place in 1819, 1821, 1825, 1830, 1833 and 1834.[5] Kussmaul [1981: 52–5] notes that on a Lincolnshire farm, complete change-overs of the servant workforce occurred eight times between 1780 and 1830. Significantly, on this farm, rates of mobility amongst the male servants were substantially lower than her quoted averages, and very similar to those in Sussex 'open' parishes, with only 54 per cent failing to work a second year.

We are surely seeing here an institution similar to that described by Ian Carter [1979: 152–4] and called in northeast Scotland the 'clean toon', in which every hired man on the farm left on a particular termday when the senior man left. The close relationship between the senior man and the rest of the men is attested to by William Marshall, who bemoaned the fact that on his Surrey farm the senior man 'all along ... has been *siding* with the men; instead of assisting me to manage them, he has been assisting them to manage me' [cited in *Kussmaul*, 1978: 94].

This institution ensured that a farmer who transgressed the norms expected of an employer stood to lose the entire labour force. Any employer who experienced complete turnovers too frequently ran the risk of being unable to get people to work for him [*Carter*, 1976: 183]. Why this form should prevail in the 'open' village is not yet clear, but we can perhaps speculate. As Mills and Short [1983: 254] make clear, the 'open' village was usually characterised by a variety of class groupings and especially by the existence of a 'peasantry' – their use of this concept will be discussed below – comprising small farmers, tradespeople and so on, who were usually absent or nearly so, from the 'closed' village. Carter [1979] has shown that where small farms were absent in northeast Scotland, servants were unable to resist reductions in their living standards, resorting to frequent mobility to counter this; but where small peasant farms prevailed, they were able to assert themselves within the farmhouse. Uncovering of the 'mechanisms' will need research, but the existence of classes or strata *other* than capital and labour allows of the possibility of forming alliances with one or more of these groups so that the servant is not so isolated socially as in the village where the class structure is polarised between capital and labour. Whatever the causes of these different patterns, there seems little doubt of their existence. We seem to be seeing different strategies developed by farm servants in different situations to exert themselves collectively, but, importantly, we still see this exercise of collective power in the 'closed' village.

Similarly, we can observe conflict in the labour process, particularly in those jobs that were sometimes done by the piece. Hobsbawm and Rude [1973: 18] claimed that being paid by time or by the piece 'hardly mattered in normal times', and they backed up their claim with reference to John Boys, who commented in the 1790s that 'the regulating medium for all task work is the value of the day's labour.' This, of course, is how piece rates are always calculated, but this does not justify the claim that it made little difference. Certainly, both farmers and workers knew better. In 1804, on a farm run by the Petworth estate of the Earl of Egremont, piecework rates for threshing were calculated on the basis that one man would thresh in a day six bushels of wheat, or three sacks of oats, or two sacks of barley, while George Mullens of Lodsworth seems to have calculated that a man would thresh a quarter of barley a day, since his piece rates are usually, though not always, the same as the current day rate. But of course, the men did not work flat out on day work and could work much harder if they wished. Ed Birt threshed barley for Mullens in 1825 at 2s. a quarter. He threshed 16¾ quarters in only ten days earnings £1 13s. 6d., around double the amount the current day rate of 1s. 8d. would have earned him. A little later, threshing barley by the day at 1s. 8d., he took 30¾ days to thresh 24½ quarters, thus costing Mullens 2s. 1d. a quarter, slightly more than the piece rate. It is worth noting that whether threshed by the day or by the piece, the farmer paid about the same per quarter, but that the worker's earnings could alter substantially. On the Earl of Egremont's farm referred to above, in 1804, James Hunt threshed 35½ quarters of oats in seven days, which the norms entered in the same account book suggest should have taken 23½ days, and for which he earned £2 13s. 3d. Robert Sopp earned just over £2 for threshing 24¼ quarters of oats in five days, rather than the 16 days the norms suggest.[6]

The foregoing demonstrates that workers could and did exercise control over the labour process, and that farms run by powerful aristocrats were not immune. We can expect to find farmers trying to wrest control from the workforce. Piecework, superficially, has much to commend it to both worker and employer. It is 'the form of wage most appropriate to the capitalist mode of production', but it is also the form of wage most likely to encourage 'constant struggle between the capitalist and the worker ...' [*Marx*, 1973: 698, 700]. Farmers seem to have preferred piece work: it cost them about the same per unit of output as day work, but was likely to be done more quickly, and freed the worker for other jobs. Farm workers, however, were less enthusiastic, despite the opportunity to earn higher wages in a shorter time [*Kebbel*, 1907: 90]. Edmund Bushby, who was hanged for arson at East Preston in western Sussex at the time of Swing, declined to do threshing by the piece, insisting on day work. After the farmer refused to allow day work, he apparently burned a corn rick.[7] Half a century later, it was noted: 'I have known labourers decline to hoe turnips on piecework by which they might earn 4s. a day, preferring to receive 2s. 6d. per day, and to limit the amount of work done [*Arnold*, 1880: 297].

The pattern of piecework seems to have changed with the supply of labour. During the war, all threshing on the Mullen's farm at Lodsworth was done by the piece, but from 1815, as the so-called 'labour surplus' grew, day work was used increasingly, so that by 1830 only about half of the labour costs for threshing went on piecework. Similar trends occurred in other tasks where piecework was common. Since piecework was to the farmer's benefit (as detailed above), and since it also rendered supervision fairly superfluous [*Marx*, 1973: 695], an important point on a large farm, and finally, since we know from other sources that Mullens was a keen advocate of piecework [*Reed*, 1982: 66–7], we can assume that it was the workers who, like Edmund Bushby, were reluctant to do piecework. During the war, there was a shortage of labour, especially since farmers were also extending the scope of their operations, and workers could perhaps afford to do great quantities of piecework and earn high wages without working themselves out of a job. With the depression following the war, and the rise in unemployment, those workers with regular jobs perhaps used their control over the labour process to maintain their employment throughout the winter by working by the day. We should perhaps see the introduction of the threshing machine as a strategy by farmers to wrest control of the work process from labour, and resistance to it as partly an attempt to retain such control. It is apparent, then, that conflict between worker and employer occurred in the countryside, as in the cities, and that neither 'closed' parishes nor the aristocracy were exempt from such problems. This kind of conflict is seldom visible to the historian, neither has it the dramatic, even romantic, appeal of 'protest', but it is no less significant, and if we are really interested in 'the study of everyday life' [*Wells*, 1981: 516/67] then it should be amongst the foremost of our priorities.

II

Let us now consider some of the forms of conflict dealt with by previous contributors to the debate. Wells [1981: 515/66] is convinced that all manifestations of overt protest, including those against the New Poor Laws as well as Swing, 'ended essentially in failure'. He is adamant that 'overt protest was limited to remarkably few years, a tiny minority in the first half of the nineteenth century'. If we confine ourselves to major regional conflagrations like those of 1816, 1822 and 1830, he is, of course, right. But to do this is to miss the frequent local manifestations of overt conflict that occurred year in and year out. Wells [1981: 515/66] sees, absolutely rightly, the defeat of Swing as 'momentous', and one might add tragic. His conclusion, though that the defeat was so demoralising that workers were totally cowed and forced into carrying out undercover forms of protest alone, is surely an overstatement. The defeat of Swing did not end collective protest. It did not prevent, in the summer of 1831, the Aldingbourne and the neighbouring work People [from] carry[ing] their claims much further than your Lordship seems to think ... this year they attempt to set up a resolution that no outparishioners at all shall be employed, however this may protract the harvest, and that instead of 8s. an Acre for which the Farmers can get the wheat reaping done, they will have 14s. and some of the Pulborough Labourers ... were so intimidated by the threats ... that they have left their jobs and returned home.[8]

The defeat did not prevent a crowd of labourers from Rudgewick in Sussex visiting the magistrates' bench at Horsham, to demand additional relief in November 1831. It did not prevent a crowd of poor from the same area in 1832 following the overseers from place to place until the demands were granted, when the overseer – rightly or wrongly – became afraid for his life. It did not prevent, at the end of 1832, crowds of labourers from Rudgewick from descending upon the magistrates' bench, to demand wage increases. Four times in as many weeks this occurred. The increases were granted, though under pressure from the farmers, they were later withdrawn. John Browne, a Horsham radical, commented:

I ask, if any thing can make the labourers unite in unions, is it not such conduct as this ... if anything can make men rise in mobs is it not to make 40 men come 7 miles four times for justice admit their claim and deny them assistance.

The defeat did not prevent Sussex workers and others setting up 'unions of the working classes' which were formed in the Horsham area, in Horsted Keynes, in Eastbourne, in Billingshurst and in Burwash:

At the latter place it was not a union of working men only there the farmers and their men join hand in hand to obtain what they well know will be an equal benefit to both, they already muster about 200 strong.[9]

Of course, these incidents seldom achieved their aims; the essential point is the fact that they took place at all. Overt protest continued frequently, if locally, even immediately after the defeat of Swing. However, Wells is surely right to insist that covert protest predominated over overt protest post-1830. Where he is wrong is in his assumption that it was the only form. He is also wrong to conclude that defeat meant total failure. Class conflict seldom works in such a schematic way. There *were* successes in Swing, which were maintained by repeated covert action. Perhaps the most significant was the thrusting back of mechanised threshing [*Hobsbawm and Rude*, 1973: 258–9]. Attempts to reintroduce the machine could be met by arson, some-times preceded, even in those areas like Wiltshire, where vengeance against Swing was most vicious, by public warning [*Hare*, 1874: 374]. The labourers succeeded for perhaps a generation in retaining control over at least that part of their work process. The limited opportunities for winter work were not further reduced, and the labourers' protests were the reason: 'The real name of King Ludd was Swing'. [*Hobsbawm and Rude*, 1973: 258]

Similarly, Wells is wrong to conclude that the actions against the New Poor Law ended in complete failure. He observes: 'open resistance to the Act did not stop its implementation' [1981: 515/66]. Well, maybe not, but *something* did. In the rural southeast, the Act simply was *not* implemented with anything like the consistency and determination that its originators had in mind [*Mosley*, 1975; *passim*]. This issue demonstrates flaws in Wells' argument. The first is his acceptance that intentions as expressed in vestry minutes actually indicate what happened [1981: 516–26/67–77]; the second, his failure to recognise the possibility of alliances between different groups within the social formation. This last mistake is not made to the same extent by Charlesworth [1980: 104–5/57–8] or Mills and Short [1983: 254/91].

The village of Lodsworth in western Sussex – incidentally, categorised by Short [1983: 154–5] as 'essentially closed' – was noted by the chairman of Midhurst Petty Sessions in 1841 to be a parish of 'much schism'.[10] In fact, conflict was rife in Lodsworth, throughout the nineteenth century [*Reed*, 1982: forthcoming]. The resident gentleman, Hasler Hollist, was the first chairman of the Midhurst Union Board of Guardians, and claimed that 'the Commissioners have requested me to allow myself to be elected for one of the parishes and to act as Chairman of the Board.'[11] His principal tenant, J. N. Farhall, was elected Guardian for the neighbouring parish of Tillington, and it was not long before Hollist was reporting arson on both his and Farhall's property, as well as on that of other Guardians. In addition, he received a number of threatening letters. He found all this slightly perplexing, believing that, 'I employ a great deal of labour at fair wages, and am generally speaking look'd up to with respect by my poorer neighbours.'[12] Moreover, as Hollist makes clear, opposition to the new law came from the Guardians themselves. In 1837, he pointed out that they 'are not going on right at present'.[13] The Midhurst Board gave out-relief on a considerable scale to the able-bodied poor, to the concern of Edwin Chadwick himself, while relief in the form of loans was given to able-bodied applicants (even non-residents), despite their declared inability to repay the loans, and despite the Assistant-Commissioner's remonstrance that it was illegal [*Mosley*, 1975: 189, 192]. Chadwick and Senior may have handpicked their chairman, but they did not get their own way with the Guardians. Able-bodied adults simply were not often placed in the workhouses. Assistant-Commissioner Hawley complained that the handmills in Sussex workhouses were 'rusting upon their stands for want of hands to turn them.' He went on: 'the number of able-bodied males found in the workhouses during the winter period is notable only for its insignificance' [*Mosley*, 1975: 143, 147).

What were the reasons for this? At present, only speculation is possible. Gentlemen, like Hollist, were seldom involved in the day to day running of the Unions. In 1847 he reported to Chadwick that 'great names may be appended to the Chairmanship of Unions, but minor men do all the work. In my Union of 70,000 acres, no owner of 500 acres except ... the Hon. G.

Ponsonby, and myself ever shows his face at the Board.'[14] The majority of active Guardians in rural Unions were tenant farmers. It was these people who were responsible for the kinds of evasions listed above. Were they simply more altruistic than Chadwick and Hollist? Were they opposed to the Act on principle? Or did the threat and actuality of arson and similar acts of protest keep them from implementing the Act in full? Had the rural poor, by their continual action against farmers, managed to prevent the full implementation of the New Poor Law?

But this was not the only form of evasion of the Act. As Mosley [1975: Ch. 5] makes clear, the most effective evasion of the law originated in the parishes. The parish was responsible for paying into the Union not only the costs of maintaining its own poor but also towards general overheads. In Lodsworth, despite vestry decisions, reached as always by the multiple votes of Hollist and the principal farmers, to pay these costs, the parish officials frequently refused to do so.[15] Moreover, the officials employed the favourite Sussex ruse of manipulating the highway rate so as to employ the poor on the Sussex roads rather than placing them in the workhouse. Assistant-Commissioner Hawley reported that in Sussex 'such practice constantly engrosses my attention ... it is beyond the power of the Commissioners to cure or control [this] enormous abuse' [*Mosley*, 1975: 221]. He further noted [*Mosley*, 1975: 227] that in Sussex and Hampshire the relieving officers' books constantly contained the phrase, 'referred to the waywardens', which he considered was 'a mere circumlocution for "set to work on the roads." '
In Lodsworth, the roads were constantly repaired following the opening of the workhouse, though an interesting and surely significant exception was the road leading to Hollist's house, and one across a heath recently enclosed by him. He resorted frequently to threats and even legal action to remedy this situation, but with little effect. The above-bodied poor of Lodsworth were far more likely to be employed on the roads than to be put in the workhouse [*Reed*, 1982: 74–6]. We should not be surprised at this. In Lodsworth, responsibility for the roads was usually firmly in the hands of local small farmers and tradespeople. In most villages, the lower and more arduous administrative posts were held by these groups. Small farmers and tradespeople, it has been recently argued, should be considered as a peasantry [*Mills*, 1980: 43–5; *Mills and Short*, 1983: 254; *Reed*, 1984]. For Mills and Short, though, the concept is used in a purely descriptive sense. Peasants are 'small rural entrepreneurs' [1983: 254] distinguished from other rural entrepreneurs merely by the scale of their enterprises. This is clearly inadequate since distinctions of this kind cannot give explanatory insights into differences of behaviour by these kinds of group as compared to other groups in the countryside. What distinguished most members of these groups during the nineteenth century from other groups in the rural social formation was their reliance upon family labour. They thus worked a different mode of production from capitalist farmers and, therefore, had different material interests [*Reed*, 1984]. We might reasonably expect, therefore, *conflicts* of material interest and alliances between these

groups and others over specific issues. Since they bore, proportionately, a larger share of the costs for maintenance of the poor, or at least probably paid a larger proportion of their income towards this purpose, than capitalist farmers and landowners, it is to be expected that they would seek to reduce the costs of maintaining the poor below that of keeping them in the work-house. In addition, they themselves were often close to poverty, which gave them additional reasons for keeping the poor from the workhouse. The children of Phillip Rapson, who was overseer of the poor for a number of years in Lodsworth, were frequently recipients of relief, as were family members of other overseers.[16]

The New Poor Law, then, was not implemented in the way intended by its creators. It was thwarted at both the parish and the Union levels, by farmers and tradespeople. It is possible to demonstrate that at least a tacit alliance between labourers and tradespeople and small farmers existed on this issue, and to speculate that protest by labourers was rather more successful than Wells admits at impeding implementation of the Act.

What we are seeing – and there are a number of issues that could demonstrate the same points [*Reed*, 1984] – is a complexity that is usually ignored by students of rural history. Conflict extends beyond the category of protest; success and failure are not to be measured in a schematic way; existence within the social formation of groups other than capital and labour allows the possibility of alliances between different groups on specific issues and the mediation of class and power relations by these groups. Decisions may have been made with repressive intent by the 'village rich', but they were not necessarily translated into action in the straightforward manner that Wells suggests.

III

How, then, does this affect the 'open' and 'closed' model? Mills and Short admit [1983: 253] that it is a static model, which, I would suggest, gives it at best descriptive value. Even at this level, the problems of measurement are formidable [*Hobsbawm and Rude*, 1973: 151–2]. Some historians [*Mills and Short*, 1983: 255–8/92–5; *Short*, 1983: 154–5; *Everitt*, 1972: 70–72] have placed considerable emphasis on the landownership classification of J.M. Wilson in *The Imperial Gazetteer* [1870 and 1875], an emphasis that seems highly dubious. A preliminary study has been made for east Kent, using the data on landownership derived from the 1831 land tax, by R.J. Grover [1980: Appendix 11], and comparing these with Wilson's classifications. Of the 52 parishes Grover refers to, Wilson gives either no information, or ambiguous information, on 24. The remaining 28 show a wide range in the numbers of owners in the different categories. Mills and Short [1983: 257/94] consider that Wilson's categories of 'most or all land in one estate', 'not much subdivided', and 'divided among a few', are 'essentially closed'. In east Kent, 17 parishes fell into the last two of these categories, and had, according to the land tax, between seven and 49 owners. For Mills and Short, 'essentially open' parishes are those Wilson classifies as 'subdivided' or 'much subdivided'. Six of the east Kent parishes were said by Wilson to be in the former category, and they had, according to the land tax, between 17 and 71 owners, while the final category was applied to five parishes, which had between 41 and 87 landowners. Thus there is an enormous overlap between Mills and Short's categories of 'essentially open' and 'essentially closed', as well as between Wilson's own categories.

Problems of measurement do not, on their own, discredit the 'open/closed' model, though they may make one pause before accepting the work so far done using the model. What does more damage to the suggestion that the model is of explanatory use is the insistence that social control was 'total' in the 'closed' village, so that conflict was nonexistent, when in fact it can be demonstrated that this is not so. As has been pointed out above, Lodsworth, an 'essentially closed' village, was riven with conflict throughout the nineteenth century. Michael Home has described how his Breckland village was 'practically all' owned by one man later in the century. Yet, below the surface of the 'necessarily subservient village' there was resistance by an 'underground', and almost all the men were poachers, whose motivation, amongst other things, was 'to get even with squires and game laws' as well as with 'Church and State' [*Home*, 1943: 27, 30, 41, 155]. Equally important, conflict occurred within employer/worker relationships in both 'open' and 'closed' villages. The appropriate research would doubtless reveal many more kinds than those described in this paper.

Mills and Short [1983: 253/90] argue that the study of social change requires comparison between conditions in one period and those of a subsequent period. They maintain that 'it is important to use all available means of static and comparative static social analyses, before passing on to dynamic analysis.' But what if the static analyses show no change? What if the 'closed' village of, say, 1830 is still 'closed' in, say, 1890? Has nothing changed? Of course, this is unfair, since Mills and Short would not base too much upon the findings derived from a single model when analysing change. But the principle remains a good one. Many, perhaps most, of the social changes of the nineteenth century were cultural, or concerned with attitudes and ideas. No changes can be separated from these cultural and ideological developments. Spatial analysis is not good at highlighting these kinds of changes. We need concepts that are dynamic from the outset, to ensure that we have some chance of asking the most appropriate questions to explain change. The model of class conflict enables us to look for, and find, conflict in every social context, and to examine how this conflict leads to change, both in the material environment, and in the realm of ideas.

Landownership is a crucial area of study with significant social implications, and one must not be overcritical of those historians who present us with detailed information on ownership patterns. What one asks for is a realisation that landownership patterns themselves are merely the outcome, at a particular moment, of perhaps centuries of conflict. Landownership is itself part of a dynamic process that cannot be reduced to a static category, still less used in a predictive capacity.

IV

In such a multifaceted debate as this, it is not possible to do much more, in the available space, than to discuss certain assertions of previous contributors. This paper has criticised all the interventions made so far. It has been suggested that conflict extends beyond protest, and that it is to be found in all social situations. Concentration on protest, whether overt or covert, misses much vital evidence that may in time give new perspectives on such . famous episodes as Swing, as well as the daily life of the rural poor. What is needed is study of how forms of conflict varied, and how the strategies of different groups within the social formation varied according to the balance of class forces within specific historical contexts. We need to find out how alliances between different groups at different times affected both the outcome of specific issues as well as the wider current of social change. Here one finds oneself closer to Charlesworth, Mills and Short than to Wells. The former do admit to the possibility of alliances affecting the outcome of some issues at least, while Wells seems imbued with a fundamental pessimism, in that his notion of social control renders all attempts at opposition and improvement ultimately pointless. And yet one must agree with Wells [1981: 526–7/77–8] that concentration on orthodox categories of 'open' and 'closed' obscures more than it reveals, and still stronger agreement is called for with his demand that 'painstaking analysis of ample documentation on a local and regional basis' is a crucial element of research into rural society. One must agree with Wells most strongly of all – though probably neither Charlesworth nor Mills and Short would disagree – that to have been a rural worker in the nineteenth century must have been to have had an existence of appalling toil, privation, and precious little joy. When working on the topic, anger seems an altogether insufficient response. It should not imply dissent from this view to suggest that the simplistic approaches to the study of the rural past that this paper has criticised actually do a disservice to the poor in the nineteenth-century countryside.

NOTES

1. Sarah Banks [1982] has argued that landlords in 'close' villages did *not* generally exercise this kind of control, playing only a passive non-interventionist role. She sees the speculative cottage builders in the 'open' villages as the key figures, who, by erecting large numbers of cottages, attracted labour into these parishes and away from 'close' parishes.
2. Calculated from West Sussex Records Office (WSRO) Add. Mss. 9422, 829 and 9447; WSRO MP 1479.
3. John Payne, a small farmer in Kirdford in the Sussex Weald, hired servants from Petworth fair well into the 1830s. See John Payne's Memo Book. I am indebted to Reg Thompson for the loan of this document.
4. WSRO Add. Ms. 9447.
5. WSRO Add. Mss. 9447 and 829.
6. Petworth House Archive (PHA) 2853; WSRO Add. Ms. 9447.

7. *Brighton Herald*, 25 December 1830. See also PRO HO 52/10, f. 295, Holmes to Melbourne, 30 November 1830.
8. PHA 8616, Tyler to Egremont, 27 July 1831.
9. Horsham Museum Collection (HMC) 813. A Poll Book for the 1832 Horsham election, published by the Horsham Union of the Working Classes, survives. HMC 2790. Horsham, of course, was a substantial market town, but the other places mentioned were only villages. See also Hobsbawm and Rude [1973: 243] for instances of collective action in other parts of the country.
10. *Sussex Agricultural Express*, 11 December 1841.
11. Hollist to Fisher, 1 May 1835, Hollist Letter Books. I am grateful to Sue and Cecil Barnes for the loan of these letter books.
12. Hollist to Phillips, 8 October 1835; Hollist to Sun Fire Office, 1 October 1835; Hollist to Nicholls, 1 October 1835; Hollist to Richmond, 1 October 1835; Hollist to Ford, 7 November 1835. All in Hollist Letter Books.
13. Hollist to Brown, 10 February 1837. Hollist Letter Books.
14. Hollist to Chadwick, 13 February 1847. Hollist Letter Books.
15. See, for example, *Sussex Agricultural Express*, 26 October 1840. See Mosley [1975: 202] for a discussion of this form of obstruction.
16. WSRO Par 128/12/2, Vestry Minute Book, Lodsworth, 1825–40.

REFERENCES

Archer, J. E., 1982, 'The Wells–Charlesworth debate: a personal comment on arson in Norfolk and Suffolk', *Journal of Peasant Studies*, Vol. 9, No. 4.
Arnold, Arthur, 1880, 'Free land and peasant proprietorship', *The Nineteenth Century*, Vol. 7.
Banks, S. J., 1982, 'Open and close parishes in nineteenth-century England', unpublished thesis, University of Reading.
Boston, Richard, 1974, *An Anatomy of Laughter*, London: Collins.
Carter, Ian, 1976, 'The peasantry of northeast Scotland', *Journal of Peasant Studies*, Vol. 3, No. 2.
Carter, Ian, 1979, *Farm Life in Northeast Scotland 1840–1914: The Poor Man's Country*, Edinburgh: John Donald.
Caunce, Stephen, 1975, 'East Riding hiring fairs', *Oral History*, Vol. 3, No. 2.
Charlesworth, Andrew, 1980, 'The development of the English rural proletariat and social protest 1700–1850: a comment', *Journal of Peasant Studies*, Vol. 8, No. 1.
Durrenberger, E. Paul, and Nicola Tannenbaum, 1979, 'A reassessment of Chayanov and his recent critics', *Peasant Studies*, Vol. 8, No. 1.
Everitt, Alan, 1972, *The Pattern of Rural Dissent: The Nineteenth Century*, Leicester: Leicester University Press.
Grover, R. J., 1980, 'The land tax in East Kent: a study in landownership and occupation with special reference to the methodological implications of the land tax assessment', unpublished M.Phil. thesis, University of Kent.
Hare, Augustus J., 1874, *Memorials of a Quiet Life*, Vol. I, London: W. Isbister.
Harris, Edwin A., 1912, *Angmering: A Study Written Expressly for Working Men*, Littlehampton.
Hobsbawm, E. J., and George Rude, 1973, *Captain Swing*, Harmondsworth: Penguin.
Home, Michael, 1943, *Autumn Fields*, London: Methuen.
Howkins, Alun, 1977, 'Structural conflict and the farmworker: Norfolk 1900–1920', *Journal of Peasant Studies*, Vol. 4, No. 3.
Kebbel, Thomas Edward, 1907, *The Agricultural Labourer: A Summary of His Position*, London: Swan Sonnenschein.
Kussmaul, A., 1978, 'Servants in husbandry in early modern England', unpublished Ph.D. thesis, University of Toronto.

Kussmaul, Ann, 1981, *Servants in Husbandry in Early Modern England*, Cambridge: Cambridge University Press.

Lemaître, Georges, 1931, *Le Weald des comtés de Kent, Surrey, Sussex, Hampshire: études de géographie économique et humaine*, Paris: Les Presses Universitaires de France.

Marx, Karl, 1973, *Capital*, Vol. I, Harmondsworth: Penguin.

Mills, Dennis R., 1980, *Lord and Peasant in Nineteenth-Century England*, London: Croom Helm.

Mills, Dennis R., and Brian M. Short, 1983, 'Social change and social conflict in nineteenth-century England: the use of the open-closed village model', *Journal of Peasant Studies*, Vol. 10, No. 4.

Mosley, John V., 1975, 'Poor law administration in England and Wales 1834–1850: with special reference to the problem of able-bodied pauperism', unpublished Ph.D. thesis, University of London.

Reed, Mick, 1982, 'Social and economic relations in a Wealden community: Lodsworth 1780–1860', unpublished M.A. thesis, University of Sussex.

Reed, Mick, forthcoming, 'The peasantry in nineteenth-century England. A neglected class?', *History Workshop*.

Short, Brian, 1982, 'The decline of living-in servants in eighteenth- and nineteenth-century Sussex: a geographical critique', unpublished typescript.

Short, Brian M., 1983, 'The changing rural society and economy of Sussex 1750–1945' in Geography Editorial Committee, *Sussex: Environment, Landscape and Society*, Gloucester: Alan Sutton.

Wells, Roger A. E., 1979, 'The development of the English rural proletariat and social protest, 1700–1850', *Journal of Peasant Studies*, Vol. 6, No. 2.

Wells, Roger A. E., 1981, 'Social conflict and protest in the English countryside in the early nineteenth century: a rejoinder', *Journal of Peasant Studies*, Vol. 8, No. 4.

Wilson, J. M., 1870 and 1875, *The Imperial Gazetteer of England and Wales*, London.

Winstanley, Michael, 1978, *Life in Kent at the Turn of the Century*, Folkestone: Wm. Dawson.

Peasants and Conflict in Nineteenth-Century Rural England: A Comment on Two Recent Articles

Dennis R. Mills*

This note replies to two previous contributions by Mick Reed in the Journal of Peasant Studies. *The author agrees with Reed on the importance of family labour to the peasantry. While recognising that subsistence was significant, he cannot, however, agree that peasants stood outside the capitalist economy, since they depended on the market for the bulk of their living. However, within the capitalist economy the distinction between the peasant and estate systems is important, making attention to the open-closed model a necessary part of studies such as those of Roger Wells and Mick Reed. In this context, the author asserts a more limited role for the concept of 'conflict', by distinguishing it from 'friction'.*

The four sections of this note concern (1) Family labour as a key characteristic of the English peasantry; (2) The open-closed village model; (3) Use of the Imperial Gazetteer in the study of English rural society; and (4) The problem of 'conflict'.

In his latest article in the long-running series on nineteenth-century rural society in England, Reed has done well to remind historians that England still contained a peasantry in that period [*Reed*, 1986]. However, with all the enthusiasm of someone who is re-inventing the wheel, he has somewhat overdrawn previous neglect of the subject, and although Reed has presented some very useful and interesting new material, he is not quite master of the existing literature. For example, he has quite rightly stressed the importance of family labour to the peasantry, but in doing so he has accused me of neglecting this very important aspect of the subject [*1986*: 79], and as this is a repetition of an earlier charge ['*84*: 118/109], it is necessary for me to refute it.

It is true that the point about family labour is not made in the brief article by Short and myself [1983], but we were very careful to cite the book in which my extended treatment of the subject is put forward, a discussion which Reed has chosen to ignore [*Mills*, 1980: especially 28, 44 and 47). In writing this book

* *17 Rectory Lane, Branston, Lincon LN4 1NA.*

I was privileged to draw on family insights, my maternal grandfather having used the unpaid and underpaid labour of my mother and her brother on his small farm in the 1920s, and this was the common experience of many such grown children even later in the present century. I make this point because it is important not to neglect the cultural aspect of the subject: attitudes handed down between the generations, often without explicit articulation because such was unnecessary in the circumstances, but the more likely to be overlooked for that reason by those who do not share the same cultural heritage.

The most serious complaint I have against Reed's articles, is that he is not merely expressing a difference of opinion, but reporting my views incorrectly. My view that family labour was essential on peasant holdings appeared in print at least as early as 1974:

> Many would agree that the life style of the peasantry was one in which an emphasis was put upon the family as a unit of production, as well as of consumption. Being above the labouring classes, who depended only on their labour, the peasant family used its own capital in conjunction with its labour. The peasant was distinguished from the large tenant farmer by virtue of the latter's considerable reliance upon hired labour [*Mills*, 1974: 201].

Compare this statement with Reed's that:

> What distinguished most members of (the peasantry) during the nineteenth century from other groups in the rural social formation was their reliance upon family labour. They thus worked a different mode of production from capitalist farmers and, therefore, had different material interests [*Reed*, 1984: 118/109].

I am, therefore, not guilty of using the concept of peasantry 'in a purely descriptive sense' [*Reed*, 1984: 118/109]. Moreover, before Reed wrote his second article in which he repeated much the same criticism [1986: 79], he had available another similar statement by me on the English peasant of the nineteenth century:

> A peasant is regarded as any self-employed man below the rank of the large tenant farmers and the yeomen (i.e. the large owner-occupier farmers). Unlike the labourer, he did not rely entirely on wages and, unlike the higher groups, he did not rely mainly on directing the work of others. His living was obtained by virtue of a combination of a modest amount of capital with family labour and, in some instances, hired help. The typical Melbourn peasant was a dual-occupationist, and this also helped to distinguish him from the full-time farmers ... [*Mills*, 1984: 481].

Reed's failure to acknowledge statements of this kind may be bound up with his apparent misunderstanding about the distinctions I have drawn between the estate and peasant systems in nineteenth century rural England. Although *both* were part of the capitalist economy, the two systems functioned in quite different ways. The estate system hinged on a partnership between large landowners (for example, 1,000 acres upwards) and large *tenant* farmers, who employed relatively large numbers of labourers. In the peasant system farms were small, many were at least partly owner-occupied, there were many small landlords (for example, below 100 acres), dual occupations were common (for example, farmer-craftsmen, or tradesmen and craftsmen with a little land for subsistence and/or draught horses) and, of course, family labour was important [*Mills*, 1980: Chaps. 2 and 3].

This English peasantry were capitalist in the sense that the bulk of their production, whether from the land, or in a craft was destined for the market. In other words, they were not principally subsistence farmers as in so many peasant countries, even though in terms of English comparisons subsistence was a more important aspect of their family economy than among the ranks of the large tenant farmers. However, the English peasantry were 'independent' of the estate system, which Reed possibly equates with the capitalist economy, since they were not dependent on big estate owners for land to cultivate, or craftsmen's premises to occupy. The desirability of this kind of independence is again a cultural trait within the peasantry, and is bound up with their leanings towards radicalism and nonconformity, which were expressions of opposition to the conservatism and Anglicanism of the gentry and their tenants. It is difficult to overemphasise the importance of notions of 'independence' in the oral record and in the literature which has encapsulated peasant culture (see, for example, Mills [1980: 62, 64, 75, 77–8]).

Associated with the peasant system were the so-called 'open' villages, those free from the restrictions imposed by large estate owners who predominated in 'closed' villages. This distinction was recognised early in the nineteenth century by Poor Law writers, and long ago passed into the literature of rural history. Reed also has difficulty with the open–closed village model which has evolved from this long discussion.

Thus he criticises Short and myself [1983] for using a model that dictates the questions asked and the answers obtained [1984: 111/102]. Such a risk has always to be taken, a point well known to social scientists, but only partially understood by some historians. This is the reason why in one respect the article by Short and myself is part of a dialogue of the deaf with Wells and Reed. In the latter's case it is particularly ironic since he falls into the same trap himself in writing that the Marxist approach suggests that conflict between masters and men '*ought* to be present in both "open" and "closed" villages' (my emphasis) [*Reed*, 1984: 111/102]. The usual way of resolving the problem is to employ more than one model, and to accept that both may summarise and explain substantial and overlapping portions of reality. Short and I were promoting the open-closed village model because, being historical geographers, we realised that a spatial model provided sufficient insights into the subject at issue to make it a model to reckon with. Indeed, by implication Reed has admitted this by using it as the basis for some of his own argument [e.g. *Reed*, 1984: 110–13/101–4].

However, one can promote a model and still be aware of its limitations. For my own part, instead of the simple dichotomy of the Poor Law writers,

I prefer at least to work with a fourfold division of parishes:
Closed parishes (a) estate villages (b) absentee landlord parishes;
Open parishes (c) divided parishes (d) peasant villages

For many purposes it is desirable to go further and to work with a continuum measured by the concentration of landownership, with as many as, say, 3,000 acres in the hands of one owner in estate villages, stretching through categories (b) and (c) into category (d), where as many as 100 owners averaging about 30 acres each can be found in the most divided peasant villages [*Mills*, 1980: especially 77, 79, and 94]. It is interesting that some very experienced writers have not had the same difficulty in accepting such uses of the open–closed model [e.g., *Obelkevich*, 1976: 12; *Roberts*, 1986: 59; and *Phythian-Adams*, 1987: 8].

It was with such thoughts as these in mind, as well as the need to persuade Wells [1981] not to rely too much on the experience of one village, however interesting, that Short and I introduced the use of the Imperial Gazetteer [*Mills and Short*, 1983], a move which has also been criticised by Reed ['84: 119/110]. The Gazetteer has the advantage of giving quick access to a wide view of the subject in the second half of the century, but I am well aware of the fact that it is not as accurate as, say, the land tax assessments which usually stop at 1832 [*Turner and Mills*, 1986: especially 4–5, 13–16 and chaps. 2, 3, 11, 12].

However, to produce an index based on these assessments would have been totally out of scale with the writing of an article of only ten pages: indeed such an exercise was once worth a Ph.D. [*Mills*, 1963]. Again, proper care in reading up our references would have saved Reed from exaggerating the sins of Short and myself. Indeed, he would have discovered that arguably the most sophisticated attempt to face up to the problems of measurement (in the open–closed model), which Reed describes as 'formidable' ['84: 119/110], can be found in my *Lord and Peasant in Nineteenth Century Britain* [*Mills*, 1980]. The 34 pages of Chapter 4 are entirely devoted to the subject and actually include a critique of the Imperial Gazetteer, which makes clear that I am aware that it is useful only for a broad-brush treatment of the subject, which is all that was intended by Short and myself [1983]. As Short and I obviously faced some 'formidable' problems in our 10 pages, it is disappointing to have such wholly negative criticism from Reed [1984: 119/110].

Finally, there is the disagreement between Reed and myself as to the use of the term 'conflict' in the context of nineteenth-century English rural society [*Mills and Short*, 1983 and *Reed*, 1984]. At the root of this disagreement is Reed's wish to give 'conflict' a much wider meaning than 'protest', and to include within 'conflict' any differences of interest between groups in rural society, no matter how mildly expressed. One dictionary defines 'conflict' as (1) a fight, a collision, (2) a struggle, a contest, (3) an opposition of interests. Clearly Reed is within his literal rights, but the emphasis is upon militancy, and this is how many earlier writers, probably the majority, have used the term in the historical context at issue.

In wishing to widen 'conflict' so far as to include day-to-day differences of interest 'between employer and worker – conflict in the labour process and in relations of employment' [*Reed*, 1984: 111/102], Reed is diluting the focus of debate unacceptably. Only those writing naively about nineteenth-century rusticity have ignored these differences of interest, while many writers have taken them as a given fact of nineteenth- and twentieth-century rural society and have rightly concentrated their attention on open conflicts and on the organisation of the separate interest groups around such institutions as village chapels, agricultural trades unions, the National Farmers' Union, and so on.

My own view of the subject is based partly on the difficulties that arose in the working lives of my father and paternal grandfather who spent many years as gardeners on estates in Lincolnshire and Nottinghamshire. Both made frequent moves, of the kind which Reed mentioned too [1984: 112–13/103–4], but if they had been asked if there had been 'conflicts' I am certain their response would have been 'No'. Again the cultural inheritance is important: in my family we knew of men who were deferential to the point of being obsequious, and equally of men who saw that it was pointless to pick a 'row' with an employer who was too powerful to be beaten, and waited for an opportunity to move on when it suited them. It is important to remember that trades unionism was very weak in the countryside, and most farm and garden labourers engaged in a very direct relationship with their employers.

Many men left for the towns and open villages, so the real problem is to understand why others moved from one estate to another. One reason was that there was an overall shortage of jobs for countrymen in the period concerned, so picking and choosing was often out of the question. Some men preferred to keep out of the towns, where there were in any case also plenty of bad employers, some of whom my own relatives worked for at various times. Another reason is that there was always the hope that a job on one of the better estates could be found, as indeed was my own father's luck in 1928.

For married men, there was the problem of the tied cottage, which contributed to the frequency with which workers on estates had to move. It was impossible to change jobs without moving from a tied cottage, and conversely it was difficult to move out of a tied cottage and retain the job that went with it. The head gardener or the farm horseman or stockman was expected to occupy the house next to his work, so that he would be available when frost threatened the arum lilies in a greenhouse, or a mare or a cow was expected to give birth at night. The tied cottage is one of the reasons why the populations of estate villages contained a lower percentage of natives than open villages [*Mills*, 1988].

To summarise my final point, Short and I have not suggested that there was never friction in the closed villages: what we have done is to point out that the totality of control made deliberate protest almost pointless. Men 'voted with their feet' instead.

REFERENCES

Mills, D. R., 1963, 'Landownership and Rural Population with Special Reference to Leicestershire in the Mid-19th Century', unpublished Ph.D. thesis, University of Leicester.

Mills, D. R., 1974, 'The Peasant Tradition', *Local Historian*, Vol. 11, No. 4, pp. 200–206.

Mills, D. R., 1980, *Lord and Peasant in Nineteenth Century Britain*, London: Croom Helm.

Mills, D. R. and B. M. Short, 1983, 'Social Change and Social Conflict in Nineteenth Century England: The Use of the Open–Closed Village Model', *Journal of Peasant Studies*, Vol. 10, No. 4, pp. 254–62.

Mills, D. R., 1984, 'The Nineteenth Century Peasantry of Melbourn, Cambridgeshire', in R. M. Smith (ed.), *Land, Kinship and Life-Cycle*, Cambridge: Cambridge University Press, pp. 481–518.

Mills, Joan and Dennis Mills, 1988, 'Rural Mobility in the Victorian Censuses: Experience with a Micro-Computer Program', *Local Historian* (Aug.), using evidence from Buckinghamshire, Lincolnshire and Nottinghamshire census enumerators' books.

Obelkevich, J., 1976, *Religion and Rural Society: South Lindsey 1825–1975*, Oxford: Clarendon Press.

Phythian-Adams, C., 1987, *Re-thinking Local History*, Leicester: Leicester University Press.

Reed, M., 1984, 'Social Change and Social Conflict in Nineteenth-Century England: A Comment', *Journal of Peasant Studies*, Vol. 12, No. 1, pp. 109–23.

Reed, M., 1986, 'Nineteenth-Century Rural England: A Case for "Peasant Studies"', *Journal of Peasant Studies*, Vol. 14, No. 1, pp. 78–99.

Roberts, B., 1986, 'Rural Settlements' in J. Langton, and R. J. Morris, (eds.), *Atlas of Industrializing Britain, 1780–1914*, London: Methuen.

Turner, M. and D. Mills (eds.), 1986, *Land and Property: The English Land Tax 1692–1832*, Gloucester: Alan Sutton.

Wells, R. A. E., 1981, 'Social Conflict and Protest in the English Countryside in the Early Nineteenth Century: A Rejoinder', *Journal of Peasant Studies*, Vol. 8, No. 4, pp. 514–30.

Social Protest, Class, Conflict and Consciousness, in the English Countryside 1700–1880

Roger Wells

I. INTRODUCTION: A REGIONAL APPROACH AND SOUTH-EASTERN ENGLAND

This contribution is not intended as a conclusion to the recent debate between historians of the English countryside, which initially focused on socio-economic change and the effects on popular protest. The aim now is to advance the debate through the presentation of further evidence deriving from subsequent research. Some of this material addresses topics central to my original article, and the criticisms it stimulated; other evidence has a relevance to the additional foci introduced into the debate, and reproduced in this volume, most notably by Mick Reed, Brian Short and Dennis Mills. Reed's fundamental revision respecting the vigour and capacity of small and family producers to survive despite a multiplicity of essentially hostile socio-economic, *and political*, factors during much of the nineteenth century, has introduced a major new element which historians of the phenomena focused on here must embrace. Short and Mills's restatements of the analytical importance of the 'close' 'open' dichotomony of English villages, necessitates reconsideration by the social historian, despite Sarah Banks's very recent demolition of their thoroughly orthodox thesis [*Banks*, 1988]. More material addresses topics essentially new to the debate as presented in the preceeding pages, though not invariably additional to the subjects of other recent publications by historians of rural England in this period. For example, John Rule has written on social crime and sheep stealing [1979 and 1982], George Rudé has advanced our knowledge of 'rural' and 'protest' crime [1978 and 1984], and the history of both the old and the new poor laws in the countryside has engaged a number of scholars, among them especially P. Dunkley [1982], Apfel and Dunkley [1985], Anthony Brundage [1978], and John Knott [1986]. One topic which surprisingly has not engaged other scholars, is the question of rural working-class consciousness, an elusive and indeed nebulous subject; a provisional examination is offered here.

Most of the evidence discussed here derives from South-eastern England, comprising the historic counties of Kent, Surrey, and West and East Sussex. Some use is also made here of Hampshire material. The use of counties to contrive regions will not necessarily comply with the sophisticated historical criteria for regionality, advanced by Professor Everitt [1979], but the current approach does have two principal advantages. First, it permits the individual researcher to present arguments emanating from an analysis of a selection of the huge volume of available sources. Secondly, this method facilitates comparative studies with other regions, and the present survey is also designed to encourage new research for comparative purposes.

However, a number of introductory observations respecting this region's agrarian history are required. There was considerable diversity, as explained in 1845 by a knowledgable authority, speaking only of Kent:

> there is perhaps no county in England whose physical and agricultural characteristics are more distinctly marked, and where productions are more varied, than those of Kent. Anyone ... in crossing this county from north to south cannot fail to be struck with the very manifest diversities of soil, varying features of the surface, different modes of culture, and almost ceaseless variety of agricultural produce.[1]

The Weald constitutes about half of the South-east. Its notoriety, as a huge area, ostensibly dominated by small farms, on essentially poor, wet, heavy, clay soils, owed something to the polemics of the two Arthur Youngs, father and son, writing at the end of the eighteenth century. The proximity of the Downland areas, to the north and the south of the Weald, with their more advanced, scientifically orientated, large scale, mixed farming, encouraged unfavourable commentary on the Weald throughout much of the nineteenth century. In the late 1870s, one of the Royal Commission on Agriculture's roving assistants, Little, opined that it was the Downland

> that has given a name and a character to Sussex as an agricultural county .... It would be difficult in the space of a few miles to find a greater contrast than is presented in the aspect and condition of farming in passing from the Weald to the South Downs. Here are large farms, extensive sheep breeding with its usual accessories, green and forage crops, and its best allies, widely extended down pastures.

The Sussex Weald, in stark contrast, was

> for the most part the country of small farmers of little inclosures, smothered with hedgerows, copses and timber; with dead fallows in the place of green crops, few sheep, and generally speaking an old fashioned style of farming.

In its Surrey extension, 'the state of the fields is generally filthy'.[2]

Orthodox castigations of Wealden farming, and the Wealden economy, cannot be accepted uncritically. First, woodland economics had several positive features which eluded prejudiced 'experts' like the Youngs, as the woods were – in fact – central to regional agrarian equilibrium: 'underwood land, properly managed and planted', stated a Tenterden land valuer in 1848, with some exaggeration, 'is the most profitable land that a man can hold as owner', and its 'great value' came in part from 'conversion into hop-poles' to meet a huge and rising demand. Other woodland products, bark, charcoal, faggots, and hoops, figured considerably in the coastal trade of Sussex throughout the century from 1740, and great volumes escaped the statistical record through overland and river carriage to London and other places. Many observers also testified that 'many men get their living in the woods', especially during the traditionally slack winter-period.[3] Another staple, hops, was strongly attacked by the Youngs and others for absorbing excessive quantities of manure and labour, to the detriment of other farm productions, and the notorious unreliability of the crop with yields damaged or even decimated regularly by insects and fungi. Oscillating productivity was symbolised by the ten acres which yielded four and a half hundredweight in 1825, and nine tons in 1826. If these characteristics meant that hops constituted a 'lottery', in some years bonanza profits were realised. One extensive planter admitted that perhaps only one in two crops proved remunerative, but added 'when you have a good year it makes up for the loss of two or three bad ones'. Moreover, hops sold speedily after picking and drying in September, and commonly provided the cash to meet Michaelmas rent demands, and underpinned farmers' liquidity throughout the autumn. In 1833, before the post-war agricultural depression lifted, an estate manager argued that 'small farms are kept in cultivation from the assistance of a small proportion ... being planted with hops', an opinion reiterated by Little. Once again, despite the fact that harvesting required a massive influx of labour, indigenous workers also benefited from this 'second' harvest after corn, and from digging, poling, manuring, and tying, earlier in the season.[4]

Another major form of Wealden agrarian diversification – into 'chicken-cramming' – was well established long before the spread of the rail network emphasised by one historian [*Short*, 1982; esp.19–24]. As early as 1789 an authority noted that Horsham was 'the great emporium for capons', the market centre of a district where they were 'fattened to an extent and in a perfection unknown any where else'.[5] Thereafter, other notable centres of the industry, including Heathfield, developed, but this should not obscure the ubiquitous proportions assumed in the Weald. A report in 1873 stated that

> coops, in some parishes, may be seen about every where – on the strips of grass at the sides of the roads, in odd corners, in front of cottages and in the field ... .every occupant of the ... small farms, almost without exception, is a chicken breeder.[6]

Dual occupancy was firmly established in the Weald; many blacksmiths, wheelwrights, and other craftsmen, together with millers, small brewers, and retailers, also farmed in a modest way. The virtual absence of parliamentary enclosure, which wrecked their equilibrium elsewhere [Martin, 1984], helped preserve them for much of the nineteenth century. Indeed, there is considerable evidence of an intensification of dual occupancies, especially through the 1830 liberalisation of the licensing laws, which enabled many smaller farmers, traders and craftsmen, to append a beer shop to their enterprise. Brickmaking, stimulated by continuous regional urbanisation, met burgeoning demand 'primarily through a multiplication of small producers', many of them lesser farmers, and others, with appropriate land, exemplified by the 'desirable little farm' of a mere nine and a half acres at Framfield, sold in 1873 for £500, together with a stock of eighteen-thousand 'clamp bricks'. The industry's fuel demands – despite greater use of coal from the 1790s – also fortified the woodland economy. But these forms of diversification – and the list could be greatly extended – were not the exclusive prerogative of hard-nosed minor agrarians and dual occupationists of all hues; Colonel Wyndham, owner of one of the largest West Sussex estates, also had his 'pipe making yard', producing on the customary seasonal basis, 'plain tiles', 'drain tiles' and 'building bricks' in the 1850s. Henry Michell, a Horsham brewer, and the epitomy of the Victorian small town entre-preneur, also invested profits in brickmaking, initially to meet demand from local railway construction.[7]

Michell also invested in four modest farms [*Neale*, 1975: 57–8] and he represented a considerable number of urban, including metropolitan, bourgeois, who bought up Wealden farms, in part to qualify for game licenses and to ape the squirearchy. Among the many examples, are the Brighton banker Wigney, who lived and farmed directly at Barcombe, the proprietor of the Railway Hotel at Maidstone, who bought a farm at Meopham, and barrister Renshaw of Lincoln's Inn, who purchased the Rookery Farm at Keymer, converted the 'old farm house' for himself, and let the land and a new house to a tenant. Many of this category of owner injected considerable funds into drainage and the clearance of hedgerows and shaws between tiny fields, without necessarily expecting a strictly viable return.[8] We should also be careful over the nature of the numerical domination of the smaller farmers; many proprietors took more than one farm. During the French wars complaints were heard about the 'monopoly of small farms by the great farmers', and the vicar of Streat asserted that 'the little farmer of £40 or £50 ... the lower class of yeomanry is diminishing yearly'. Nor was this restricted to the 1793 to 1815 period. In 1834 'some persons' at Sedlescombe 'occupy two or three or even four' farms. Moreover, many Wealden villages, contained a whole range of farms, typified again by Sedlescombe, where 'Farms vary from 20 to 270 acres'. At the same time, a third of the 5,500 acres comprising Ewhurst parish were occupied by three men, and the remainder divided into what were *called* 'small Farms', though several contained about a hundred acres. Ticehurst, another huge parish, was 'much divided', but despite this description its author postulated two categories, farms of between 150 and 200 acres, and 'many smaller holdings'. He additionally calculated that thirty-nine farmers employed labour, while only eleven did not. Substantial agriculturalists included Jerimiah Smith who owned only 1,300 of the 6,000 acres he farmed in 1848. Nor were Mick Reed's 'peasant' farmers the only ones to vary their holdings commensurately with family considerations. Tenant farmer John Robinson, extended his 422 acres to 785 in the 1870s because he had

> sons who are now quite old enough to be learning practical farming, and I could not get them to fancy anything else .... I undertook this large farm in addition, hoping that I should be doing the best for my children.[9]

This evidence fortifies rather than confronts Reed's emphasis of the tenacity of the small farming sector. So too does the confusion amongst contemporary experts on the main victims of the later nineteenth-century agricultural depression. Little, referring to Sussex, reported that

> I have heard the most opposite and apparently irreconcilable opinions expressed ... where large farms and small farms are brought into close juxtaposition with each other as to the comparative pressure of adverse times on those two classes; on the one hand I am told that 'undoubtedly the little men have felt it most': on the other ... that 'the little man has escaped, he has no expenses, no labour bill'.

Identical observations about the significance of labour costs were common, and owed something to agrarian trade union pressure in the 1870s, but the Earl of Chichester was nevertheless flabbergasted that 'some of our best down farms are unlet', and he ascribed this in part to insolvency among big 'farmers who farmed largely with borrowed capital'. Once the nation's consumption of so much of the staples of big agrarian capitalism's production – cereals and meat – was increasingly met by imports, another major farmer, Charles Whitehead of Barming, argued that all 'farmers will have to turn their attention to the production of these smaller things ... butter, milk, eggs, poultry, fruit and vegetables' to ensure survival. It was, of course, what lesser Wealden farmers had been doing for well over a century.[10]

Finally, one major feature of Wealden society has largely escaped historical notice, namely the degree of entrepreneurial activity notably at the lower end of the social hierarchy. Many farmworkers – and their wives – as suggested by the citation respecting cramming, reared modest numbers of chickens; one witness, asked about Wealden employment for women and children in 1843, replied that there was little outside the hop-gardens except 'rearing poultry for the market', and some cottagers were said in 1874 to annually produce 200 birds. Frant 'labourer' Field recounted in 1844 that 'for some years past ... [he] followed the business of collecting Chickens and fattening them for the London Markets'. Others who managed to rent plots of land, produced, including the keeper of Flimwell Turnpike Gate and a farmworker's wife, who are encountered selling 500 and 225 cabbage seedlings to the governor of Ticehurst workhouse in 1860, and Burwash stonemason Thompson who had 'a small plantation of Hops (consisting of three Hills)' with thirteen poles and twenty-six bines 'growing in a Garden' in 1837. Profits from such enterprise were used by some to join the burgeoning ranks of the ubiquitous hucksters who constantly toured the villages buying up principally perishable farm goods, for sale in town marts. Possession of rudimentary transport, a mule or the equally ubiquitous dog-cart – 'generally used by poor persons and small Ratepayers' – could enable those with little or no resources to get a foot on the lowest rungs of the entrepreneurial ladder, including 'labourer' Smith of Chevening who used a donkey and 'light cart' to convey 'small parcels' on commission to Sevenoaks. Smith's economic status was reflected in his beast's value, £1–12–6, and the fact that it 'used to eat about the road side with his legs tied'. James Crunder was just one dog-cart owner who traversed a district buying up scrap iron, and Mrs Welch a typical customer at Robertsbridge, 'who keeps a shop and buys old metal', no doubt in competition with local blacksmiths. James Bond of Northiam, represented thousands more, 'not in constant field Employment ... is generally a hawker of fish & Brooms'. The more successful, among them Charles Diplock of Heathfield, became small-scale employers; he hired Hiram Holland 'to collect chickens for me', and Lindfield huckster Welfare employed a man 'to deliver goods about ... when I came to Brighton market'. This vigorous petty entrepreneurship within, and transcending beyond, the nineteenth-century Wealden economy, was promiscuously symbolised; 'butcher and publican' Couchman of Leeds, Kent, additionally 'dealt in any thing when he could see his way clear' to a profit: William Friend of Salehurst, self-righteously described his 'little Colling':

> i ... do the best i Can to get my Living ... wiCh is gethering of Rags and Rabits Skings and Car[ry]ing of SCKand.

A working-class lad, saved from drowning at Fulking in 1860, could wish only to reward his plebeian rescuer with 'a whip and a donkey for taking me out of the water': that might comprise the first step to upward social mobility – though he would not have put it quite like that![1]

II. THE QUESTION OF RURAL ISOLATION

None of this economic evidence suggests that Wealden and other South-eastern rural communities were isolated; Professor Chaloner was forced to remark, over a decade ago, that 'There is still an unjustified tendency to regard the English rural population of the deep south, c.1815 as "still largely isolated and inward looking" a statement not borne out' by evidence from parish registers and settlement examinations [*Chaloner*, 1977: 68]. Yet this notion is still reiterated. Professor Bagwell concludes that it was only the 'rapid innovation in modes of transport', namely the railways and motorised road traffic which 'undermined the age-old isolation of villages and hamlets' [*Bagwell*, 1981: *passim*]. Dr Short, referring to the rapid increase in hop-culture in the seventeenth-century South-east, asserts that 'by 1670 many isolated Wealden parishes had established a thriving London trade'; within forty pages, Short claims that 'In terms of rural population, few regions could have been less self-contained', a statement closely followed by the allegation that the 'rural south east before 1750 was still an intensely parochial world' [*Short*, 1984: 273, 313]. In fact, each market town, themselves components of an interlocking hierarchy headed by London, had its rural hinterland, and these economic enforcers of regionality were strengthened – and often transposed – by the political, judicial, and administrative functions, of several urban centres. And it was not simply farmers, considerable and petty dealers in agrarian produce, who dealt in urban markets. A glance at the diary of the mid-eighteenth-century Wealden shopkeeper, Thomas Turner, reveals that he relied on both Lewes based wholesalers, and also obtained merchandise elsewhere, including directly from London [*Vaisey*, 1984: *passim*]. Ironically, contemporary notions of isolation were even fuelled – or redefined – by the railways; a Brightonian described Henfield as 'a secluded out-of-the-way place' in 1860 because 'the nearest railroad is seven miles off'.[12]

Almost every village had its craftsmen. Even 'close' Glynde, with a population of 212 in 1789, had its 'carpenters, wheelwrights, blacksmiths, bricklayers', admittedly all 'connected with, and dependent on agri-culture', bar a shoemaker who in addition to supplying villagers, 'sells ... to people at large in fairs and markets'.[13] Everitt observes that 'the domestic world of mid-Victorian England was still the hand-made world of the craftsmen ... to a greater extent than is sometimes realised'; trade directories invariably underestimate the numbers of rural craftsmen, because their imperfect listings of masters, take no cognizance of the numbers of their employees [*Everitt*, 1979: esp.105; cf. *Horn*, 1976: 90–91]. These occupational groups certainly survived what could be described as the de-industrialisation of the rural South, with the collapse of the iron industry, and the slightly later erosion of the previously wide-spread textile industry [*Wells*, 1988a; *Kenyon*, 1958: esp. 69]. Indeed, a fair proportion were considerable business men. William Kenwood of Holtye, Sussex, was a blacksmith employing several journeymen; he kept an inn, dealt in several commodities, including fuel, and like so many of his genre, also farmed. Employers like Kenwood facilitated consider-able movement by journeymen craftsmen between town and country. Edmund Prudence, a shoemaker who temporarily worked for master craftsmen Barnard of Burwash in 1820, was 'well-known about Lewes, Eastgrinstead and Fletching'. Tailor Sam Butler left London in the same year, worked in Brighton until January 1822, when he too secured employment in Burwash, until the following December when he worked in Lewes for two months, before returning to Brighton. When journeyman stone-mason Bell from Somerset arrived at Lamberhurst in 1838, he secured 'ready furnished lodgings' where he resided until 1844.[14] Boys from the villages were often apprenticed to market town and metropolitan craftsmen, and those trained there were especially favoured by rural employers, if they returned.[15] London craftsmen were regularly contracted to do the more skilled work, especially on country mansions, as at Stanmer house in the 1720s, on the new county hall at Lewes in 1808, and on Hadley rectory in 1830.[16] Nor was this traffic one way, as revealed for example by advertisements for bricklayers and hod-carriers placed in the Sussex press by the London Dock Company in 1801. Such migrations even had an impact on patterns of criminality, revealed for example, by London plumber Hazle, employed by a Lewes builder on a job at Firle Place, who was detected in carting off eight hundredweight of lead, 'intended for the London market by way of Alfriston'.[17]

The road transport industry continued to grow even if the railways altered road haulage patterns [*Everitt*, 1976]. Many combined carting with specialist dealing to link town and country, exemplified by 'fish carrier' King of Broadwater, who was 'known at Billingsgate'.[18] A further reflection of this constant communication is encountered in the distribution of literature. The nature of illiteracy is commonly distorted, for if perhaps only a minority of rural workers "'got the hang'" of writing, many more could read [*Colson*, 1937: 127, note 18]. Labourer Hills of Hartfield was said to be 'fond of a Newspaper' in 1828, and deep in rural Buckinghamshire labourer Mayett's Christian convictions were shaken in 1820 by exposure to 'Cobbet Woler and Carlile'. Eight people domiciled at Ditchling in the same year subscribed to Wooler's radical *British Gazette*. Hawkers were important in this dissemination, and itinerant booksellers did a steady Wealden trade in the 1840s.[19] Although there are examples of intense parochialism, represented by two Wadhurst labourers aged eighty-one and sixty-four in 1864, who respectively said that they had 'never worked' and had 'never lived out of the parish', the case for rural isolation, on any criteria, is a figment of imaginations – contemporary and historical.[20]

III. THE AGRICULTURAL DEPRESSION, 1815–37

The wartime inflation of cereal prices stimulated a considerable increase in corn acreages throughout the South-east, including the Weald where much essentially unsuitable land was brought under the plough; the latter brand of agrarian economics was sustainable only while prices remained high [*Henderson*, 1952: 58]. Dr Wilks has recently emphasised that the intensity of the subsequent depression was geographically and chronologically uneven [*Wilks*, 1980]. If no part of the South-east escaped, none was affected so severely and for such a prolonged period as the Weald.

From 1815–16, the Wealden economy exhibited all the symptoms of perennial crisis. Cereal acreages contracted markedly, and much remaining arable land was farmed less intensively; 'the farmer does not ditch it, nor grub it, nor trunk it', encouraging complaints that they 'grew weeds'. This generated a vicious circle; it became difficult, if not impossible, 'to get tenants at all; the farms are not in condition and nobody will take them'. David Rowland, estate-owner at Frant, said that his 'Small Farms' let 'readily' during the war at 15/– per acre, but afterwards he experienced a reluctance to take them despite reducing the rent to 7/–, and doubling customary annual tenancies, and he was reduced to costly advertising. In 1823 farms were offered rent-free in the Battle district by landlords trying to evade the phenomenon whereby 'many thousands of acres are getting out of cultivation daily'. Smaller tenants' children were said to be more 'hungered' than paupers', while their fathers 'worked harder than ... labourers'. Avoiding bankruptcy dictated numerous expedients. Many 'pledged' hay and corn stacks to their landlords 'for arrears of rent'. Increased resort was had to exchange to combat recurrent liquidity crises. One casual labourer was typically paid 'in Wheat' as his employer had 'no Money' in 1825.[21] The press teemed with reports of bankruptcies, and scores of reports confirmed that hundreds of 'tenants ... became paupers'. Some years were clearly worse than others, notably 1821–23, but there are signs of only uneven and partial recoveries, which proved ephemeral. Recurrently wet seasons between 1825 and 1828 posed additional problems, precisely because much land was 'less drained than it used to be', which was in part responsible for the widespread sheep rot of 1828–29, generating another crisis which severely compromised downland agrarian profits too. In January 1830, one Wealden estate steward depicted the depression's renewed intensity engulfing entire communities.

> The Rents, Timber and Wood Money, I am grieved to state ... how slackly they come in ... . The Timber Merchant, as well as all the principal Tenants, are craving, not for abatement, but for indulgence of further time. The year, it is allow'd on all Hands, to be the most disasterous, and about here, the almost total failure of the Crop mainly depended on (the Hop) together with the great deficiency of all the others, and added thereto the dreadful Havoc in the Stock of Sheep, by the Rot ... caused a general dismay amongst the Farmers.[22]

This 'unprecedented agricultural distress' from 1815, according to one Southern landowner, 'compelled ... farmers generally ... to reduce to the lowest limit the numbers of their labourers'.[23] Reducing labour costs in this climate also entailed a considerable resort to threshing machines by big farmers everywhere [*Fox*, 1978: 26–8; *MacDonald*, 1975: *passim*.

MacDonald, 1978: 29–31], none more so in districts including East Kent, the Downs, and the Sussex coastal plain, favourable areas where farmers countered the depression by increasing cereal production [*Wilks*, 1980: 93–100]. Traditional historical accounts of the depression have focused exclusively on the impact on farmers and their labourers. This is too narrow, for it had equally dire consequences for rural and market town traders and master craftsmen, and their skilled employees. As one witness retrospectively put it:

> I never knew the country doing so well as when corn was selling at the high prices ... all the little tradesmen ... were doing very well ... the farmers could get money ... lay it out, and their daughters were fond of dressing, and the tradesmen were doing extremely well in consequence,

in stark contrast to the post-war situation obtaining in 1833. Those with a principally plebeian clientele, notably shoemakers, suffered severely, but they were joined by most trades serving farmers, who reduced outlays on new farming implements and repairs to all manner of things, including fencing, gates, waggons, harnesses, barns and houses. Farmers also forced wheelwrights, blacksmiths and builders, to reduce their prices. In addition tradesmen had to confront delayed payments and bad debts. Detailed accounts of one bailiff between 1821 and 1828 prove that tradesmen's complaints were real, not rhetorical: '6 Months Bricklayers Bills Due at Midsummer 1822', totalling nearly £32 were paid in March 1823. Over £154 owed to a carpenter on 1 January 1821 was not paid until 9 November, and a subsequent invoice for £65 submitted on 1 July 1823 was not honoured until March 1824. Only the blacksmith invariably received settlement within three months. Tradesmen retaliated by reducing the quality of their products, but this served principally to generate undercutting and price wars. Those who resorted to parish contracts, especially the tailors, shoemakers and joiners, were forced to accept miserly terms for the supply of paupers, and repairs to parish properties.[24] Brede was – as the vestry put it in May 1829 – 'over done with Carpenters'; 'many mechanics and persons employed in trade' experienced under- and unemployment, and were forced to seek public aid. When wheelwright John Reed of Battle 'applied for Money to seek Work' he was 'offered work at grubbing' in the hop-garden of a parish-owned farm. Others received allowances in-aid-of wages, and Goudhurst recipients included bricklayers, brickmakers, sawyers, shoemakers, and a journeyman miller.[25] Retailers, especially butchers, also suffered. Lesser traders chopped and changed, both their businesses and their locations, as they tried to find a profitable niche, like Mr Brook who told a friend on taking premises at Chailey in 1830, that 'he is out of Business at present, he talks of going to butchering again'. At this moment, the reformed licensing laws were perceived as a saviour:

> the Beer Business is all the talk with us we have plenty of Beer Shops

all selling the 4d and 5d therefore we must do the same we dont know what to think but if we cant git Bread at one Business we must do something else ... .Henderson Cartling is one of the Beer Shops, they have 3 at Newick, John talks of letting his house for one.[26]

Professor Wrigley has argued that demographic statistics and census materials reveal a marked expansion in men engaged in ten major rural trades. As there was 'very little expansion of employment on the farm', at most ten percent, during the unprecedented post-war demographic explosion, Wrigley suggests that the huge human increment was principally absorbed by the trade and craft sectors of the rural economy. If we add the considerable range of petty entrepreneurial activities previously encountered to Wrigley's main trades, his argument has an importance, and we may also endorse his complementary point that 'the probable ... overall majority' of these 'new' traders were self-employed. Wrigley's empirical evidence excludes that from the South-east, but it does include materials from – among other counties – Dorset and Buckinghamshire. The rural history of these counties between the later 1810s and 1830s is very similar, including close parallels in events comprising the Swing revolt [*Cirket*, 1978: 75–88; *Agar*, 1981: 49–79; *Kerr*, 1962; *Bawn*, 1984: Ch.4]. But Wrigley's conclusion that these developments reveal that

> rural England retained sufficient economic momentum ... to permit notable increases in employment in many classes of occupation which could only flourish if the local economy was healthy since they depended on a local market,

is manifest nonsense [*Wrigley*, 1986: 295–6, 302–3, 335–6]. In aggregate, master craftsmen reduced their labour force, thus encouraging attempts to survive through self-employment, but the severe difficulties encountered are reflected by thousands of whom John Reed is a typical representative, and also in the resort of parishes including Burwash and Edenbridge to Roundsmen and Labour Rate schemes to combat the almost insuperable difficulties these occupational classes encountered.[27] These did not begin to lift until the later 1830s when agrarian profitability returned.

IV. THE CENTRALITY OF THE OLD POOR LAW

The centrality of the old poor law to rural society in general, and to agrarian labour in particular, was underestimated in my original article; my rejoinder may have done justice to this centrality, but coverage extended only to the 1815–34 period, and concentrated almost exclusively on one Sussex village. Dr Archer's stricture – that the entire debate might dissolve into a myopic concentration on Burwash, reiterated by Drs Mills and Short, questions Burwash's typicality [*Archer*, 1983: 282/87; *Mills and Short*, 1985: 254/91]. Challenges to the representative quality of the evidence seriously weakens any thesis. The original underestimation, and the several limitations of the rejoinder, dictate a more substantial treatment of the old poor law. Moreover, neither piece dealt substantially with the old law's successor, the system created by the notorious 1834 Poor Law Amendment Act, that statutory embodiment of so many Victorian values, which aimed to sanitise agrarian labour through the enforcement of laissez-faire economic principles. The radical and lofty ideological objectives of the new system ensured that the poor law retained – be it in altered form – its key significance in the countryside for most of the nineteenth century. Social protest – in its many moulds – was greatly conditioned by successive social security systems, as indeed were many other aspects of rural life in the eighteenth and nineteenth centuries.

The history of the old poor law in the South-eastern countryside can be interpreted as an almost inexorable progression engendering the multi-faceted crisis engulfing the system in the economically depressed post-war years of the early nineteenth century, a crisis belatedly confronted by the utilitarian dominated Whig party on its return to office after fifty years. This thesis turns on the unremitting demographic growth from the early eighteenth century, dovetailing with subsidiary forces, generating proletarianisation, with the supply of agrarian labour increasingly outstripping demand. Old poor-law administrations were forced to grapple with forces outside their control, a process responsible for a fundamental expansion of the system's original focus on the ill, the disabled, the elderly, widowed mothers and orphans, to embrace the regulation of employment, wages, family income, indeed almost all facets of plebeian life, including housing accommodation for farmworkers. Such a panorama does little violence to the bare outlines, but analysis and explanation are better served when the last hundred years of the old law's operations are periodised, whereby changing conditional circumstances are projected into sharper relief. Three periods can be detected. The first was ushered in by the beginnings of the population explosion from the 1730s, the so-called golden age of the labourer, and lasted until the start of the war with revolutionary France (1793) which virtually coincided with the critically significant famine of 1794–96. The second period embraces the bulk of the war years, 1794–1815, when unprecedented mobilisation reversed some of the effects of demographic growth. The final period, 1815–34, includes the agricultural depression, at its fiercest in the Weald during these years, but severely felt throughout the South-east for most of them.

1700–1794

Evidence that rural employers speedily exploited the burgeoning labour supply derives from the golden age itself. As early as 1756 Thomas Turner, the shopkeeping diarist of East Hoathly in Sussex, complained that 'the richest and leading men of our parish' were reducing 'poor men's wages' by 'bringing in many poor ... from other parishes ... until the parish is full of poor'. In 1761 he registered further wage reductions and complained that current rates constituted 'oppression, fraud and grinding the face of the poor'. Turner represented that sector of the community, including small farmers dependent on family labour, which had no economic interest in reducing wages; they feared that immigrants might become poor-law claimants, and their children parishioners, thereby inflating the poor rates in the medium and long term. This conflict of interests between the greater farmers and other ratepayers was commonly, if reluctantly, resolved through what was effectively a compromise based on the settlement laws. Only immigrants possessing settlement certificates from their home parishes, which absolved their host village from welfare responsibilities, for them, and their children who automatically took the parents' settlement, were permitted to obtain work. Certification under the settlement system also facilitated migration in search of work; it offered protection against the vagrancy laws, permitted unchallenged residence once employment was secured, and preserved migrants from summary removal to their home parish. Parochial authorities had a vested interest in granting certificates to villagers who could not secure employment locally; when such people required temporary relief, granting parishes had every inducement to relieve them where they were domiciled, as there was little point in insisting on their returning home where there might be neither work nor housing accommodation. If certification increased markedly during the eighteenth century, its use remained discriminatory, not least because parishes may have hoped that those insubordinate or inadequate workers who migrated in search of work without documentation might at some indefinite future point clandestinely secure a settlement through residence elsewhere. Constant and effective policing of migrants was not an invaried feature of rural communities. Every crisis exerting pressure on the poor-rates precipitated investigations; in 1748 Northiam vestry typically ordered non-settled residents to obtain certificates, and in 1795 their Icklesham counterparts ordered 'the People that have Intruded into the Parish' to provide documentation or risk legal expulsion 'as soon as it can be conveniently done'. Certification certainly put a brake on the increasing resort to removals in the eighteenth century, and equally certainly facilitated the exploitation of the labour supply by the larger farmers; the resultant irritation was neatly expressed in 1754 by the Ticehurst vestry – dominated numerically by small farmers and petty entrepreneurs – that the village was 'obliged to admit Several Famileys under Certificates from other Parishes'.[28]

A combination of the abundant labour supply, and an aversion to unnecessary creation of new settlements, challenged the traditional living-in system of farm service for young and unmarried workers, and other annual hirings of labourers, which were increasingly restricted to those already formally settled. The use of fifty-one week hirings probably spread from Berkshire after the 1750s. About 'a Week before Mich[aelm]as Day 1776', one Kent labourer was informed 'that if he chose to stay another year ... he ... might ... he must leave his Service on Michas Day and take away his Cloaths and must return again in two or three days', thereby ensuring a break in the year's service. Half-year contracts were another commonly used device, notably from Ladyday to Michaelmas which embraced the busiest times in the agrarian calendar.[29] Debate continues over the decline of the classic living-in system, but it did not collapse, especially not in its non-settlement achieving form before the 1790s [*Snell*, 1985: Ch.2; *Kussmaul*, 1981; *Short*, 1984; *Reed*, 1985]. The evidence suggests that the system was increasingly unable to absorb youthful workers. This meant that a growing proportion of farmworkers did not experience living-in, despite the growing intervention of vestries over the employment of adolescents and youths.

Traditionally, official intervention over juvenile employment was confined to securing apprenticeships, or farmwork for the fatherless and orphaned. These obligations survived, but the importance of securing work for children increased, not simply with population, but also with farmworkers' declining post-1750 living standards, which aggravated pressure on larger families. Prior to the 1740s, Northiam arranged the odd contract, invariably supplying clothes for the child to use in service, but these interventions were restricted to the traditional category of juvenile. However, from the mid-1740s the vestry made *ad hoc* contracts respecting an increasing number of children, and finally systematised the process from 1753 when 'Candlemas day hereafter' was designated as annual contracting day. Five children were placed in 1753, eight in 1754, six in 1755 and nine in 1756. Within 20 years even this system was inadequate; in 1772 escalating expenditure was ascribed to 'many of the Aged Poor and Children ... destitute of employ', and the parish created a 'manufactory' to put them to work. Unemployment among ageing males is a sure sign that farmers were meeting their labour requirements from younger, fitter men, and all these problems indicate that the local economy was already glutted by labour.[30]

Population pressure, contractions of living-in, and farmers' growing preference for day labour, combined to intensify pressures on rural housing stocks. There is no evidence of a commensurate rise in housing, despite the notorious speculative jerry-building by tradesmen and other petty entrepreneurs in more open villages, and even by some substantial landowners like the Sanctuary's in the Horsham district.[31] Ultimately, accommodating homeless but legally settled people devolved on the vestry, a responsibility reflected in such workhouse – or more strictly poorhouse – provision inherited by eighteenth-century administrators. The expansion of vestry participation in the housing market is usually ignored by historians,[32] but was commonly revealed by failed attempts to implement Knatchbull's Act of 1723 which permitted all relief to be confined to workhouse inmates. Northiam tried to implement the Act by building a new workhouse, but by the late 1730s relief was granted on condition that recipients 'keep out of the Poorhouse', and in the 1740s rents were wholly or partly paid for several male inhabitants in addition to traditional aid towards widows' housing costs. In the process several houses became permanently rented directly by the parish, and under its auspices densities in these buildings increased. In the 1780s the parish built new houses, and the debts incurred were still being serviced in the early nineteenth century. Parallel responses are found elsewhere, including Icklesham where existing premises were enlarged in 1787 'to Contain the Poor that the Parish shall think proper to put therein', and in 1791 another parish house was converted 'into two Dwellings'.[33]

Vestry action over under- and unemployment, notably the introduction of Roundsmen schemes, whereby unemployed labourers were distributed round the farmers, with wages paid principally from the rates, made their appearance in some counties in the 1770s and 1780s; in October 1794, it was said of Buckinghamshire and Oxfordshire that this 'abominable practice' was enforced on 'all the Labourers ... as soon as the Harvest is finished' for the duration of the winter. Although wages were varied according to individual's family responsibilities, incomes were invariably 'inadequate to the common ... necessaries of life'.[34] There is little evidence of pre-war Roundsmen schemes in the South-east, but experimentation with systems designed to ensure basic subsistence living standards in response to rising, if volatile food prices, which comprise the antecedents of the notorious Speenhamland scales, was made in 1791–92 in some rural Southern counties, among them Dorset and Berkshire [*Neuman*, 1969; *Neuman*, 1972: 100–101; *Body*, 1966: 90, 205]. These precedents, whereby poor-law authorities began to address the problems of depressed wages, rising food prices, seasonal unemployment, and housing, constituted a practical charter for a massive extension of parochial intervention with labouring families, which commenced in the unique circumstances obtaining in the mid-1790s.

1794–1815

Famine conditions in 1794–96, 1799–1801, and again in 1810–13, were key factors in this process. I have offered a reinterpretation elsewhere of the origins, spread, speedy contraction, and virtual extinction of the Speenhamland system of sliding scales of relief [*Wells*, 1988b: 290–301]. A combination of factors ensured that by the first decade of the nineteenth century the radical expansion of poor relief embraced most farmworkers with families, notably with the regular payment of *de facto* child subsidies. The famines were also important for a massive extension of relief payments to non-resident claimants.[35] Allegations that farmworkers accepted this dependency and sought to exploit it as a right, followed almost immediately, and were frequently reiterated. In 1805 an observer typically asserted that the famines obliged many to apply ... who before felt the conscious pride of independence, and that pride having been once broken, has not yet been, nor probably ever will be recovered. No more disgrace is now attached to such applications, than as if they were for the regular earnings of industry.[36]

Such statements, even when shorn of their moralistic overtones, do not dovetail with the common assumptions of historians, that the duration and unprecedented scale of wartime mobilisation, generated an agrarian labour shortage which forced wages and living standards up. This erroneous analysis is based on a handful of biased sources, notably farmers writing in the agricultural press. In fact concrete evidence is virtually non-existent in the first phase of the war [1793–1801],[37] and elusive for the second [1803–15]. Localised shortages, principally for major but non-agrarian labour-intensive schemes, occurred occasionally,[38] and rising harvest earnings after 1805 suggest some fragility in the supply but only during the short season of peak demand. The only detectable retreat of poor-law officials' profile relates to a decline in Roundsmen systems. Nevertheless changes in the structure of the labour market had important effects. The war certainly creamed off a considerable proportion of younger men, whose physical capacities always gave them an advantage in the market. Mobilisation served to put a greater premium on younger farmworkers, who exploited the situation notably by eschewing in-service and by increasingly insisting on piece work, to the serious disadvantage of less fit and especially elderly counterparts.

As early as 1796 a Wrotham labourer 'worked more by the Great [piece] than by the Day', even while permanently employed on the same farm; his son, John Lawrence, who also worked on the farm from the age of fourteen to eighteen on a daily rate which increased from 8d to 1/6 in four yearly increments, thereafter worked 'sometimes by the Day & sometimes by the Great with his Father'. John also 'never considered himself bound to work ... for any particular time, but was always at Liberty to leave when he pleased'.[39] John's employment record also testifies to the shrinkage in in-service. The Wealden landowner George Courthope later reported that 'the feeling of both man and servant during ... the war led to the same result', with the

good workman desirous of independent labor and the farmer was ... improving his circumstances, he found his farming servants residence in the house interfere materially with the comforts of his family.

Other witnesses confirmed that younger, unmarried but adult workers finally 'broke through' the traditional living-in system. Conversely there is some evidence that inflated living costs deterred farmers from hiring in-servants. Joseph Mayett was unable to secure such a position in 1801, though he also testified that it was commonly irksome, indeed repressive, despite the romantic – and later – claims of the system's supporters. Farmers and their wives were dictatorial, and the young resented prohibitions on socialising. All farm servants were vulnerable to abuse, physical and otherwise, and lasses were often the sexual targets of their masters.[40] Hirings came under the criminal code, but appeals to magistrates by workers were traumatic occasions accompanied by the chance of subsequent victimisation. Conversely, employers used the courts rather more often to deal – usually harshly – with errant living-in servants. When farmer Dixon summoned three of his men for alleged pilfering – which he could not prove – justice Brockman 'discharge[d] them from ye Mastr's service & abate[d] most of their wages', which in this case meant almost all money owed to them for seven months work.[41] The wartime labour market enabled many young workers to escape these restrictions and often oppressive working environments, relatively secure in their ability to obtain piece work, perhaps interrupted by short periods of unemployment, when poor relief would be available.[42]

The war years witnessed little retreat by vestries from organising contracts for juveniles; indeed, some parishes including Pevensey from 1805, and West Firle from 1813, were reduced to costly advertisements in the county press to find employers willing to enter into hirings. Vestries also became increasingly intolerant of relief recipients with unemployed children, typified by a decision at Brede to terminate one regular claimant's aid until his eldest lad obtained work.[43] Many parishes expanded their activities in the housing market. In 1802, Framfield 'Resolved that as the Parish is Distressed for Houses for the Poor families ... a Number of Cottages shall be Erected'; further initiatives followed in 1808 and 1809. In 1811 more family accommodation derived from clearing the poorhouse of aged persons – who were put out as lodgers in private homes – but this policy failed to end the problem, and further cottages were built before the end of the war.[44] Other parishes resorted to a variety of expedients, included loaning or sharing the costs of new houses with individuals, and making relief conditional on cottage owners handing over their houses to the parish on their deaths. Desperation is frequently evinced, as at Hartfield where in 1808 the vestry bought 'a Hut' – previously used to dress flax – for £3, and promptly added 'a Chimney and oven'. This 'Damp' rudimentary accommodation was still occupied by a non-rent paying parish tenant in 1830.[45]

The costs of these latter developments were but a supplementary factor to the major causes of escalating wartime poor-law expenditure, namely general inflation and allowances in-aid-of wages. Every component was essentially an adoption and expansion of pre-war practices to deal with rural poverty, and supports the conventional interpretation that especially the affluent farmers exploited the situation. Almost every contemporary authority, among them Arthur Young, Robert Malthus, and the Treasury minister, George Rose, acknowledged that 'the farmers, although they bear themselves a large proportion of the assessments, have already learned ... to prefer low wages and high rates, to low rates and high wages'. In 1805 Rose published statistics of those relieved in 'agricultural counties', which varied between 13 and 23 per cent of the entire populations of Surrey, Hampshire, Kent and Sussex; he emphasised that the cause was the farmers, 'solicitous to restrain the price of labour' [*Malthus*, 1807: 201; *Rose*, 1805: 14; *Young*, 1812: 90–91; *Young*, 1815: 175, 210]. However, the reasons are more complex than ostensibly suggested by this monocausal explanation. The costs to employers paying wages adequate to the support of men in different categories is easily illustrated by the basic incomes calculated by some Petty Sessions; the West Malling Bench designated weekly incomes of five shillings for a single man, and 12/3 for a childless married couple: families with two and eight children required 15/9 and £1–5–3 respectively.[46] It is difficult to imagine a greater disincentive to the payment of wages adequate to the support of considerable families. Moreover, just as war stimulated prices, peace would depress them, and action to restrain wartime wages, had the additional advantage of negating peacetime needs to force them down again. But the rationale was even more sophisticated than anything suggested by these figures, though it was rarely articulated contemporaneously. High poor rates had two additional, crucial advantages; first they comprised an important vehicle for clawing back some of the costs of tithes, as tithes were assessed to the poor rates. Secondly, they were a defence against huge rent increases by landlords anxious to cash in on agrarian profitability. Landowners accepted poor-rate levels as criteria in negotiations over rents, but not wage levels:

> If the tenant answers 'Rates are low but wages are high', the valuer says 'I have nothing to do with wages, that is your affair, but rates are a positive thing, and I allow for them'.[47]

1815–35

Rapid demobilisation in 1815 helped fuel the fastest demographic growth ever experienced in England over the next two decades. The collapse of farm produce prices ushered in twenty years of agricultural depression, omnipresent, as we have seen, but at its fiercest in the Weald. Apparently chronic employment difficulties constituted the major problem for poor-law authorities, and the massive extension in their role reveals one great consistency in the struggles between various interest groups to seize some advantage in the resultant melee. Examples include the larger farmers' attempts to effectively force public authorities to meet more and more of their wages bill, and cottage proprietors' insistence that vestries under-write the inflated rents charged for plebeian tenancies. Incessant battles within vestries, and between poor-law officials and claimants, turned parochial politics into an unremittant frenzy which threatened the very fabric of rural communities. Only campaigns to reduce farm-rents, taxes and tithes provided forums for expressions of residual cohesion.

The return of demobilised serviceman precipitated a fierce recourse to the settlement laws; parish followed parish in agreements to employ only settled workers, and those who had migrated during previous years were expelled creating 'more individual misery than can be conceived by those who were not eye witnesses'.[48] Such action predictably failed to solve the 'surplus labour' problem in any district; instead desperation encouraged wholesale resort to contested removals between parishes which generated the 'proverb that if you could gain one appeal out of three, it was worthwhile' despite the heavy costs.[49] But the contemporary castigation of this litigation, and the views of those historians who have echoed them, are essentially unreal. Vestrymen were not simply concerned with current relief levels, nor with the difficulties of housing those removed; these families were correctly seen as the major source for additional and for-ever expanding generations of paupers in the future. Not surprisingly, many parishes also sought to pre-empt removals by paying poor relief to non-resident claimants, often under the spur of threats from them to 'bring my Family down to the Parish'; as one claimant put it, 'if I leave my work to cum for my right I shall be out of Work all the winter and that will be a sad thing'. Non-resident claimants advanced many reasons, including indebtedness and the necessity to preserve credit arrangements, a broken friendly society, threatened seizures of household goods, and evictions. But such appeals were not invariably successful; many had to write repeatedly, while others who abandoned their families in desperation were prosecuted. Nevertheless, many did end up with regular allowances in-aid-of wages; in 1834, Goudhurst, for example, was paying them to 174 able-bodied men domiciled in 36 locations, mostly in Kent and Sussex, with some in Essex and London, of whom 133 were farmworkers.[50]

Removal and housing were often inseperable, as represented by Henry Climpson's case. Removed with his family from Winchelsea in 1816 he was temporarily put into Pevensey workhouse before he was placed in a furnished, parish-'hired' house where he lived for the next seven-teen years.[51] Financial restraints put a virtual stop to house-building by vestries.[52] The trend was in the opposite direction with many parishes mortgaging properties to ease liquidity problems, typified by Ripe's £250 mortgage on one house, equal to 'nearly or quite ... its full value'. Every device was seized upon to increase village housing stocks, symbolised by Hartfield's savagely-worded minute directing the officers to ascertain if the house of the late Henry Mitchell, now occupied by his widow in receipt of the miserly but customary weekly pension of 1/6,

> be so far gone from any Claim of this Parish ... as to preclude by Will or otherwise the Right of the Parish ... of recovering the said House ... for the benefit of the Parish.

Financial restraints eroded vestrymen's options. John Bartholomew of

Goudhurst was £23 in debt and 'receiving constant relief'; he offered his 'freehold Cottage of small value' to the parish for £40, 'on condition he was allowed to reside in it during his life'. The parish accepted the offer, but found a parishioner with the cash to invest, rather than commit public funds to the transaction. Parochial actions over housing were rarely adequate as reflected in magisterial interventions. The Battle Bench ordered that parish 'to provide some Place of Shelter' for a family of five 'living in a tent', and Wartling authorities 'to get quarters' for Samuel Fairhall currently 'obliged to be at a public House at ... 5s a Week', half of which was paid by the overseer of the poor.[53] All this evidence proves that the old poor law in its last years of perennial crisis was unable to undertake adequate responsibilities for housing; instead, authorities were forced by their own and plebeian poverty to subdivide and further overcrowd existing property,[54] and to greatly increase intervention in the rented market.

Goudhurst parish, unable to find the £40 stipulated, was forced to pay the new owner an annual £4 to house Bartholomew. At Framfield, Fred Fielder's small family was turfed out of a parish house to make way for a larger family, and the overseers instructed to 'offer an increased Rent to any Person that ... will Accomodate ... Fielder with a House'.[55] Increased intervention drove rents up, and led landlords to prefer pauper tenants, or at least those who got the parish to underwrite their rents. Grocer Adams of Edenbridge who owned houses at Hartfield, approached the overseers respecting William Hoath's prospective tenancy of 'a Cottage ... 4 Guineas and if you like to stand engaged for the Rent ... I have no Objection'; Hartfield replied that 'this parish will be acountable' without even questioning the price. The 1834 Poor Law Report rightly insisted that 'Paupers have ... become a very desirable class of tenants', notably for landlords drawn from that petty entrepreneurial class represented by Adams.[56]

Increased concern with housing through guaranteed rents, parish houses, poorhouses, unreformed workhouses, and almshouses, in the last twenty years of the old poor law, represented a climax to a long tradition. In 1834, West Grinstead with 1,292 inhabitants, subsidised the rents of 56 families. Populous Battle [2,999] had 20 properties, while smaller villages, including 'closed' Ashburnham [721] and 'open' Brightling [656] had seven and eight respectively. Subdivision and serious overcrowding obscures the actual numbers of people involved, but financial restraints and other factors ensured that parochial properties were in the main of poor and deteriorating quality. At Hollington, Sussex, one cottage was 'in a very dilapidated state and not worth repairing', and two more required at least £20 spent on urgent repairs. Assistant Poor-Law Commissioner Colonel A'Court compiled reports on parochial housing in parts of Hampshire. At Compton, 'upwards of 40' of the total population of 255, lived in 'a miserable mud building ... one story high with three chambers in the thatched roof'. At Owslebury, '7 wretched tenements', and at

Broughton-with-Frenchmoor nine tumble-down cottages, were 'allotted to needy families rent free', from their respective populations of 664 and 897. A 'Court discovered few exceptions, though he recorded '4 brick built decent cottages' at Upham Woodcut Common, and seven more in 'decent repair' – occupied by fifty people – at Selbourne.[57]

Under- and unemployment remained the major problem in rural England. According to one southern landowner, 'nearly the whole of the well-conducted, honest and industrious labourers were employed at the usual wages'; he added that

> the persons out of employ consisted principally ... of individuals who had absented themselves from their parishes during the summer and working months for the purposes of obtaining higher wages and returning to be maintained by their own parishes in the winter.

There was some truth in these statements; micro-studies have revealed a core of regularly-employed farmworkers, and here lays the origins of the division of local labour forces into 'roughs and respectables' which was later to achieve some notoriety.[58] But this apologist's statement unwittingly testified to the fact that full employment was confined to the harvest, and that some had to migrate to ensure they participated in work even at this juncture. The fraility of demand, even at harvest time, is further revealed by localised outbreaks of violence between migrants and indigenous workers.[59] Downward pressure on wages was exerted by a combination of the over-supply of labour and the ever-burgeoning system of allowances in-aid-of wages; not only was it 'contrary to reason that any person should pay a man for his work sufficient to support a whole family, which in some cases would be 20s a week', double most and treble some current wage-levels, but as a Kent observer put it, parochial responsibility for poor-law funding generated a 'jealousy ... among the farmers', who 'frequently turn off a man because a neighbour does not employ a proportionate quantity with themselves'. The resultant recourse to wage supplementation was so universal that one farmer on the favoured and still prosperous Sussex coastal plain, achieved an obituary notice in 1830 – rare for the early nineteenth-century press – because he was 'one of the liberal few who paid his labourers out of his own pocket, rather than any part ... from the poor's rate'.[60]

In parish after parish schemes to combat unemployment were tried, reviewed, amended and abandoned often in rapid succession, as the problem proved practically insoluble. These histories require establishing at village level. Framfield vestry convened on 10 December 1816 and elected a committee 'to plan for the Employment' of out-of-work labourers during the winter; their deliberations produced only a simple assertion that the 'principal Inhabitants' must aid the overseers in organising 'Works of public Utility'. Full employment recurrently appeared to be a thing of the past. In June 1817 farmers 'reluctantly assented' to increase the numbers hired on a commonly used ratio based on farm size, and the overseers were instructed to use every endeavour to 'put out ... the boys ... with those who will employ them'. Despite haymaking, the road surveyors were permitted to take as many hands as they required, with the costs funded from the poor rate. After the harvest all the unemployed were assigned to the surveyors, but this scheme was hotly and recurrently debated and narrowly survived five separate referrals to formal vestry votes between 8 December and 10 February. Attempts to simply reintroduce this plan in the autumn of 1818 foundered because the surveyors could not find work for the numbers eligible. Thereafter repetitive negotiations turned on trying to devise quotas which each farmer 'ought to employ according to their rental'. Inevitably, the 'very small Occupiers' considered that they got a raw deal under these type of arrangements, which were manipulated time after time in attempts to establish workable compromises. They all failed, and on 22 November 1821 a symbolic motion was formally passed on the workless:

> that as no other plan can be thought of to Employ them those who cannot get work must be kept by the Overseers.

Six days later this charter for work-free benefits was itself overturned with the reintroduction of a quota scheme; it soon collapsed as revealed by the vestry's despondent motion on 11 March 1822:

> that as no other plan can be thought of the Surveyors be requested to employ the Superfluous Hands and to pay them as much as their [straitened financial] Circumstances will admit of.

Scapegoats were now found in the labourers themselves, many of whom were accused of courting the sack 'by their bad conduct'; employers were to document reasons for future dismissals, and the work-discipline problem was further addressed in the following autumn when a new scheme based on parish directed farmwork on piece rates was tried. The situation improved in 1823 owing to a major road improvement project at nearby Uckfield, which Framfield exploited by renting a quarry to supply stone using the labour of the unemployed. Therefter, quarrying, combined with permutations of previous schemes, absorbed the unemployed during the winters, and tentative steps were taken to promote parish-funded emigration. In 1829 Framfield adopted the 'Oundle plan' which encouraged farmers to maintain men in work through calculating their poor-rate contributions against their labour bill. In 1832 the parish implemented the Labour Employment Act of that year which legitimised the Oundle plan by giving statutory authority for the raising of a labour rate.[61]

The records of scores of parishes reveal parallel histories, including the repeated failures of initiatives like Hartfield's make-work scheme to 'Inclose and Cultivate' parts of Ashdown Forest. Some villages financed temporary migrations in search of work, and one Sussex parish even paid two men 'their Expenses' to find winter employment in Hampshire.

Almost every poor-law authority increased its commitment to arranging work for children. Icklesham's wartime annual totals never exceeded ten, but by 1820 the vestry had twenty-six to place. Hartfield kept a record of its children's conduct and progress, which also reveals that many of the younger ones were not placed despite the reductions in numbers eligible achieved through upping the starting age from ten to eleven. Brede tried to make its youthful charges more attractive propositions by abandoning previous insistence that employers undertook responsibility for clothing, with the introduction of Saturday night laundering under the overseer's superintendance. Several parishes brushed aside parental objections and insisted that the offspring of poor-law claimants came into the workhouse; unemployed adolescents comprised one important category, but a handful of parishes adopted the same expedient with children aged seven to nine, whose workhouse residence was aimed to school them for future employment. Nevertheless, circumstances invariably ensured that employers retained the advantage, exemplified by the confident note penned by Mrs Ann Norman of Lye Green to 'the Gentleman Overseers of Hartfield' in May 1833; she

> Would be extreme Oblidged … if they would allow Mary Crowhurst a pair of Shoes and a New Gown, as She is a Good Girl and Suits me pretty well and I think of keeping her some Time if they will allow her a few Nessassry Articles to go clean and Decent but cannot Possible think of keeping her so Destitute as she is.

The recipients endorsed this missive, 'A pr Shoes – a Gown – and a few necessary Articles 2 checked Aprons 2 Changes' of underwear.[62]

Widespread resort to labour rates, despite all the permutations and difficult vestry politics, with larger farmers being opposed by their smaller counterparts and many tradesmen, dictated a broad South-eastern adoption of the Labour Employment Act; at least 107 parishes implemented it within weeks of its parliamentary passage, with 'dirty fellows' in one village seizing on the opportunity this provided to wring greater rate contributions from the tithe-owner. Although there were problems, especially with non-resident claimants who were generally excluded, successes were achieved. Rate reductions were normal; roadworkers were reduced from thirty to two at Bosham, winter unemployment was conquered at Warnham, and extensive land drainage which otherwise would not have been even contemplated, was carried out at Henfield. The regional Tory press extolled the Act's virtues, and several MPs fought hard but unsuccessfully against the Act's inevitable demise, in the parliamentary manoeuvres preceeding the passage of the Poor Law Amendment Act.[63]

The administrative records of the old poor law, and the judicial records of its ultimate control by the magistracy, reveal a picture at considerable variance with that contrived by the manipulations of the Poor Law Commission behind their 1834 report. Despite their concentration on rural England, the Commissioners eschewed systematic analysis of the agricultural depression, and their attention to tradesmen focused on their alleged exploitation of poor-law contracts for the supply of basic necessities. In fact, four basic considerations dictated increasing resort to contracts. First, the payment of relief in kind reduced claimants' opportunities to spend benefits on alcohol. Second, contracting allowed economies of scale. Third, many decisions to enter into contracts were taken in response to liquidity problems, and therefore eased – be it temporarily – vestries' cash-flow problems. Fourth, contracts represented negotiations whereby non-farming interest groups could be accommodated and compensated in various ways. The nature of compensation to shopkeepers and millers is obvious, but that to other tradesmen less clear; contracts with shoemakers and tailors to supply poor-law claimants, and with carpenters, plumbers and builders to repair parish and other properties owned by claimants, were also manipulated as a form of public aid without the stigma of poor-relief, and was important for hard-pressed family businesses. This is not to deny the validity of the Commissioners' identification of nepotism and corruption. The history of contracting at Framfield reveals the manoeuvres of a 'combination of Millers to fleece the parish', recurrent furious vestry debates with contradictory terminations and renewals of contracts, and further complications deriving from repeated appeals to the magistracy; the record permits a rare insight into the opaque world of vestry politics, and serves to emphasise the ferocity of disputes between interest groups where negotiations failed to establish mutually acceptable compensations.[64]

Hartfield represented hundreds of vestries which lurched from liquidity crisis to liquidity crisis. In 1817 a majority voted to summons rate defaulters, 'Determined that it must be done for the want of Money to pay the Poor'. Cash-flow problems were repeatedly advanced in explanation of delayed payments, notably to non-resident claimants, one of whom was informed that 'The Money Matters of this parish get Worse and Worse'. An emergency vestry convened in June 1826 to agree ways of 'preventing the impending Ruin now hanging over their Heads', and decided to seek a £200 loan, only to be told by the leading Lewes bank – in a response which speaks volumes – that 'it is not our Practice to advance any Sum beyond three Months, and in no Cases for Parish purposes'. The loan eventually materialised from a private source which required the intervention of the village's most prestigious resident, the Dean of Chichester, who normally remained aloof from vestry affairs. Continued desperation drove the vestry to compound bastardy payments, including that obtained from Richard Thomas who handed over £36 – in annual payments of £5 – which saved him at least £25, and effectively created a breach for the parish to bridge at some point in the future. A major assault on Hartfield's financial morass came in 1830–31 under the auspices of a local grandee, Earl Delawarr, who designed a package comprising an emigration fund, a labour rate, and a major reallocation of workhouse facilities to permit

'Classification of the Inmates', which effectively implemented a central tenet of utilitarian thought on social security.[65]

Cost-containment characterised old poor-law administrations in the last two decades of the system when the numbers of claimants rose dramatically. The most poignant strategy in this cause was the appointment of salaried, assistant overseers, who were expected to effect economies through having a global overview of parochial social-security affairs. The breadth of duties was typically specified by Brede which first appointed an assistant in 1826. For an annual salary of £70, and expenses of five shillings for attendance at the Petty Sessions, he was to supervise pauper labour on the roads, distribute workers under the labour rate, govern the workhouse, and collect the rates; he was also to thoroughly investigate the precise circumstances of all existing and new claimants, and inform himself of any changes, so that his employers would be equipped with detailed intelligence when taking further vestry decisions. A majority of parishes who experimented with such appointments were convinced that an overall, and some said considerable, saving was achieved, despite the salary paid.[66]

The South-eastern magistracy fully entered into this spirit despite the strictures, alleging that they over-ruled cost-conscious parish officers and vestries, advanced by the Poor Law Commissioners.[67] Although the Battle Bench had on occasion to specifically order 'the Overseer to see that the Paupers do not suffer', and on others supported claimants who protested, including the four bachelors who refused work offered by the Northiam vestry at derisory wages,[68] none of their decisions in the post-war period represents liberal let alone generous treatment of appellants. Many had no orders made at all.[69] The Bench enquired into earnings, and those like Spears of Sedlescombe who 'earned 12s a Week until Whitsuntide and since has had Work in Harvest', and another who it was 'proved ... had earned 65£ in the last Year', were unsuccessful. Bricklayer Harmer of Ashburnham who had 'earned 19s a Week all the Summer & probably £1–10s a Week – now earns but 10s a Week', had his appeal dismissed in January 1826. James Briant's appeal was also rejected as 'when he is breaking Horses he earns 15/6' weekly. Samuel Pollard's 'Wife's Hopping Money' was ordered to be handed over 'for Rent for the House bel[ongin]g to the Parish'.[70] The Bench certainly supported vestries who penalised the insubordinate. Failed appeals included three Ewhurst men who 'Misbehaved & neglected to apply their Earnings', and butcher Springett of the same village as the assistant 'Overseer proved that he was drunk a few Days before'. Claimant Buggins of Hooe got his new hat and shoes, but was ordered to repay the parish and warned that 'if he does not support himself' he would 'be sent to Prison'. Appellants who 'refused to answer the Magistrates questions', got short shrift; on Samuel Shardwell's 'Impertinent' response – 'There is no Justice done here' – he was 'committed to Gaol', and his release made conditional on providing 'Sureties for good Behaviour'. The Bench also threatened innkeepers, who permitted 'tippling ... by Paupers who are notoriously chargeable to Parishes', with the loss of their licenses, and decreed that publicans displayed parochial lists of claimants. Marital irregularities invariably evoked a harsh response; the Bench endorsed Bexhill's decision to 'refuse Work' to John Evenden 'in Consequence' of his having 'parted with his Wife & lives with another Woman'. William Catt was instructed to 'live together' with his wife before any aid would be considered, and Charlotte Brett, whose labouring 'Husband ... turned her out of doors', was given 'No order for dress beyond a Pauper's Station'. Considerations relating to property and affluent relations also evoked further judicial hardness. In November 1821 the Bench ruled that

> In future Orders to be made on Parents & Grandfathers to maintain there Children & Grand Children wholly as long as they have any Property,

a ruling subsequently enforced against the father-in-law of a transportee. The Bench ruled that Thomas Coleman's 'House be sold & then to be entitled to Relief'; as Henry Freeland 'has expectation of' inheriting 'Property', Sedlescombe was 'To find him Work or advance him Money on loan'.[71]

In this context the experiences of Sir Charles Goring, a West Sussex magistrate since the 1770s, are symbolic. In the 1790s Goring chaired the Steyning Petty Sessions, and secured agreement that child allowances should be paid for the third, and further children, in labourers' families. This was challenged in the high price year of 1812, when a ratepayers' action group formed to 'oppose the interference of Magistrates respecting poor relief'. The dispute went on for years, and became acerbic once the depression commenced. Goring was accused of failing to discriminate between 'deserving and undeserving' claimants, and a committee – chaired by an Anglican clergyman – took to pamphleteering. The Committee boasted that

> they have not shrank from remonstrance with the magistrates, and asserting the right they possess of making *such* allowance only to the poor as they, in conjunction with the parish officers, deem reasonable.

Handbills were also distributed warning claimants against appeals to the Bench, as they would incur the legal costs, 'loose their day's work ... and in all probability have their allowance further reduced'. The committee engineered a test case, and challenged the validity of Goring's orders at the Quarter Sessions. Goring lost, the committee's chairman was voted a 50 guinea piece of plate, by 22 local luminaries, led by Lieutenant-General Sir R. Jones.[72] Some Benches were not only conscious of experimentation elsewhere with utilitarian principles, but implemented them. The Battle Bench purchased a copy of C.D. Brereton's pamphlet on the poor law on publication in 1825, and three copies of the Rev. Becher's 1828 *Anti-*

Pauper System.[73] Their East Grinstead counterparts distributed handbills detailing economies made in Berkshire and publicised in the *Quarterly Review.*[74] In May 1826 this Bench launched a major initiative, advising parishes to cease direct hiring of cottages, and aid with rent payments, to which was added an instruction to terminate automatic child allowances for the fourth and further children in families, and take them into the workhouse for employment with 'Religious and useful Instruction'. Unemployment pay was to be restricted to those with documentary proof that they had unsuccessfully applied for work to the 'twelve principal Occupiers of Land' in the village.[75] In this climate vestries could confidently stand up to claimants like John Standen of Fittleworth who 'threatened to go to the Bench', and respond to characters like William Price who refused to leave the workhouse by ordering his eviction by the police, and 'came to the Conclusion not to relieve him until ordered to do so by A Magistrate'. There was more than polemic in the claim, that for those

> indebted to their parish for a meagre weekly pittance, that scarcely suffices to keep off starvation ... apply to the Bench who ... treat their complaints with indifference, frequently with hautiness and severe reproof, coldly admonishing them to make great exertions to get work in their own parish.[76]

It must be emphasised that these findings, especially the contradictions between the actual history of judicial intervention as revealed by Petty Sessions' minutes, and the claims of utilitarian polemicists, including the Poor Law Commissioners themselves, are of major significance for the pre-1834–5 expansion of the social-security system, *and* its effective contraction under the Poor Law Amendment Act. Much more research is required to assess whether the actual history established here is representative of other rural regions.

V. THE NEW POOR LAW

In Nassau Senior's eyes the radicalism of the Poor Law Amendment Act focused on 'the most extensive and most important of all *political* relationships, the relation between the employer and the labourer' [cited, *Dunkley*, 1981; 139]. Despite South-eastern attempts by administrative and judicial authorities to minimise costs, the assistant poor-law commissioners who arrived over the winter of 1834–5, correctly emphasised the old system's deep entrenchment in the region and the scale of dependency on it. Able-bodied males' outdoor relief in its many forms was the Act's principal target, and those who were unable to survive independently – with the sole exception of medical aid – faced incarceration in the deterrent workhouse. Much recent writing on the Act's implementation and subsequent administration has had an urban focus [*Fraser*, 1976; *Rose*, 1972 and 1985]. Rural studies have 'emphasized

continuity between pre- and post reform administration', thereby mini-
mising the radical impact of the new law in stark contrast to its radical
intent: scholars' emphasis has been on circumvention and evasion of the
key components through several major expedients, with charity filling
some of the voids created by the demise of the old system. While there is
much supporting evidence, and if we need more local and regional studies,
recent investigators of Buckinghamshire, have correctly complained that
'we are now confronted with a new orthodoxy that threatens to explain
away the significance of the New Poor Law altogether' [*Apfel and
Dunkley*, 1985: 37–8, 67–8]. This would do great violence to realities, as
the following discussion of the very rich South-eastern evidence reveals.[77]

The new system was bitterly hated and induced 'an undefined terror'
from its inception amongst its principal targets:

> the poor are stunned; a law has come upon them, for which they are
> not prepared ... .poorhouses are suddenly springing up ... with the
> outward appearance of a prison ... .the consequence is that they are
> completely stunned ... that feeling ought [not] to be supposed to rise
> from any acquiescence on the part of the poor in the new law.

Even after five years 'many men are found abusing the new Poor Law ...
with the most violent and unmitigated rancour'; Boards of Guardians
were said to treat appellants 'as criminals', notably *ex officio* members,
the magistrates, whose judicial functions encouraged them 'to suppose
that every ... applicant must be a "Liar and a Vagabond" '.[78]

Distressing scenes were everyday occurrences at workhouses. When a
family of ten arrived at Westhampnett workhouse 'all crying together',
the mother broke down completely when routinely subjected to medical
examination and became

> very much excited and expressed a great dislike to have her hands
> and arms examined and said it would break her heart to remain there
> four and twenty hours ... .she would not have come into the Union
> only she was in hopes the Guardians would have allowed her
> something out of the house.

The impressive catalogue of workhouse scandals publicised by *The Times*,
could be greatly extended by those achieving but a local notoriety,
including the Horsham workhouse chaplain who prevented unmarried
mothers attending their babies' christenings to impose a 'marked distinction ... between honest & respectable women and abandoned &
worthless ... Females'. Deaths of inmates repeatedly galvanised hostile
rumours which were countered only by 'useful post mortems and
inquests'; so too could alleged deaths from starvation outside the house,
as 'when the public sympathy was excited, it was usual to cast odium on
public' authorities.[79] Fear of imminent incarceration – 'coming to the
union' – lay behind scores of suicide attempts, many of which succeeded.[80]

The new law put a priceless premium on employment, reflected in 'a general improvement in the Conduct of Agricultural Labourers and a great wish to procure and keep Employment for themselves and Children'. Labourer Cox agreed that 'the men had to be more submissive ... because there were so many out of employment', and this encouraged employers to discriminate; 'we have made friends of our best labourers', opined John Ellman, 'and put the others at defiance, and that is as the thing should be'.[81] Yet a high proportion of farmers adhered to traditional practices, namely winter-time lay-offs, and in the later 1830s many farmworkers were driven into workhouses at some point in the winter; the Uckfield Union even rationalised expenditure on the workhouse chapel as it could be converted to additional dormitory space to cope with winter peaks. Gradually farmers realised that incarcerating family men inflated parochial contributions to Union funds, and 'tacit understandings' at village level dictated the discriminatory employment of married men, at the expense of bachelors. The latter were assumed to be able to survive through summer and harvest wages, and any casual earnings obtained during the remainder of the year. Although it was said that 'idle and profligate' able-bodied men refused to enter workhouses, it was also confidently claimed that 'labourers of bad character' were 'kept in a workhouse by farmers ... who will not employ men of bad character'.[82]

The Act had a confused and contradictory effect on the housing market. It terminated public aid towards rent payments for the able-bodied, and it encouraged parishes to sell off cottages, notably to finance parochial contributions to the cost of erecting the new workhouses. But such sales had their dangers when bought by speculators who further sub-divided properties and increased densities of poor inhabitants; some philanthropic individuals purchased these premises for conversion to a 'properly conducted Alms House'. Other parishes, unable to sell dilapidated houses, turned a blind eye, and sitting tenants went on living in rent-free tumbledown premises for years; time eroded legal arrangements, as at East Grinstead, where 'Parties transferred their right' to what originally were 'almshouses by selling the key', assuming 'that buying the key was the same as buying and selling the property'. The occupiers used 'every contrivance for keeping falling and tottering walls together' for decades.[83] Nevertheless, the Act's implementation was accompanied by numerous evictions, both by public and private owners, and this dual offensive accounted for some of the earliest workhouse inmates, many of whom were elderly. Henry Climpson, whom we encountered living rent-free in a parish house at Pevensey, soon gave up the struggle to pay the rent imposed after 1835, and left. Some major landlords, including Lord Egremont, recognised changed economic realities, and reduced rents, but speculative cottage proprietors were 'generally' able to exploit the unremitting demand to preserve 'exorbitantly high' rents, while being disinclined to attempt even urgent repairs. In this situation, the most squalid accommodation retained its value, and it was only in the relatively few South-eastern 'close' parishes that dominant landlords were able to reduce the impoverished sector of the population by demolishing hovels. ' "We must get rid of these people" ', opined Colonel Wyndham to the Duke of Richmond, a fellow owner of broad West Sussex acres, with reference to 'surplus labour' in 1845.[84]

Market conditions ensured that the provision of adequate housing for farmworkers remained uneconomic. In 1843 it was estimated that a single cottage cost £80 to erect, while in 1863 the building of 'double-tenement cottages' with brick walls and a tiled roof was costed at £160; adding a third bedroom brought the sum to £200, and by 1870 other estimates put it even higher at £400. New buildings were principally erected by speculative 'little tradesmen' in the long-established tradition of the 'old lath and plaster or rattle and dab rubbish', and even those 'brick and stone cottages' built were 'indifferently ... run up'. Many conversions led to three or more tenement dwellers sharing an oven. Reports also abound of working families living in 'mud cottages, not of any value, which if uninhabited would fall down within ... a very few months'. At Burpham farmworker Knight paid a weekly shilling for a windowless place with 'the rafters ... falling in', and the Stoner family lived near Horsham in a hovel, erected in 1860, '12 ft by 8 ft and about $4\frac{1}{2}$ ft high, with a hole at the top for the smoke to go out when they had a fire'. One of farmer Hinchnott's tied cottages on Tunbridge Wells Common – inhabited in 1847 by an employee of 'many years' – was rented at three shillings weekly.

> The windows were all broken in; the tiles were off the roof; the stairs were so broken down that it was scarcely safe to ascend them: there were neither sewers nor privy.[85]

The new Act's aggravation of the economically and demographically determined pressures on plebeian housing also had environmental ramifications. High rents dictated the taking of lodgers, and entire families regularly shared one bedroom. Additional overcrowding often derived from the Act's stipulation that children contributed to the costs of maintaining elderly parents; at Cudham between 1840 and 1854, ploughman Beagley's mother shared one of the two bedrooms with his four children. Landlords commonly discriminated against fathers of big families, fearing that their living costs would lead to difficulty with rent payments; typically, 'no one' at Staplehurst 'seemed disposed to accept' Isaac Bromley 'as a tenant ... as he had a large family'. Housing was a severe problem for family men who were forced into workhouses; if household goods could be stored by relatives and friends, tenancies could not be maintained, and getting out of the workhouse necessitated obtaining a job and a house. Two families from Chalvington and Selmeston, with thirteen children between them, had resided in West Firle workhouse for 'a long time', but their heads refused jobs offered as 'they cannot any where get a House'; despite the fact that ratepayers from both parishes registered 'great complaint' at the costs incurred, 'no one in either ... will let them a Cottage'.[86]

Rents maintained an upward spiral across the rural South-east until the 1880s, when depopulation at last reduced pressures revealed by unprecedented untenanted cottages. By then campaigns in the 1860s and 1870s had emphasised loathsome housing conditions, and equally abysmal environmental contexts,[87] echoing less-well publicised exposures under the stimulus of cholera in the later 1840s. At Hurst Green in the High Weald, with a population of only 300 in 1853,

> divers most extensive nuisances of the most pernicious & offensive kinds, consisting of over-flowing privies, drains, cess pools, pig sties & the filthy emanations of a slaughter house, are in existence contiguous to many houses in the locality, resulting in the most noxious gases & contaminating the wells from which the water for all domestic purposes is procured.

Rural Boards of Guardians principally eshewed using their new powers under the public health legislation rushed through during the cholera epidemic in 1848, and later additions were rarely used, not least because of ratepayer resistance to incurring the costs of any initiative. Continued indifference characterised the rest of our period, with one main exception, namely such owners of extensive estates, who rebuilt cottage accommodation and introduced adequate sewage facilities in their villages; their cottage rents, it was tellingly said, 'do not represent anything like their value ... extremely low rents in proportion to the cost of building' and sanitation.[88]

Discriminatory employment and housing usually went together to benefit the same workers. 'In the country villages' in the Alton district of Hampshire,

> the cottages are kept for the choicest men; those who are remarkable for strength, skill or character. The reduced cottage room in the close parishes, with the selection of the tenants, acts as a premium for good character, as the superior men always have the preference for a cottage when one falls vacant.

The Act permitted social sanitisation. At Fletching for example, the Rev. Wilde targeted six families, the girls from three of which were 'avowed Prostitutes', resident in a publicly-owned tenement building which functioned as the 'Parish Brothel', and arranged their eviction to create 'a more orderly & moral population in the Village'. The result here was no doubt a permutation of the situation at Alton, where 'The inferior labourers ... are compelled to reside at a distance, mostly ... at the market town, and walk to and from their work daily'. The Act also directly stimulated a panic migration to the towns; Brighton was inundated with 'poor persons from neighbouring villages' desperately seeking work as early as March 1836, and Fordington, the 'poor suburb' of Dorchester, was swamped 'by an influx of surplus agricultural labourers, discontented and disowned'. When Rye resorted to the settlement laws in 1840, expulsions to twelve Kent and Sussex villages transpired. Climpson left his Pevensey parish cottage to reside in Eastbourne, where he worked as a builder's labourer, and William Trigwell, a New Poor Law protester from Ringmer, went via a spell in Chailey workhouse to a job at a Brighton laundry. Others, like William Frost, took a town tenement, and walked daily to their farmwork, in his case the five mile round trip from Chichester to Westhampnett. The ratio of men like Frost, to those like Climpson and Trigwell is undiscoverable, but the latter category was sufficiently large in Brighton for radicals to denounce the 'consequence ... wages were reduced'.[89]

This influx also aggravated poor urban conditions, typified by those at Maidstone, which included abysmal housing and an environment traditionally associated with Victorian London and the industrial cities. The Medway was a giant sewer and 'received ... the filth of the town', especially 'decomposing animal and vegetable substances' from the premises of butchers, fellmongers and dyers; huge deposits of this effluent was periodically swept away by opening the sluices, but the stench was perennial. Much plebeian accommodation was located in numerous 'narrow courts and alleys', characterised by

> accumulation of ashes and filth, and the almost total want or neglect of drainage in all of them with ... open pools in several; the total abandonment of decency and cleanliness, in the limited number and construction, and filthy condition of the privies; and the nuisance arising ... from the overflowing of the same, and leakage into dwelling houses and wells ... .the home drainage, and even the underground drainage ... appears to be totally neglected or from faulty construction have become worst than useless.

Sharp's Yard typically contained thirteen houses and a beershop, with the occupants and customers competing to use the four privies, which were also used for 'slops', and were – not surprisingly – in an 'offensive and unwholesome condition'. A huge rubbish tip, with a leaven of human excrement deriving from pressure on the lavatories, comprised the central feature of this location. St Faith's Green houses were 'over-run with ... rats' who attacked sleeping children. In 1849 fifty percent of working-class infants died by the age of five. Herculean efforts by civic leaders to sanitise the town recurrently foundered on the antipathy of the rate-payers, with the result that even by 1872 the 'sanitary conditions are very far from efficient'. Migration to such towns may have improved agricultural labourers' purchasing powers, through the greater availability of women's and child's work, even for those who continued in farmwork, though even poorer housing and environmental conditions cannot have improved living standards.[90]

Social conditions were commensurately horrendous. Teenagers Eliza Beach and Sophia Headen, who may have originated from places like the Fletching brothel, rented rooms with board at ten shillings a week along with 'the rest of the girls' from widow Harris in Stone Street; Harris lamely expressed surprise that 'the watchman made any complaint', as 'When the Girls get a little drink they will sing', but Eliza deposed that

> it frequently happens that Men send for Liquor and Mrs Harris fetches it and she always keeps the Change – and it was my agreement with her that she was to have the privelege [profit] of the Drink.

Sailor John Little, reduced to 'travelling about the Country selling Matches and Ballads..took up ... Lodgings' in the same district, in a room containing three beds shared by six occupants, including William White; Little awoke to find White 'playing with my prick', and a major brawl erupted. William Stroud was the proprietor of another Stone Street lodging house, and 'occasionally employed' widow Arnold 'to make the Beds'; one of her more erotic experiences came when she encountered two seriously maimed and drunken men, rollicking in the straw, each literally legless on two counts, and observed that 'Gill had George's Tool in his hand. I mean his Private Parts'. The Broyle Row in Chichester resembled Stone Street, and hosted an exotic miscellany of characters in addition to farmworker Frost; they included Joe Sims who obtained a 'living by selling Books and Songs', and Bill Singer who made a livelihood 'by mending Umbrellas and buying and selling old rags': among the other neighbours were 'a crockery ware man', a 'wireworker', a 'Cordwainer & Broker', together with more hawkers, chimney sweeps, and casual labourers, several of whom 'can lodge at the Wellington' with Sims, where he amused customers with pornographic ditties in exchange for drinks. Petty disturbances were so common on the Row that Mary Town did not 'take much notice of a Scuffle as they are often quarrelling'. The Row's counterpart at Lewes – Castle Banks – was said in 1863 to be 'worse than St Giles', the notorious metropolitan rookery, 'as the neighbourhood was in ... continual uproar' generated by argumentative residents.[91]

These details emphasise that country towns were a magnet for vagrants. The mendicancy problem was not new; one climax was experienced in the immediate post-war years, but the Amendment Act served to seriously aggravate an existing problem, in both urban and rural locations. The vicar of Rumboldswick, Sussex, reported a huge increase in mendicants in 1837, principally 'agricultural labourers ... driven from their own parish', and the chief of Chichester police confirmed that numerous 'able-bodied, young men of very decent appearance ... repeatedly' told his officers that 'they cannot procure work in their own parishes, and say, they are told to go about the country and seek for employment'. But the Act's impact was not restricted to youngsters. Evicted families took up residence in barns, or went on the road living in tents and vans. The numbers of families abandoned by fathers increased dramatically. Even West Firle Union 'lying out of a direct line from one great Town to any other', and 'not in the direct road' for seasonal migrants, experienced an 'increase ... a great many more applications for a nights lodgings ... than we ought to have, according to the spirit of the New Poor Law'. In April 1841 the Uckfield Union converted its workhouse stables to a vagrant ward, and farmers in the same Wealden district responded to the 'many who travel and lay about' by insisting that such people slept in outbuildings, rather than barns, and lit fires only in the open air. In the 1840s the scale of mendicancy was immeasurably inflated by vast numbers of Irish escaping famine conditions at home.[92]

Police reform, commencing with the creation of the Metropolitan Police in 1829, served to aggravate the vagrancy problem in the country-side prior to the 1834 Act. In 1833 the chair of the Hampshire Sessions claimed that police activity in London served to drive mendicants into his rural domain. By the mid-1830s a seasonal pattern was observable with youths from 'St Giles and other infamous neighbourhoods, pour[ing] themselves periodically over the face of the country'. The creation of rural police forces under the 1839–40 legislation, which was initially adopted by Hampshire and East Sussex, was said to have a similar effect, with the latter for example 'driving all our rogues into the Western Division' of the county. Occasional offensives by urban forces, including that mounted by the Brighton police in 1844, had a similar effect. Pressure on mendicants increased with the passage of the compulsory 1856 legis-lation which established professional police forces universally. 'Before', claimed a West Sussex JP in 1863, 'these vagrants used to stop in hovels and outbuildings. Now they were dislodged from these places … and were driven to the union house'. Rural unions, among them Steyning and Thakeham, saw the numbers of wanderers admitted over-night, rise from half yearly totals of 289 and thirteen, to 1185 and 790 respectively.[93]

It is difficult to distinguish between itinerants, gypsies and vagrants, not least because so many reports lumped them together. 'Hoards of wander-ing gypsies' were relentlessly reported, and if they had a distinguishing feature, it was their caravans, horses. cattle and pigs, 'encamped where they please' on roadsides, commons, woodland clearances, and waste land. Most dealt promiscuously in goods ranging from horses to baskets. An experienced poor-law official noted in 1850 that wayfarers originating from 'London and other large Towns' were intermixed with 'idle and dissolute persons … who systematically passed the summer months in wandering' through the countryside. The latter often came from the villages, and suggest that younger people, especially those discriminated against by employers, adopted a semi-mendicant life, with recourse to workhouse vagrant wards, notably during the most adverse winter-time weather.[94]

Two critical factors militated against the full and potentially explosive, if not revolutionary impact of the Amendment Act. First, the strict letter of the law was evaded. Secondly, the survival of outdoor relief to non-able-bodied males meant that the vast majority of those still seen to have a legitimate claim on the state, survived outside the workhouse. When the Croydon Union insisted that all recipients of outdoor relief presented themselves for inspection in 1839, over a thousand materialised:

> Widows and orphans, the aged, the lame and the blind, in short all those who, by favour or the interference of friends, could obtain the smallest relief, and such an accumulation of poverty and misery combined could hardly have equalled – the sight was heart sickening in the highest degree.

The scale of human misery and personal disaster was far too huge for the free market or unrestrained agrarian capitalism; it was beyond the resources actually tappable by utilitarian philosophy. The essential failure of the state to rigorously reinforce the main elements of the Victorian Poor Law – at least before the 1870s – derived not simply from all the internal contradictions trapped within the fusion of the capitalist economy and the utilitarian social security system, but also from socio-political considerations emanating from the resistance to, and protest at the new law. A combination of protest and social-security logistics ultimately played a part in preventing further progress down the road towards institutionalised solutions to the poverty problem. If they thus ensured some continuties between the old and new systems as theatres of conflict and protest, there were significant shifts in both to which we must now turn.[95]

VI. SOCIAL PROTEST

Historians of social protest commonly attempt to quantify their findings, and assume – erroneously – that disturbances invariably leave traces in the sources [*Williams*, 1976; cf. *Wells*, 1978]. The scale of eighteenth-century conflict over poaching, and the inexorable strengthening of statute law for its repression, has been recognised [*Munsche*, 1981]. Conversely, the apparent absence of protest against parliamentary enclosure, comprises a major unanswered problem, notably now when a general consensus concedes that the enclosure of commons, waste and forest-land, seriously disadvantaged both the lesser dual occupationists and the burgeoning rural proletariat, by removing customary sources of supplementary income;[96] if protest was so muted, then English land privatisation emerges as unique on the world's stage. In fact many enclosure experts concentrate on costs, precise legal ownership, diffusion and chronology, and protest is rarely registered in their sources; however, specific enquiry, notably by Dr Neeson in Northamptonshire, reveals miscellaneous hostile reactions, both overt and covert protest, if with little serious social violence.[97] Dr Bushaway's inspiring study of popular customs, includes St Andring, when rampaging crowds ostensibly squirrel-hunting, in fact had a secretive 'primary aim', damaging fences and hedges. Indeed, the English customary calendar provided numerous opportunities for 'robust, aggressive, demanding and far from deferential' collective celebration, which invariably symbolised conflict between groups and facilitated 'ritual demonstration of strength by the labouring poor' [*Bushaway*, 1982: 180–81]. Although, as we have mentioned, the South-east experienced relatively little parliamentary enclosure, it is surely significant that at least one exceptional area, on the West Sussex–Hampshire border, was so recurrently disturbed by St Andring celebrations, that a sustained legal offensive was launched against it in the 1790s.[98] There is little published evidence of the poor-law as a centre for pre-1790 conflict, but this may reflect the absence of Petty Sessions' records [*Neuman*, 1982: 166 and n.77]; where they are extant, as for Battle and West Malling, a pronounced contrast emerges between judicial intervention, before and after the French Wars. But conflict did erupt before the 1790s; Thomas Court 'behaved ... scurrilously ... indecently and in a contemptuous manner' when his 1787 appeal was rejected by the Malling Bench, and he was locked up 'for abusing us ... in the execution of our Office'. If vestry room squabbles largely eluded the minutes, they were regularly logged in Thomas Turner's diaries; 'all noise and discord' characterised many meetings, with 'volleys of execrable oaths' juxtaposed with 'obscenity and raillery', 'resound[ing] from all sides of the room'.[99]

The defects in our knowledge of the scale and incidence of social protest can be exemplified by a re-examination of food rioting in the South-east. Professor Clark established that Kent witnessed repeated mobilisations – principally by cloth and iron workers – to implement the 'moral economy' over subsistence matters in the sixteenth and seventeenth centuries [*Clark*, 1976]. Andrew Charlesworth's *Atlas* of social protest reveals no South-eastern food rioting between 1660 and 1737, only one in the famine year of 1740, and a mere three in 1756–57, a national crisis galvanising disturbances 'amongst the most severe of the eighteenth century' [*Charlesworth*, 1983: 80–85]. There were none in 1766–7, an even worse crisis, and that responsible for the fiercest rioting nationally, before the 1790s. Such relative South-eastern tranquillity could be attributed to the virtual demise of the cloth and iron industries, and such an interpretation is fortified by the 1772 disturbances in rural Essex, in which textile workers predominated.[100] Moreover, the conservation of local grain stocks and their sale at reduced prices under the auspices of poor-law authorities, was relatively easy in rural parishes, as exemplified by the response of the Uffington vestry in Berkshire to the autumn 1766 crisis; two emergency rates were voted to purchase wheat for sale to labourers at prices conditioned by family size.[101] While in-service persisted on the farms, a smaller percentage of the agrarian workforce was exposed to market prices. However, Charlesworth's catalogues are deficient; additional South-eastern incidents include an attack on a Surrey market gardener in 1740, attempts to mobilise the populace of Tenterden against farmers and millers in 1768, the same year in which the Hastings crowd descended on farmers in the adjacent countryside. In 1757 the Lewes district experienced repetitive disturbances. Turner accused 'many great farmers' of withholding corn despite 'very dear' prices, and noted that massive purchases by one merchant sparked appeals to the Bench; several farmers were summonsed for refusals to sell corn, but this failed to remedy all grievances, and cereal shipments were stopped from leaving the ports and also interrupted in a number of inland locations. This suggests the involvement of farmworkers, as does the intelligence that Lewes activists were drawn from 'several neighbouring parishes'.[102]

No revision of the scale of eighteenth-century social protest in the South-east is likely to alter the identification of the 1790s as a watershed in rural history. However, the diversity of the regional response to the famines and other problems of that decade, was underestimated in my original article. Many market towns experienced disturbances in the spring of 1795, and the intensity of riot was inflated by the participation of several Militia regiments on the side of the populace, which culminated in the spectacular mutiny of the Oxfordshire Militia and its two-day take-over of Newhaven to prevent coastal shipments of corn. The scale of disturbances is not revealed by reports sent to the Home Office by magistrates, press coverage, or resort to legal repression, but in the severance of mercantile contracts to supply grain to the South-west, and the recourse of local millers to secret, overland carriage of flour to the London market during the summer months. South-eastern market towns provided the foci for further food-rioting in the spring of 1796, the spring and autumn of 1800, and early in 1801; farmworkers were regular participants, and they also figured in the widespread protests against a short-lived economy measure, the Brown Bread Act, which facilitated adulteration.[103]

The 1790s did not witness a simple resort to food rioting on the traditional model; food prices, wages and – crucially – poor relief levels were increasingly juxtaposed. On 2 February 1795 a petition signed by forty-three men 'was presented to the Overseer and other Inhabitants' of Hartfield:

> Gentlemen. We ... do give this as a Humble Petition to bag the faver that you will think and Consider to Lower the Price of flour to Six Shillings pr. Bushell – Otherwise we are under great Nessety of Raising our Wages 6d pr Day as Every Commodity is so Dear that it is impossoble for we poor Men to Maintain our familys.

Farmworkers in some Kent and Sussex villages struck for higher wages during the 1794–95 winter, and in the following spring; at Edenbridge a number were prosecuted for conspiring to 'force and compel the Farmers ... to raise the Wages and prices of work', a demarcation reflecting the growing importance of piece-work. Sussex also saw prosecutions, and farmworkers' adoption of trade unionist tactics foundered on the convictions brought in at the Sessions and Assizes by juries dominated by farmers. Nevertheless, the strike option survived, as revealed by the invasion of Lewes in February 1801 by 300 workers from Chiddingly, East Hoathly, Framfield and Buxted. The latter contingent 'had set out with the Determination of lowering the price of Provisions' in orthodox style, but the Framfield component 'had determined unless they lived better "to throw off labour"'. The remainder insisted on increased parochial relief. Justice Shadwell

> After remonstrating with them on the Impropriety & Illegality of coming in such numerous Bodies ... ordered the Parish Officers who did not appear to be wrote to ordering them to call Vestries for ... enlarging the Relief.

During the nineties, the Bench took a relatively firm line with those who resorted to riotous means to prise out greater aid payments, for example by imprisoning men who mobbed the Cocking vestry for an increase in allowances in-aid-of wages, but responded favourably to peaceful lobbying, exemplified by orders to Hurstpierpoint overseers to pay between two and eight shillings a week to the 25 family men who collectively presented their case to the magistrates in March 1795.[104]

My original identification of the escalating importance of arson in this wartime scenario of protest requires some revision. Incendiarism in earlier crises, including 1740 and 1766, was clearly designed to enforce 'moral economy'.[105] Arson was also a weapon deployed against enclosure [*Neeson*, 1984: 345, 352–3], and attempts to restrict commoners' rights in Ashdown Forest in 1810–11, galvanised so many 'threatening letters, and the burning of buildings and stacks', that an Anglican vicar was alleged to have used it as a cover for firing his own house in order to claim the insurance.[106] The threat of arson – 'which was expected to be done' – was made against an early experimenter with a threshing machine in Surrey in 1791. Moreover, in the 1790s poor-law officials who were also farmers, were not the sole targets of arsonists; incendiarism was adopted in other disputes, including that between hop-growers and itinerant hop-pickers at Farnham in 1801.[107] South-eastern incendiarism declined between 1802 and 1809, reflecting more stable prices, the successful mediation of the Bench between capital and labour in the form of systemised relief schemes, and some improvement – notably for younger farmworkers – in living standards when compared to the nineties. The recurrence of subsistence problems in 1810–2 stimulated further significant recourse to arson. The strength of the incendiary tradition locally, can be seen in tenant farmer Hodson's creation of a night 'watch ... from fear' stimulated by arson threats in 1813; his predecessor had been a victim in 1806.[108]

The post-war erosion of the judiciary's successful mediation between labour and capital, as poor-law authorities desperately tried to reduce expenditure while at the same time becoming responsible for an ever-increasing proportion of working-class inhabitants, turned relief administration into a battleground. Burwash's experiences here were typical, as revealed by the geographical spread of examples across Sussex, which I have catalogued elsewhere [*Wells*, 1988a]. However, my critics correctly suggested that covert protest was accompanied by overt forms. If South-eastern events of 1816–17 were a mere echo of the fiercer East Anglian revolt, the former included thoroughly orthodox resort to food-rioting, intermixed with incendiarism again in defence of common rights, and also against threshing-machine users.[109] Comparisons between the two regions, suggest that Charlesworth's identification of the importance of textile workers – their industry now in terminal decline – in the East Anglian protests was accurate [*Charlesworth*, 1980: 107–9/60–62; cf. *Evans*, 1985: esp.152–9]. The 1822 crisis, universally the worst year of the agricultural depression, reveals greater similarity between the two regions; arson dominated protests in both, and victims included poor-law officials, threshing-machine owners, and in Sussex, at least one tithe-owner, reflecting the growing antipathy to the clergy's exactions. If protest was less fierce in the South-east, it precipitated a rush by farmers to insure their properties despite this additional drain on their diminished resources.[110]

Manipulations ensured that press coverage of incendiarism was mini-mised. Somewhat later an insurance company informed the Home Secretary that

> We have endeavoured to discourage the frequent mention of these Acts in the Newspapers, thinking that such descriptions might set others on to produce similar devastations.

Later, between 1832 and 1834, Cobbett used his *Political Register* to circumvent this device.[111] Animal maiming in Sussex in 1802 was casti-gated as un-English, but by 1815 no such emotive responses seemed relevant.[112] The scale of malicious damage, which appears to have peaked in 1822, was also seriously under-reported, as privately admitted by the editor of the *Maidstone Gazette*.[113] The record of overt protest is probably almost equally defective. Minor affrays, notably against overseers and vestrymen, were common, and reflected in the notorious unwillingness of victims to prosecute, for fear of inviting covert reprisals.

A whole range of post-war factors enhanced the importance of the parish, especially recourse to the settlement laws, decisions to employ only the legally settled, and parochial public employment of 'surplus labourers', served to ensure that perceptions were restricted to parochial boundaries. This transformed attitudes to migrant labour. The greatest influx of migrant workers to the south-east concerned the hop harvest, but the region's cereal harvest also customarily required a considerable augmentation of the indigenous labour force. The Irish – aided by cheaper steamship travel across the water – formed a considerable proportion of migrant labour in the post-war decades, but whereas they might be tolerated amongst hop-pickers, their willingess to reap for lower wages brought them into direct confrontation with indigenous labour. One magistrate put it succinctly:

> The great influx of Irish labourers and the numerous itinerant wanderers with the increased population in some places, in no small degree creates competition and injures the resident and Industrious Labourer who is incumbered with large families struggles in vain … .while many resident Labourers are wanting employ there are literally colonies of itinerant Labourers, Men, Women, and Children who are employed by the Farmers, at reduced wages consequently the Parish Poor are distressed.

A typical July report stated that the roads leading 'to the weald swarm with half-clad Irish vagrants', and farmers exploited the resultant 'competition' between indigenous labour and 'their wretched Irish brethren', and harvest wages fell further; this jeopardised the sole remaining source of additional income for farmworkers struggling to retain some independence, by paying their own rents, the cost of replacement clothes and shoes, and the clearance of cumulative debts. Excess supply, was reported in 1827 and 1828, but Irish competition was doubly disastrous in years of lighter harvests, especially 1829, 1830 and 1831. At Lewes in the first week of August 1830,

> Hordes of Irish and other labourers, with their wives and children, have infested the neighbourhood of this town for many days past. At Winterbourne, just without the precincts … there is an encampment of between two and three hundred,

who dispersed gradually 'in different directions' as harvesting commenced, but not before 'a number of home labourers saluted them with a volley of large stones', and more fercious attacks followed elsewhere. The adverse impact of Irish competition that year was highlighted by the peculiarly wet cereal harvest, being quickly followed by an abysmally light hop-picking.[114]

The 12 months prior to the Swing insurrection were characterised by enhanced protest, and Cobbett correctly identified the start of Swing in the Isle of Thanet mobilisations against the Irish, commencing in July 1830. The 'same principle', namely job protection, 'pointed out the necessity of putting down the threshing machine', attacks on which formed the second phase of East Kent militancy in October 1830.[115] This is not the place for a major review of our knowledge of the so-called last labourers' revolt; yet the rightly famous account by Hobsbawm and Rudé [1973], and its refinement by Charlesworth [1979], with his emphasis on the significance of rural radical groupings, firmly located within the burgeoning national *political* Reform Bill crisis, still eschew a number of considerations requiring some commentary here. The precise politics of Swing are reserved for our final consideration of class and consciousness; other factors, notably those linking post-Swing developments with the

anti-New Poor Law demonstrations of 1835–36, can be usefully – if briefly
– touched upon.

The insurrectionary character of Swing facilitated many interests,
labourers', craftsmen's, and small farmers', to try to remedy grievances,
only one of which – the tithe – united all sectors towards the bottom
of the social hierarchy. The intensity of Swing, especially from a local
perspective, is commonly ignored. On 9 November 1830 the Hastings
postmaster confirmed that,

> The neighbourhood is in the utmost alarm and confusion, indeed the
> labourers have had the complete dominion for several days and we
> have neither Military or Civil power to venture at collision.

A Wealden observer spoke of

> the resolute temper of the people, and the natural strength of the
> country, which is woodland, and quite a la Vendée ... force is useless
> against a whole population broke loose from all restraint. There is
> not a soldier for a thousand men; and every one knows, that in a
> woodland country, the labourers can hardly ever be caught.

These visions were partially sustained by the very mobility of some
crowds. One which bypassed Frant to destroy a threshing machine, went
on to Withyham to force a tithe reduction, and aimed to return via Eridge
Castle, an itinary of over fifteen miles. Another, initially convening at
Ticehurst, despatched parties to raise neighbouring villages, regrouped
on the two consecutive days, and at one moment was expected to invade
Tunbridge Wells on the market day 'to bully or reduce the farmers'. In the
event it descended on Tonbridge, though predictions were virtually
useless as 'The meetings of the labourers still increase in all directions',
and the Home Office was advised that only 'irregular Detail' could be
transmitted in these circumstances. In some places, Swing crowds carrying tricolours, stopped stage coaches, and forced the passengers to make
cash donations. After a week's continuous action, one of the most
determined magistrates, George Courthope, was 'so fatigued that I can
scarcely put two connected sentences together'. Petty Sessions meetings
were abandoned. Some towns, including Canterbury were invaded by
Swing crowds. One massive assembly, reputedly 'about one thousand'
strong, drawn from north Kent and north Surrey, entered Southwark, and
was stopped from crossing the river and into the City, only by a huge
posse of Metropolitan policemen. At this moment on the morning of 9
November, many more 'Groups of from 3 to 10 ... Labourers and
Mechanics are pouring into Town from the Greenwich Clapham and
Brixton Roads', and some 'Countrymen with Sticks' managed to get 'over
Blackfriars Bridge'. Brighton was divided into districts, each with a force
of special constables, as fears grew of urban mobilisations. Wellington's
government, literally on its last legs, was unable to restore ruling-class
confidence. The Home Office was besieged by magisterial supplications

beyond its capacity to respond, though the South-east received favoured treatment with the despatch of Treasury Solicitor Maude to 'give spirit and courage to the Magistrates'. In the towns 'The Word Swing is now in the Mouth of every dirty boy in the Streets': one 'indiscreet ... act', calculated Courthope, would 'hazard ... the whole Peace of the Country'.[116]

In many locations farmers encouraged mobilisations, either openly or secretly, notably against tithe-owners, in opportunistic manoeuvres to shift responsibility on to the Anglican clergy, and enforce tithe reductions. At Brede, farmworkers' spokesman Joseph Bryant, said that 'a day or two before Mr Hele's Tithe Audit', farmer Bowne

> came to me in ... the Fields where I was at work for him and said that he should like us to go down to the Tithe Audit and see if we could get a little of the Tithe off for them and we were to go altogether but to behave very civil and only to show ourselves. Other men in the Parish have told me that their Masters spoke to them in the same way.

Three other farmers were named, but Bryant did much of the negotiation with Hele 'to throw something off for us and our poor Children'. By contrast, at Wrotham and Herstmonceux, farmers acted as spokesmen, and at the latter adopted common plebeian tactics, 'dragging ... small farmer' Miller 'to the scene of the Riot'. Some considerable farmers were also implicated, as at Robertsbridge, Salehurst, and Barcombe. The Rev. Matthews – who took an unusually firm stand – 'reprobated ... the Farmers' of Herstmonceux 'for their disgraceful conduct', and told 'the Labourers that they were the dupes of their Masters' cupidity'. Matthews pursued the matter, and four farmers ended up in the Assize dock, to be reprobated through the judge's telling observations:

> As holders of property themselves, they ought to have respected the property of others, for if tumultuous assemblies in the defendants rank of life, were thus permitted to enforce a reduction of tithes the farmers themselves would the next day be forced to yield to the demands of their labourers, and thus an indiscriminate confusion would ensue.[117]

Small farmers also supported crowd actions against threshing machines and assistant overseers. Robert Avery, 'yeoman' of Wartling played a major role in the ceremonial carting of Ninfield assistant-overseer Skinner to Battle, and several farmers treated the labourers who performed a similar ritual on his Brede counterpart, as they 'had done such a great thing'.[118] At Upper Hadres, one of the Kentish epicentres of the campaigns against threshing machines, a decision to destroy '"the first Machine that comes into the Parish"', was assumed to derive from 'labouring People', but in fact – according to publican Woollett – was orchestrated by '"a ... small farmer who has no ploughing Land"', namely Henry Atwood who 'keeps 2 or 3 Cows' and owned 'a little

Land'. Atwood probably periodically laboured for others, and certainly symbolises that class of petty proprietors who had nothing to gain from mechanised threshing. In this campaign, machine-breakers 'appeared not to be all of the labouring Class – Some appeared above', including the archetypal jolly butcher Carswell, 'called the Fat one', and blacksmith Arnold.[119] Reviewing High Wealden events, justice Collingwood asserted that 'The Mechanics throughout the whole business have been the leaders & plotters of the whole mischief'; carpenters, blacksmiths, tailors, shoemakers, glovers, sawyers and bricklayers were prominent, and a baker, a butcher, and even a trainee solicitor, were also mentioned.[120] Farmworkers breaking threshing machines in the Chichester district, were joined by city artisans, a posse of sawyers from Oving, and another of bricklayers from Fishbourne, together with a groom, and another butcher, Goble.[121] Most magistrates were dumbfounded by the participation of artisans, because they believed that 'mechanics' had no direct interest in Swing objectives and targets; Collingwood typically 'thought it expedient to select not Agricultural Labourers, but artisans' for prosecution, 'because I thought they had nothing to do with a threshing machine'. The Home Office disapproved of such discrimination, but the fact that many local Swing leaders were artisans, coupled with magisterial prejudices, were responsible for the disproportionate number of non-farmworkers among indicted Swing participants.[122]

The explanation for such involvement – other than political reasons discussed below – is relatively obvious. The agricultural depression had undermined the economic equilibrium of many small masters, bankrupted some, and reduced hundreds of journeymen to claiming poor relief, and even labourer status. Shoemaker Taylor of Bridge in Kent, 'not being able to procure full employment ... has occasionally gone to agricultural labour', and was so depressed that he 'didn't care what happened to him, as his condition in life could not be made worse'. At Bosham, butcher Goble's turnover had suffered, and tenants of his cottages were in arrears which the parish refused to cover; he castigated farmer Farndell for employing non-parochial labour, using a threshing machine, and for 'never attending ... Vestries' to advance the case of his pauperised neighbours. Shopkeepers and master tradesmen's sympathies for the labourers were also revealed by the provision of bail for arrested labourers, even for serious offences, including the assault on High Sheriff Mabbott.[123]

The participation of some categories of worker, notably from the brickmaking and building industries, and especially in attacks on threshing machines, was a partial reflection of occupational fluidity, and seasonal factors, which dictated periodic resort to farmwork by non-agricultural labourers. Others, like the sawyers, had their own direct experience of new technology, namely machine sawing, and almost all those in skilled occupations were doubtlessly victims of the virtually omnipresent early nineteenth-century fear in plebeian circles of the deskilling potential inherent in mechanisation. The threat extended directly to country blacksmiths too, notably those who felt unequal to developing engineering skills commensurate with the repair of threshing machines. Some engineering firms' premises were attacked, as at Bosham and Crowborough, where 'a large quantity of machinery was destroyed'. Technological advances in paper-milling underpinned attacks on new milling machinery elsewhere during Swing, and if this was not a feature of the revolt in the South-east, a Surrey justice who relayed his expectations that a nearby mill 'will very probably be attacked' by itinerant 'Paper-makers ... on the tramp through Kent & Sussex' had good reason, as they were 'sworn foes to machinery of all kinds'. The crowd stopped from crossing the Thames 'said they would return in an hour with a Reinforce-ment and burn all the Machinery of the Saw Mills.[124]

Swing's use of arson facilitated the settling of numerous scores, some deriving from the rising itself. It is difficult to distinguish between public and personal motives, not least because they commonly overlapped. John Boys, Kent's incisive Clerk of the Peace, believed that arson had 'more of a personal than a political nature, & consequently was less alarming'. He gave two examples. One victim suffered after a 'bold & meritorious' resistance to machine-breakers. The other, the overseer of Ash, had done his utmost to deter claimants, including making an unemployed tailor, and father of five, John Fordred, domiciled in Margate, walk the 26-mile round trip to his settlement, *daily* barring Sundays, to receive payments of 1/6 instead of sending nine shillings weekly; after nine weeks, Fordred was forced by ill-health to give up, and he took 'any little Job of work nearer Home at reduced Pay, so as to be almost starving'. William Kenward, whom we encountered as a multi-occupationist at Holtye, Sussex, was another arson victim. He was also a salaried assistant-overseer, much given to swearing at claimants, but his business interests were an additional source of friction. In October 1830, when farmworkers suffered from abnormally low harvest earnings, he threatened to 'force' the customary clearance of debts incurred for firewood; some labourers boycotted his pub, and on 17 October his barn was fired. There was no suggestion that Fordred was the incendiary at Ash, but George Bucknall was prosecuted for the Holtye blaze, largely on the grounds of his relationship with Kenward; Bucknall was indebted for fuel, had joined the boycott, and had been forcibly ejected from Kenward's premises when appealing for poor relief. Yet, the trigger for the alleged arson attack was the non-renewal of Buckland's lad's in-service; 'ever since', the father 'said there was no use trying to get a living'.[125]

Parallel perceptions of hopelessness, notably the refusal of workers to acquiesce in another winter of underemployment and 'insufficient' parish relief after their dire experiences of 1829–30, were identified as key causal factors behind the timing of the revolt. But it is erroneous to see Swing as an inevitable rising of depressed innocents; rather more had criminal records than suggested by the standard authorities [*Hobsbawm and*

Rudé, 1973: 208–11]. The fact that many, almost certainly a majority, had lengthy histories as recipients of poor relief, causes no surprise, but a significant proportion had also been involved in fierce – and commonly recurrent – disputes over public aid. Of the sixteen rioters tried for offences at Bosham and Funtingdon, at least seven had criminal records. Butcher Goble had assault convictions dating from 1819 and 1826. Two colleagues had convictions for theft, another two for poaching offences, one for abandoning his family, and another had spent months in jail while sureties were arranged in a bastardy case. Another had been acquitted of theft. George Hurlock Crockford, self-confessed Swing 'Captain', had been jailed in 1823 for assault; he received occasional parish cash payments to fund work-seeking expeditions to Brighton and elsewhere (1820 and 1823), 'to buy ... Rushes ... to employ himself as a Travelling Rush chair bottom maker' (1823, thrice, 1825, 1827 and 1829), in addition to periodic parish employment, and casual payments in every year between 1821 and 1830, during which period he was accused of refusing to work on five occasions, and on one taken before a magistrate. In 1823 he refused the offer of farmwork for the summer, and had his relief terminated when this was compounded by being spotted in a public house. In 1828 the vestry again ruled that 'from the testimony of a respectable Parishioner that he has refused work he is not an object of charity' – a euphemism for poor relief. Thomas Reed – who was transported with Crockford – also came from a rebellious family. Father John had refused vestry directions to work on an enclosure in 1822 and 'declared in a threatening manner' that he would appeal to the Bench. That year, Thomas was despatched by the vestry to work as a London chimney-sweep; he adopted an itinerant life on leaving this employ following a dispute, but periodically returned home when ill, and to request further funds to seek work, including aid with the purchase of a donkey. He was involved in at least four altercations; in 1825 he refused to accept a mere 1/6 to travel for work to Worthing; in 1829 his relief was restricted 'as he has Soot in his possession to sell if he pleases', and later that year the vestry decided that he was 'not entitled to any [relief] other than a loaf of bread'. In 1830 he returned again, this time with a wife, and demanded accommodation; incarcerated in the workhouse, he simply 'refused therein to work'.[126]

Local sources can be exploited to reveal richer pictures of Swing activists, and their histories within their villages. Burwash was one of the first Sussex communities to rise; on 7 November the 'the labouring population ... assembled en masse', but were denied the opportunity to expel assistant-overseer Freeman, who pre-emptively fled thirty miles to Rochester. Thereafter, Burwash folk participated for days in events in other villages.[127] Involvement outside the home parish gave activists some protection, as victims elsewhere were less likely to know 'strangers', reflected in the absence of Burwash people from legal proceedings [*Wells*, 1985b: 136–7]. Curiously, while Burwash is mentioned twice in Hobsbawm and Rudé's text, on evidence derived from Home Office sources and the 1834 Poor Law Report, it is not listed in their copious 'Table of Incidents' comprising Appendix 3 [*Hobsbawm and Rudé*, 1973: 54, 79]. It would be uncharitable to blame these distinguished authors for either a bureaucratic slip, or for missing incidents in the extensive sources consulted. But the numbers of unrecorded events – for one county alone – in the standard work is not insignificant. They include the invasion of Tonbridge 'by some parties', from across the Sussex border, on 12 November, a fierce mobilisation of the crowd at Cuckfield aimed to prevent the committal of a prisoner which required military intervention on the 18th, a riotous assembly demanding cash at Beeding the same day, considerable assemblies over wages at Henfield and Newick on the 24th, and another at Kirdford on the 30th; all of these were reported in the county press, as were arson cases at Hellingly and Kingston, none of which are tabulated in Appendix 3.[128] Also absent are events revealed by Assize documentation, including the Twineham labourer accused of assaulting fire-fighters. Similarly, the records of Quarter and Petty Sessions, together with private archival sources, reveal additional incidents. These include a riotous attack on the overseer of East Grinstead by a party of thatchers employed with others in a parish gravel pit, other typical Swing incidents at Thakeham, Walberton, Eartham, Aldingbourne, Castle Goring, Lancing, Treyford, Kirdford, Wisborough Green, Edburton, Ferring, and West Chiltington, and evidence of further violence in North Kent at the very end of November, when the revolt had swept on towards the West, and round into East Anglia.[129] These additional incidents, together with the considerable mobility of several crowds, the fact that many villages were in turmoil for days on end, must jeopardise both Hobsbawm and Rudé's demarcation between riotous and non-riotous parishes, and the spatial diffusion analysis advanced by Charlesworth through reworking the tabulations in the appendices to *Captain Swing* [*Charlesworth*, 1979].

The immediate post-Swing years, 1831–34, witnessed contradictions in agrarian labour's responses to the revolt's suppression. Although the South-east was preserved from the scale of harsh sentences meeted out in those counties subjected to the notorious Special Commission, and the Kent Bench was contemporaneously castigated for its initial light sentencing of the first batch of Swing defendants, severe sentences were passed subsequently by courts in both Kent and Sussex. There was considerable indignation even over minor punishments, exemplified by the tone of a letter from one prisoner's wife, to her landlord: ' "I cannot ... pay my rent as my Husban taken up and send to prison for 3 months for standen up for more wages" '. All actors in Swing's repression were subsequently seen as legitimate targets for populist reprisals. At the execution of a Sussex incendiary, a 'relative ... was heard to leave the fatal scene with threats of vengeance'. An 'uproar began' at the William IV pub in Bridge on the entry of labourer Bartholomew, a prosecution witness; customers called me an Informer and said I had split against the Party – and that it was all through me that the Machine Breakers had got ... transported.

Bartholomew was assaulted, and a gallon of beer offered to lynch him, in an incident terminated only by the intervention of 'Two Gentlemen', and which – significantly – required the passage of a fortnight before judicial investigations commenced. It was repeatedly said during the post-Swing years that farmers were too intimidated to have recourse to the law over criminal matters, and that 'The local constables dare not act. The Magistrates must execute their own warrants'. Among the recipients of letters threatening their lives, were a number of prosecution witnesses, and magistrates who had acted decisively against the Swing rioters.[130]

Nevertheless, very real gains, increased wages, enhanced social-security payments, reduced deployment of threshing machines, and understandings to give preference to parishioners for work, had been achieved by Swing, and they required defending. In Kent, the summer of 1831 saw a renewed campaign against threshing machines, which engulfed some parishes, including Hurst, which seemingly escaped the 1830 rising. Other South-eastern offensives were mounted against the replacement of the labour-intensive sickle by the economising scythe, and farmers were again warned against the employment of Irish reapers; the latter campaign even deterred parties of Surrey labourers who customarily contracted for harvesting work on the Sussex coastal plain from coming in 1831. Tensions increased, reflected in press reports of continuing 'SYMPTOMS OF THE RURAL WAR', and the re-appearance of 'The ominous monosyllable Swing ... written with chalk on most of the walls and buildings' in some trouble spots.[131] Conflict continued to rage in the crucial theatre of poor-relief throughout the 1831–34 period. Although some protesters were jailed for short spells, many magistrates adopted a mediatory strategy, typified by the Battle Bench's response to the eight parish-employed labourers accused of besetting the overseer in his own house, and 'extorting £2 from him'; their worships 'solicited them over and over again to beg pardon', or be sent for trial. When apologies were belatedly offered 'in a stubborn and ungracious manner', the vestry insisted on a further hearing, and one man, Jack Wood, was committed for withdrawing his apology. Six months later, Wood and six others were fined for another 'Rout ... and Assault' on the overseer.[132] At village level anybody who 'dared to publicly' castigate claimants became 'immediately a marked object, and spitefully injured', and burnings in effigy seem to have become common. Many magistrates calculated that full use of their judicial powers would regalvanise Swing, and this attitude probably extended to jurors, as reflected in the acquittals of machine-breakers tried in Surrey in 1832 and Kent in 1833.[133] In Dorset, James Frampton JP who had orchestrated the repression of Swing, adopted a different approach to the 'uneasiness amongst the lower orders' in 1831, by encouraging informers to relay intelligence of discussions in plebeian circles, thereby creating the source of his early warning in 1833 of the Grand National Consolidated Trade Union's thrust into the countryside, which soon played itself out with the notorious prosecution of the Tolpuddle Martyrs [*Bawn*, 1984: 58–9; *Wells*, 1988a].

Overt protest was much more intense between 1831 and 1834 than suggested in my rejoinder, but was nevertheless overshadowed by the scale of arson. Hobsbawm and Rudé's tabulations for 1831 are hopelessly defective, and their respective totals of one and five for Sussex and Kent can be increased to nineteen and twenty on evidence principally from the provincial press.[134] In the autumn, Cobbett published the first of his claims that the metropolitan press ignored the incidence of arson, and correctly asserted that incendiarism was prompted by wage reductions. Cobbett doubtlessly knew of the case of thatcher Robert Dixon, executed for arson at Eastry, a case which revealed debate in plebeian groupings, 'as to whether a "good fire" would not "set things to right"'; a proportion of Dixon's mates believed that 'dread of having their stacks fired would induce the farmers to advance ... wages'. Cobbett reiterated his claims of non-press reportage each year, and in 1834 calculated that arson was more prevalent than in the autumn of 1830; meanwhile insurance companies largely stopped offering – and therefore advertising – rewards for information leading to convictions of arsonists, and also refused to reinsure their victims.[135] Other observers offered analyses of the perpetrators, based on the details revealed by trials. The *Maidstone Gazette* claimed that incendiaries were all

> idle and worthless vagabonds ... long habituated to crime ... in whose brutal and perverted minds the firing of a farm yard raised no compunctious feelings. These persons belonged to the scum and refuse of society.

Creating a successful prosecution case against arsonists was problematic, commonly hinging on establishing a motive to support circumstantial evidence, and the legal process leant itself to dredging up materials which sustained interpretations emphasising the 'scum' of society.[136] The *Gazette* additionally acknowledged the 'indifference if not the complacency' with which farmworkers viewed arson, revealed by their 'brutal jeers' in response to 'demands for assistance' to fight fires, which symbolised their 'acquiescence in the *principle* of the outrage'. Conceptual gymnastics were required to square this type of observation with the 'scum' thesis, and this journalist was reduced to claim that 'many ... agricultural labourers are ... ignorant and degraded', and admit his incapacity 'to account for their apathy but by some strange obliguity in their moral judgements'.[137]

The confusion and the fears continued, fuelled repeatedly by fires at a distance, and solidified by local incidents; 'I know of no means by which the parish can be cleaned up', opined one Petty Sessions Clerk after a blaze at Wartling.[138] Where the Oundle system, and its statutory enactment in the 1832 Labourers Employment Act, were implemented, incendiarism appeared inexplicable: 'there is not a man unemployed in ... Rainham', wrote a mystified Rev. Poore. The press periodically emphasised incendiarism in its repeated attacks on the beer shops, creating a picture of conspiracies of criminal clienteles, using arson to warn neighbourhood farmers against informing on perennial law-breaking by beershop proprietors and their customers, and a parallel imagery was used by Benches of baffled magistrates.[139] The aborted attempt to reduce arson to a non-capital offence in 1834 provoked claims that farmworkers in their 'common discourse' said 'that there is to be no hanging for firing', but Lord John Russell soldiered on, seemingly correct in his assertion that the crime's capital status discouraged prosecution, rather than the incendiaries themselves.[140]

Any evaluation of social protest between Swing and the implementation of the New Poor Law encounters inconsistencies. Some overseers – including several actually expelled during Swing – even had the temerity to penalise activists who subsequently sought relief, among them assistant-overseer Smith of Buxted, who prosecuted for assault, and insisted on his assailants entering recognizances to keep the peace, despite threats to 'burn you out'; the historian of Swing in Hampshire argued that once 'order was restored the wage agreements were generally abandoned'.[141] Conversely, a Wealden observer claimed in 1833 that wage-rates were maintained by intimidation, a view reiterated by an assistant poor-law commissioner in 1835. Nor was this phenomenon peculiarly Wealden; it prevented wages paid on the Sussex coastal plain being reduced 'in proportion to the fall in the price of wheat', and in East Kent incendiarism 'is one great reason why we cannot reduce our labour'. It was said that threshing machines were 'generally exploded', and 'it is considered that where they are kept they may expect a visit'. Elsewhere 'men came into the rick-yards half a dozen at a time, and ... used three words "Work, money or fire"'. The *Poor Man's Guardian* repeated Cobbettite claims of a conspiracy of silence in November 1834, and argued that incendiarism required redefinition:

> setting fire to property, without any private grudge or malicious design towards the proprietor himself, but solely with a view to ulterior objects, or as an indirect *means* to an *end* ... an improvement in the labourer's condition through the fears of his oppressor.

The *Guardian* anticipated intensified incendiarism with the implementation of the

> New Poor Law Act, which divests poverty of hope ... Swing is inexorable ... Swing continues his triumphant progress without check or fear.[142]

The radical reformation of the social-security system provoked fierce responses in the form of scattered riots, resort to trade unionism, and much more prolonged and embittered covert protest, with a combination of arson, animal maiming, and miscellaneous malicious damage. Only the geographically piecemeal implementation, and the staggered enforcement of the deterrent clauses, prevented a riotous eruption on a scale paralleling Swing. The South-eastern essay in trade unionism in the shadow of the Tolpuddle Martyrs failed, despite assistance from urban and industrial unions, and the eschewal of secret oaths which had entrapped the Dorset men. The farmers' resort to a lock-out of union members, and their sudden and peculiar vulnerability to the less eligibility clauses of the new legislation, at once popularised the Act in employers' eyes, and immeasurably aggravated farmworkers' fears. Resort to covert protest in this atmosphere was guaranteed. Lord Templemore typically had 'all my Stacks placed in different parts of my farm' in 1836, but such precautions offered limited security. If open protest against the New Poor Law was suppressed, its covert alternative achieved some circumvention of the strict letter of the Law by Poor Law Union Boards, and this success was partially responsible for the endemic nature of incendiarism and the South-east for much of the remainder of the nineteenth century.[143]

South-eastern incendiarism peaked between 1835 and 1840, and in the 1840s was eclipsed on the national stage by *The Times*' exposures of its notorious East Anglian counterpart, but its endemic nature is proved by Table 1, which is derived exclusively from reports in the *Brighton Gazette*. Detection was facilitated by neither the end of its capital status, nor by the introduction of professional policing. Although criminal fraternities, like the Collins gang at Alfriston, used arson to intimidate [*Wells*, forthcoming], and smugglers elsewhere fired stacks to distract the authorities while contraband was run ashore,[144] incendiarism remained largely the tactic of individuals. As one said, 'The best way was to go by yourself, because they could not trust one another'. Rewards, therefore, rarely worked, and became discredited. Hardly any incendiaries were caught red-handed, and the difficulties attendant on establishing a motive to bring home convictions, remained, especially when model employers like Squire Phipps of River, Kent, were victims.[145] Many victims were reduced to accusing anybody seen in the vicinity, which simply operated to deter innocent parties from being first on the scene,[146] or any plebeian with whom they had had a dispute in the past. Hence the regularity with which ex- and current employees, and the locally notorious were arrested, and on occasion the interrogation of a crop of suspects served principally to generate legal confusion.[147] When newly elected poor-law Guardian Ide's barn was fired at West Wittering in 1835, two lads whom he had refused work were arrested, but further evidence led suspicion falling on Ide's foreman, whose son lost his parish employment under the Amendment Act; the foreman was committed by a divided Bench, only to be acquitted at the Assizes. Where trials revealed an 'entire want of Motive', judge followed judge, before and after the end of arson's capital status, and during and outside periods of incendiary peaks, to virtually secure acquittals through their emphasis on this dimension to the case. Time after time, judges complained that prosecutions were mounted 'upon bare suspicion' against those 'most liable to suspicion', and Grand Jurors were repeatedly advised not to let cases go forward on flimsy evidence, not least because acquittals allegedly encouraged incendiarism. Such views filtered down the legal system, with the Cuckfield Bench, for example, discharging a suspect from 'inconclusive' evidence, despite the 'moral certainty of his Guilt' which legitimised only 'a very severe admonition'. By way of contrast, some convictions came directly from divisions within proletarian communities; smuggler and incendiary Thomas Bufford of Guestling was convicted on the evidence of plebeian witnesses, whose testimony derived from hatred of Bufford for giving evidence against those responsible for the murder of an excise officer.[148] Professional policeman, including the Bow Street Runners who were often sent down in the 1830s, scored few successes. Sergeant Stead 'made every enquiry' in Edenbridge and district, during an eight-day investigation, but was unable to penetrate plebeian society, and drew a blank.[149] Runner Goddard's investigation into the 1836 firing of Sheffield Grace's barn at Frant, identified his own butler, and his poaching pal, the notorious James Poulter; although Goddard exacted a confession from the butler, which an Assize judge admitted as evidence, Poulter was acquitted – to his own amazement – largely owing to the jury's dislike of the Runner's heavy-handed methods, leaving Grace to enter into an acerbic dialogue with the Home Office over the costs of Goddard's services, and Poulter to embark on a relentless reprisal campaign against Grace's sheep.[150] Nor were professional policemen invariably adept at effective presentation of key evidence, and cases were compromised to the point of collapse when suspects' footprints and footwear were not categorically collated. The first Chief Constable of East Sussex did categorically state in 1844 that

> no police establishment could stem ... incendiarism ... It originated in causes not always to be traced; by employment of labourers was the chief thing to repress the crime.[151]

The introduction of lucifer matches certainly aided arsonists as suggested by Dr Archer; 'We all know', said a magistrate in 1851, 'that lucifer matches have become very cheap ... they are not only in the cottage, but in the pockets of every labourer'. John Ellman testified in 1845 that 'smoking ... is now general' among farmworkers, and a Kent lad carried matches on the farm 'because the men sometimes want one to light their pipes with'. Greater match availability and smoking also served to increase both accidents and childish pranks. Ellman banned smoking, but his men still carried pipes, and some arsonists probably escaped conviction through advancing accidental causes. In 1854 another JP acknowledged the 'considerable damage ... done by children under seven ... setting fire to stacks and farm buildings'. But as an Assize judge observed at the trial of two ten-year olds for incinerating 120 tons of straw, it was difficult to demarcate between malicious intent and a 'mischievous act which boys indulge in'; young George Tiller told the police that he and mate Miles 'were both as bad as one another but Miles struck the match'. Employers, on the whole, were anxious to avoid extremes with children, exemplified by different farmers agreeing to punishments of overnight incarceration in Steyning lock-up, and two days jail and a whipping, for juveniles guilty of pranks rather than incendiary intent in 1854 and 1859. Childish larks and carelessness gave some innocent parties nasty moments, including two men arrested on suspicion at Horsham which further enquiries laid at the door of a seven-year old, and the arrest of all one farmer's workforce prior to a farm-lad's belated admission that he had dropped a lanthern.[152]

Many of the same problems recurred over two other major categories of suspected arsonists, tramps and itinerant workers. Among the latter, hop-pickers were notorious; Superintendant Dance's first response to incendiarism at Tonbridge was to enquire 'whether there had been quarrelling amongst the hoppers', a group of whom on another occasion 'were all talking together ... about fires'. Many minor disputes stimulated incendiarism by hop-pickers; to give but one example, Henry Dine's immediate response to an employer who refused an advance of wages was to threaten to 'set fire to one of his stacks, or steal something for ... supper'. Mr Justice Piggott commenting in 1863 on the numbers of tramps before him on arson charges, said that when refused food, or permission to sleep overnight in barns, 'they did not know what else to do' except 'set fire to the first stack ... in their way'. One commonly repeated explanation claimed that tramps' apparent addiction to incendiarism was 'for ... terrifying the farmers, and forcing them to comply in future' with solicitations. Some vagrants, as might be expected, were unmistakable villains. Job Snook, in addition to a dishonourable discharge from the army, had twelve criminal convictions when he pleaded guilty to firing a stack in 1864; he responded defiantly to the imposition of a ten-year prison sentence – ' "I have been flogged a dozen times, and you can do no more than flog me to death" ' – and it took four constables to remove him from the dock.[153]

While it survived, defence lawyers played on the death sentence in arson trials, and many witnesses were reluctant to volunteer evidence; one eye-witness admitted that 'I never spoke a word ... for seven months ... I didn't like to take a man's life away'. Plebeian witnesses were also difficult to come by because so many sympathised with this dominant brand of protest, attitudes which survived the death sentence. Examples include farmworkers' 'ill-concealed pleasure' at Aldbourne, the cheers at the fall of every beam during barn-blaze at Clinton, 'the great apathy if not something worse' perceived by Ellman near Seaford, the sabotage of fire engines at Tonbridge, amongst scores of identical cases, and the 'manifold disposition ... among the labourers generally to attempt a rescue' of prisoners taken at Eastry. But even these situations were more complicated than suggested. Fires, especially the more spectacular, drew hordes of spectators, including 'many idlers ... more to obtain drink than to render assistance'. Those who did fight fires often worked long and hard, and damaged their clothing. The refusal of some arson victims and their insurance companies to pay firefighters' wages, and for ruined clothes, was also a cause of indifference. The press castigated the parsimonious, and applauded those who 'handsomely rewarded' firefighters.[154]

The problems confronting would-be prosecutors also create analytical difficulties for the historian. Nevertheless, a motivational miscellany emerges. Deprivation galvanised many incendiary attacks. The introduction of a parochial policeman at Chobham stimulated a criminal fraternity to threaten arson, unless the decision was revoked, and obdurate vestrymen were shaken by seven blazes in one week; other thieves who used arson as a terrorist ploy reasoned that as '"they had ... steady work ... they would not be suspected"'. New technology continued to provoke incendiarism, as exemplified by cases following the introduction of a horse-powered thresher at West Dean in 1839, and the arrival of a steam variant at Mountfield in 1864; entrepreneurial engineers antagonised different sectors of the rural workforce, and a Hurst Green manufacturer who made agricultural machinery and used steam-saws on his premises, was a recurrent arson victim. Other grievances stimulating arsonists include at least one attack on a tax-collector, and the distinctly Irish-flavoured case of victim, farmer Rendall of Cocking, whose hayricks went up after taking 'a farm over a man's head'. The history of incendiarism in Ashdown Forest, suggests that it maintained its traditional role in defence of common right until the end of the nineteenth century.[155] The campaign of the Kent and Sussex Labourer's Union in the early 1870s was also accompanied by considerable incendiarism, though as far as can be known, no members were convicted of the offence.[156]

Arson also retained its attractions as a mode of private vengeance. Cowkeeper Chapman fired farmer Dauber's ricks for threatening legal action over debts, and hoop-shaver Hillier incinerated hoop-maker and publican Morris's 'shaving house' in retaliation for stopping beer on credit. Labourer Savage ignited brickmaker Gravett's thirty-thousand faggot stack for prosecuting him for robbery, and permanently employed farmworker Shepard, sacked for having '"struck work"' in the 1850s, started three fires on his ex-employer's property, despite having taken a beershop some miles distant in Chichester.[157] Farmworkers Crowhurst of Ash and Pettit of Lamberhurst, and itinerant bookbinder Clarke, claimed to have committed arson in order to get transported, and in the early 1860s several judges stressed the futility of this ploy, as the system neared its end.[158]

VII. CRIME

Those contemporaries who linked both arson and other crime with the new beershops of course had their empirical evidence, including that from executed incendiary Goodsell, who lodged at his sister's licensed establishment, admitted that she fenced stolen property, and agreed that his participation in at least sixteen robberies made him a 'confirmed thief'.[159] My original identification of a relationship between larceny and protest is confirmed by masses of South-eastern evidence. Jack Wood, whom we encountered as an old-poor law protester at Battle, was subsequently acquitted of arson, only to be convicted of crimes committed as the leader of a criminal gang some six years later. Henry Dine, jailed for arson in 1839, was transported for theft in 1843.[160] The rejoinder emphasised on evidence derived from Burwash, that there was some correlation between the scale of criminal activity and the worst years of the post-war agrarian depression; but, as the first essay also acknowledged, theft from the poor by the poor was common, and it became endemic after the war, only to intensify after the implementation of the New Poor Law.

Every crisis, from the relatively short-term wartime famines, to the sustained post-war depression, was accompanied by contemporary identifications of crime waves. For example, during the 1795–6 winter the press denounced 'nocturnal marauders' active throughout the region who amassed such 'booties in corn and poultry' that smugglers were thought to be behind it. In 1800, one country clergyman noted what he believed to be a new criminal phenomenon, theft from workers' vegetable patches, and decided on personal intervention 'or we shall be overrun with thieves'. The post-war press teemed with evidence supporting identifications of crime waves, in which violent offences assumed an unprecedented profile; nor was this journalistic hyperbole, for the topic was etched on the minds of ordinary folk, as revealed by a conversation between two men at Bexhill – 'there are so many rough Fellows about they would not mind murdering him for his Watch': 'they would do anything for a shilling'.[161] Desperation seems to have undermined key plebeian norms, typified by a debate between Edward Morgan who 'knew where there was a pull' and approached John Boots for assistance to rob a small shopkeeper; Boots 'didn't like to ... take anything from a poor man like this', but succumbed to Morgan's riposte – 'those that hadn't got it couldn't lose it' – and the proceeds were used to finance a twenty mile trip seeing work.[162] But if crime was endemic, and some of it violent, theft by farmworkers at work continued to dominate. The Iford vestry, one of the few which supported the introduction of professional policing in 1839, while communicating their approbation, asserted that 'the absolute suppression of crime by detection or watching in a rural district' was 'out of the Question'. The Rev. Butler, addressing the scale of 'trifling offences of wood-stealing, or turnip stealing and ... poaching', suggested that few were really 'aware how common dishonesty is among the lower classes, or rather, how very uncommon strict honesty is among ... agricultural labourers'.[163]

Raw criminal statistics derived from prosecutions comprise an inadequate tool for any assessment of the crucial question of the direct enhancement of criminality by the Poor Law Amendment Act. Calculations are bedevilled by many extraneous factors, commonly operative in contradiction. Some believed that the abolition of the death penalty at least encouraged prosecutions for some crimes, including sheep-stealing, as did more generous financial help with the costs.[164] Conversely, levels of incendiarism did deter many victims, as did the replacement of so many capital by transportation punishments; victims commonly would not bring cases 'for fear of throwing the whole family into the workhouse' with its inescapable cost to the parish.[165] The permissive police acts of 1839–40 had an effect on prosecution patterns, but the evidence is ambiguous for East Sussex, the sole south-eastern authority implementing the legislation.[166] Moreover, only a small proportion of petty crimes 'ever came before the eyes of the public' owing to the regularity with which detected offenders 'made up' or compounded with their victims; the record is hopelessly defective, and details usually emerge only when extra-legal arrangements were dishonoured. Young Emily Hill, sentenced to two months for thieving pickled pork in 1855, remonstrated with her accuser, ' "You know you forgave me on my father paying you 2s" '. The non-payment of £3 'compensation for a violent blow' agreed between protagonists at Sidlesham Mill, 'three months ago', led to renewed fighting and a court appearance. Another victim offered 'the value of his property' by the lawyer representing the accused, replied 'he should be satisfied with that and think no more about it'. Some characters achieved a local notoriety unreflected in legal records, including the Hadlow man who 'had been in prison, and he begged pardon 12 times besides, for different offences'. Defence lawyers resorted to exploiting such detail to discredit prosecution witnesses, one of whom typically being forced to admit that he 'Took some carrots once, but was let off'. The Rev. Butler said that even within the confines of his Hampshire parish, 'crimes ... occur without my knowledge, unless a man is brought before a magistrate'; this informal system meant that a *considerable proportion* of even *detected* crimes evaded the statistical record.[167]

Contemporaries were convinced that the Amendment Act directly enhanced criminality; in 1839 a radical journalist exclaimed that

> no sane man can attend any quarter session or sittings of the magistrates, and see the amazing number of persons reduced to a state of squalid misery brought for trial for the most paltry offences, such as stealing a little fire-wood, a few potatoes, or a loaf of bread, but must be convinced that distress in a great majority of cases, is the parent of these crimes.

In the Eastbourne Union 'many of the surplus labourers' openly said that they preferred the risk of imprisonment to taking their families to the workhouse:

> The stealing of wheat from barns, sheep, geese, fowls, tame rabbits … almost anything that constitutes an article of food is … [a] nightly occurrence. Go into any town or village, and you will see the walls placarded with handbills, offering rewards for the apprehension and conviction of offenders of this description.

Observers said that most 'criminals thieve to live, not live to thieve', and noted that offenders had 'no more pity for the poor than the rich': the poor 'actually prey on one another'. Nor were these class-based or ideologically determined perceptions. The Bench coined the expressions 'cottage robbery' and 'cottage plunder' to designate this variety of robbery, exemplified by the break-in at widow Munnery's house at West Grinstead, and the theft of clothes, 'bits' of food and even jars of 'preserved blackcurrants and gooseberries'. Even the intensely propagandist early annual reports of the Poor Law Commission candidly admitted that their new system operated 'to swell the catalogue of criminality', though they managed to pervert this into an attack on the old, not the new poor law. By the early 1840s many senior magistrates were drawing a stark picture; the unemployed went either to the workhouse, or existed independently 'by unlawful means … crime must and did increase', and they repeated these claims until the early 1860s, when 'graver offences' declined. Even then young farmworkers retained their propensity for 'idleness and dissipation'.[168]

The relationship between the New Poor Law and crime is further illuminated through a brief look at the new workhouses themselves. They speedily developed a distinct culture, conditioned in part by inmates' defensive mechanisms, which turned on rule evasion. In the North Aylesford house, some men frequently visited their wives and other females at night, by getting up the chimney of the male ward and descending the chimney of the women's ward, returning by the same means in the morning. Inmates resorted to sabotage, especially against the despised penal dietaries; putting beatles and cats' heads in gruels was one favourite, as one governor exclaimed, ' "they have done me today and they must have bread and cheese" '. Virtually everything had its price, even 'skimmed fat from soup' which when 'cold they sold for baccy'. Theft was rampant, Hellingly workhouse officials typically discovering potatoes secreted all over the house, even in the 'air holes in the ceiling'. Many institutions were characterised by perennial insubordination and defiance, ranging from slipping 'into a shop to purchase some snuff' while en route to church, 'whistling in the chapel', and playing cards rather than addressing allotted tasks. 'Clapping … hands in approbation' of inmates confronting officials, was endemic, and at many workhouses the inmates 'fancy that they can act in the manner they please'. Violence, between inmates, and against officials, was endemic; when one inmate typically squared up to the governor, he 'forseeing that we were likely to have a Scuffle ... began to move ... the many full Chamber Pots in the room'. Violence was commonly met by violence, and this was often condoned by the Bench: ' "if a pauper came to the House and was insolent ... he deserved a licking" ' stated a magistrate, and a colleague observed that 'if every petty case of assault in the house' came to court, the cost of imprisoning the convicted would be astronomical. It was surely significant that the porter at the Ticehurst Union, dutifully recorded the names of all visitors in his day book, except the glazier's, whose repetitive visits exhausted the porter's bureaucratic enthusiasms. Every workhouse had its 'Black hole' or 'lock up Ward', and most minor transgressions were punished by arbitrary incarceration and dietary penalties, and handcuffs were available in many institutions.[169]

Workhouses had an adverse impact on children whether their entire childhood was institutionalised, or they were merely temporary residents, including those from large families, put in as a semi-disguised form of short-term out-relief for their parents.[170] Overcrowding produced abysmal exigency procedures, typified by Goudhurst, where 'one man usually sleeps in the same Bed with two younger persons'. The young were exposed to the 'anger, ignorance, prejudice, want of discretion and discrimination' of governors and schoolmasters, and minor scandals forced many Boards to institute formal records of the 'number of stripes' inflicted in order to monitor physical chastisement. Bed-wetting was a perennial problem, which exposed the limitations of officials, some of whom could respond only 'by obliging those ... guilty ... to stand ... before their fellows ... with their blanket in its wet state pinned around them'. The anti-authoritarian popular workhouse culture was both transmitted to, and fuelled by the young. Training was rudimentary, 'mere palliatives partially and unsystematically adopted', commonly basic instruction in over-supplied trades like shoemaking and tailoring. Few rural Unions possessed the estimated ten to twenty acres required to teach boys 'garden or field-work', the most appropiate 'industrial teaching' in the countryside. 'The utmost that is ever done' for girls comprised 'teaching to make straw hats, mats, sacking ... usually to knit their own clothes', and 'to clean their own rooms'; moreover, 'a most objectionable practice prevails ... of sending the elder girls to nurse the children of single women, whilst the latter are employed ... in the ordinary labours of the house'. Critically, 'the moral atmosphere ... tends to create depression and apathy in the numerous orphans, bastards and deserted Children'. The juxtaposition of inmates of 'good and bad character' constituted 'palpable ... evils', and even where daytime segregation prevailed, nocturnal 'excesses ... are ... for more revolting than any of which they would venture in the day'. Classification did not separate adults and children all day long. An experienced inspector, with a primarily rural jurisdiction, concluded in 1851 that

> the most inveterate paupers have hitherto been the Children of
> Paupers, and ... but a small proportion of the Children trained in
> Workhouses can be brought to apply themselves permanently to
> hard labour.

They commonly became 'confirmed vagrants and paupers'.[171]

The practice of imprisoning inmates – including children – for serious
workhouse offences solidified the links between the workhouse,
vagrancy, and crime. Prison governors repeatedly attributed serious
overcrowding to a huge, if oscillating flow of summarily convicted
inmates. Many stressed that a high proportion of 'agricultural criminals
alternate between the workhouse and the prison'. George Roberts represented those who preferred the latter, and his robust statement to that
effect to the Hailsham Bench was entirely creditable, as his 1859 transfer
to Lewes jail was his sixth. The radical press said that workhouses,
'conducted as they may be', were the same as model metropolitan
penetentiaries, namely criminal seminaries.[172] Yet historians, notably
those on the left, have castigated mid-nineteenth century identifications
of 'vagrant crime' as 'erroneous as historical fact', to claim that such were
convenient 'social theory' in campaigns for a universal 'efficient police'
[*Steedman*, 1984: 25–6]. But it was not simply senior justices, like the Earl
of Chichester, who made this connection; the press, including the radical
newspapers, united in this analysis. The *Brighton Patriot* reported
'numerous depredations' at Horsham in July 1838, incorporating fowl-
stealing, burglaries, and pony-thefts, which was typically attributed to
'the raff' attending the two fairs held in one week. Most concurred that
'The great part of those who beg by day, steal by night': 'to prevent
felonies it is important ... to get rid of beggars', and in 1866 the Poor Law
Board asserted that two-thirds of beggars were thieves. Even after the
creation of the professional police, farmers worried over the pragmatics of
removing mendicants' encampments; ' "Do you think we had better leave
them alone for another night" '?, said a Falmer farmer to another, as they
might retaliate through larceny. Two from an enormous number of case
histories available should suffice to establish the point. Thirty-two-year-
old Joseph Gains, a labourer sentenced to seven years transportation for
fowl-thieving at West Grinstead in 1845, had been imprisoned sixteen
times for vagrancy. The mother of a fourteen year old lass, who pleaded
guilty to the theft of miscellanous articles, while hop-picking in the High
Weald in 1842, informed a court that

> she got her living by hop-picking, or selling articles when she could;
> at other times she begged, and did not see any harm in that.[173]

A high proportion of the numerous hawkers who worked the market
towns and their hinterlands were also said to be continuously on the look-
out for targets to rob and burgle; as I have shown elsewhere, on occasion
criminal gangs represented a fusion between semi-nomadics, including

hawkers, and unemployed farmworkers, to become virtually professional thieves. One fraternity, with widespread contacts in places as distant as Tunbridge Wells, Hastings, Guildford, Frome and London, were active, principally as burglars, with a penchant for country mansions, in the late 1840s and early 1850s [*Wells*, forthcoming].

However, if there are firmly identifiable links between underemployment, poverty, vagrancy, workhouses, criminal gangs and professional thieves, analyses of 'social crime' and 'rural crime', are more problematic. Case studies highlight the complexities. Sheep-stealing was endemic in the countryside [*Rule*, 1982; *Wells*, 1984]. But the virtual coincidence of the Amendment Act and the end of the crime's capital status raises difficulties, as do the survival of customary rights. Shepherds had rights to rear orphaned and rejected lambs. The proprietors of sheep on jointly-stocked commons filched each others lambs, and on some commons, including Framfield, the carcass of a dead lamb belonged to the finder. But compared with the North, or the West Country, there were few South-eastern commons, and most land was enclosed, with fewer, rather than no problems with strays.[174] In the later 1830s and throughout the 1840s, the regional press recurrently reported waves of rustling, lamented the rarity of convictions, and began to speak of the winter 'season' for the crime; journalists, and the police, attributed it to unemployment and farmworkers' 'necessitous condition'.[175] Sheep-stealers rarely worked alone, but in twos and threes; beasts were almost never sold; carcases were cut up, and divided between the thieves, and detections commonly involved the discovery 'of an unusual quantity to be found in a labourer's cottage'. This emphasises that sheep-stealers took beasts as a source of meat, and many of those caught plausibly claimed that 'they were driven to the crime by want'. Many thieves were relatively skilfull. Skins, with their markings, were almost invariably abandoned, and care taken to conceal footprints, 'so that the b[ugga]rs could not track us'.[176] Some rustlers were also protesters. George Clear of Angmering repeatedly killed Guardian Heasman's sheep, but never stole the carcasses of the animals, though on one occasion, he hacked off the rear legs; Clear, and his associates, stole sheep for consumption, from other local farmers.[177]

Hunger, and diet supplementation, by distressed labourers and other rural workers, were not the sole motivations. Wholesale rustling was not unknown, and Portsmouth achieved a post-war notoriety as a market for parcels of stolen animals, and there is some evidence of the participation of impoverished small farmers.[178] Butchers, from town and country, were quite active rustlers, typified by 'small butcher' Hylands of Ringmer, convicted in 1846 of two raids which netted seven beasts, valued at £14. Butcher Golds of Brighton was accompanied on sheep-stealing expeditions into the adjacent countryside by neighbour Wadey, pork-butcher, greengrocer, and beerhouse proprietor. Others involved included another Brighton butcher, who also 'goes about pig-killing', and his son, a 'smith and boiler maker'. This crew were among the few to owe their exposure to trading in the skins, with 'the ears cut off ... a very uncommon thing'. Few farmers were implicated, though the cases of a handful who were prosecuted, reveal resort to the criminal law by frustrated losers in commercial disputes. But there were enough cases of 'systematic' rustling by men travelling in carts, who left the skins of slaughtered animals revealing 'evidence of a practised hand' to conclude that some 'robbers have not been driven by want'.[179]

Fowl thieving grew to endemic proportions in the wake of the massive increase in the South-eastern chicken-cramming industry in the later eighteenth and early nineteenth centuries. The industry's omnipresence, and the broad range of occupations engaged, has been noted. Fowl-stealing displayed similarities with poaching, it being typically said in 1823, that if poulterers were 'more circumspect' when purchasing, the crime would decline. In 1846, Colonel Mackay, the Chief Constable of East Sussex, stated that the difficulty of detection derived from

> the facility of removing stolen property ... by carts and waggons which could not be searched without a warrant and ... the difficulty of identifying poultry.

His West Sussex counterpart, identified fowl stealing as the 'principal ... of the small robberies' soon after the force's creation in 1856. The Amendment Act appears to have aggravated an existing serious criminal problem; owners fought a losing battle. Most locked their birds up nightly and 'counted' them 'every night and morning'. Labourer Wren of May-field 'placed ... two strings amongst the poultry which communicate with Bells in my Bedroom'. At Ninfield farmer Fox 'chained up two fierce dogs in the hen house' in 1838, 'but the thieves stole dogs, chains, collars', and forty chickens.[180]

If fowls, like sheep, were commonly stolen for personal consumption, a multitude of petty dealers encouraged their theft by farmworkers for sale. When farmer Farrance of Ticehurst arrested his labouring neighbour Henry Wheeler at gun-point, caught red-handed thieving six birds valued at ten shillings, Wheeler eloquently ' "wished there wasn't a damned Higler in the World" '. Many hucksters, were themselves, perennial thieves, including Jesse Smith of Lewes, who rented a multi-roomed building for business and domestic accommodation; labouring brother, Henry, knew that Buxted farmer Martin had fowls 'just fit for the market', and the two raided the farm, and stole thirty-five birds, valued at seventy shillings.[181] Many urban-based fowl-stealers commonly raided the adjacent countryside. William Packenham of Brighton, had a 'dog ... produced in court ... its teeth filed down' to help it seize birds. Such 'marauders' found a ready sale for their hauls, either privately, or to poulterers. Although the police occasionally learned about clandestine dealings, and magistrates publicly, and severely castigated private individuals and business folk, who purchased at suspiciously low prices, the authorities believed that not 'a tithe' of stolen birds were recovered.

Farmer Weller's response to the loss of seven chickens was typical; 'I had no clue, no suspicion & did nothing'. Fowl-thieves also regularly disposed of birds by ' "raffling" ' them in the beershops, the thieves pocketing the cash, and the winners getting a cheap dinner. Occasionally, an element of flambuoyance, defiance or even protest, can be detected, as at Magnam Down, where farmer Woodhouse 'found the heads and legs of his seven geese suspended from the knocker of his front door'.[182]

Philip Coley, a young farmworker, who broke into a Lindfield shop and stole £30 in cash in 1840, clearly hoped that high earnings on railway construction, would provide a cover for his ostentacious living on the proceeds of crime. But the nature of that ostentation is significant. He treated several friends to heavy-drinking bouts, spent £5 on a watch, and more on 'guns, dogs, ferrets etc'. Coley's conduct exemplifies George Rudé's important identification of the ' "acquisitive" criminal, who is merely concerned to line his pockets at another's expense'; crime represented 'the most readily available' course to accepting the norms of an 'acquisitive society' for 'a man without property or means'.[183] Some of the details from this discussion of crime, also challenges the usefulness of concepts of "rural crime"; much property stolen in the countryside was disposed of in towns, so much so that an experienced Quarter Sessions chairman observed that 'all crime was more or less connected with towns'. It was easier, however, for rural employers to discriminate against village, than urban, villains; it was said of farmworker Ginman, sacked for thieving, that 'Men of his description ought not to meet favour ... after committing Robbery on their ... employer'.[184] The Burwash material published earlier, established that there was something approaching a semi-distinct, criminal element in the 1820s. Further research has extended the chronology, and provisional analysis suggests that this demarcation intensified after 1835. But the details also prove that the criminal sector did not comprise exclusively farmworkers, but included others, notably the extensive Eastwood family, whose successful road-haulage business leant itself easily to criminal activity, especially the carriage of, and dealings in both stolen and smuggled goods, supplying unlicensed liquor-dealers with beer as well as spirits, in addition to direct theft; much of the latter category of goods was disposed of through Lewes fences.[185]

VIII. WORKING-CLASS CONSCIOUSNESS

This catalogue of qualifications to analyses of "rural crime", "social crime", and "popular protest", together with the identification of a criminal class in the countryside, present difficulties for identifications of rural working-class consciousness. E.P. Thompson's famous thesis, that 'between 1780 and 1832 most English working people came to feel an identity of interest as between themselves and as against their rulers and employers', compromised itself through the non-integration of the largest occupational group, namely farmworkers [*Thompson*, 1968: 10 and Ch.7]. Elsewhere, Thompson insists that 'the poor were not altogether the losers' in the eighteenth-century struggle against the gentry, backed by the state, and he assigns a principal role to rural proletarians in the defence of 'traditional culture', notably resistance to invasions of customary rights, enforcement of traditional rights integral to the 'moral economy', and 'they perhaps enlarged the scope of the Poor Law'. However, 'We move out of the eighteenth-century field-of-force and enter a period in which there is a structural reordering of class relations and ideology'. Is it possible to use rural evidence, 'to analyse the historical process in terms of nineteenth-century notations of class', to broaden the application of Thompson's key thesis, relating to class formation [*Thompson*, 1978: esp.164; *Thompson*, 1974, and 1971: *passim*].

There are two central facets. First, did rural plebeians believe that their interests were opposed to those of their employers? Second, was the state and its apparatus perceived as hostile to working-class interests, and did they see reform on democratic principles a precondition for necessary changes? Superficially, both questions could be negated, as Chartism, the first genuinely working-class mass movement, failed to penetrate the countryside, and this could be interpreted as a ramification of the lack of rural working-class consciousness; the evidence does not sustain such a peculiar geographical or occupational analysis.

Part of the proof lays in another of Thompson's assertions about the nature of the 'defeat' of the first democratic movement in the 1790s: 'Throughout the war years there were' lower-class democrats 'in every town and many villages ... biding their time, putting in an odd word at the tavern, the chapel, the smithy, the shoemaker's shop, waiting for the movement to revive' [*Thompson*, 1968: 201]. Men like stonemason and 'ardent republican' Joseph Harmer of Heathfield, who emigrated to the United States in 1796, but returned in 1800 to inherit his father's business; Harmer was a a keen folklorist, but also active in populist causes, among them the 1833 creation of a Friendly Society [*Lucas*, 1910: 104–6]. Men like cobbler John Gower of Lindfield, 1779–1857, renowned as a local historian and champion of working-class causes. Others, like fellow shoemaker William Hayden of Faversham (1778–1847), whose brief obituary in the Whig press described him as 'an ardent and sincere reformer of long standing', who 'dared to avow the principle of civil and religious liberty when such avowals were dangerous'.[186] Such men had their disciples, including Clement Hoare, eventually a school-master at Sidlesham, active since at least 1818 when he too founded a Friendly Society. He was still secretary in 1837, with an enviable reputation among local farmworkers, notably for advising them in poor-relief, housing and employment disputes; he also composed petitions on behalf of those convicted of petty felonies. Hoare gave a magnificent, if at times pragmatically evasive, performance as a witness to a parliamentary enquiry into the New Poor Law in 1837, which unfortunately did not enquire into his admission that the Anglican clergyman refused to preach at his Society's anniversary dinners. On this occasion Hoare kept his democratic principles to himself, but in the midst of Swing he tried to transmute the protests into a political movement, by holding a rally, chaired by butcher Gray, in the regional capital of Chichester.[187] If evidential problems pre-empt coherent histories, these details resonate on occasions, to permit glimpses into barely opaque societies, to reveal the accuracy of Thompson's key point.

Perceptions of the politics of the agricultural depression are customarily restricted to the issues faced by successive Tory ministries, laced with some recognition of Cobbett's countryside campaigning. The intense and recurrent lobbying, especially by South-eastern farmers, throughout the 1817–30 period is rarely recognised [cf. *Crosby*, 1977: Ch.3.] Hundreds of petitions praying for relief through reductions or abolition of the hop, malt and other taxes, flooded to parliament and ministers during these years, only to be ignored or rejected, which galvanised fiercer representations. In 1823 Northiam hop-planters again protested, stressing that Sussex hop-acreages had shrunk by nearly a quarter, and

> it would not be prudent to carry the displanting further than it had already gone, until the army in Ireland had executed its duties, and could be spared, for that Sussex would become the counter-part of Ireland, if the labourer were still more to be deprived of his employ.

This was rebuffed with a typical *laissez-faire* rationale; repeal of the hop-duty would 'only encourage a cultivation which could hardly fail to lead to a recurrence of the evil'.[188] Some politicians feared the extension of radicalism to the countryside, and were shocked at Cobbett's favourable reception by tenant farmers, but the restoration of agrarian capital's equilibrium proved beyond governmental policies. Petitioning achieved a new crescendo in the months preceeding Swing, with over 50 from Kent alone, many of which detailed horrendous proportions of village populations receiving poor relief. George Courthope, the perceptive Wealden squire, asserted that

> a very general feeling of dissatisfaction against government prevailed in this part of the country amongst the farmers in the supposed inattention to or neglect of the petitions, which I impute to ... a mischievous practice of parochial petitioning too generally adopted for other purposes than the benefit of the Petitioners ... The Petitions ... were principally in the subject of the hop duty which Government must be aware has never been paid since 1822 without remonstrance & petition.

These experiences underlay farmers' notorious reluctance and refusal to act against Swing. Courthope additionally emphasised that further conflict between farmers, vestries, and tithe-owners, had 'invariably produced the worst of consequences amongst the labouring population'.[189]

A fortuitous combination of factors over the summer of 1830, including the continental revolutions, the death of George IV, the resultant general election, and the burgeoning national crisis over the issue of reform, generated the millenial atmosphere in which Swing exploded. Radical groupings in several locations acclaimed the French Revolution. A convention at Maidstone despatched £23 for the families of the men killed in Paris, together with an address:

> 'Nous n'avons pas oublié et c'est avec douleur que nous nous rappleons que l'or de l'Angleterre a autrefois liqué contre vos libertés les despots armés de l'Europe.'

The adjacent Hampshire villages of Wonston, Sutton Scotney, Bullington and Barton Stacey hosted a 'combined Radical and Musical Society', which also regularly and collectively read Cobbett's *Political Register;* in October, they drafted a petition which was taken by one member to the king, at Brighton. This superbly intellectual and articulate document graphically described the 176 petitioners' poverty, which they argued

> proceeds from a misrepresentation in the Commons ... by which the present system being confined to the rich; in consequence of which, men have been returned to sit in parliament in whom the people have no confidence,

including the current Hampshire representatives, who supported the present exhorbitant taxes 'on those articles which are necessaries of the poor man's life ... malt, hops, tea, sugar, tobacco. soap, candles etc'. The money raised was squandered on liquidating debts 'contracted by unnecessary wars', the 'grants, pensions, sinecures ... wantonly heaped on the ... aristocracy', and a massive 'standing army'. Huge sums also went – via the tithe – to the fabulously 'rich men in the church', at the expense of 'poor curates' who actually ministered; finally, a battery of law,

> forbids us to take for our own use the wild birds and animals that inhabit the woods and fields, or the fish that swim in the water, those things being kept for the support of the rich.

Until 'reform' through 'annual Parliaments, universal suffrage, and vote by ballot' was implemented, 'the humblest of petitioners, can never have the full enjoyment of our hard earned little'.[190] At Battle, a democratic grouping of journeymen – some of whom were on the tramp – and 'tinkers', publicly praised the 'glorious actions of ... humble operatives' responsible for manning the Parisian barricades, before returning to their vociferous campaign behind the embattled editor of the radical *Brighton Guardian*. Rising socio-political tensions in London, as radicals mobilised and galvanised Wellington's notorious 3 November declaration against reform, coincided with the escalation of Swing. Cobbett's South-eastern lecture tour helped to heighten political perceptions. The countryside could not be immunised; as the doughty octogenerian Lord Lieutenant of Sussex explained,

> the county swarms with tramps & travellers who converse with the Cottagers & their wives & always speaking of the Revolution as certain, next year when I call, you will have a glass of wine to give me & such language whether intended for mischief or only a joke, makes a deep impression ... general excitement may provoke very serious mischief.

Timothy Willcocks, a Swing activist in Kent, said – on 8 October – 'that this country would soon come to the same state as France'; simultaneously Courthope acknowledged that the rural workforce believed that 'the means of redressing their grievances were in their own hands'.[191]

These events preceded Swing, but similar manifestations accompanied the rising. The mass lobby of the Rev. Hele's tithe audit at Brede forced him to admit that he 'was in possession of a large share of the fruits of the labour of the industrious classes'; in the midst of these protracted events, Brede was one of ten parishes which quickly

> formed themselves into Association, to promote local and general Reform; they have committees to direct them, and subscribe one penny per week to raise a fund upon the same principles as the Catholic Rent.

It is interesting that several of the main activists at Brede initially evaded imprisonment through flight to Norwich – a notorious radical centre.[192] Political radicalism was also promoted through the enormous distribution of handbills, published in London, entitled 'Nice Pickings', which detailed the incomes of state pensioners and senior ecclesiastics; several hawkers concerned were arrested, but not before the contents achieved an even greater circulation through their incorporation in Swing placards, and in the litany of the protesters themselves; at Benenden, for example, one JP was told 'that pensions and tithes should not be paid longer and' reference was made 'to a paper stating ... the income of different Noblemen and others'. Swing crowd followed crowd in insisting that steps were taken so that all 'may live by their labour'. Many activists claimed that the only acceptable remedy was political; merely reducing tithes, rents and taxes, according to sawyer Eaves, would be useless, as 'the farmers would pocket the money, and the labourer would be no better off'. Robert Price, an itinerant Swing activist, responsible for at least three distinct mobilisations, 'came to enlighten the people; they had been long enough in darkness'. They 'should alter the Laws':

> 'the burnings were necessary to bring people to their senses; it is your dandy houses, your dandy habits, and your sinecure places that have brought the country to this state. The gentlemen must take

down their equippages .... It is only now for the farmers to rise against their landlords .... There will be no more gaols, no tread-mills, much longer .... There must be an alteration altogether ... that the poor may live by their labour".[193]

Price was neither idiosyncratic nor unique, just one, according to a bewildered hostile observer – like the 'patriotic shoemakers in Maidstone' – who had 'no cause to complain of the distresses of the times'. Charles Inskipp was unusual – in that he had resigned from the Metropolitan Police in bizarre circumstances – and returned to his native Battle, to embark on 'lecturing the Paupers after Cobbett's fashion', replete with 'a Cap decorated with *tri-coloured Ribbards*', thoroughly befitting 'a person of notoriously revolutionary principles'. Inskipp decanted on the imminence of a British revolution in imitation of France, and several other radicals and groupings, seized on the rising to mount politicisation campaigns. On 1 November, Maidstone papermakers struck for the day, to attend a rally on Peneneden Heath, where speakers spoke on ' "Reform in the Commons ... vote by ballot" '; they also condemned the magistracy for arresting Swing activists. At Southfleet farmer Andrus received the news as 'no doubt the fore-runner of a glorious revolution'.[194] At Horsham, an ugly mass intimidation of the tithe-owner, was followed within days by a meeting summoned by 'the influential agitating party' to petition 'for Radical Reform'; a belligerently worded document was drafted. Ironically, at Chichester, those who did – unusually – enroll as special constables, also demanded a reform meeting, though they were defeated by mayoral fiat. Elsewhere, as at Lewes, Rochester and many villages, reform meetings were held in the midst, or wake of Swing, and petitions drafted accordingly.[195] Not surprisingly, the *political temperature* rose commensurately, to be expressed in many ways. In a Lewes pub, toasts were drunk,

> 'May God above send down his love, with swords as sharp as sickles,
> To cut the throats of gentle folks, who grudge poor men their victuals'.

A handwritten petition, sent by 33 Dallington inhabitants,

> Implore[d] his Majesty's Government if they value the Existence of the middle Class of Society, to take off all Taxes, which press on the Industrious Classes, otherwise there will be but two Classes the one the most misserable Poor and the other the most Extremely Rich.

When justice Collingwood lamented the leading role of 'disaffected ... Mechanics', and his view that 'the mob' was effectively controlling matters 'instead of Parliament' to a wealthy Kent yeoman, he received a rebuff in the form of a distorted historical perception: ' "Parliament has deluded & conned us. It is such Conduct as that of Parliament which

before now has led to Civil War" '. Once the Whigs acceded to government, Collingwood insisted that

> If Parliament attempt to delude & mystify them now, or if the new
> [Tory] opposition throw facetious difficulties in the way of amend-
> ment, in my conscience I believe, that we shall have to get our Swords
> & muskets ready, & prepare for the field.[196]

In parts of West Kent and East Sussex tax collections were stopped, and
the gatherers forced to return the cash to the farmers; only strategic
deployment of the available troops nipped this clear revolutionary
development in the bud.[197]

The Whigs' ruthless suppression of Swing severely compromised the
new government in the eyes of radicals everywhere; petitions demanding
clemency came from many industrial cities, and supported their counterparts in market towns including Shaftsbury, who implored that

> a new administration pledged ... to the immediate and efficient
> redress of grievances should not commence their rule with evil
> auspices, by measures of severity ... leniency may still be con-
> sistently ... extended to our ... offenders ... goaded by suffering.

Some politicised Swing activists bore the brunt of the repression in places,
including Hampshire where 18 of those signing the petition to the king
were indicted for offences committed during the rising. Of these, sixteen
were convicted, an unusually high proportion for Swing trials; all were
transported. Another from the same locality, nineteen year-old Henry
Cook, accused of a murderous attack on justice Baring, was sentenced to
death, together with a handful of arsonists. Cook's sentence caused a
furore, but even local dignatories who advised clemency to halt mass
alienation, excluded the youth from their entreaties. After his execution,
Cook's parents were subjected to heavy pressure from the Barings to
admit that their son was 'stirred' by Cobbett's *Register*. In his mother's
estimation, Cook 'was no scholar' and 'ran headlong with the rest'. The
local rector who argued that only commutations 'would paralyse the
power of seditious spirits', was correct, because the executions put the
entire plebeian community 'in that state of mind ... likely to render them
the easy dupes of the vile agitators who are so industriously at work'. The
government's support of judicial severities, brought the question of rural
workers to the front of both the democratic and labour movements; this
new awareness led directly, if eventually, to the encouragement of rural
political unions, and the attempt to incorporate farmworkers under the
giant umbrella intended by the Grand National Consolidated Trade
Union.[198]

The state assumed a new centrality in the perceptions of rural workers;
when the Home Secretary revealed an iota of clemency, through the early
release of Kent machine-breakers, the local

> Peasantry openly state that it has arisen from the conviction of

> Government that they cannot punish Machine breaking by Law & that consequently Orders are sent out to New South Wales to release & send home those that were transported for that offence.

Many country observers reported a marked increase in the circulation of Cobbett's *Register*, and some magistrates, including those confronting renewed attacks on threshing machines in Kent, sought to blame the journal for all forms of protest.[199] The rapid development of the Reform Bill crisis in the context and aftermath of Swing, served to fertilise the seeds of politicisation sown during the rising. The parliamentary progress of reform dominated public affairs everywhere: it was the 'all absorbing' topic in rural communities, and most public events generated pro-reform demonstrations, like the first anniversary of William IV's coronation, celebrated at Aylesford inns, where 'but one toast was given ... "The Reform Bill, and in God's name may it pass"'. Local Tories who refused to illuminate their windows to honour such rejoicings had their houses attacked by stone-throwers, and the odd MP who dared to publicly explain their reactionary posture, was accorded parallel treatment.[200] Major peaks in tension, generated by the Lords' October 1831 rejection of the Bill, and Wellington's attempt to formulate an anti-reform ministry in the following spring, provoked further rounds of intense petitioning which absorbed entire rural communities for days on end, to reinforce populist perceptions of the Ultras and their episcopal supporters, as the implaccable enemy.[201] Nor were these confined to the enfranchised, exemplified by the bills flooded through East Sussex allegedly to 'inflame the minds of the lower orders', in October 1831: simultaneously, a taxman in rural Surrey advised that collections be suspended 'until the great excitement and agitation now existing be tranquilised'.[202] A meeting of Ultras at Cranbrook in May 1832 was greeted by 'A low rabble', who 'paraded the streets the whole afternoon, with music and effigies of ... Wellington, and a Bishop suspended from a beam in a waggon'. An exasperated clergyman seized on a funeral to deliver a revealing condemnatory oration, replete with

> a most violent strain of invectives against the inhabitants at large, assuring them that his health, rest, and comfort were destroyed by the prevailing wickedness of many of the inhabitants, and abruptly concluded 'Reform Reform! under this word has well nigh broken all the bonds of social order'.[203]

Extravagant anticipations over the potential of post-reform developments became the norm; as one contributor typically informed a Kent county meeting,

> why is a change required? Because the people are too generally in a state of poverty, dissatisfaction, and destitution beyond that known to their forefathers ... the probability is, that we shall enjoy a cheaper government, lower taxes, lower tithes.

This atmosphere helped to spawn working-class political organisations in the countryside, and several grandees passed on private intelligence of 'affiliations', 'delegations', collective readings of the radical press in beershops, with the invaried result that farmworkers 'have of late listened to Politics & shewn much discontent & ill will to their employers': not only was there 'much more' popular politics 'in villages', but 'some are for the first time invaded by politics'. Frampton's response in Dorset was not an isolated example of a rural JP creating localised spy networks in conscious imitation of the tactics pioneered by magistrates in urban and industrial districts since the 1790s. The Duke of Buckingham and Chandos reacted to the start of a Political Union at tiny and 'close' Itchen Abbas [population 243] in Hampshire, with the establishment of a 'system of espionage'.[204]

Some of these manifestations derived from Political Unions; created in several southern towns in 1831 and 1832, branches were established in their rural hinterlands. The aggressive Winchester Union confirmed the political anticipations of those who had warned against the severity meeted out to Swing;

> deputations are sent to the neighbouring villages to instruct the labourers in their political rights, and to recruit the Union by an accession of new members and funds from the surrounding country ... .the deputations had a considerable success, for ... they obtained a 'great many members' and roused the farm labourers to 'exert themselves' and 'unite together',

much to the chagrin of the farmers to whom 'The idea of common clodhoppers – the serfs of the soil – presuming to think for themselves, was a species of rebellious pride they could not understand'. Secretary Stripp of the 'Winchester National Union' wrote, 'by order of the Committee', to village publicans to arrange parochial venues for inaugural meetings, requesting 'an answer by the Carrier'. One magistrate confirmed that 'the Union extends ... from Winchester by the Villages of Woonston, Sutton [Scotney], Bellingham, Barton Stacey & Whelwall to Andover'; in these 'the Numbers in *each* uniting themselves vary from one half of the Labourers, and upwards'. At least one procession – 'conducted ... very quietly' – attracted 'six or seven hundred' participants. The first general election under the Reform Act was seized upon to publicise the unaltered radical demand for manhood suffrage, the 'vote by ballot, annual Parliaments, abolition of Tithes, repeal of assessed Taxes'. Almost simultaneously, the membership squared up to widespread attempts by farmers to reduce wages, by threats of a strike. The Brighton Union responded positively to requests – allegedly from 'the Paupers' of 'very remote Agricultural' Horsted Keynes' – to inaugurate 'a branch'; a public meeting was scheduled, and the district flooded with bills headed '"Union is Strength and Knowledge is Power"':

> It is earnestly requested that all persons who feel the bitter pains of having their pockets picked by the holy and emalculated tribe of Priests, Sinecurists, Pentioners, and a long and dismal list of their supporters who have for years been living riotously, and faring sumptuously every day, on the hard earned pittance of the Working Classes, will attend this Meeting, and judge for themselves.[205]

Horsham was another epicentre, responsible for orchestrating 'nearly a dozen agricultural Political Unions ... in the vicinity', including Billingshurst and West Chiltington. The latter, like other Sussex and Hampshire bodies, had Swing associations:

> The West Chiltington Union is held at the House of a Publican whose Principles both of Politics and Religion are notorious and at whose House a very violent Riot was hatch'd in Novr. 1830.

Thomas Baverstock of Sutton Scotney signed the 1830 petition to the king, was one of the only two of those eighteen signatories prosecuted for Swing offences to be acquitted, and in 1832 he is encountered informing the *Poor Man's Guardian* of political unionism in his district.[206]

Local counter-offensives were launched in some places. The Horsted Keynes meeting was interrupted by a magisterial posse. The Hampshire Bench had launched a new series of trials earlier in 1832 against Swing activists; four Barton Stacey men were convicted of incendiarism, one of whom – Henry Hunt – had signed the 1830 petition. Later, in October 1832, the Duke of Wellington as Lord Lieutenant orchestrated the interchange of intelligence between magistrates, and with his customary brusqueness, swept aside the traditional independence of Borough authorities from county governance, with orders to the Mayors of Winchester and Andover to participate. Although 'the farmers were much alarmed', they counter-attacked in places, including Chilbolton, where thirteen members of the Union were sacked, and the threat extended to fifty more. Vestry decisions to deny poor relief to the victims, and to withdraw allowances in-aid-of wages from all members, were supported by the magistracy, one of whom 'gave out ... that I will order no relief ... to any individual that ... belongs to these Unions', on the grounds that the penny weekly subscription comprised a 'malappropriation of the poor rate'. These tough initiatives stimulated defiance; one claimant who appealed to Sir John Potton's 'Petty Sessions ... threatened if we did not give him relief "the Union he belonged to would see him righted"', and the rural branches refused to dissolve. These developments served to dramatically increase tensions, and provoked magisterial anticipations of a recurrence of Swing. Army detachments were rushed across from Dorset, in an episode obscured by the press; the *Poor Man's Guardian* explained – with reference to the lock-out – that

> To appeal to the press would be useless. Except the *True Sun*, there is not a daily paper in London which would publish a syllable of the

affair. The *Times*, or *Herald* would give us whole columns of Belgian protocols ... but not one half inch ... to illustrate the insolence of wealth, or the sufferings of the poor.[207]

Nevertheless, much evidence derived from the 1832–35 period suggests that beershops were the forging houses of an emergent, radicalised, rural plebeian culture, in part through the supply of 'newspapers which could not be procured by the poor at their own houses'. Moreover, the increased numbers of labourers employed on public make-work schemes transformed many farmworkers experiences, because for periods they exchanged the relative isolation of farm-work, for employment in gangs:

> In one field 30 to 40 are set to work breaking stones ... at meal times, one of the most learned may be seen reading aloud ... and expounding ... to his fellow workmen ... they are all politicians.

Magistrates repeatedly said that the radical press 'produced pernicious effects on the minds of those incapable of judging for themselves', and one detected – rather more perceptively – 'An increase of information among the peasantry'.[208] Several witnesses to yet further parliamentary enquiries into agricultural conditions in 1833 and 1837 made similar comments: farmworkers' 'minds were too much occupied with politics', and there was a

> great deal of evil caused among the agricultural population by the political excitement of the last years ... ever since the Reform Bill was first talked of in the neighbourhood it ... has produced a great deal of disorder and the immoral state of the population.[209]

'It is my decided conviction that the labourers *as a class* are ready for any mischief', opined Henry Drummond in rural Surrey late in 1830. In July 1831, the Earl of Brecknock enjoined farmers in the newly formed West Kent Yeomanry to 'remember that we are "marked men" by the labouring classes'. In 1837, farmer Stapley of South Bersted, Sussex, noted that 'the relationship ... is broken between the farmer and the labourer'; asked 'Since when', by a committee of parliamentarians, he replied,

> Since about 1818 the tie has been broken in the greatest measure; the farmer looks upon the labourer as a burthen ... because they are so many more than he wants; and the labourer who can hardly exist ... looks upon the farmer as his oppressor ... that is the feeling in our neighbourhood.

The proletarian poet, Abraham Blair of Overton, penned his 'Swing Redivivus' in 1832:

> *Johnny Swing* is not yet dead,
> Soon again he'll raise his head;
> How will the tyrants stare,
> When they see their ricks flare,

And all their ill-got property with ruin overspread.
Swing's renown each landlord hears,
Swing's advance each despot fears;
With more than royal glare,
Swing marches every where,
And laughs at bailiffs, beadles, watchmen, guards and overseers.
Swing knows how the intellect to whet,
Of any poor man by hunger met;
Idlers eat pheasant and hare,
Cold potatoes are *our* fare;
But every monopoly Jack Swing will overset.
Rich men make (what they call) 'Law',
But in this Swing finds a flaw;
What "Equal Rights" are there?
How can the laws be fair,
Which, without poor men's *rights*,
Would poor men overawe?

Late in 1834, assistant poor-law commissioner Head, wrote of a large part of Wealden Kent, to the effect that

> the peasantry ... have succeeded in intimidating the upper classes, and the balance of social life being thus far disordered, the demands of the labourer are rising in the one scale, precisely as the authority of the upper classes is sinking in the other ... The fact is admitted by all parties ... most respectable people (strange as it may sound) acknowledge that they are afraid of the peasantry, with the same shameless simplicity with which the peasantry openly declare that they are *not afraid* of those above them.[210]

The formation of the National Union of the Working Classes was perceived by South-eastern observers as a manifestation of the 'deep-rooted hatred' of proletarians 'towards all those who have been placed by their own industry or talent, or by the care of their predecessors, in better circumstances'.[211] Agrarian class-struggles are revealed by campaigns including that waged by the *Poor Man's Guardian* on behalf of victimised rural political unionists, and the Grand National Consolidated Trade Union intention to exploit it; the latter's promoters argued that 'All the trades have an Union', and an informer revealed their strategy:

> They are trying to get up a Union amongst the agricultural labourers ... the subject of wages [is] only a subterfuge ... they have an ulterior object,

namely, to consolidate politicisation amongst farmworkers, still the largest sector of the English proletariat. Then they would have the capacity to 'paralyse all the Efforts of ... Government'.[212]

That initiative partially foundered at Tolpuddle [*Wells*, 1988a] but the Poor Law Amendment Act was implemented in the atmosphere described by Head and confirmed by many others. Although initially, only the gentry and some of the greater farmers, supported the measure, this broad-based social opposition collapsed within two or three years; by 1838 it comprised a rump of 'small farmers ... a few shopkeepers ... and a few well-intentioned and benevolent but unreasoning people', together with the entire rural proletariat.[213] The implementation provoked widespread if intermittent overt protest, with some major and rather more minor disturbances, and longer enduring covert protests. It also stimulated an important South-eastern essay in farmworker trade unionism, which collapsed owing to a debilitating combination of the over-supply of labour, a powerful lock-out, and the capacity to use the new social security system – including incarceration in the workhouse – to penalise both leaders and members [*Wells*, 1985a: 24–9].

But the Act also served, more importantly, to bring home the realities of class-based legislation, passed by the newly-reformed state, to the hearth of every rural proletarian, in a fashion, arguably that no other measure could. A farmworkers' union meeting at Heathfield was typically informed that

> We have got Reform have your expectations been realised [the] first reformd parliament passed the poor Law Bill places & punishment assign'd to you directly you become poor you are punished [as] a common fellon who would have thought the first reformd parliament would have passed this despotic Measure.

Local employment realities were ably woven into this representation of the global political context:

> Your labour is exacted by Oppression by the ... Farmers ... The Farmers are your immediate Oppressors ... you are the victims of Petty Tyrants.

One widow, whose outdoor relief was savagely, but representatively reduced by nearly half, said that 'the people in general are Greatly disturd abaught it as they expected it better instead of worse'. Another observer said in 1841 that the 'Poor Law experiments ... have half alienated the poor from the rich, the labourer from his employer, the servant from the master'.[214] In the countryside, employers – notably the farmers – were, through their domination of most Boards of Guardians, also the principal administrators of the new system. It was they who benefitted from reduced rates; conversely, under the Act, most cottages were assessed, and if many were excused payment, this required supplication, and increased the resentment; the Act, coming so immediately after the other phenomena we have discussed, finally forged rural working-class consciousness, symbolised by a Hambledon well-digger's response. He purchased an abstract from one of the many hawkers peddling them in handbill form, and observed, that as he was a man of pretty good head, and he had got the Act, and read it, and he was counsel for the rest of them, and he said he thought the face or odour of it very bad, and he should go to America.[215]

If there were any residual vestiges of the magistracy's historic role as mediators between labour and capital which we encountered during the war years, after the titanic struggles in the poor-law theatre throughout the post-war depression, and the Bench's onslaught against Swing, political and trade unionism, judicial support of the 'Robbery Bill' – as ordered by the reformed state – proved to be the final nail in the coffin of rural paternalism. Workers believed that ' "Government is not the Poor man's Friend" ', as

> 'a cruel and unjust law has been pased, that they are deprived of their rights, & that the Magistrates are disgraced for having not taken their parts against their Oppressors'.[216]

However, in some regions including relatively restricted ones like the valleys of the Test, and the Stoke, the epicentres of Hampshire rural politicisation in the early 1830s, and huge ones, notably the Weald, where smaller farmers, rural craftsmen and petty entrepreneurs, were numerically very significant, their very concentration served to mediate class relations. Thomas Attree, who had over thirty years experience as a salaried overseer at Maresfield, noted at this time that

> the smaller farmers are almost universally connected with the labourers by relationship, or in some other way, so that the labourers have an influence over them, which they have not over the larger farmers. The small farmer will not for the sake of the parish, be strict with a relation ... Besides, a refusal [of poor relief] from a person who is nearly an equal, excites more animosity, than from a person who is more of a stranger, and has greater authority.

The Rev. Harvey of East Grinstead put it differently: 'here are many yeomen and labourers families who have been located here since Henry the VIII time, and by intermarriages all blended together', so that 'we retain a great deal of the ancient ruggedness of the Wealden' population.[217] Major ramifications of this situation include elements of class collaboration during Swing, again during the prolonged Reform Bill crisis, and to a reduced extent during the post-Reform political agitations. Hampshire radicalism embraced many craftsmen and small farmers; Robert and Joseph Mason possessed a few acres each, and were market gardeners, of whom it was said that they were of 'superior education and intelligence'. After his transportation, Robert wrote from Sydney saying that he wished 'to come home to put my tools away as I left them about very carelessly'. Enos Didums said of the assembly which despatched the petition to the king that 'It was a meeting of the middle and lower classes'.[218] In 1833 one Wealden Political Union contained some farmers [*Reed*, 1984: 116/107]. The same phenomena materialised, initially, during the furore unleashed by the implementation of the Poor Law Amendment Act. The Rev. Harvey stated that his entire community 'very cordially disliked ... the Bill, the Board & the Commis[ione]rs'. William Day, squire of Maresfield, and soon to be an assistant-commissioner himself, typically reported 'much discontent, not only with the Labourers ... but of the people generally ... Shop keepers & small ratepayers as leagued with the labourers'. Assistant-commissioner Hawley agreed that 'The little Shopkeepers, the Millers & Beershop keepers ... everywhere ... are at the bottom of all the disaffection', and during the disturbances there were further echoes of Swing in the refusal of non-labourers to enrol as special constables, forcing Day to swear in relieving officers and workhouse officials. Another assistant commissioner, Tufnell, claimed that most farmers tried to manipulate the situation to their advantage, and score political points, with their adherence to traditional mass lay-offs during winter-time bad weather. These

> farmers ... have not the heart to pay half labour price, that is make a job in the snow to keep men from starving. All this class are crafty. They continue to throw the blame on the Landlord, the Parson, or the taxes, [say] 'they have no money'. And when they do employ, by giving plenty of coarse cider ... they contrive to get the name of good masters and actually acquire popularity, the bulk of these men being against 'the rich, the gentry' what the lower classes always like to hear; and the swinish multitude is led wonderfully by drink.[219]

However, a number of factors ensured that these expressions of class collaboration emated from a short transitory phase. First, the Chandos Clause in the Reform Act extended the vote to a high proportion of tenant farmers, who thus became part of the rural electorate, together with most of even modest property owners. Second, whatever the shortcomings of the Tithe Commutation Act of 1836, it reduced some of the frictions between payers and receivers, not least through tying payments to cereal prices, and was perceived as a very positive state intervention with the agrarian problem [*Evans*, 1976: Chs.6 and 7]. Third, the significant rise in the prices of farm produce in the later 1830s restored economic equilibrium in the countryside, at least as far as capital was concerned, and this restored profitability to the craft sector too. Fourth, the Amendment Act did succeed in radically reducing the poor rates, and this benefited all existing ratepayers, though ironically it extended liability to working people. The Act's provisions helped to speedily smash agrarian trade unionism in the South-east in 1835, raised the *per capita* productivity of agrarian labour, and operated to fundamentally increase employers' powers over farmworkers, while at the same time greatly reducing conflict at parochial level over social security. This was largely transferred to the much larger unit namely the Unions, who plausibly represented themselves as mere agents for the central power, over which they had no influence.[220] A combination of property qualifications, plural voting, to which in the early years at least fear must be added, generated a marked reluctance even among the qualified to volunteer candidacies for Poor Law Guardianships. Not only were contested elections extremely rare in rural parishes, a proportion experienced recurrent difficulties in finding anyone who would stand. The Boards speedily became dominated by larger tenant farmers almost everywhere, and if there was considerable variation between Unions, in many, most of the decisions were taken by a small number of regular attenders. The social-security system, despite the well-known but in aggregate essentially petty warping of the Act's strict provisions, took on a regularised momentum, almost beyond the parochial pale in stark contrast to its predeccesor.[221] In the countryside the Victorian Poor Law haunted only those liable to be on the receiving end, namely the working class, as revealed by the vehemence with which it was repeatedly denounced by farmworkers' trade union leaders in the 1870s, among a mass of other evidence.[222] Fifth, the central tenet of popular radicalism, universal suffrage became more ominous in the later 1830s. It directly threatened to abolish not only the clear class advantages of the new social-security system, but also the Corn Laws, as yet perceived to underwrite the agricultural economy. Moreover, land nationalisation speedily assumed prominence, with some major Chartist orators, including Bronterre O'Brien, who campaigned in the South [*Wells*, 1985b: 152–4].

The relatively rapid dissolution of class collaboration is variously evinced. From Hampshire assistant poor-law commissioner A'Court reported that 'the rather extensive circulation of Cobbett's Journal ... has had the effect of unsettling the minds of many respectable yeomen, who know not now what to think on the subject' of the new law in October 1835; however, within a month he was reporting that these employers were sufficiently astute to opportunistically test the Act's immediate impact by reducing wages, confident that

> Violence was never contemplated by the labourers: their plan was to lay up sufficient means to supply their wants for a fortnight or three weeks & to endeavour, by declining any work during that period, to compel their employers to return to the former ... wages. The folly of such a plan was too apparent to allow of its execution.

The proposed 'union of the middle and working classes' for West Kent failed to get off the ground, about the same time as the West Chiltington Political Union was reduced to selective trading 'to compel the little Tradesmen to join them'. Within a year of the Amendment Act's implementation, an opponent who had the temerity to speak against it at the Hailsham Cattle Show dinner, was howled down amidst scenes of 'much uproar and hissing'; a radical journalist noted that 'Such conduct ... exasperates the people. They feel that they are not only neglected, but insulted. Every agricultural labourer in East Sussex was insulted'.[223]

Southern Chartism awaits its historian, but this is no place to supply the omission. In 1838–39 the Chartist leadership acknowledged that the depressed farmworkers of the South represented a huge potential accretion of strength. Addresses specifically 'to the agricultural labourers' were distributed enjoining farmworkers 'to form yourselves into societies, upon the plan of the London Working Men's Association, in all your villages. Let the labourers join together and meet in each other's cottages'. Chartist organisations were formed in many, but not all southern towns, and a number took specific initiatives to spread the movement to villages in their hinterlands. Lecture tours by national Chartist speakers, notably O'Brien, principally under the auspices of urban groupings, nevertheless exposed rural workers who flocked in to hear these deliveries, to some of the more militant assertions. In one of his addresses in Brighton O'Brien denounced the middle class as 'traitors and robbers of the people'. There appear to have been even a smaller proportion of non-working class folk among Southern Chartists than elsewhere, though there were inevitably the exceptions, including 'shambling' pork-butcher Bob Sutton of Bromley, and the congregationalist minister, tanner and shopkeeper Charles Brooker of Alfriston, both of whom came into the movement through their hatred of the poor law and notably the policy of splitting husbands from wives in the workhouses. O'Brien also asked,

> Why did he mention arms? Because, if there were a month's strike, though the people should be as meek as angels and as peaceable as doves, their enemies would find means to drive them to some act which would give them an opportunity of attacking them as traitors. He ... always wished that every adult man should have arms.

If such speeches galvanised repeated cheerings, they also had the effect of embracing the South in a apparently potentially revolutionary movement. If the establishment was essentially weak in Chartism's urban and industrial midland and northern centres, their southern counterparts were powerfully placed to ensure that the movement encountered massive opposition when it tried to penetrate the countryside. Squires, parsons and farmers, joined to maximise a counter-offensive. Workers who even attended meetings were sacked, or threatened with dismissal, while others were simply denied customary perks, especially joints of mutton at Christmas. Publicans who permitted Chartist gatherings on their premises were summarily informed that their licenses would not be renewed. Rural Chartist experiences proved that these naked expressions of power could not be confronted, not that ingredients central to class war were somehow absent. Countryside Chartism was speedily driven underground, symbolised by eighty year-old potter Jonathan Farmer of Heathfield, who wrote to his daughter in the USA in 1842 that

> I wish you to consult your American Newspapers for the progress of political events in England they will far better detail them than I at present dare.[224]

If no organised working-class movement gave expression to class war in the rural South-east, before the remarkably successful Kent and Sussex Labourers Union in the 1870s, rural communities' class structure was reflected in all manner of things. When farmer Mead of Chart, Kent, casually encountered and hired labourer Dyke to drive some bullocks some distance, they called at the Buffalo's Head; Mead gave Dyke 'some allowance and he went into the tap room and I sent him a pint of porter' from the other bar. The tap was clearly for plebeians. Although beershops are customarily seen as solidly plebeian – one at Burwash in the 1840s was called 'The Labour in Vain' – others developed class-based internal arrangements, as revealed when a proletarian 'came tumbling into' the 'bar parlour, which was not for labourers, but for superior people' in Mr Rusbridger's establishment at Epsom. 'It was usual for the tradesmen' of Rotherfield 'to have a private party in the Half Moon parlour on a Saturday evening', stated postmaster Gosling.[225] Assemblies of youths, and young men, who blocked village walkways in the evenings, and especially church and chapel paths on Sundays, forcing the more respectable members of the community to walk in the mud, while insulting them, constituted a recurrent and very widespread phenomenon throughout the nineteenth century.[226] Nor was such behaviour confined to youths; after Major Gilmore of Grove Cottage, Maybury, near Woking, obtained warrants against the 'ringleaders of a gang of roughs who gathered round his residence and caused most hideous disturbances, thereby endangering the lives of members of his family', John and George Howard, father and son, appeared before the Bench to be bound over for using threatening language. Customary riotous celebrations of Guy Fawkes's Day in the South were never completely tamed, despite recurrent police campaigns, and on occasions the deployment of troops, but it was reported in 1863 that it was

> not the only day on which these ebulitions of passion and ill-feeling are exhibited; indeed, the occurrence of any public event in which the lower orders participate is taken advantage of as presenting a favourable opportunity for indulging in licentiousness and *retributive behaviour.*[227]

See Table on pp.200–201.

NOTES

1. Huzel, 1975, citing G. Buckland, 'On the Farming of Kent', *Journal of the Royal Agricultural Society* IV (1845), pp.251–2.
2. B[ritish] P[arliamentary] P[apers], 'Report of the Royal Commissioners on Agriculture', vol. XIV (1881), Q[uestion]s, 370–1.
3. Farrant, 1976, pp.108–9. *BPP*, loc.cit., Q.55, 982. cf. *BPP*, 'Reports of the Poor Law Board on the Laws of Settlement and Removing of the Poor', 1850 (1152), vol. XXVII, p.80.
4. *Annals of Agriculture*, 22 (1794), pp.380–1. *Farmer's Magazine*, 1, 2 (June 1834), p.149. *BPP*, 'House of Commons Select Committee on Agriculture', 612 (1833), vol. 5, Qs.11,836–8, 11, 849. *BPP*, 'Royal Commissioners on Agriculture', vol. XVI (1882), p.403; vol. XVII (1883), Qs.51,049, 51, 080–2. Vance, 1838, esp. pp.25, 99, 105–8, 113, 128–9.
5. *Annals of Agriculture*, 11 (1789), p.291.
6. *Sussex Advertiser*, 9 April 1873, citing *Wright's Book of Poultry*.
7. Samuel, 1977, esp. pp.4–5, 10–2, 32–3. *Sussex Advertiser*, 2 July 1873. *Sussex Notes and Queries*, 5 (1934–5), p.621. Neale, 1975, pp.57–8. *Brighton Gazette*, 16 Sept. 1852 and 11 Jan. 1855. *Sussex Weekly Advertiser*, 7 Jan. 1793.
8. *BPP*, 'Royal Commission ...', vol. XIV, pp.405–7. Wells, forthcoming. *Kent Messenger and Maidstone Telegraph*, 12 Oct. 1872. *Sussex Advertiser*, 29 March 1864.
9. *BPP*, 'Poor Law Report', (1834), Appendix A, pp.503, 506, 528–9. Henderson, 1952, p.57. *BPP*, 'Select Committee of the House of Commons on Agricultural Customs', 461 (1848), Qs.5074–6. *BPP*, 'Royal Commissioners ...', vol. XIV, Q.577; vol. XVII, (1883), Qs.51,122–50.
10. Ibid., XIV, Qs.556–8, 577; vol. XVI, pp.396, 405–7; vol. XVII, Qs.55, 740–4, 56, 181, 56, 593, 58, 205.
11. *BPP*, 'Poor Law ...', Appendix A, p.511. Letters to the P[oor] L[aw] C[ommissioners] from, Clerk, Ticehurst Union, 30 June 1836, and 2 March 1844, and Friend, 3 Jan. 1843; enquiry, March 1860, into Ticehurst Workhouse Governor's fraudulent practices; Clerk, Ticehurst Union, to the P[oor] L[aw] B[oard], 8 Dec. 1864, and PLB Inspector Cave's report, 12 Aug. 1865, P[ublic] R[ecord] O[ffice], M[inistry of] H[ealth], 12/13,138, 13,142, 13,147. Depositions, Thompson, 29 Aug. 1837, and Diplock, 30 Oct. 1846 E[ast] S[ussex] C[ounty] RO., QR/E847, 920. *Brighton Gazette*, 8 Jan. 1857 and 14 June 1860. *Sussex Advertiser*, 9 April 1873. *Maidstone Gazette*, 14 Feb. 1832 and 22 March 1842.
12. *Brighton Gazette*, 5 Jan. 1860.
13. *Annals of Agriculture* 11 (1789), pp.142–3.
14. Prosecution brief against G. Buckwell, Dec. 1830, PRO. T[reasury] S[olicitor], 11/1007/4051. Examination of S.D. Butler, 2 July 1823, ESCRO. QR/E776.
15. Ayres, 1986, p.119. Turner, 1862, p.11. Harting apprenticeship records, 1770 and 1791; Lewes St. Michael, vestry minutes, 11 April and 20 Oct. 1748, and memoranda, 1751–2, 1766–7, ESCRO. Par.360/14/18/2, 4; 414/12/1. *Brighton Gazette*, 11 May 1848.
16. Farrant, 1979, p.197. Dell, 1962, p.6. Patmore, 1885, pp.49–51. *The Times*, 28 Dec. 1830.
17. *Sussex Weekly Advertiser*, 9 May 1791 and 24 Aug. 1801.
18. *Ibid.*, 20 Feb. 1818.
19. Kussmaul, 1986, pp.70–1. Furley, 1874, vol. II, p.675. *Brighton Gazette*, 14 April 1842. John Browne papers, Oct. 1820, W[est]SCRO. Add[itional] Mss.29205. Hartfield vestry minute, 16 Nov. 1828, ESCRO. Par.360/10/1/1.
20. *Sussex Advertiser*, 29 March 1864.
21. W. Weston, deposition, 5 Nov. 1825, ESCRO. QR/E786.
22. *Sussex Weekly Advertiser*, 22 May, 2 and 9 Oct. and 20 Nov. 1815, 15 and 29 Jan., 5, 12 and 26 Feb., 11 March, 6 May, 7 Oct. and 11 Nov. 1816, 16 June 1823 and 9 Dec. 1826. *BPP*, 'House of Commons Select Committee on Agriculture', 612 (1833), vol. 5,

TABLE 1

ARSON IN SUSSEX 1850–1859

Date	Place	Target	Victim	Value	Accused	Verdict
7.2.1850	South Mundham	2 Ricks	Farmer			
10.5.1850	Pagham	House	Farmer		Domestic servant aged 14	1 yr. HL
4.9.1850	Toddington	Rick	Farmer			
25.11.1850	Patcham	Haystack	Farmer		Indebted small agriculturalist	Not guilty
15.2.1851	Boxgrove	Carthouse	Higgler			
15.5.1851	Warbleton	Wood stack	Publican/hoop-maker		Employee	Not guilty
5.9.1851	Hoe	Rick	Farmer			
16.9.1851	Felpham	Farmyard	Farmer	£300		
19.9.1851	Bexhill	Barn	Farmer			
27.9.1851	Great Belhurst	Barn	Farmer			
19.2.1852	Levant	Straw stack	Farmer		Two vagrants	Fined
23.2.1852	Luggleshall	Stubble	Small farmer		Labourer	Not guilty
29-2-1852	Petworth	Furze	Landowner		Two labourers	Not guilty
23.3.1852	Harting	Furze	Landowner		Labourer	1 yr. HL
12.4.1852	Westbourne	Barn/ricks	Farmer		Labourer(previous arson conviction).	Transported
16.4.1852	Westbourne	Faggot stack/sheds	Brickmaker		(Two men; one tried for offences).	Not guilty
20.4.1852	Easebourne	Outbuildings	Farmer			
26.4.1852	Easebourne	Barn	Farmer			
19.5.1852	Harting	Barns/outbuildings	Estate bailiff		Two men	Not committed
Oct. 1852	Midhurst	Outbuildings	Farmer			
Winter of 1852-3	West Grinstead)Burwash	Barn	Farmer		Seaman	Not guilty
		Straw stack	Farmer	£2	Boy, aged 12	2 days/birched
17.4.1853	Fulking	Furze/faggots 5th attack	Farmer		2 Brighton hotel workers	1 discharged 1 not guilty
20.5.1853	Hellingly	Stack	Farmer		Female domestic servant aged 18	Not guilty
10.6.1853	"	Part of house	Same victim		Boy, aged 13	committed/not indicted
23.6.1853	Mountfield	Haystack	Farmer			

Date	Place	Property	Owner	Accused	Sentence
11.2.1854	Angmering	Hayrick	Farmer	Tramper	Not guilty
14.4.1854	Goring	Wheat rick	Farmer	Young labourer	18 months HL
15.4.1854	Loxwood	Wood stack	Squire		
7.9.1855	Landport	Wheat stack	Farmer		
15.9.1855	Rumboldswyke	Barn/hayrick	Farmer		
18.9.1855	West Wittering	Barn	Farmer		
23.9.1855	Aldingbourne	Wheat stack	Farmer	Boy	2 months HL
29.9.1855	Pagham	Live hedge	Farmer	Labourer	Transported
6.11.1855	Racton	Rick yard	Farmer		
6.4.1856	Lower Beeding	Forest land	Landowner		
21.4.1856	Balcombe	Heath	Landowner	Labourer	Not committed
25.4.1856	Amberley	Plantation/shed	Landowner	Labourer	6 years
23.7.1856	Bexhill	House	Labourer-tenant		
4.10.1856	Littlehampton	Barn	Farmer	£100	
12.10.1856	Eastbourne	Oak stack	farmer	2 boys aged 14	Not guilty
25.11.1856	Slindon	Furze	Landowner	£40 Elderly man	Insane
7.11.1857	Preston	Cottage/straw-stack	Farmer		
19.12.1857	Wadhurst	Shed/outbuildings	Publican	Labourer	5 years
26.7.1858	Findon	Haystack	Farmer	Labourer	Not guilty
13.1.1859	Heyshott	Hayshed	Farmer	2 lads	Not guilty
30.6.1859	Lancing	Straw stack	Farmer	2 10 year old employees	
12.11.1859	Horsted Keynes	2 wheat ricks	Farmer	Shoemaker	Not guilty
12.11.1859	Lurgashall	Cart shed	Farmer	Blacksmith	Not guilty

Qs.7234–74, 12,682–4, 12,700–14, 12,718, 12,724, 12,805, 12,847. *BPP*, 'Poor Law ...', Appendix C, p.505. *BPP*, 'House of Commons Select Committee on Emigration', 404 (1826), vol. IV, p.114. Steward Bishop, Northiam, to Mrs Frewen Turner, 21 Jan. 12 March and 16 Aug. 1830, ESCRO. Frewen Mss. 7859–60, 7918. Wells, 1985b, p.130 and note 29.

23. Cited, Northbrook, 1905, vol. I, p.102.
24. Brockman, miscellaneous account and estate book, 1821–9, B[ritish] L[ibrary] Add. Mss. 42, 705.
25. Minutes, Battle Petty Sessions, 10 June 1828, and Brede overseers to the authorities at St. Thomas à Beckett, Lewes, 10 May 1829, ESCRO. PBSA.5; Par.253/12/3. Goudhurst, list of non-resident receivers of allowances in-aid-of wages, 1834–5, PRO. MH.12/4911.
26. Mary Weston to Mrs Gosling, 18 Oct. 1830, ESCRO. AMS.5774/4/1.
27. *Sussex Weekly Advertiser*, 26 March 1826. Vestry minutes, Burwash, 5 March and Heathfield, 7 Feb. 1831, ESCRO. Par.284/12/1; 372/12/1. *Brighton Gazette*, 1 Dec. 1831.
28. Northiam vestry minutes, 11 April 1748, 5 April 1769 and 3 Feb. 1772; Ticehurst legal case statement, 1754, ESCRO. Par.431/12/1; 492/35/7–8. Viasey, 1984, pp.67–8, 238–9.
29. West Malling Petty Sessions minutes, 5 Dec. 1778, 6 July 1789, and 2 Jan. 1796, K[ent]CRO. PS/Ma3. Merryman, 1973, p.17. Snell, 1985, ch.2, esp. pp.67–84, and p.77 note. Snell's attempt to quantify the evidence deriving from settlement examinations is of dubious value, not least because he fails to even acknowledge the key problematic, namely the typicality of those, who for whatever reason, incurred legal scrutiny. They certainly represented but a minority of migrant farmworkers.
30. Northiam vestry minutes, 1738–1774, ESCRO. Par.431/12/1, 2.
31. T. Sanctuary to the Home Office, with enclosure, 18 Nov. 1830, PRO. HO.52/10, ff.536–7.
32. For example, Oxley, 1974, pp.61–2, 107–8, mentions the topic with the utmost brevity, twice. The subject virtually eluded Tate, 1946. Melling, 1964, pp.31–2, 144, notes disputes over cottage erection on manorial wastes in 1601, a parish building a house for a homeless family in 1634, and the 1742 conversion of a workhouse into family tenements.
33. Vestry minutes, Icklesham, 14 April 1798, and Northiam, 1738–94, ESCRO. Par.400/12/2; 431/12/1, 2.
34. Oxley, 1974, pp.110–11. Victoria County History, 1948, p.97. Sir C. Willoughby to Henry Dundas, 19 Nov. 1794, Scottish RO. Edinburgh, Melville Mass. GD. 51/1/372. *Reading Mercury*, 13 Oct. 1794.
35. The West Malling decision emerged from a prolonged debate between May and September 1795; this division restricted its directive to component parishes to urging them to aid non-settled residents on the same principle as the settled, in 1799 during the renewed subsistence crisis. Minutes, 1794–1800, KCRO. PS/Ma. 4, 5.
36. Rudge, 1805, p.346. Cf. Sir G.O. Paul to the Duke of Portland, 7 Aug. 1795, PRO. Privy Council, 1/29/A64, and Vicar of Sutton Berger, acreage return, 27 Oct. 1801, PRO. IIO.67/23, f.245.
37. An isolated threat of a shortage occurred in Sussex in 1794 owing to freak weather conditions delaying the completion of haymaking almost to the start of the normal harvest period, *Sussex Weekly Advertiser*, 7 July 1794. Some observers' claims of labour shortages refer to workers willing to take annual hirings, including William Gordon to Lord Romney, 26 March 1798, KCRO. Q/SB.1798.
38. Including the construction of the Kent Military Canal in 1804, and the new Tonbridge–Igtham turnpike in 1810. *Sussex Weekly Advertiser*, 27 Nov. 1804 and 16 April 1810.
39. Lawrence settlement examination, West Malling Petty Sessions, 2 May 1795, KCRO. PS/Ma4.
40. Justice Brockman in Kent released Elizabeth Norrington from her contract after she was assaulted 'with a Horsewhip' by her employer, and Martha Cornelius from her's

after master, George Bromley, 'came into her Bedchamber & attempted to have carnal Knowledge of her Body ... she resisted & got away 7 [said] she is afraid of returning to his House'; Brockman diary entries, 25 March 1771 and 9 July 1781, B[ritish] L[ibrary] Add. Mss. 42, 599.

41. Ibid., 16 Oct. 1775 and cf. 22 May 1776.
42. *BPP.*, 'Report of the House of Commons Select Committee on the Poor Law Amendment Act' (1837), vol. XVII, Qs. 2926, 3008, 14, 905. *BPP*, 'Report of the House of Commons Select Committee on Emigration', (1826–7), vol. V, Q. 1208. Draft reply to the PLC. by Courthope, Nov. 1832, ESCRO. SAS. Co/C/230. Kussmaul, 1982, pp.121–2, and 1986, p.11.
43. *Sussex Weekly Advertiser*, 18 March 1805, 6 March 1809, 19 April 1813. Brede vestry minute, 14 July 1812, ESCRO. Par.253/12/1.
44. Framfield vestry minutes, 20 Feb. 1800, 24 and 27 July 1808, 15 Aug. 1809, 10 May and 8 Aug. 1811, ESCRO. Par.343/12/1. Internal evidence suggests that this record does not fully embrace parish construction.
45. Clerk, Ticehurst Union, to the PLC., 18 July 1836; Survey, Lamberhurst parish property, 1858, PRO. MH.12/12,747, 13,146. W. Morphew to solicitor Hartie, 13 Feb. 1830, and list of parish property, 1833, ESCRO. Par.360/10/1/1; 360/14/11.
46. KCRO. PS/Ma.5.
47. Checkland, 1974, pp.136–8. This topic requires systematic investigation. Developments in poor-law practices may correlate closely with regional and local leasing arrangements. Farmers in districts like the Weald, where lengthy leases were rare, probably resorted more speedily to allowances in-aid-of wages than their counterparts in areas where long leases were the norm.
48. Ibid. Courthope reply, loc.cit.
49. *Brighton Gazette*, 18 Aug. 1842. Extant Petty Sessions minutes, including those from Battle, reveal business choked by settlement cases, ESCRO. PBSA.7
50. Letters to Burwash parish officers from B. Brooks, Wrotham, 3 March and 12 Dec. 1831, M. Jackson, J. Andrews, and W. Cornford, all domiciled in Brighton, 13 Jan., 9 June 1831, and undated; Harriott to Hallingdale, 25 June 1816, ESCRO. Par.284/35/12/3, 6, 10, 28, 33, 39; QR/E748. Goudhurst, list of outdoor relief paid to non-residents, 1834–35, PRO. MH.12/4911.
51. Settlement examination, Sept. 1843, ESCRO. QR/E898.
52. Slinfold's contraction of a £112 debt through the erection of 'New Parish Houses' as late as 1834, was exceptional; Slinfold to the Horsham Board of Guardians, entered in Board minutes, Nov. 1836, WSCRO. WG.6/1/1.
53. Goudhurst statement on parish property, 6 Jan. 1842, PRO. MH.12/4913. Battle Petty Sessions minutes, 25 July 1826 and 20 June 1831; Hartfield vestry minute, 22 Sept. 1826, ESCRO. PBSA. 5; Par.360/10/2/3.
54. Wells, 1981, pp.518–19. An experienced Wealden land surveyor said in 1833, that he did 'not know of any new cottages built in villages on speculation for agricultural labourers', and several other witnesses confirmed a 'great want of cottages', and severe overcrowding. *BPP*, 'Report of the House of Commons Select Committee on Agriculture', 612 (1833), vol. V, Qs. 9486–90, 9896–7, 9908.
55. Goudhurst statement, *loc.cit.* Framfield vestry minute, 17 March, 1817, ESCRO. Par.343/12/1.
56. Parsons to the Hartfield overseers, March, and reply, 3 April 1826, ESCRO. Par.360/10/1/1. Checkland, 1974, pp.82–5.
57. West Grinstead overseers' accounts, 1834–5, WSCRO. Par.95/38/1. Battle Union, details of component parish properties, 1837; A'Court's surveys of Winchester and Alton divisions, Nov. 1834 and Jan. 1835, PRO. MH.12/12,747; 32/1, 2.
58. Northbrook, 1905, vol. I, p.102. Wells, 1981, pp.525–6/76–7.
59. See below for violence between English and Irish labourers.
60. *Kent Herald*, 11 June 1835. *Sussex Advertiser*, 27 Sept. 1830. Checkland, 1974, pp.166, 198.
61. Framfield vestry minutes, 1816–32, ESCRO. Par.343/12/1, 2. Cowherd, 1977,

pp.142–3. Rose, 1970, pp.57–8.
62. Mrs Norman to Hartfield overseers, May 1833; vestry minutes, Brede, 30 Jan. 1807, 13 May 1811, 9 March and 10 Aug. 1812, 8 March, 12 April and 10 May 1813, and 20 Jan. 1818; Framfield, 9 June 1817, 4 and 11 March 1819, and 26 Feb. 1820; Hartfield, 1819–26; Icklesham, 26 Jan. 1820, West Grinstead (and overseers' accounts) 1830–35, ESCRO. Par.253/12/1, 2; 360/10/1/1; 360/10/2/1–3; 343/12/1; 401/12/3: WSCRO. Par.95/38/1.
63. R.H. Hurst, n.d.(1833), and Sir Charles Burrell, to the Duke of Richmond, 7 May 1833 and 14 April 1834; précis of letters from the Act's supporters to Burrell, 1832–3; Lansdowne to Richmond, 23 March 1833, and draft reply: printed return to the House of Commons re. Act's implementation, 2 April 1833, WSCRO. Goodwood Mss. 638, 642, 665. Brenchley, printed regulations, 1 Dec. 1833, ESCRO. SAS. Co/C/230. *Brighton Gazette*, 16 Aug. 1832, 24 Oct., 7 and 21 Nov. 1833. 16 Jan., 20 Feb., 29 May and 12 June 1834. *Kent Herald*, 24 Jan. 1833. *Hampshire Telegraph*, 20 Jan. and 3 March 1834. Brundage, 1978, pp.15–19.
64. Framfield vestry minutes, 4 and 11 March 1819, 29 May 1821, 9 Dec. 1824, 19 Oct 1825; J. Smith to R. Newenham, n.d; H.B. Hughes to J. Woodward JP, 1 June 1822, ESCRO. Par.343/12/1; 343/37/2/2, 5.
65. Hartfield vestry minutes, 21 Dec. 1817, 11 June 1826, 12 Feb., 30 April and 17 Nov. 1830, and 25 March 1831: overseer Morphew to claimant Austin, domiciled Leatherhead Common, Surrey, 14 April 1826; Harley and Co., Lewes bankers, to Morphew, 28 Aug. 1826, ESCRO. Par.360/10/2/1; 360/10/1/1.
66. *BPP*, 'Poor Law Report' (1834), Appendix B, rural queries, 32–5. Brede vestry minutes, 20 April 1826, 15 March and 21 May 1829, ESCRO. Par.253/12/3.
67. Checkland, 1974, pp.133–47, 220–23.
68. Battle Petty Sessions minutes, 24 July 1821 and 13 Dec. 1825, ESCRO. PBSA.4; the Bench ordered the weekly 1/6 and a gallon loaf to be raised to 'at least 5s. ... to include Lodging & washing' costs.
69. See for example, minutes, 9 and 23 Oct. and 27 Nov. 1821, ibid.
70. Minutes, 9 July and 13 Aug. 1822, 24 Jan. 1826 and 23 Jan. 1828, ESCRO. PBSA.4, 5.
71. Minutes, 13 Nov. 1821, 12 Mar, 25 June and 20 Oct. 1822, 28 Jan. and 11 Nov. 1823, 13 July 1824, 13 Sept. 1825, 23 May, 13 June and 24 Oct. 1826, 14 Aug. and 11 Dec. 1827, 8 Jan. 1828, 10 March 1829 and 14 June 1831, ibid.
72. *Sussex Weekly Advertiser*, 26 Oct. 1812, 18 Jan., 1 and 8 Feb. 1819.
73. Battle Petty Sessions minutes, ESCRO. PBSA.5. Poynter, 1969, pp.313–4.
74. Copy, rules and expenditure revealing a cut in annual costs from £3133 to £1155 between 1819 and 1829, ESCRO. Par.360//14/11. Poynter, 1969, pp.268 (and note 37), 311, 315.
75. Hartfield vestry minute, 3 May; circular to 'every Landlord & Lady' of 'cottages or Tenements', 6 June 1826: East Grinstead Special Petty Sessions handbill, 25 Jan. 1828, ESCRO. Par.360/10/1/1; 360/14/11.
76. Vestry minutes, Brede, 26 Oct. 1823; Fittleworth, 16 Aug. 1827, ESCRO. Par.253/12/ 1; WSCRO. Par.86/12/1. *Kent Herald*, 25 Nov. 1830.
77. The detailed correspondence between each poor-law Union and the PLC, and its succeeding central body, the PLB, supplemented by that of the assistant commissioners (subsequently inspectors), in PRO. MH.12 and 32 series, is powerfully reinforced by the contents of the commonly considerable archives generated by individual Unions, now principally deposited in CROs. The extra evidence in the press is also massive and rich.
78. Chichester, and Day, to the PLC, 28 April and 9 May 1835, PRO. MH.12/12, 854, 13, 157. *BPP*, 'Report of the Select Committee of the House of Commons on the Poor Law Amendment Act'. (1837), vol. XVII. evidence of the Rev. Soberton, Q.5680. *Sussex Advertiser*, 7 Dec. 1840. *Brighton Patriot*, 12 Feb. 1839.
79. Statement by Clerk, Westhampnett Union, 8 June 1839: Horsham Union minutes, 3 and 8 Nov. 1841, and 30 Nov. 1842, WSCRO. Goodwood Mss. 1608: WG.6/1/5. *Brighton Gazette*, 13 Dec. 1849, 5 June 1857 and 4 Feb. 1858.

80. Among the numerous examples, *Brighton Gazette*, 1 Aug. 1844 and 6 Sept. 1860. *Maidstone Gazette*, 26 Dec. 1848.
81. Horsham Union draft reply to PLC. circular, minutes, 27 July 1836, WSCRO. WG.6/1/1. Day to the PLC, 9 May 1835, PRO. MH.12/13, 157. *Brighton Gazette*, 8 June 1843. BPP, 'Second Report of the Select Committee of the House of Commons on Agricultural Distress', 189 (1836), vol. VIII, Qs.4528–9. BPP, 'Report of the Select Committee of the House of Commons on the State of Agriculture', 464 (1837), vol. V, Qs.1478–80. BPP, 'Report of the Select Committee of the House of Commons on the Poor Law Amendment Act' (1837), vol. XVII, Q.8903.
82. *Brighton Patriot*, 27 Feb. 1838. Uckfield Union minute, 28 Oct. 1837, ESCRO. G.11/1a/1. BPP, 'Second Annual Report of the PLC' (1836), pp.212–3. BPP, 'Report of the Select Committee of the House of Commons on the Laws of Settlement and Poor Removal' (1847), vol. XI, Qs.3161, 3468, 7130. Hawley to the PLC, 31 Oct. 1837, PRO. MH.32/39.
83. Frant vestry minute, 1 Jan., enclosed by D. Rowland, to the PLC, 11 May 1836; Etchingham parish property sale documents, 1861; Hawley to the PLC , 9 Oct. 1835, PRO. MH. 12/13,138, 13,147; 32/39. Horsham Union minute, 22 March 1842, WSCRO. G1/1/5. BPP, 'Report of the Royal Commission on Agriculture', 3rd vol. (1883), vol. XVII, Q.64, 531. *Brighton Gazette*, 22 July 1841 and 6 Sept. 1855. *Illustrated London News*, 1 Sept. 1846.
84. The claim by an assistant poor-law commissioner that the end of subsidies reduced cottage rents by a third, was a propagandist exaggeration; Tufnell, 1842, p.36. *Brighton Patriot*, 13 Oct. 1835. Uckfield Union minute, 9 July 1836; settlement examination of H. Climpson, Sept. 1843, ESCRO. G.11/1a/1; QR/E898. BPP, 'Report of the Select Committee of the House of Commons on the Poor Law Amendment Act' (1837), vol. XVII, p.14.
85. *Sussex Advertiser*, 10 Nov. 1843, 21 March and 8 Dec. 1863. *Maidstone Gazette*, 23 and 30 Nov. 1847. *Brighton Gazette*, 9 Aug., 21 Nov. 1844 and 21 June 1849. BPP, 'Report of the Royal Commission on Agriculture', 1st vol. (1881), vol. XIV, Q.637; 3rd. vol. (1883), vol. XVII, Qs.47,071; cf. Qs.55,283–55,306, 55,405–6, 55,485. BPP, 'Report of the Special Assistant Poor-Law Commissioners on the Employement of Women and Children in Agriculture' (1843), pp.148–9. BPP, 'Report of the Select Committee of the House of Commons on Emigration' (1826–7), vol. V, Q.1572. Tufnell, 1842, pp.37–8.
86. BPP, '... Employment of Women and Children...', p.195. *Brighton Gazette*, 31 July 1851 and 15 April 1852. *Maidstone Gazette*, 6 June 1848. Ticehurst Union workhouse report, 11 Dec. 1850; Clerk, West Firle Union, to the PLB, 14 Sept. 1850; Piggott to the PLB, 12 June 1849, PRO. MH.12/13,144, 13,190; 32/61. Tufnell, 1842, p.40. Beagley's deposition, Aug. 1854, PRO. Assi.36/8.
87. For example, *The Times*, Sept. to Nov. 1863, which stimulated simultaneous investigation by the regional press, including the *Sussex Advertiser*. Cf. *Kent Messenger and Maidstone Times*, Jan. 1873.
88. *Sussex Advertiser*, 14 April 1863. Piggott to the PLB, 26 Jan. 1859, PRO. MH.32/62. Rev. Wrench to Dr Manley, 22 Sept. 1853, PRO. MH.12/13,145, and cf. report on South Malling, *Maidstone Gazette*, 25 April 1848. BPP, 'Report of the Royal Commission on Agriculture', 3rd vol. (1883), vol. XVII, Qs.47,071, 51,214–21. Bawn, 1984, p.157. Lowerson, 1980, pp.161–2. Smith, 1971, pp.40–1, 69, 88. Carlton, 1977, p.35.
89. BPP, 'Report of the Royal Commission on Agriculture', 3rd vol. (1883), vol. XVII, Q.55,399. BPP, 'Report of the Select Committee of the House of Commons on the Laws of Settlement and the Removal of the Poor', 1152 (1850), vol. XXVII, p.95. Clerk, Eastbourne Union, to the PLC, 4 July; Wilde to Chadwick, 27 Oct. and 23 Nov. 1835, PRO. MH.12/12, 854, 13, 157. List of Settlement cases, 1840–1, and Climpson's examination, Sept. 1843, ESCRO. QR/E875, 898. Frost, deposition, Sept. 1837, PRO. Assi.36/3. *Sussex Advertiser*, 8 June 1835 and 21 March 1836. *Brighton Gazette*, 2 June 1842 and 9 Feb. 1843. Roberts, 1979, pp.119–21. Bawn, 1984, pp.182, 247.

90. *Maidstone Gazette*, 28 March, 2 and 23 May 1848, 30 Jan., 27 Feb., 13 March, 3 July, 4 and 25 Sept. 1849. *Kent Messenger and Maidstone Times*, 24 Feb. 1872. Cf. Barker-Read, 1982.

91. Maidstone Petty Sessions, minutes of evidence, 2 July 1827, 4 Aug. 1829, 27 Dec. 1831 and 10 Dec. 1836, KCRO. PS/Md, 1, 2. For Chichester see the numerous depositions respecting a murder case, Sept. 1837, PRO. Assi.36/3. *Sussex Advertiser*, 30 June 1863.

92. *BPP*, 'Report of the Select Committee of the House of Commons on the Poor Law Amendment Act' (1837), vol. XVII, Qs.225–8, 514–54, 3049–50, 11,709, 15,489, 15, 492. *BPP*, 'Report of the Select Committee of the House of Commons on the Laws of Settlement and Poor Removal' (1847), vol. XI, Qs.6309–12. *BPP*, 'Report of the Select Committee of the House of Commons on the Laws of Settlement and the Removal of the Poor', 1152 (1850), vol. XXVII, p.97. *Kentish Gazette*, 23 June 1835. *Brighton Patriot*, 3 Jan. 1837. *Brighton Gazette*, 4 July 1844. Deposition, Etchingham labourer Henry Kind, 16 Dec. 1840; Clerk, West Firle Union, to the PLC, 2 Feb. 1848, and the PLB, 23 June 1852, PRO. MH. 12/13,141, 13,190. Uckfield Union minute, 17 April 1841, ESCRO. G. 11/1a/2.

93. *Hampshire Telegraph*, 21 Oct. 1833 and 6 Jan. 1834. W.A. Miles, Chatham, and the Earl of Chichester, to the Duke of Richmond, 30 Sept. 1835, and 14 Dec. 1840, WSCRO. Goodwood Mss. 1578, 1610. *Sussex Advertiser*, 27 Oct. 1863.

94. *BPP*, 'Report of the Select Committee of the House of Commons on the Laws of Settlement and the Removal of the Poor', 1152 (1850), vol. XXVII, p.97. Piggott to the PLB, 1 Feb. 1850, PRO. MH.32/61. J. Croker to Peel, 29 May 1830, PRO. HO.52/ 10, ff.153–4. *Sussex Advertiser*, 11 May 1840. *Brighton Gazette*, 6 May 1839 and 29 June 1843.

95. *Sussex Agricultural Express*, 20 April 1839. Wells, 1985a, *passim*.

96. Walton, 1976, pp.139–42, for example, argues that 'There is sufficient evidence to suggest that enclosure may have contributed directly to the pauperisation of the agricultural labour force between 1776 and 1783', and again between 1807 and 1815, both periods of intensive enclosure in the county, and interestingly, both times of war when mobilisation militated against unemployment. Cf. the temperate conclusions covering 1700–1780, in Malcolmson, 1981, pp.140–44.

97. Neeson, 1984. Turner, 1988, reports even less protest for Buckinghamshire, but his picture is drawn without apparent reference to local newspapers, a source effectively exploited by Neeson, and is therefore a highly questionable contribution to this difficult topic.

98. Quarter Sessions minute book, 1797–99, ESCRO. QO/EW33.

99. Petty Sessions minutes, Battle, 1789–96, West Malling, esp. 2 April 1787, ESCRO. PBSA; KCRO. PS/Ma.3. Viasey, 1984, pp.143, 145, 147–8, 173, 181, 204.

100. Charlesworth, 1980, pp.92–6. *London Evening Post*, 21 and 25 April 1772. Essex Assize indictments, 1772, PRO. Assi.35/212. I have to thank Mr Charlesworth for identifying details of the diffusion of these disturbances.

101. Uffington vestry minutes, 13 Oct. 1766, Berkshire CRO. DP.134/8/1.

102. Home Circuit Assize minute book, 1740; indictments, 1757, PRO. Assi.31/1, f.123; 35/197/10. *Annual Register* (1768), p.114. Vaisey, 1984, pp.82, 107.

103. Wells, 1982, *passim*. Wells, 1988b, pp.99–105. A. Shelley, Lewes, to the Duke of Richmond, and Receiver of Corn Returns, Atkinson, to the Home Office, 20 June and 2 July 1795, PRO. HO.42/35. *Kentish Chronicle*, 24 April 1795. *Sussex Weekly Advertiser*, 13 July 1795, March to May 1796, 1800 and 1801.

104. Hartfield petition, annotated by overseer Morphew, 2 Feb. 1795; Hurstpierpoint parish records, ESCRO. Par.360/14/11; 400/39/33–62, 400/21/12. Kent Lent Assize 1795, minute book and indictments, PRO. Assi.31/17, f.158; 35/234/10. West Sussex Quarter Sessions rolls, indictments, 1794–95, WSCRO. QR/608, ff.58, 62; 609, ff.51– 3. Shadwell to Richmond, 5 and 15 Feb. 1801, PRO. HO.42/61. *Sussex Weekly Advertiser*, 2, 9 and 16 Feb., and 16 March 1801. Wells, 1988b, pp.219–29.

105. See esp. inhabitants of Blewbury, Berkshire, pardon petition, 8 Jan. 1740, and letters

to Secretaries of State from, Mr Justice Chappel, re. Hampshire arsonist, n.d. but 1740, and J. Tucker, Gloucester, with enclosures, 11 Jan. 1767, PRO. State Papers 36/ 50, f.88; 36/54, ff.90–91; 37/6, ff.7–9. *Gloucester Journal*, 13 Oct. 1766. *Ipswich Journal*, 18 Oct. 1766.

106. Indictments, Sussex Lent Assize, 1811, PRO. Assi.35/251/4. *Sussex Weekly Advertiser*, 21 and 28 Jan., and 1 April 1811. Baxter, 1811.

107. *Annals of Agriculture*, 17 (1792), pp.169–70. *Sussex Weekly Advertiser*, 28 Sept. 1801.

108. *Sussex Weekly Advertiser*, 1 Feb. and 19 March 1802, 7 and 14 April 1806, 2 July, 24 Sept. and 22 Oct. 1810, 4 Feb. and 29 Nov. 1811, and 11 Oct. 1813. Depositions of J. Hodson and J. Chapman, Sept. 1813, ESCRO. QR/E737.

109. *Sussex Weekly Advertiser*, 1 April, 13 and 27 May, 10 June, 1 July and 15 Aug. 1816, and 7 July 1817.

110. *Ibid.*, 1, 8 and 22 April, 7 Oct., 11 and 18 Nov. 1822. King and Fell, Lewes, to E.J. Curties MP, with enclosures, 15 May 1822, PRO. HO.64/1, ff.205–7. Muskett, 1984. Charlesworth, 1982.

111. B. Beaumont, County Fire Office, to Melbourne, 15 Dec. 1831, PRO. HO.40/29(2), ff.533–4. Spater, 1982, vol. II, p.608 and note 86.

112. *Sussex Weekly Advertiser*, 17 May 1802, 7 and 14 Nov. 1808, 27 Feb. 1809, 3 Sept. 1810, and 23 Feb. 1818.

113. For example, R. Monies, re. events in the Dover district, to the Home Office, 22 Feb. 1822, PRO. HO.64/1, ff.246–7. H. Beddell to Peel, 23 July 1822, PRO. HO.52/3, f.175. *Maidstone Gazette*, 23 July 1822.

114. *Sussex Advertiser*, 17 Sept. 1827, 8 Sept. 1828, Aug. to Sept. 1830, and 6 July 1835. *Maidstone Gazette*, 1 March 1831. W. Maxfield, Sunbury, to Melbourne, 25 June 1831, PRO. HO.52/14, ff.297–302. BPP, 'Poor Law Report' (1834), Appendix B, pp.266, 505. BPP, 'Report of the Select Committee of the House of Commons on Agricultural Customs', 461, (1848), Q.5497. BPP, 'Report of the Special Assistant Poor Law Commissioners on the Employment of Women and Children in Agriculture' (1843), p.175. Perkins, 1976–77, pp.52–3. Barber, 1982, pp.10–11. Bagley, 1962, p.27. Clift, 1908, p.64.

115. Spater, 1982, vol. II, pp.473–5 and esp. notes 73–4. See also *Morning Chronicle*, 3 Dec. 1830, and *Sussex Advertiser*, 29 Nov. 1830.

116. *The Prompter*, 20 Nov. 1830. Col. Rowan, Metropolitan Police Commissioner, to Phillipps, 9 Nov. (twice); letters to Rowan from E.T. Smith, and Inspector Lean, both 9 Nov; Sir Charles Blunt to Peel, 10 (with enclosure), 11 and 14 Nov; F. Manger to Camden, 10 Nov; unknown JP, at Tunbridge Wells to the Home Office, 15 Nov; Battle Bench to Peel, 12 Nov; Courthope to Phillipps, 11 and 14 Nov; Hastings postmaster, and A. Scott, Brighton, to F. Freeling, 11 Oct., and 12 Dec. 1830; J.M. Scott, Brighton, to Melbourne, 3 Jan. 1831, PRO. HO.40/25(1), ff.160–2, 174, 185; 52/8, ff.16–7; 52/10, ff.235–6, 340–4, 390–1, 394–5, 407–8, 523–9, 635. Battle Petty Sessions minutes, July to Dec. 1830, ESCRO. PBSA.5. *Rochester Gazette*, 16 Nov. 1830. *Maidstone Gazette*, 16 Nov. 1830. *Kent Herald*, 18 Nov. 1830. *Morning Chronicle*, 25 Nov. 1830.

117. Bryant's deposition 19 Nov; letters to Melbourne, from R.Devonport,2 Dec. 1830, Matthews, and Rev. Allen, 3 and 15 Feb. 1831, PRO. HO.52/10, ff.422–3, 438–9, 610–3; 52/15, ff.11–12. *Maidstone Gazette*, 28 Dec. 1830 and 4 Jan. 1831. *Kent Herald*, 6 Jan. 1831.

118. Wartling recognizances, Nov. 1830, ESCRO. QR/E806. Ninfield indictments, Dec. 1830, PRO. Assi.35/270/5. *Kent Herald*, 30 Dec. 1830. Bryant's deposition, 19 Nov. 1830, PRO. HO.52/10, ff.422–3.

119. Depositions of F. Castle and six others, 18 to 21 Sept. 1830, KCRO. Q/SBe/120.

120. Collingwood to Phillipps, 18, 19 and 22 Nov. 1830, PRO. HO.52/8, ff.91–2; 52/10, ff.303–6. *Maidstone Gazette*, 11 Jan. 1831. Prosecutor's brief against five Hawkhurst men for machine-breaking, Kent Winter Assize 1830, PRO. T[reasury] S[olicitor] 11/ 943/3412.

121. *Sussex Advertiser*, 22 Nov. 1830. J.B. Freeland, lawyer and agent, to the Duke of

Richmond, ten letters 23 Nov. 1830 to 6 Jan. 1831, enclosing numerous depositions and Quarter Sessions conviction notices, WSCRO. Goodwood Mss. 1477a.

122. Collingwood to Phillipps, 18 and 19, and reply 19 Nov. 1830, PRO. HO.41/8, pp.73–4; 52/8, ff.91–2; 52/10, ff.303–4. Cf. Freeland to Richmond, 9 Dec. 1830, WSCRO. Goodwood Mss., 1477a.

123. *Maidstone Gazette*, 16 Nov. 1830. Wilmshurst, 1981, citing land tax microfilm 628 (1830), WSCRO. Recognizances, James Izzard and Edward Avery, Rotherfield, in £50 to keep the peace for one year towards M.C. Mabbott, JP, 19 Nov. 1830, and ten more, taken by Sir G. Webster, 9 to 23 Nov. 1830, ESCRO. QR/E866. Mabbot, obituary, *Brighton Gazette*, 20 Sept. 1860.

124. Rowan to Phillipps, 9 Nov. and Drummond, Abby Park, to Peel, 17 Nov. 1830, PRO. HO.40/25(1), f.185; 52/10, ff.199–200. Henry Meddon, machine-maker, deposition, 18 Nov. 1830, WSCRO. QR/W758. *Hastings and Cinque Ports Iris*, 20 Nov. 1830. Wells, 1985b, p.132.

125. Boys to Peel, 17 Oct. 1830, PRO. HO.52/8, ff.209–10. Prosecution brief against George Buckwell, Sussex Winter Assize, 1830, PRO. TS.11/1007/4051.

126. Wilmshurst, 1985. I have to thank Mick Reed for much of this detail, which is extracted principally from Quarter Sessions rolls, Westbourne parish, WSCRO. QR/ W755; Par.206/12/4–6,and Australian convict records, namely Tasmanian Convict record book, New South Wales, CON. 31/4, 7, 10, 37; AO. Ref.40/417, Reel 905.

127. *Rochester Gazette*, 16 Nov. 1830. Blunt to Peel, 10, 11 and 14 Nov. 1830, PRO. HO.52/ 10, ff.523–9.

128. *Sussex Advertiser*, 22 and 29 Nov., and 6 Dec. 1830.

129. I have to again thank Mick Reed for supplying some of these references. *Kent Herald*, 2 and 9 Dec. 1830. T. Mitchenor, Kirdford, to W. Tyler, 26 Nov. 1830, Petworth House Archives, [uncatalogued]. R. Prime to J. Hawkins, 16 Nov; Quarter Sessions, Dec. 1830, WSCRO. Hawkins Papers, 6f. 1769; QR/W758. Diary of Lady Brooke-Pechell, Parham House, typed transcript of Parham papers, vol.33. North Aylesford Petty Sessions minutes, 3 Dec. 1830, KCRO. PS/NA/16. Labourer Reeves' indict-ment, Dec. 1830, PRO. Assi.35/270/5. Depositions against East Grinstead men, Nov. 1830 ESCRO. QR/E 806 *Hampshire Telegraph*, 22 Nov. 1830. Diary of John Payne, privately held. Caldecott, 1918, pp.30–32.

130. Colson, 1937, pp.97–8. *Sussex Advertiser*, 31 Jan. 1831. Depositions of Bartholomew, and innkeeper Moors, 10 Dec. 1830, KCRO. Q/SBe/122. Letters to Melbourne from justices, Monypenny, Hadlow, 5 Feb., and Plumptree, 9 and 13 Sept. 1831, PRO. HO.52/13, ff.13–4, 50–51; 64/2, ff.219–22.

131. *Maidstone Gazette*, 31 May, 12 July, 9, 16 and 30 Aug., 6 Sept. and 25 Oct. 1831. Letters to Melbourne from Dr Poore, Murston, 4, 5 and 8 Aug., W. Stringer, New Romney, 16, 17 and 18 (with enclosed depositions) Aug; T. Badley, Sittingbourne, to Earl Camden, 6 Aug. 1831, PRO. HO.52/13, ff.70–3, 78, 87–99. Freeland, Chichester, to Richmond, 14 and 29 July 1831, WSCRO. Goodwood. Mss. 635.

132. Recognizances, returns of summary convictions, 1833, and cf. deposition of overseer Barrow, 18 Nov. 1834, ESCRO. QR/E817–8, 825. *Kent Herald*, 3 Jan. 1833. *Sussex Advertiser*, 24 Oct. 1833.

133. *Sussex Advertiser*, 26 Feb. 1835. Earl Delawarr to Melbourne, 10 Sept. 1831. *Kent Herald*, 24 Oct. 1833.

134. Figures from, *Maidstone Gazette, Brighton Gazette,* and *Sussex Advertiser*, and additional Sussex evidence from, C.J. Sackham, to Phillipps, 16 Sept., R. Pomfret to T.L. Hodges MP, 12 Oct., and letters to Melbourne from, W. Borrer, and T. Baker, 5 and 25 May, T.C. Bellingham, 2 June, and W. Jenner, 4 Nov. 1831, PRO. HO.52/15, ff.13–4, 35–6; 62/2, ff.132–4, 151–2, 178–80, 350–52, 570–78.

135. Spater, 1982, vol. II, p.608 and note 86. *Maidstone Gazette*, 23 Nov., 6 and 27 Dec. 1831. R. Lasse, Melton, to J. Bell, 9 Nov. 1834, PRO. HO. 64/4, ff.184–5. Poore to Camden, 11 June 1831, KCRO. U840/0236/8.

136. See also below.

137. *Maidstone Gazette*, 29 Nov. and 6 Dec. 1831.

138. J. Bellingham, Battle, to H.B. Curteis MP, 27 Aug. 1831; Rev. Mayne, Crowhurst, to Melbourne, 27 Nov. 1832, PRO. HO.64/2, ff.209–12; 64/3, ff.194–5.
139. Poore to Camden, 13 June 1831, PRO. HO.52/13, ff.159–65. *Brighton Gazette*, 22 Nov. 1832, 9 and 16 Jan. 1834.
140. Radzinowicz, 1948–68, vol. IV, pp.308, 321. Beaumont to Melbourne, 31 Oct. 1834, PRO. HO.64/4, ff.103–4.
141. Colson, 1937, pp.97–8, 264. Case against John Thomas of Buxted, 30 July 1831, ESCRO. QR/E809.
142. Hawley to the PLC, 19 May 1835, PRO. MH.12/12,747. *BPP*, 'Report of the Select Committee of the House of Commons on Agriculture', 612 (1833), vol. V, Qs.7285–7309. *BPP*, 'Report of the Select Committee of the House of Commons on Agricultural Distress', 465 (1836), Vol. VIII, Qs.13,170–74. *BPP*, 'Report of the Select Committee of the House of Lords on the State of Agriculture', 464 (1837), vol. V, Qs.93–6, 117, 132–6. *BPP*, 'Report of the Select Committee of the House of Commons on the Poor Law Amendment Act', 138 (1838) Vol. XVIII, Qs.361–3. *Poor Man's Guardian*, 15 Nov. 1834.
143. Templeman to Russell, 31 Aug. 1836, PRO. HO.64/6, ff.117–18. Wells, 1985a. Wells, 1988a.]
144. Justices Twopenny and Essell, Rochester, to Russell, 24 Dec. 1835, PRO. HO.52/26, f.118.
145. *Maidstone Gazette*, 27 Dec. 1831. Dover Chronicle, 7 July 1849.
146. *Sussex Advertiser*, 28 March 1836. *Brighton Patriot*, 22 Dec. 1835.
147. Lewes Bench to Melbourne, 24 April 1831, PRO. HO.64/2, ff.132–4.
148. Freeland to Richmond, 5 and 7 July 1835, WSCRO. Goodwood Mss. 1575. *Brighton Patriot*, 7 July 1835. *Sussex Advertiser*, 6 July and 10 Aug. 1835, and 3 Aug. 1840 *Brighton Gazette*, 15 Dec. 1831, 5 Jan. 1832, 1 Aug. 1833, 27 May 1847 and 21 July 1853.
149. Rowan to Chadwick, 6 Feb. 1836, PRO. MH.12/5315.
150. Grace to Russell, 22 Oct.(with enclosure), 24 Oct. and 2 Nov. (with enclosure) 1836, PRO. HO.64/2, ff.86–97; 64/7, ff.15–8, 24–7. Goddard, 1956, pp.125–30.
151. *Brighton Gazette*, 19 Dec. 1833, 24 Oct. 1844 and 31 July 1845. *Kent Messenger and Maidstone Times*, 3 and 10 Feb., and 16 March 1872.
152. *Brighton Gazette*, 20 Oct. 1845, 24 and 31 Oct. 1850, 16 Oct. 1851, 18 March 1852, 24 March 1853, 19 Oct. 1854, 24 March and 7 July 1859. *Maidstone Gazette*, 20 March 1849. *Berkshire Chronicle*, 12 Oct. 1850. *Sussex Advertiser*, 31 March 1863.
153. *Sussex Advertiser*, 25 March 1839, 10 March, 29 Sept. and 22 Dec. 1863, 27 Sept. and 4 Oct. 1864. *Kent Herald*, 14 Nov. 1833. *The Champion*, 1 March 1840.
154. *Sussex Advertiser*, 28 March 1836. G.W. Hughes D'Arth to Melbourne, 16 Nov. 1831; D. Rowland, Frant, to Russell, 28 March 1837, PRO. HO.64/2. ff.421–4; 64/7, ff.15–6. Ellman to Richmond, 16 Sept. 1835, WSCRO. Goodwood Mss. 1578. *Maidstone Gazette*, 17 May 1831, 10 Jan. 1832, 20 June 1848 and 24 April 1849. *Brighton Patriot*, 4 Aug. and 29 Sept. 1835. *Brighton Gazette*, 10 April 1856. *Kent Herald*, 21 Feb. 1833. *The Champion*, 29 March 1840.
155. *Maidstone Gazette*, 8 Aug. 1848, 16, 23 and 30 Jan., and 20 March 1849. C.J. Sandham, Washington, to the Home Office, 21 Sept. 1831; R. Micklethwaite to Russell, 16 Oct. 1837, PRO. HO.52/15, ff.13–14; 64/7, ff.68–9. *Sussex Advertiser*, 8 Aug. 1825, 7 Oct. 1839, 26 July and 22 Sept. 1864. *Brighton Patriot*, 24 Oct. 1837.
156. *Kent Messenger and Maidstone Telegraph*, March 1872 to Aug. 1873.
157. *Brighton Gazette*, 28 Nov. 1850, 7 Aug. 1851, 29 April, 13 May and 29 July 1852.
158. *Brighton Gazette*, 22 March 1849 and 27 March 1863. *Maidstone Gazette*, 8 May 1849.
159. *Brighton Gazette*, 9 and 16 Jan. 1834.
160. Wood's indictment, Sussex Winter Assize, 1833, PRO. Assi.35/273/5. *Brighton Guardian*, 18 March 1840. Dine, depositions against and jail calendar, April and May 1843, ESCRO. QR/E892.
161. *Sussex Weekly Advertiser*, 21 Dec. 1795, 8 Feb. and 14 March 1796. Depositions, A. Brook, and E. Daw, Dec. 1824, PRO. Assi.36/1. Ayres, 1986, p.25.

162. Confession of Boots, and depositions against Morgan, April 1832, ESCRO. QR/ E812.
163. Iford return, Nov. 1839, ESCRO. QAC/1/E1. *BPP*, 'Report of the Select Committee of the House of Commons on the Poor Law Amendment Act', (1837), vol. XVII, Q.5013.
164. Lord Chief Justice Denham, address to Sussex Assize Grand Jury, *Brighton Patriot*, 31 July 1838.
165. Assistant Poor-Law Commissioner Tufnell to the PLC, 6 Nov. 1838, PRO. MH.32/ 70.
166. This conclusion emerges from the unpublished work of Shirley Chase who has kindly permitted me to draw upon it.
167. *Brighton Patriot*, 18 Dec. 1838 and 4 June 1839. *Brighton Gazette*, 8 Feb. 1855, 1 and 8 Jan. 1857. J. Skinner, deposition, 1835, ESCRO. QR/E827. *Sussex Advertiser*, 13 April 1840. *BPP*, 'Report of the Select Committee of the House of Commons on the Poor Law Amendment Act' (1837), vol. XVII, Q.5408. *BPP*, 'Report of the Select Committee of the House of Lords on the Allotment of Land and Agricultural Statistics', 402 (1843), vol. VII, Q.80. White, 1891, cited Bawn, 1984, p.3.
168. *Brighton Patriot*, 17 Nov. 1835, 25 Feb. 1836, 2 May, 19 Sept. and 5 Dec. 1837, 2 Jan., 6 and 27 Feb., 1 May, 2 Oct. and 13 Nov. 1838, and 4 June 1839. *Sussex Advertiser*, 9 May 1836 and 27 Oct. 1863. Depositions of E. and J. Munnery, and J. Brooker, 27 Oct. 1838, WSCRO. QR/W791. *Brighton Gazette*, 8 Dec. 1842. *BPP*, 'Second Annual Report of the PLC' (1836), vol. XXIX, p.215.
169. *Maidstone Gazette*, 8 Feb. 1848. *Brighton Gazette*, 8 Dec. 1856, 4 June 1857 and 24 March 1859. Summary convictions, Battle, 17 March 1838; depositions against Hellingly inmates, Acton, 23 Dec. 1842, and James Cook, 18 Oct. 1851, ESCRO. QR/ E854, 889, 960. Disciplinary hearings against Ticehurst Union schoolmaster, April 1857, PRO. MH.12/13,146. *Kent Herald*, 4 March 1847. *Berkshire Chronicle*, 16 Nov. 1850. *Brighton Patriot*, 20 Feb. 1838. *Sussex Advertiser*, 20 Oct. 1863.
170. Wells, 1985a, p.45. The Cranbrook Union even extended this arrangement for families domiciled in London; Clerk to Chadwick, 27 Aug. 1842, PRO. MH.12/4913.
171. Deposition of Goudhurst workhouse governor, 29 Jan. 1838; Hawley to the PLC, 9 Oct. 1837; Piggott to the PLC, 30 March 1847, and the PLB. 16 Jan. 1851, 11 Dec. 1852, 31 Dec. 1854, 9 Jan. and 12 April 1858, PRO. MH.12/4911; 32/39, 61–2.
172. *Brighton Patriot*, 2 June 1835 and 24 Jan. 1837. *Brighton Gazette*, 7 April 1842 and 24 Nov. 1859. *Sussex Advertiser*, 13 Jan. 1863.
173. *Brighton Patriot*, July 1838. *Sussex Advertiser*, 29 April 1839, 5 Oct. and 23 Nov. 1840. *Brighton Gazette*, 18 Sept. 1842, 15 Jan. 1846 and 14 Aug. 1851. Gibson, 1978, p.48.
174. *Brighton Gazette*, 18 May 1843. *BPP*, 'Report of the Select Committee of the House of Commons on the Inclosure of Commons' (1844), vol. V, Q.2684. Depositions against Alfriston shepherd Weaver, May 1866, ESCRO. QR/E1034.
175. *Brighton Patriot*, 8 Sept. 1835, 31 Jan. 1837, 20 Feb., 26 June, 17 July and 21 Aug. 1838. *Sussex Advertiser*, 26 Jan. and 16 Dec. 1839, 27 Jan. and 2 March 1840. *Brighton Gazette*, 12 April 1849 and 11 April 1850. *Maidstone Gazette*, 9 Jan. and 17 April 1849.
176. Depositions against George Watson, Aug. 1841, carter Sawyers and others of Icklesham, 16 Aug. 1851, and journeyman butcher Head of Ore, Oct. 1853; deposition of F. Marshall, and police constable Jeffery, 10 and 16 Aug. 1851, ESCRO. QR/ E958, 974, 976, 978. *Brighton Gazette*, 23 Feb. 1843, 4 May 1848, 7 June 1849, 5 Jan. 1854 and 4 Dec. 1856. *Maidstone Gazette*, 11 April 1848.
177. Heasman, enclosing a very lengthy confession by Clear's mate John Field, to Tufnell, 15 Jan. 1841, after his conviction for sheep-stealing, PRO. MH.32/61.
178. *Sussex Weekly Advertiser*, 6 and 13 April 1818, 17 and 24 May, 7 June, 2, 16 and 30 Aug. 1819.
179. Depositions against Hylands, May 1846, ESCRO. QR/E916. *Brighton Gazette*, 7 and 21 May 1846, 2 and 9 Jan., 20 Feb. and 27 March 1862. *Sussex Advertiser*, 1 and 29 March 1863. *Maidstone Gazette*, 7 March and 3 Oct. 1848, and 20 March 1849.
180. *Sussex Weekly Advertiser*, 24 Nov. 1823. *Sussex Advertiser*, 9 Nov. 1835, 4 Jan. 1836

and 28 Jan. 1839. *Brighton Gazette*, 8 Jan. 1846 and 15 April 1858. *Brighton Patriot*, 29 May 1838. Depositions of Wren, Feb. 1835, and J. Vigor, 12 Nov. 1838, ESCRO. QR/ E827, 857.

181. Depositions against Wheeler, 18 Nov. 1839, and J. and H. Smith, 24 Nov. 1853, ESCRO. QR/E865, 970.

182. Depositions by Wren, Feb. 1835, Weller, April 1838, and constable Duly, 8 Nov. 1838, ESCRO. QR/E827, 853, 857. *Brighton Patriot*, 23 Feb. 1836. *Brighton Gazette*, 4 Nov. 1841, 17 Nov. 1842, 11 April 1849, 29 Nov. 1855 and 17 Feb. 1859. *Sussex Advertiser*, 27 Oct. 1863.

183. *Sussex Advertiser*, 13 April 1840. Rudé, 1985, pp.78–9.

184. *Brighton Gazette*, 21 Oct. 1841 and 16 Oct. 1845. Rusbridger to Richmond, 11 March 1839, WSCRO. Goodwood Mss. 1863. *Sussex Advertiser*, 15 July 1839.

185. Details extracted from the local press, the records of Petty and Quarter Sessions, and the Assizes.

186. *Brighton Gazette*, 24 Sept. 1857. *Kent Herald*, 1 April 1847.

187. *BPP*, 'Report of the Select Committee of the House of Commons on the Poor Law Amendment Act' (1837), vol. XVII, Qs.13,704–14,112. Freeland to Richmond, 16 Dec. 1830, WSCRO. Goodwood Mss. 1477a.

188. *Sussex Weekly Advertiser*, 10 March and 17 April 1823.

189. Anon., *England in 1830 being a Letter to Lord Grey* (1831), esp. pp.3, 38–51. Courthope, draft to the PLC, Nov. 1832, ESCRO. SAS. Co/C/230.

190. *Maidstone Gazette*, 16 Aug. 1831. W.E. Tallents to Melbourne, 13 Dec; Capt. Thompson, Longparish, to Lord Melville, with enclosure, 10 Nov. 1830, PRO, HO. 40/27(6), ff.580–5; 52/7, ff.235–8. *Twopenny Trash*, 1 July 1832. Colson, 1937, pp.146–7.

191. *Sussex Advertiser*, 13 and 20 Sept. 1830. Postmaster, Maidstone, to F. Freeling, 14 Oct; Egremont, Petworth, to Peel, 13 Nov. 1830, PRO. HO.52/8, f.333; 52/10, ff.621–2. Prosecution against Willcocks for arson on 8 Oct. 1830, PRO. TS.11/943/3412. BL. Place Newspaper Collection, vol. 21, f.82. Courthope to the PLC, *loc. cit.*

192. *Kent Herald*, 18 Nov. 1830. J. Bryant, deposition, 19 Nov; Courthope to Peel, 5, 6 (with enclosure) and 17 Nov: letters to Melbourne from Norfolk JPs, J. Stacey, 7 Dec., and G. Pellow, 14 Dec., Battle Clerk of the Peace, 11 Dec: undated London police officers' report; Phillips to Courthope, 8 Dec. 1830, PRO. HO.41/8, pp.425–6; 52/9, ff.12–3; 52/10, ff.369–70, 373–4, 413–14, 422–3, 447–8. Indictments of Thomas Noakes and four others, Sussex Winter Assize, 1830, PRO. Assi.35/270/5.

193. Charles Perrot, arrested near Lewes for distributing handbills in the district, deposed that 'he saw the statement in Bells Life in London, & took that Paper to Patching', a Brighton printer, 'to extract something from it for sale – but it did not have the heading "successful Expedient" – that was added by Patching'. Copies of bills, printed by Harrison, and Hetherington; Maidstone postmaster to F. Freeling, 14 Oct; T.L. Hodges MP to the Home Office, 11 Nov; letters to Peel from Webster, and Blunt, 12 and 14 Nov., Kell and Sons, Lewes, 19 Dec., Lord Arden, Epsom, to Melbourne, 29 Dec. 1830, with enclosures including handbill, 'Conversation between two labourers', printed by Cohen of Brighton, PRO. HO.52/8, ff.33, 171–2, 320, 334; 52/ 10, ff.278–85, 397–9, 528–9, 584–5. Prosecutor's brief against three Goudhurst rioters, West Kent Quarter Sessions, Dec. 1831, PRO. TS.11/943/3412. Depositions against Price, Nov. 1830, KCRO. Q/SBw/124. *Maidstone Gazette*, 4 Jan. 1831.

194. *Maidstone Gazette*, 16 Nov. 1830 and 16 Aug. 1831. Prosecution brief against Inskipp, Sussex Winter Assize 1830, PRO. TS.11/1007/4051. Maule to Phillipps, 1, 2 and 8 Nov; Battle postmaster to F. Freeling, 27 Nov and 1 Dec; letters to Melbourne from, Clerk of the Peace, Battle, 26 Nov., and chairman Sussex Assize Grand Jury, 24 Dec. 1830, PRO. HO.40/27(2), ff.54–7, 62–3; 52/10. ff.431–7, 607–8. *Hastings and Cinque Ports Iris*, 6 Nov. 1830. Andrus, 1984, p.376.

195. At Mayfield, the Rev. Kirby refused to reduce his tithes, 'but they made up their minds not to separate without doing something, and consequently they resolved to petition ... the ... Commons'. *Morning Chronicle*, 9 Dec. 1830. Letters to the Home Office

from T. Sanctuary, 18 (with enclosure) and 19 Nov., W, Burrell, 19 and 21 Nov., R.H. Hurst, 28 Nov. and C.M. Burrell, 5 Dec. 1830, PRO. HO.52/10, ff.534–45, 555–6, 565–6. *Political Register*, 11 Dec. 1830. *Sussex Advertiser*, 15 Nov. and 6 Dec. 1830. BL. Place Newspaper Collection, vol. 21, f.83. *Maidstone Gazette*, 16 Nov. 1830.

196. Prosecutor's brief against Richard Hodd and three others, PRO. TS.11/1007/4051. *Kent Herald*, 9 Dec. 1830. Undated Dallington petition c.17 Nov. and Collingwood to Phillipps, 22 Nov. 1830, PRO. HO.52/10, ff.305–6, 420.

197. Prosecutor's brief against J. and W. King, Sussex Winter Assize 1830, PRO. TS.11/1007/4051. Collingwood to the Home Office, n.d., signed statement by T.T. Hodges, Benenden, 11 Nov., Courthope to Peel, 18 Nov. (thrice) 1830, and Clerk of the Peace, Battle, enclosing itemised prosecution costs of prisoners from the Rape of Hastings, 4 Feb. 1831, PRO. HO.52/8, ff.171–2, 455–8; 52/10, ff.415–19, 448–52

198. Letters to Melbourne from Rev. Dallas, 8 Jan. and Rev. B. Donne, enclosing petition, 16 Jan. 1831: handbill, 'Henry Hunt's Address to the Radical Reformers of England, Ireland and Scotland', 20 Oct. 1831: 'S.S.' reports on meetings at the Rotunda, three undated letters, but late Dec. 1830 and June 1831, PRO. HO.52/12, ff.5–7; 52/13, ff.113–5; 52/14, ff.318–21; 64/11, ff.189, 191–2, 221. *Poor Man's Guardian*, 24 Sept. 1831. Wells, 1988a. Hammond, 1966, p.321.

199. Letters to Melbourne from Lord Carnarvon, Hampshire, 5 Feb., the Deal Bench, 5 and 9 Aug., and Dymchurch JPs, 19 Aug. 183 (with enclosure), PRO. HO.52/13, ff.124–5; 52/1, ff.75–6, 79–82.

200. *Maidstone Gazette*, 15 March, 19 April and 20 Sept. 1831.

201. For pro-Reform meetings in the autumn of 1831 at Chatham, Dover, Gravesend, Dartford, Tonbridge, Cranbrook, and Tenterden, all of which drew crowds from adjacent villages, and the Kent County meeting on Penenden Heath, see the *Maidstone Gazette*, 27 Sept., 18 and 25 Oct., and 4 Nov. 1831. Moreover, 'In several villages petitions have been signed without the formality of calling meetings. At Appledore ... every villager who could wield a pen has subscribed'. Meetings in the spring of 1832 included the rally on Blackheath, with 'Processions of tradesmen and others from the various districts', and another at Hythe comprising large groups from all 26 parishes in the Elham division; many village rallies were also held again, as at Wrotham and Hawkhurst; ibid., 29 May 1832.

202. Letters to Melbourne from 'Moderate Reformer', Eastbourne, 31 Oct., and W. Robinson, Reigate, 5 Nov. 1831, PRO. HO.40/29(2), ff.343–4, 364.

203. *Maidstone Gazette*, 5 and 12 May 1832. *Church Examiner and Ecclesiastical Record*, 1 Nov. 1832.

204. *Maidstone Gazette*, 29 March and 4 Nov. 1831. Lettrs to Melbourne from Webster, 28 March, and Mayor of Rye, 7 and 9 Nov. 1831, PRO. HO.52/15, 15, ff.22–3, 39–40. Aspinall, 1952, p.154. Buckingham and Chandos to the Duke of Wellington, 20 Nov. 1832, S[outhampton] U[niversity] L[ibrary], Wellington Papers, 4/1/4/1/39.

205. Letters to Wellington from Sir J. Pollon, 28 Oct. and Rev. W.R. Wright, 5 Nov. 1832, and 1 Jan. 1833; H. Stripp to the 'Landlord of the White Lion, Werwell', 26 Oct. 1832, SUL. Wellington Papers, 4/1/4/3/29, 34, 44; 4/1/5/3/1. Letters to Melbourne from Wright, Itchen Abbey, 29 May, with enclosed depositions relating to the 'monstrous attacks upon the King & Nobility' made by plcbeian orators in the district, W.C. Mabbott, 20 (with enclosure) and 29 Nov., and 12 Dec., and eleven Sussex JPs, 28 Nov. 1832, PRO. HO.52/17, ff.126–7; 52/20, ff.8, 12–13, 21–5. *Poor Man's Guardian*, 1 Dec. 1832. *Brighton Gazette*, 22 and 29 Nov. 1832.

206. *Twopenny Trash*, 1 July 1832. *Poor Man's Guardian*, 29 Sept. 1832. Borlee to Melbourne, 5 May 1833, PRO. HO.52/23, ff.12–13. *Brighton Guardian*, 28 Feb. 1833. Colson, 1937, pp.146–7.

207. *Poor Man's Guardian*, 29 Sept., 1 and 8 Dec. 1832. *Brighton Gazette*, 22 Nov. 1832. Wellington to H. Pierrepoint, Pollon, and the Mayor of Andover, all 3 Nov., to Woodham, 20 Nov. and Blount, 3 Dec; letters to Wellington from Pollon, 28 Oct. and 5 Nov., the Mayor of Winchester, 6 Nov. and Melbourne, 1 Dec. 1832, SUL. Wellington Papers, 4/1/4/1/20–1; 4/1/4/3/, 29, 32, 34–5, 41.

208. *Kent Herald,* 11 April 1833. *Brighton Gazette,* 31 May 1832, 16 Jan. and 10 July 1834. J. Broadwood, Lydd, Sussex, to Richmond, 30 July 1835, WSCRO. Goodwood Mss. 1575. I. Thomas to Chadwick, 20 Sept. 1834, PRO. MH.12/12,854.
209. *BPP,* 'Report of the Select Committee of the House of Commons on Agriculture', 612, (1833), vol. V, Q.10,977. *BPP,* Report of the Select Committee of the House of Commons on the State of Agriculture', 464 (1837), vol. V, Q.4957.
210. H. Drummond to Peel, 15 Nov. 1830, BL. Add. Mss.40401, ff.271–2. *Maidstone Gazette,* 26 July 1831. *Poor Man's Guardian,* 20 Oct. 1832. Head, Sundridge, to the PLC, 29 Oct. 1834, PRO. MH.12/5315. *BPP,* 'Report of the Select Committee of the House of Commons on the Poor Law Amendment Act' (1837), vol. XVII, Qs.17,000–1.
211. *Brighton Gazette,* 8 Nov. 1832.
212. G.M. Ball to Commander Rowan, 11 and n.d. Feb., and 5 April 1834, PRO. HO.64/15, 105–8.
213. Tufnell to the PLC, 2 Dec. 1838, PRO. MH.32/70.
214. J.P. Durant, who inflitrated the Heathfield meeting, to Day, 25 July; S. Ayling to Richmond, 23 May 1835, WSCRO. Goodwood Mss. 1573, 1575. *Brighton Gazette,* 17 June 1841.
215. *BPP,* 'Report of the Select Committee of the House of Commons on the Poor Law Amendment Act' (1837), vol. XXVII, Q.4195.
216. Thomas to Chadwick, 25 Sept. 1834, PRO. MH.12/12,854.
217. Hawley to the PLC, 10 Sept; Col. A'Court, Hampshire, to Lefevre, 21 June, 14 Oct. and 17 Nov. 1835, PRO. MH.12/5315; 32/2. *BPP,* 'Poor Law Report' (1834), Appendix A. p.18.
218. *The Times,* 25 Dec. 1830 and 3 Jan. 1831. Letters to Melbourne from W.E. Tallents, 11 Dec., and Capt. Thompson, 15 Dec. 1830, PRO. HO.40/27(6), ff.580–85; 52/7, ff.233–8. R. Mason to his family, 27 July 1831, cited Colson, 1937, pp.293–302.
219. Day to Chadwick, 11 May, and to Melbourne, 13 May; Hawley to Nicholls, 8 July 1835; Tufnell to the PLC, 30 Jan. 1837, PRO. MH.32/38, 69; HO.52/27, ff.175–6.
220. By December 1835 the chairman of the Uckfield Union was satisfied that the rigorous implementation of the Act had taught the poor, and their anti-Poor Law supporters among the small ratepayers, that the Board of Guardians was unable to modify the Act's provisions. The Board was now unanimous, as those previously hostile Guardians were also convinced that rate reductions had been achieved 'without any undue suffering to the Classes that were operated upon'; Day to the PLC, 22 Dec. 1835, PRO. MH.12/13,157.
221. This is an impressionistic provisional appraisal deriving from a mass of South-eastern New Poor Law material from the records of the PLC and PLB, local Unions, and the press. But see esp. *Brighton Gazette,* 30 Nov. 1832. Horsham Board of Guardians minute, 20 April 1842, WSCRO. WG.6/1/5. Hawley to the PLC, 20 April 1836; Piggot to the PLB., 30 April 1849, and undated quarterly report, 1860, PRO. MH.12/12,747; 32/61–2. Fraser, 1976, p.11. Horn, 1976, pp.199–202. Brundage, 1975, pp.201–2, 205, 207–10. *BPP,* 'Report of the Select Committee of the House of Commons on the Settlement Laws and the Removal of the Poor' (1847), vol. XI, Q.3544. *BPP,* 'Report of the Select Committee of the House of Commons on the Poor Law Amendment Act' (1837), vol. XVII, Qs.9966, 9971, 9987–9. *BPP.,* 'Report of the Royal Commission on Agriculture', (1881), vol. XIV, Q.9605.
222. *Kent Messenger and Maidstone Telegraph,* 25 May, 1 June 1872 and 17 May 1873.
223. A'Court to Lefevre, 14 Oct., 7 Nov., 13 and 20 Dec. 1835, PRO. MH.32/2. Borlee to Melbourne, 4 May 1833, PRO. HO.52/23, ff.12–3. *Maidstone Gazette,* 28 June 1832. *Brighton Patriot,* 20 Dec. 1836.
224. Wells, 1985b, pp.150–54. *Brighton Guardian,* 21 Aug. 1839. Farmer to Urania, 9 April 1842. Henry Vincent, 'An Address to the agricultural labourers ...', Birmingham Public Library, Lovett Collection, vol. II, f.291. Norman, 1900, p.147. *Sussex Advertiser,* 10 Nov. 1863.
225. Prosecution brief against Dyke, 1831, PRO. TS.11/943/3412. *Sussex Advertiser,* 23

June and 29 Sept. 1863. Deposition of shoemaker Aaron Apps, of the 'Labour in Vain', Oct. 1848, ESCRO. QR/E935.
226. Brede vestry minute, 16 Nov. 1828, ESCRO. Par.253/12/3. *Brighton Gazette*, 15 Jan. and 2 April 1846, 28 March 1850, 21 July 1853 and 23 April 1857. *Kentish Express*, 1 Sept. 1883.
227. *Sussex Agricultural Express*, 26 Feb. and 5 March 1878. *Sussex Advertiser*, 10 Nov. 1863.

An Agenda for Modern English Rural History?

Mick Reed and Roger Wells

Historical debates engross the participants. The appearance of issues, and the positions of individuals in print, commonly masks a longer, invigorating process of discussion and debate in research seminars and conferences, as well as in the convivialities which invariably follow, involving many more people than those whose names appear as contributors. In these situations, the capacity of those who publicly nail their colours to the mast, to stand back and try to evaluate what has been achieved, is open to doubt. However, we are satisfied that the debate to date has achieved something, if nothing more than some acceptance that the study of the history of rural communities should comprise much more than the traditional emphasis on agriculture and its development. Naive, ahistorical accounts and analyses which imply an inexorable and linear intensification of agrarian capitalism, are simply inadequate, even where this approach pays at least lip service to those who were so manifestly the losers in such transitions. Indeed, there is much which can be lost by exclusive concentration on the losers, even where this embraces such spectacular manifestations of their reactions as the Swing explosion. What Edward Thompson described in one of his most memorable phrases, as 'the enormous condescension of posterity', in fact extends – as he would be the first to agree – way beyond the domestic outworkers to whom it referred.

The historians' craft demands some focus on change, but at its more refined it must also involve an attempt at the re-construction of past communities, so that their internal mechanisms can be understood, as well as – and this is crucial – their relationships with what is usually portrayed as the national society. Such a combination of objectives, when applied to the social history of the English countryside, dictates an holistic approach to rural communities. It also requires a theoretical and empirical definition of what precisely a 'community' was. Though one might not fully agree with the suggestions of Charles Phythian-Adams [1987] in this respect, his definitional quest is admirable.

Indeed, although there will always be space for the competent and thorough, but *empiricist*, historian, there is no logical reason for empiricism to exist in a vacuum; all historians should become more aware and explicit about the conceptual bases of their work. We need to *think* about theory very much more than we are used to doing. Theoretical thinking is not simply about the way that historians use concepts such as class, but includes at a most general level, an awareness of the ultimate objectives. The answer to that will dictate the way in which we approach research, the questions raised, and the answers that are obtained. Different historians will reach different conclusions about these epistemological issues, and for the moment we can only indicate, what appear to us, partly as a result of the debate, to be major empirical and conceptual lacunae in our knowledge. The debate, even more so in its broadened form, has exposed areas of empirical weakness and ignorance. It has thrown up, though not resolved, important conceptual, methodological and ideological issues. Moreover, even where the debate has succeeded in generating more empirical evidence, this has principally derived from historians working on specific regions and localities. There is no guarantee that the findings, especially of the new contributions by the editors, who have concentrated on southern England, with a principal focus on the south-east, have a general applicability. We would, however insist that our priorities, methodologies, and concepts have a much wider relevance. The list could be extended by us, and doubtlessly by the other contributors here, as well as the many other historians who have enlivened the discussions previously mentioned. However, while we recognise all this, and the ramifications of the crucial regional characteristics of rural England as a whole, we wish to suggest an agenda of topics that we consider are crying out for further research work. The fundamental broadening of the issues by contributors to the debate, together with other publications over the past decade, dictate these observations. However, this modicum of satisfaction at developments should not be interpreted as complacency; there are, with one partial exception, neither conclusions nor conclusive statements here.

Clearly, the traditional tripartite division of rural society between agricultural labourers, tenant farmers, and their landlords, to which historians are so attached, is totally inadequate. Most villages hosted numbers of country trades and craftspeople as well as small-scale agriculturalists, and their activities were of central importance to the community. Yet their existence has been virtually overlooked by myopic historians content with the odd platitudious reference, with the partial exception of the recognition of village craftsmen [*Kerr*, 1968; *Holderness*, 1972; *Chartres*, 1981; *Chartres and Turnbull*, 1971]. A potentially richer – though still only emergent – picture of rural communities, has established the importance of household producers, dual occupationists, and small-scale farmers. Indeed, Professor Wrigley has suggested that demographic evidence reveals a considerable expansion in the numbers of, principally though certainly not exclusively, self-employed craftsmen in the early nineteenth-century countryside, though he makes no reference to recent revisionist literature on rural social structures. We can no longer ignore the vigour and scale of small-scale trade, craft and agricultural activity; if demobilisation after 1815, fiercely reinforced by unprecedented population growth, stimulated this sector, the hypothesis advanced in chapter eight of this volume, of probable significant further expansion owing to the impact of the Poor Law Amendment Act, requires much deeper investigation.

Moreover, this important sector of village communities rarely perceived themselves or their immediate successors, as the inevitable victims of what some in the nineteenth century thought of as scientifically determined progress. Much more empirical work of course needs to be done on these neglected groups, some of it highly appropriate given Thatcherism's devotion to an exotic combination of notions of individual independence, enterprise, entrepreneurship, and supposed Victorian values. This social category's role within parish politics, notably at vestry level, was of some significance, and indeed the opaque world of vestry politics, notably under the Old Poor Law, but also after the implementation of its successor, warrants sustained analysis. Again, much conceptual elaboration is required. The editors are at odds as to whether the activity of these groups should properly be considered entrepreneurial or not. But the explicit elaboration of such differences is the very catalyst that can provoke a more thorough and informed investigation of these and other issues. Moreover, although we may be confident that household producers were ubiquitous in the early nineteenth century countryside, whether their histories and significance, were similar in all regions during the remainder of the period covered by this book is still unknown. But from such clearly-defined positions, debate can proceed, and knowledge accrue.

If these small producers can be seen as a distinct class (however unclear at the perimeters), how is it that, at least at times, they appear to identify socially, politically, and even perhaps more momentarily, economically, with proletarians, than with the more affluent rural bourgeoisie, including the greater farmers? Why indeed, should they ally with either? David Blackbourn's [1984: 43, 49] approach to a major facet of this problem is certainly less than satisfactory. He designates the 'petite bourgeoisie' as an 'uneasy' and 'contradictory' class, sharing some values with the proletariat, and some with the bourgeiosie. Such a view can only come from seeing this class from the standpoint of either capital or labour, and as something of an anachronism. A more fruitful avenue might be to try to see the class from its own standpoint – as having its own specific and relatively consistent class interests, that at times coincide with those of labour; at times with those of capital; and at times with neither. Blackbourn's approach guarantees a failure to recognise the latter, and historians of conservative/liberal and Marxist persuasions should use the facility to perceive changing and shifting allegiances across time, to avoid the same trap.

Many of our projections here hinge on the view that rural communities did not exist in either the isolation posited by so many historians, or the apparent vacuum implied by such conceptions. A glance at the account book of even the humblest tradesperson will demonstrate, in addition to neighbourhood networks, links with nearby, *as well as distant*, towns and cities. An analysis of poor law records will show the constant movement over many miles of many of the claimants for relief. This interaction is also central to the case, which may have been established here, for the genesis of a working-class consciousness in southern villages, at least for a brief period of time. We are aware of any number of problematics in this regard. Did the state's apparent neglect of the agricultural sector's fundamental difficulties during the prolonged post-war depression, and the escalating problem of poverty, generate a unity of analysis and purpose, which was expressed in demands for radical political reform of the state? But how representative is the projection of our southern evidence of political developments, and the genesis of a rural working-class consciousness, about the time of the recurrent crises galvanised by Captain Swing, the issues of the Reform Bill, and the Poor Law Amendment Act? To what extent did the encroachments of the market drive those who bore the harshest brunt of it, farmworkers, journeymen craftsmen and their small masters, modest farmers and equally modest dual-occupationists – whether 'entrepreneurial' or not – into closer collaboration that was expressed through a 'working class' consciousness. Mention of the state reminds us that it was – at least on occasion – a very intrusive agent. After all, it provided a framework for governance and of *law* if not invariably of order, and defined many of the contexts in which all English rural communities existed. There was a constant interaction between the state and society and at times the decisions by the state could assume a paramountcy in the village, and have medium as well as long term significance. Was the state's role in the early nineteenth century unique? How important was its part as one, if but one, of the determinants as to *perceptions* of class interests? These determinants demand further enquiry; again the question of significant regional variations warrants specific investigation.

Was this socio-political alliance as transient as it appeared to be? Was it split, and if so how irrevocably by new factors, among which we would include the Chandos clause of the Reform Act which extended the vote to inhabitants of county constituencies paying rents of 50 pounds, or more, together with relatively rapid emergence of the manifestly divisive inter-locking effects of the Poor Law Amendment Act? Was this experience shared with other regions, and was what one distinguished Welsh historian, Gwyn A. Williams, once polemically described as the 'un-making of the English working class', a feature of rural societies in other parts of the country? Were these apparent fragmentations major con-tributory forces to the farmworkers' incapacity to organise collectively, to participate in burgeoning Victorian trade unionism before the 1870s?

This debate derived from an attempt to chart changes in the nature of social protest in the countryside, especially the development of incendiarism as a peculiarly rural form in England. While some satis-faction must be taken from the considerable volume of literature on the subject of social protest, inspired by the seminal studies of George Rudé and Edward Thompson, and published completely independently of our debate, together with an iota of pride that some scholars even advanced issues central to the debate through doctoral theses [*Archer*, 1982; *Bawn*, 1984], there are still important gaps in our knowledge of rural protest. Paramount are the largely unanswered questions over enclosure. Why was it, that land privatisation through the mechanism of parliamentary intervention in the eighteenth and nineteenth century, apparently failed to evoke social responses parallel to both sixteenth and seventeenth century English precedents, and to similar reactions to dispossession on literally the global stage? With relatively rare, and apparently isolated exceptions, of which the best known is the example of Otmoor in Oxfordshire [*Hammonds*, 1966, 83–92]. England experienced none of the 'phenomenon of the mass invasion or occupation of land', which Eric Hobsbawm correctly insists 'is familiar' to 'whoever studies peasant movements' [*Hobsbawm*, 1974 esp. 120; cf. *Te Brake*, 1981: 70, note 12]. The nature of British colonialism itself, was probably partially conditioned by this key experience of the English ruling class. To give but one example, the historian of the Malabar rebellions in the nineteenth and early twentieth centuries notes that this experience 'possible rendered' colonial authorities 'sympathetic to eviction of tenants by Hindu landlords'; from the 1790s 'the recognition of the *jenmi* as an absolute owner or "lord of the soil" formed the lasting basis of British land policy ... and throughout the nineteenth century, British administrative and judicial institutions ... worked directly to restore the landed aristocracy of the ... *jenmis*' [*Dhanagare*, 1977, 118, 120]. Historians of English parliamentary enclosure must emulate Neeson's Northamptonshire study [1984], and this will mean changing their orthodox focus, methodology, and evidential sources, for the range of additional local and regional work required. The fact that the topic does have a directly global significance ought to provide a further spur.

Other facets of social protest in the English countryside are perhaps less elevated, but several topics warrant additional investigation. As yet animal maiming – that 'un-English' phenomenon – has received systematic treatment for East Anglia only [*Archer*, 1984]. The relationship between social protest and crime remains unclear, and our picture could be enriched through re-examination of concepts of 'rural crime' too. The same must be said of the relationship between vagrancy and crime, and the scale and nature of organised crime.

One early development in the debate was the identification of a need to begin a 'study of everyday life' [*Wells*, 1981: 514/65]. Much remains to be done. We know virtually nothing about the kinds of everyday manifestations of conflict between the suppliers of capital and the suppliers of labour, despite the work of Alun Howkins [1977; 1985: 15–38], and Mick Reed [1984a: 110–15/101–6]. What kinds of 'informal' institutions existed among rural workforces both during the era of trades unionism, and even more importantly, before it, are largely unexplored with the significant exception of Morgan's identification of the harvest of a forum for commonly intensive but highly localised negotiations between labour and capital over piece rates [*Morgan*, 1982: Ch. 8]. Micro studies clearly have enormous potential here, but whether we actually find manifestations of these phenomena will depend on whether we look for them; and whether we look for them will depend upon our models. It is surely a disservice to our craft as well as those we purport to study, to assume some things as 'given', and therefore of no interest to us.

Models are a crucial area for further thought as to their general role, and to the specific value of particular examples. Sarah Banks has recently [1988] presented a consummate challenge to the usefulness of the 'open/close' model. It seems to us, as principally social historians, that the model enforces a restrictive and damaging approach, which is so *prescriptive* that its devotees are blinded to the full range of possibilities. Endlessly refining the model, so that there are numerous descriptive categories of 'openness' and 'closeness' will succeed only in creating still more confusion, as the model collapses in upon itself. The fact that nineteenth-century commentators used the *term* ensures the need to attach some importance to it. What needs further enquiry is whether their use of the term constitutes a model that can have some explanatory value, which the apparently endless permutations threatened by Dennis Mills cannot. This really is a case where historians need to ask just what it is that they are trying to do. Models do not have universal validity, and the old axiom, 'horses for courses' should be recalled here.

Such considerations lead directly to many other topics within English rural history where contemporary polemic has been uncritically adopted by historians to define their own frameworks. The Old Poor Law is one major example. The actual history of the pre-1834 system virtually demolishes many of the hostile arguments advanced by its critics, especially of the Poor Law Commissioners themselves, and incorporated so readily in much later historical writing . This extends from the cost-cutting initiatives of vestry after vestry, in the most 'open' of parishes in contemporary parlance, to Benches of magistrates with clear utilitarian-minded majorities in the 20 years following Waterloo. But proving the typicality of the notoriously impoverished parishes of Kent and Sussex, and that of their increasingly hard-nosed, economising, local judicial authorities, requires considerable regional and local research, freed from the pre-emptive biases so easily assumed by historians. We need local and regional analyses that look at poor law administration not only as part of a *national* relief system, but within the context of local and regional power structures.

Much of the same must be said about one other key functions of the Old Poor Law, namely housing provision. Of all the other interventions by public authorities in the market, that concerned with housing for the rural working class, is the category where our ignorance is most profound. The

topic is not mentioned in Dr Rule's otherwise excellent brief survey of
rural working-class housing [1986: 76–81]. As it is we are not even in the
position of being able to estimate the numbers of working people who
received some form of housing aid, still less explore regional and local
variations. Yet this is a subject of monumental importance, because here,
despite the most "advanced" social-security system in the eighteenth-
century world, housing a rapidly expanding proletarian population
proved beyond the ability or inclination of those in power within an
equally rapidly intensifying capitalist system.

Conversely, to what extent did the New Poor Law lead to a shrinkage or
withdrawal of that intervention? Did it contribute to the generation of a
housing crisis at the start of the Victorian era? Did it, together with the
new premium on jobs, particularly for farmworkers, intensify the already
considerable problems of homelessness and vagrancy? What was the
impact of this essentially rural problem, through that key phenomenon of
migration and eventual depopulation of the countryside, on the nation's
urban and indeed industrial history? To pose but one of so many potential
questions, to what extent did the market towns of rural England share with
their industrial counterparts the twin problems of poor overcrowded
housing provision, and unsanitary environments in distinct proletarian
districts?

How did the rural proletariat itself fragment into the contemporary
categories of 'roughs' and 'respectables', which certainly seems to have a
greater factual validity than other Victorian perceptions of social (and
structural) features of the mid- and later-nineteenth century countryside?
If the history of the 1840–70 period remains the dark age as far as our
knowledge of rural history in general, the comment can be made with even
greater conviction about its key proletarian dimension. The contributors
to this volume have hardly touched upon this chronology, with the partial
exceptions of crime and incendiarism. While Morgan [1982] presents
interesting material on harvesting, Howkins' [1985] passionate engage-
ment with the proletarians of rural Norfolk, lacks incision, and begs
essential questions, both over 'roughs' and 'respectables', and the *timing*
of the take-off of agrarian trade unionism in the 1870s. For example, did
'roughs' or 'respectables' make the more stalwart trade unionists, and why
did agrarian trade unionism take off so spectacularly in the early spring of
1872? [*Wells*, 1985c]. Moreover, the paucity of studies on farmworkers'
trade unionism in the later nineteenth century is a disgrace, symbolised by
the fact that Alfred Simmons, the general secretary from 1872 to 1887 of
the Kent and Sussex Labourers' Union, which at moments had more
members than Joseph Arch's nominally national union, is mentioned
twice in Professor Armstrong's recent 300-page study of *Farm-workers. A
Social and Economic History 1770–1980*; namely, Simmons was 'more
artful' than some other farmworkers' union leaders, and gave evidence to
the Royal Commission on Agriculture in 1881 [1988: 119, 127, cf. *Arnold*,
1974; and *Carlton*, 1977]. What is demonstrably obvious, even at this

stage, and in spite of what Dr Mills learned while perched on grandad's knee [*Mills*, 1988: 399/119], is that there were a great many men in the 1870s who made a huge point of picking a row with their farming employers. And, in Kent at least, many labourers' wives attempted collective action.[1] Mills' grandfather inherited the lessons of organised labour's late nineteenth-century defeat, but the grandson is too little of a historian to perceive that at times in their history, farmworkers did *not* surrender to anticipations of failure. Detailed study of agrarian trade unionism will throw massive light on many of the issues raised, but unanswered here. Until such is tackled, we are once more confronted with a massive lack of knowledge and understanding of what class means – and meant.

The period from 1840 to 1870, is fraught with problems for the historian of rural labour. In the main, apart from copious coverage of criminal cases before the courts, which begins to include arson after the traumas of the 1830s, and the partial exception of the workhouse and housing scandals in the 1840s and 1860s respectively, the provincial press in this period ignores rural labour issues, probably studiously. Chartism in the countryside has, with something of an exception respecting Suffolk and Essex [*Brown*, 1969], been ignored by historians who have submitted to the screen imposed by the editors of the establishment press. Yet Bronterre O'Brien's *Southern Star* was aimed at least in part at rural inhabitants. If Chartism really had little rural impact, then it would be useful to know why. Certainly it can no longer be attributed to either rural isolation or rural ignorance. It would be interesting to know something as well of the initiatives taken by post-Chartist radicals, among them Ernest Jones [*Saville*, 1952: 57], to extend urban working-class organisations to rural England in the 1850s.

Equally fascinating – as a problematic – is the apparent reluctance of the leaders of organised farmworkers in the 1870s to speak about their own history, except in subjective ways that turned on poverty induced through low wages, the callousness of farmers over unemployment, wet weather lay-offs, and the abysmal quality of working-class housing. Much rhetoric was expended on denouncing the current Poor Law, with poignant aspersions cast on ageing farmworkers' visions encompassing only the workhouse. Extensive research on the sources for the Kent and Sussex Labourers' Union, has revealed no recollection of the revolts against the New Poor Law, which included the failed essay in agrarian trade unionism in the mid-1830s, and just one reference to the Swing episode marginally over forty years previously. At one of the earliest rallies, an elderly labourer recalled the farmers saying in 1830 that wage increases were prevented only by tithe exactions; he pointed out that once Swing forced tithe reductions, wages did not improve because the savings were pocketed by the employers.[2] And this absence continued even after this Union was firmly established, with over ten thousand members, secure funds, and some successes on both the wages and hours worked fronts.

There may be several explanations for this, including the Union leadership's determined stance against militant tactics and their aversion to the evocation of precedents of popular social disorder, but – ostensibly at least – this feature encapsulates the curiously low profile of the mid-Victorian farmworker.

And what about the bourgeiosie – landowners, capitalist tenant farmers, the grander owner-occupiers – as well as annuitants, clergy, and many others? We have more knowledge here. The work of F.M.L. Thompson [1963], David Spring [1963], Travis Crosby [1977], John Beckett [1986], to name only a few, has told us much. But still we know all to little about the divisions of interest, of opinion, and of action, at the local level. Why were there divisions between fractions of capital over Swing, the poor law, and the repeal of the corn laws, to give only three examples? Yet these interests, opinions and actions, had enormous significance locally. The responses of labour and small producers to the pressures of the times varied enormously even within relatively small areas. To a degree these responses were conditioned by *local* conditions; by the *personalities* of local representatives of capital; by the presence or absence of particular class fractions; in a word by the complexities of class.

There is much to be discovered about the Georgian and Victorian countryside. Social protest and class conflict certainly oscillated, and were equally certainly perennial. The scale of strife and sheer poverty were such, that perhaps only one feature of a much more thorough picture can be predicted, namely that the romantic assumptions of Victorian urban man and the equivalents from certain twentieth-century historians, will not be rehabilitated.

NOTES

1. *Kent Messenger and Maidstone Telegraph*, 8 Feb., 15 Feb., 8 March, 15 March, 5 April, 15 April, 3 May, 7 June 1873.
2. *Kent Messenger and Maidstone Telegraph*, 11 May 1873.

Consolidated Bibliography

Agar, N.E., 1981, *The Bedfordshire Farm Worker in the Nineteenth Century*, Publications of the Bedfordshire Historical Record Society, Vol. 60.

Amos, S.W., 1971, 'Social Discontent and Agrarian Disturbances in Essex, 1795–1850' (unpublished M.A. thesis, University of Durham).

Andrus, F.S., 1984, 'Extracts from the Miscellany and Farm Accounts of Francis Andrus of Scadbury in the Parish of Southfleet', *Archaeologia Cantiana*, Vol.100.

Apfel, A., and Dunkley, P., 1985, 'English Rural Society and the New Poor Law; Bedfordshire 1834–47', *Social History*, Vol. 10.

Archer, J.E., 1985, '"A Fiendish Outrage?": A Study of Animal Maiming in East Anglia, 1830–1870', *Agricultural History Review*, Vol. 33.

Archer, J.E., 1982a, 'The Wells–Charlesworth Debate: A Personal Comment on Arson in Norfolk and Suffolk', *Journal of Peasant Studies*, Vol. 9 No. 4.

Archer, J.E., 1982b, 'Rural Protest in Norfolk and Suffolk 1830–1870' (unpublished Ph.D. thesis, University of East Anglia).

Armstrong, Alan, 1988, *Farmworkers: A Social and Economic History 1770–1980*, London: B.T. Batsford.

Arnold, Arthur, 1880, 'Free Land and Peasant Proprietorship', *The Nineteenth Century*, Vol. 7.

Arnold, R, 1974, 'The "Revolt of the Field" in Kent 1872–1879', *Past and Present*, Vol. 64.

Ashworth, G.J., 1970, 'A Note on the Decline of the Wealden Iron Industry', *Surrey Archaeological Collections*, Vol. 67.

Aspinall, A. (ed.), 1952, *Three Early Nineteenth-Century Diaries*, London: Williams & Norgate.

Athreya, Venkatesh, Boklin, Gustav, Djurfeldt, Goran, and Staffen Lindberg, 1987, 'Identification of Agrarian Classes: A Methodological Essay with Empirical Material from South India', *Journal of Peasant Studies*, Vol. 14, No. 2.

Ayres, J. (ed.), 1986, *Paupers and Pig Killers: The Diary of William Holland a Somerset Parson 1799–1818*, Harmondsworth: Penguin.

Bacon, R.N., 1844, *Report on the Agriculture of Norfolk*, Norwich.

Bagley, G.S., 1962, 'The Life and Times of William Holloway, Historian of Rye', *Sussex Archaeological Collections*, Vol.100.

Bagwell, P.S., 1981, 'The Decline of Rural Isolation', in G.E. Mingay (ed.), *The Victorian Countryside*, 2 vols, London: Routledge & Kegan Paul.

Bainbridge, A., and Jones, D.J.V., 1975, *Crime in Nineteenth-Century Wales*, SSRC Report.

Banks, S.J., 1982, 'Open and Close Parishes in Nineteenth-Century England' (unpublished Ph.D. thesis, University of Reading).

Banks, Sarah, 1988, 'Nineteenth-century Scandal or Twentieth-century Model?: A New Look at 'Open' and 'Close' Parishes', *Economic History Review*, 2nd ser., Vol. 41.

Barber, S. 1982, 'Irish Migrant Agricultural Labourers in Nineteenth-Century Lincolnshire', *Saothar*, Vol. 8.

Barker-Reed, M. 1982, 'The Public Health Question in the Nineteenth Century; Public Health in a Kentish Market Town, Tonbridge, 1850–1875', *Southern History*, Vol. 4.

Barnett, D.C., 1967, 'Allotments and the Problem of Rural Poverty, 1780–1840', in G.E. Mingay and E.L. Jones (eds.), *Land, Labour and Population in the Industrial Revolution*, London: Edward Arnold.

Baugh, D.A., 1975, 'The Cost of Poor Relief in South-East England, 1790–1834', *Economic History Review*, 2nd ser. Vol. 28.

Bawn, K.D., 1984, 'Social Protest, Popular Disturbance and Public Order in Dorset, 1790–

1838' (unpublished Ph.D. thesis, University of Reading).

Baxter, R., 1811, *The Trial of the Rev. Robert Bingham*, Lewes: Baxter.

Beattie, J.M., 1974, 'The Pattern of Crime in England, 1660–1800', *Past and Present*, No. 62.

Beavington, F. 1975, 'The Development of Market Gardening in Bedfordshire', *Agricultural History Review*, Vol. 23.

Beckett, J.V., 1984, 'The Peasant in England: A Case of Terminological Confusion?', *Agricultural History Review*, Vol. 57.

Beckett, J.V., 1986, *The Aristocracy in England, 1660–1914*, Oxford: Blackwell.

Behagg, Clive, 1979, 'Custom, Class and Change: The Trade Societies of Birmingham', *Social History*, Vol. 4, No. 3.

Bellesiles, Michael A., 1986, 'The World of the Account Book: The Frontier Economy of the Upper Connecticut River Valley, 1760–1800' (unpubished paper presented to the Conference of the Organisation of American Historians).

Bernstein, Henry, 1979, 'African Peasantries: A Theoretical Framework', *Journal of Peasant Studies*, Vol. 6, No. 4.

Berryman, B. (ed.), 1973, 'Mitcham Settlement Examinations 1784–1814', *Surrey Record Society*, Vol. 27.

Blackbourn, David, 1984, 'Between Resignation and Volatility: The German Petite Bourgeoisie in the Nineteenth Century', in Geoffrey Crossick and Heinz-Gerhard Haupt (eds.), *Shopkeepers and Master Artisans in Nineteenth-Century Europe*, London: Methuen.

Body, G.A., 1966, 'The Administration of the Poor Law in Dorset 1760–1834, with Special Reference to Agrarian Distress' (unpublished Ph.D. thesis, University of Southampton).

Bohstedt. J.H., 1972, 'Riots in England, 1790–1810, with Special Reference to Devonshire' (unublished Ph.D. thesis, Harvard University).

Booth, A. 1977, 'Food Riots in the North-west of England, 1790–1801', *Past and Present*, No. 77.

Boston, Richard, 1974, *An Anatomy of Laughter*, London: Collins.

Brown, A.F.J., 1969, *Essex at Work, 1700–1815*, Chelmsford: Essex County Council.

Brown, A.F.J., *Chartism in Essex and Suffolk*.

Brundage, A. 1975, 'Reform of the Poor Law Electoral System, 1834–95', *Albion*, Vol. 7.

Brundage, A., 1978, *The Making of the New Poor Law, 1832–1839*, London: Hutchinson.

Burgess, John, 1982, *The Journal and Correspondence of John Burgess 1785–1819*, edited and published privately by Leonard J. Maguire, Ditchling: The Old Meeting House.

Burnett, J., 1966, 'Trends in Bread Consumption', in T.L. Barker, J.L. Mackenzie and J. Yudkin (eds.), *Our Changing Fare*, London: MacGibbon & Kee.

Bushaway, Bob, 1982, *By Rite: Custom, Ceremony and Community in England, 1700–1880*, London: Junction Books.

Byres, T.J., 1977, 'Agrarian Transition and the Agrarian Question', *Journal of Peasant Studies*, Vol. 4, No. 3.

Byres, T.J., 1986, 'The Agrarian Question, Forms of Capitalist Agrarian Transition and the State: An Essay with Reference to Asia', *Social Scientist*, Vol. 14, Nos. 11/12.

Carlton, F., 1977, ' "A Substantial and Sterling Friend to the Labouring Man"; The Kent and Sussex Labourers' Union 1872–1895' (unpblished M.Phil. thesis, University of Sussex).

Carter, Ian, 1976, 'The Peasantry of North-east Scotland', *Journal of Peasant Studies*, Vol. 3, No. 2.

Carter, Ian, 1979, *Farm Life in North-east Scotland 1840–1914: The Poor Man's Country*, Edinburgh: John Donald.

Caunce, Stephen, 1975, 'East Riding Hiring Fairs', *Oral History*, Vol. 3, No. 2.

Chaloner, W.H. 1977, review of E.O.A. and S.G. Checkland (eds.), *The Poor Law Report of 1834*, in the *Agricultural History Review*, Vol. 25.

Chambers J.D. 1940, 'Enclosure and the Small Landowner', *Economic History Review*, 1st ser. Vol. 10.

Chambers J.D., and Mingay, G.E., 1966, *The Agricultural Revolution 1750–1880*, London: Batsford.

Chambers, J.D. 1953, 'Enclosure and the Labour Supply in the Industrial Revolution', in E.L. Jones (ed.), *Agriculture and Economic Growth 1650–1815*, London: Methuen.

Charlesworth, A. (ed.), 1983, *An Atlas of Rural Protest in Britain 1549–1900*, London: Croom Helm.

Charlesworth, A. 1979, *Social Protest in a Rural Society: the Spatial Diffusion of the Captain Swing Disturbances of 1830–1831*, Historical Geography Research Series, No. 1. Norwich.

Charlesworth, A., 1980, 'The Development of the English Rural Proletariat and Social Protest, 1700–1850: A Comment', *Journal of Peasant Studies*, Vol. 8 No. 1.

Charlesworth, A. 1982, *A Comparative Study of the Spread of the Agricultural Disturbances of 1816, 1822 and 1830*, Liverpool Papers in Human Geography, No. 9.

Chartres, J.A., 1981, 'Country Tradesmen', in G.E. Mingay (ed.), *The Victorian Countryside*, 2 Vols. London: Routledge & Kegan Paul.

Charters, J.A., and Turnbull, G.L., 'Country Craftsmen', in G.E.Mingay (ed.), *The Victorian Countryside*, 2 Vols. London: Routledge & Kegan Paul.

Checkland, S.G. and E.O.A. (eds.), 1974, *The Poor Law Report of 1834*, Harmondsworth: Penguin.

Chevalier, J., 1982, *Civilisation and the Stolen Gift: Capital, Kin and Cult in Eastern Peru*, Toronto: University of Toronto Press.

Chevalier, J., 1983, 'There is Nothing Simple about Simple Commodity Production', *Journal of Peasant Studies*, Vol. 10, No. 4.

Chivers, Keith, 1983, 'The Supply of Horses in Great Britain in the Nineteenth Century', in F.M.L. Thompson (ed.), *Horses in European History: A Preliminary Canter*, Reading: British Agricultural History Society.

Cirket, A.F., 1978, *The 1830 Riots in Bedfordshire, Background and Events*, Publications of the Bedfordshire Historical Record Society, Vol. 57.

Claridge, R., 1793, *A General View of the Agriculture of the County of Dorset*, London: Board of Agriculture.

Clark, Christopher F., 1978, 'The Household Mode of Production: A Comment', *Radical History Review*, No. 18.

Clark, Christopher F., 1979, 'Household Economy, Market Exchange and the Rise of Capitalism in the Connecticut Valley, 1800–1860', *Journal of Social History*, Vol. 13, No. 2.

Clark, Christopher F., 1982, 'Household, Market and Capital: The Process of Economic Change in the Connecticut Valley of Massachussetts, 1800–1860' (unpublished Ph.D. thesis, Harvard University).

Clark, Christopher F., 1987, 'Economics and Culture: Change in Rural Massachussetts, 1780–1860' (unpublished paper presented to the Peasants Seminar, Institute of Commonwealth Studies, University of London. 13 March).

Clark, P., 1976, 'Popular Protest and Disturbance in Kent 1558–1640', *Economic History Review*, 2nd ser., Vol. 29.

Clift, W., 1908, *Reminicenses of William Clift*, Basingstoke: Bird Bros.

Cobbett, W., 1853, *Rural Rides*, London: A. Cobbett.

Collins, K., 1967, 'Marx on the English Agricultural Revolution', *History and Theory*, Vol. 5.

Colson, A.M., 1937, 'The Revolt of the Hampshire Agricultural Labourers and its Causes 1812–1831' (unpublished M.A. thesis, University of London).

Cook, Scott, 1984a, *Peasant Capitalist Industry. Piecework and Enterprise in Southern Mexican Brickyards*, Lanham, NY: University Press of America.

Cook, Scott, 1984b, 'Rural Industry, Social Differentiation and the Contradictions of Provincial Mexican Capitalism', *Latin American Perspectives*, Issue 43, Vol. 11, No. 4.

Cook, Scott, 1984c, 'Peasant Economy, Rural Industry and Capitalist Development in the Oaxaca valley, Mexico', *Journal of Peasant Studies*, Vol. 12, No. 1.

Cowherd, R.G. 1977, *Political Economists and the English Poor Laws*, Ohio: Ohio

University Press.

Crosby, T.L. 1977, *English Farmers and the Politics of Protection 1815–52*, Hassocks: Harvester Press.

Crossick, Geoffrey, 1984, 'The Petite Bourgeiosie in Nineteenth-Century Britain: The Urban and Liberal Case', in Geoffrey Crossick and Heinz-Gerhard Haupt (eds.), *Shopkeepers and Master Artisans in Nineteenth-Century Europe*, London: Methuen.

Crummett, Mario de los Angeles, 1987, 'Class, Household Structure, and the Peasantry: An Empirical Approach', *Journal of Peasant Studies*, Vol. 14, No. 3.

Dalton, George, 1974, 'Peasant Markets', *Journal of Peasant Studies*, Vol. 1, No. 2.

Davies, D. 1795, *The Case of the Labourers in Husbandry*, London: C. G. and T. Robinson.

Davies, M.F., 1909, *Life in an English Village: An Economic and Historical Survey of the Parish of Corsley in Wiltshire*, London: Fisher Unwin.

Deane, P. and Cole, W.A., 1962, *British Economic Growth, 1688–1959*, Cambridge: CUP.

Dell, R.F., 1962, 'The Building of County Hall Lewes 1808–12', *Sussex Archaeological Collections*, Vol. 100.

Digby, A., 1978, *Pauper Palaces*, London: Routledge & Kegan Paul.

Dunbabin, J.P.D., 1974, *Rural Discontent in Nineteenth Century Britain*, London: Faber.

Dunkley, P., 1981, 'Whigs and Paupers; the Reform of the English Poor Laws, 1830–1834', *Journal of British Studies*, 20.

Durrenberger, E. Paul, 1982, 'Chayanov and Marx', *Peasant Studies*, Vol. 9, No. 2.

Durrenberger, E. Paul, and Tannenbaum, Nicola, 1979, 'A Reassessment of Chayanov and his Recent Critics', *Peasant Studies*, Vol. 8, No. 1.

Dutt, M., 1966, 'The Agricultural Labourers' Revolt of 1830 in Kent, Surrey and Sussex' (unpublished Ph.D. thesis, University of London).

Edsall, N.C., 1971, *The Anti-Poor Law Movement*, Manchester: Manchester University Press.

Emsley, C., 1979, *British Society and the French Wars, 1793–1815*, London: Macmillan.

Ennew, Judith, Hirst, Paul, and Keith Tribe, 1977, '"Peasantry" as an Economic Category', *Journal of Peasant Studies*, Vol. 4, No. 4.

Evans, E.J., 1975, 'Some Reasons for the Growth of English Rural Anti-Clericalism, 1750–1850', *Past and Present*, No. 66.

Evans, N., 1985, *The East Anglian Linen Industry*, Aldershot: Gower.

Everitt, A., 1979, 'Country, County and Town; Patterns of Regional Evolution in England', *Transactions of the Royal Historical Society*, 5th ser. No. 29.

Everitt, Alan, 1972, *The Pattern of Rural Dissent: The Nineteenth Century*, Leicester: Leicester University Press.

Farrant, J.H. 1976, 'The Seaboard Trade of Sussex 1720–1845', *Sussex Archaeological Collections*, Vol. 114.

Farrant, S. 1979, 'The Building of Stanmer House and the Early Development of the Park 1720–50', *Sussex Archaeological Collections*, Vol. 117.

Flinn, M.W., 1970, *British Population Growth, 1700–1850*, London: Macmillan.

Fox, N.E. 1978, 'The Spread of the Threshing Machine in Central Southern England', *Agricultural History Review*, Vol. 26.

Franklin, S.H., 1965, 'Systems of Production: Systems of Appropriation', *Pacific Viewpoint*, Vol. 6.

Fraser, D. (ed.), 1976, *The New Poor Law in the Nineteenth Century*, London: Macmillan.

Fraser, D. 1976, 'The Poor Law as a Political Institution', in D. Fraser (ed.), *The New Poor Law in the Nineteenth Century*, London: Macmillan.

Friedmann, Harriet, 1978a, 'World Market, State, and Family Farm: Social Bases of Household Production in the Era of Wage Labour', *Comparative Studies in Society and History*, Vol. 20.

Friedmann, Harriet, 1978b, 'Simple Commodity Production and Wage Labour in the American Plains', *Journal of Peasant Studies*, Vol. 7, No. 2.

Friedmann, Harriet, 1980, 'Household Production and the National Economy: Concepts for the Analysis of Agrarian Formations', *Journal of Peasant Studies*, Vol. 7, No. 2.

Furley, R., 1874, *A History of the Weald of Kent*, 2 vols, Ashford.

Fussell, G.E., 1968, *The Dairy Farmer, 1500–1900*, London: Frank Cass.

George, M.D., 1966, *London Life in the Eighteenth Century*, London: Peregrine.

Gibbon Peter, and Neocosmos, Michael, 1985, 'Some Problems in the Political Economy of "African Socialism"', in Henry Bernstein and B.K. Campbell (eds.), *Contradictions of Accumulation in Africa: Studies in Economy and State*, Beverley Hills: Sage.

Gibson, M., 1978, 'The Treatment of the Poor in Surrey under the Operation of the New Poor Law between 1834 and 1871' (unpublished Ph.D. thesis, University of Surrey).

Gilboy, E.W., 1934, *Wages in Eighteenth Century England*, New York: Russell & Russell.

Glen, R., 1984, *Urban Workers in the Early Industrial Revolution*, London: Croom Helm.

Glyde, J., 1894, *Suffolk in the Nineteenth Century*, London.

Goddard, H., 1956, *Memoirs of a Bow Street Runner*, London.

Grover, R.J., 1980, 'The Land Tax in East Kent: A Study in Landownership and Occupation with Special Reference to the Methodological Implications of the Land Tax Assessment' (unpublished M.Phil thesis, University of Kent.)

Hammond, J.L. and B., 1911, *The Village Labourer*, London: Longmans.

Hammond, J.L. and B., 1966, *The Village Labourer*, London: Longmans.

Harber, J., 1972, 'Rural Incendiarism in Suffolk, 1840–1845' (unpublished M.A. thesis, University of Essex).

Hardy, le, W. (ed.) 1935, *Hertfordshire County Records: Calendar to the Quarter Sessions Minute Books, 1752–1798*, Hertford: Hertfordshire County Council.

Hare, Augustus J., 1874, *Memorials of a Quiet Life*, Vol. 1, London: W. Isbister.

Harris, Edwin A., 1912, *Angmering: A Study Written Expressly for Working Men*, Littlehampton.

Hart, J., 1956, 'The Reform of the Borough Police 1835–56', *English Historical Review*, Vol. 70.

Hasbach, W., 1908, *A History of the English Agricultural Labourer*, London: P. S. King.

Henderson, H.C.K., 1952, 'The 1801 Crop Returns for Sussex', *Sussex Archaeological Collections*, Vol. 90.

Henretta, James A., 1978, 'Families and Farms: "Mentalité" in Pre-Industrial America', *The William and Mary Quarterly*, Third Ser., Vol. 35.

Henretta, James A., 1980, 'Reply to James T. Lemon', *The William and Mary Quarterly*, Third Ser., Vol. 37.

Hill, Christopher, 1942, Review of V.M. Lavrovsky, *Parliamentary Enclosure of the Common Fields in England at the End of the Eighteenth and Beginning of the Nineteenth Century*, *Economic History Review*, 1st ser., Vol. 12.

Hobsbawm, E.J., 1969, *Industry and Empire*, Harmondsworth: Penguin.

Hobsbawm, E.J., 1974, 'Peasant Land Occupations', *Past and Present*, No. 62.

Hobsbawm E.J., and Rudé, George, 1973, *Captain Swing*, Harmondsworth: Penguin.

Holderness, B.A. 1972, '"Open" and "Close" Parishes in England in the Eighteenth and Nineteenth Centuries', *Agricultural History Review*, Vol. 20.

Holderness, B.A., 1975, 'Credit in a Rural Community 1660–1800: Some Neglected Aspects of Probate Inventories', *Midland History*, Vol. 3 No. 2.

Holderness, B.A., 1981, 'The Victorian Farmer', in G.E. Mingay (ed.), *The Victorian Countryside*, London: Routledge & Kegan Paul.

Home, Michael, 1943, *Autumn Fields*, London: Methuen.

Horn, Pamela, 1971, *Joseph Arch, 1826–1919: The Farm Workers' Leader*, Kineton: Roundwood Press.

Horn, Pamela, 1976, *Labouring Life in the Victorian Countryside*, Dublin: Gill & Macmillan.

Horn, Pamela, 1980, *The Rural World 1780–1850: Social Change in the English Countryside*, London: Hutchinson.

Horn, Pamela, 1982, 'An Eighteenth-Century Land Agent: The Career of Nathaniel Kent (1737–1810), *Agricultural History Review*, Vol. 30 Pt. 1.

Horn, Pamela, 1984, *The Changing Countryside in Victorian and Edwardian England and Wales*, London: Athlone Press.

Horn, Pamela, 1987, *Life and Labour in Rural England 1760–1850*, London: Macmillan.

Hoskins, W.G., 1957, *The Midland Peasant: The Economic and Social History of a Leicestershire Village*, London: Macmillan.

Howkins, Alun, 1977, 'Structural Conflict and the Farm Worker: Norfolk, 1900–1920', *Journal of Peasant Studies*, Vol. 4, No. 3.

Howkins, Alun, 1985, *Poor Labouring Men: Rural Radicalism in Norfolk 1870–1920*, London: Routledge & Kegan Paul.

Huckel, G., 1976, 'English Farming Profits during the Napoleonic Wars, 1793–1815', *Explorations in Economic History*, Vol. 13.

Huzel, J.P., 1976, 'A Quantative Approach to the Agricultural Labourers' Riots of 1830 in Kent' (abstract), *Peasant Studies*, Vol. 5.

Huzel, J.P., 1975, 'Aspects of the Old Poor Law, Population and Agrarian Protest in early Nineteenth-Century England, with Particular Reference to the County of Kent' (unpublished Ph.D. thesis, University of Kent).

John, A.H., 1967, 'Farming in Wartime, 1793–1815', in G.E. Mingay and E.L. Jones (eds.), *Land, Labour and Population in the Industrial Revolution*, London: Edward Arnold.

Jones, D. J. V. 1976, 'Thomas Campbell Foster and the Rural Labourer: Incendiarism in East Anglia in the 1840s', *Social History*, Vol. 1.

Jones, E.L., 1965, 'The Agricultural Labour Market in England, 1793–1872', *Economic History Review*, 2nd ser. Vol. 17.

Jones, E.L., 1975, 'The Constraints on Economic Growth in Southern England', *Third International Conference of Economic History*, Paris.

Karsky, Barbara, 1983, 'Le Paysan Americain et la Terre a la fin du XVIIIe Siecle', *Annales ESC*.

Kebbel, Thomas Edward, 1907, *The Agricultural Labourer: A Summary of his Position*, London: Swan Sonnenschein.

Kent, J.H., 1844, *Remarks on the Injuriousness of the Consolidation of Small Farms and the Benefit of Small Occupations and Allotments; with some Observations on the Past and the Present State of the Agricultural Labourer. On the Physical and Moral Condition of the Agricultural Labourer*, Bury St, Edmunds.

Kenyon, G.H., 1958, 'Petworth Town and Trades, 1610–1760', Part I, *Sussex Archaeological Collections*, Vol. 96.

Kerr, B. 1962, 'The Dorset Agricultural Labourer 1750–1850', *Proceedings of the Dorset Natural History and Archaeological Society*, Vol. 84

Knott, J., 1986, *Popular Opposition to the 1834 Poor Law*, London: Croom Helm.

Kussmaul, Ann, 1981, *Servants in Husbandry in Early-Modern England*, Cambridge: Cambridge University Press.

Kussmaul, A., (ed.), 1986, 'The Autobigraphy of Joseph Mayett of Quainton 1783–1839', *Bedfordshire Record Society*, Vol. 23.

Lance, E.J., *The Hop Farmer, or a Complete Account of the Hop Culture*, London: J. Ridgeway.

Landau, N., 1984, *The Justices of the Peace, 1679–1760*, London: University of California Press.

Langare, D.N., 1977, 'Agrarian Conflict, Religion and Politics: The Mophah Rebellions in Malabar in the Nineteenth and Early Twentieth Centuries', *Past and Present*, No. 74.

Laurance, E., 1731, *The Duty and Office of a Land Steward* (2nd edition), London: John Shuckbrugh.

Leeds, Anthony, 1977, 'Mythos and Pathos: Some Unpleasantries on Peasantries', in R. Halperin and J.Dow (eds.), *Peasant Livelihood: Studies in Economic Anthropology and Cultural Ecology*, New York: St. Martin's Press.

Lemaître, Georges, 1931, *Le Weald des Comtes de Kent, Surrey, Sussex, Hampshire: Etudes de Geographie Economique et Humaine*, Paris: Presses Universitaires de France.

Lemon, James T., 1980, 'Comment on James A. Henretta's "Families and Farms: Mentalité in Pre-industrial America"', *The William and Mary Quarterly*, Third Ser., Vol. 37.

Lenin, V.I., 1966, 'Preliminary Draft Theses on the Agrarian Question', *Collected Works*, Vol. 29, Moscow: Progress Publishers.

Littlejohn, Gary, 1977, 'Peasant Economy and Society', in Barry Hindess (ed.), *Sociological Theories of the Economy*, London: Macmillan.

Llambi, Luis, 1988, 'Small Modern Farmers: Neither Peasants nor Fully-Fledged Capitalists? A Theoretical and Historical Discussion', *Journal of Peasant Studies*, Vol. 15, No. 3.

Lowerson, J.R., 1977, 'The Aftermath of Swing; Anti-Poor Law Movements and Rural Trades Unions in the South-East', subsequently published in Charlesworth [1983].

Lowerson, J., 1980, *A Short History of Sussex*, Folkestone: Dawson.

MacDonald, S., 1975, 'The Progress of the Early Threshing Machine', *Agricultural History Review*, Vol. 23.

MacDonald, S., 1978, 'Further Progress with the Early Threshing Machine; a Rejoinder', *Agricultural History Review*, Vol. 26.

MacMahon, K.A., 1964, *Roads and Turnpike Trusts in the East Riding of Yorkshire*, East Yorkshire Local History Series, No. 18.

Mackie, C., 1901, *Norfolk Annals*, Norwich: Norwich Chronicle.

Malcolmson, R.W., 1981, *Life and Labour in England 1700–1780*, London: Hutchinson.

Malthus, T.R., 1807, 'A Letter to Samuel Whitbread, Esq. MP', in D.V. Glass (ed.), *Introduction to Malthus* (1953), London: Watts.

Marlow, J., 1974, *The Tolpuddle Martyrs*, London: Panther.

Marshall, J.D. 1968, *The Old Poor Law, 1795–1834*, London: Macmillan.

Martin, E.W. 1972, 'From Parish to Union: Poor Law Administration, 1601–1834', in E.W. Martin (ed.), *Comparative Development in Social Welfare*, London: George, Allen & Unwin.

Martin, J.M. 1964, 'The Cost of Parliamentary Enclosure in Warwickshire', in E.L. Jones (ed.), *Agriculture and Economic Growth in England, 1650–1815* (1967), London: Methuen.

Martin, J.M., 1984, 'Village Traders and the Emergence of a Proletariat in South Warwickshire, 1750–1851', *Agricultural History Review*, Vol. 32.

Marx, Karl, 1973, *Capital* Vol. 1, Harmondsworth: Penguin.

Melling, E. (ed.), 1964, *Kentish Sources; the Poor*, Maidstone: Kent County Council.

Merrill, Michael, 1977, '"Cash is Good to Eat": Self-Sufficency and Exchange in the Rural Economy of the United States', *Radical History Review*, No. 16.

Merrill, Michael, 1979–80, 'So What's Wrong with the "Household Mode of Production"', *Radical History Review*, No. 22.

Merrill, Michael, 1985, 'Gifts, Barter and Commerce in Early America: An Ethnology of Exchange' (unpublished paper presented to the 78th Annual Convention of the Organisation of American Historians, Minneapolis).

Mills, D.R., 1963, 'Landownership and Rural Population with Special Reference to Leicestershire in the Mid-19th. Century' (unpublished Ph.D. thesis, University of Leicester).

Mills, Dennis R., 1974, 'The Peasant Tradition', *Local Historian*, Vol. 11.

Mills, D.R., 1979, 'The Court of Arches and Church Rates Disputes as Sources of Social History', *Bulletin of Local History: East Midland Region*, Vol. 14.

Mills, Dennis R., 1980, *Lord and Peasant in Nineteenth-Century Britain*, London: Croom Helm.

Mills, D.R., and Short, B.M., 1983, 'Social Change and Social Conflict in Nineteenth-Century England: The Use of the Open-Closed Village Model', *Journal of Peasant Studies*, Vol. 10, No. 4.

Mills, Dennis R., 1984, 'The Nineteenth-Century Peasantry of Melbourn, Cambridgeshire', in Richard M. Smith (ed.), *Land, Kinship and Lifecycle*, Cambridge, Cambridge University Press.

Mills, D.R., 1988, 'Peasants and Conflict in Nineteenth-Century Rural England: A Comment on Two Recent Articles', *Journal of Peasant Studies*, Vol. 15, No. 3.

Mills, Joan and Dennis, 1988, 'Rural Mobility in the Victorian Censuses: Experience with a

Micro-Computer Program', *Local Historian*, Aug.

Mingay, G.E., 1956, 'The Agricultural Depression 1730–50', in E.M. Carus-Wilson (ed.), *Essays in Economic History*, 3 vols. (1954–62), II, London: Edward Arnold.

Mingay, G.E., 1961–62, 'The Size of Farms in the Eighteenth Century', *Economic History Review*, 2nd ser. Vol. 14.

Mingay, G.E., 1963, *English Landed Society in the Eighteenth Century*, London: Routledge & Kegan Paul.

Mingay, G.E., 1968, *Enclosure and the Small Farmer in the Age of the Industrial Revolution*, London: Macmillan.

Mintz, Sidney, 1973, 'A Note on the Definition of Peasantries', *Journal of Peasant Studies*, Vol. 1, No. 1.

Mitchell, B.R.,1962, *Abstract of British Historical Statistics*, Cambridge: Cambridge University Press.

Mosley, John V., 1975, 'Poor Law Administration in England and Wales 1834–1850: with Special Reference to the Problem of Able-Bodied Pauperism' (unpublished Ph.D. thesis, University of London).

Munsche, P.B. 1981, *Gentlemen and Poachers; the English Game Laws 1671–1831*, Cambridge: Cambridge University Press.

Muskett, P., 1984, 'The East Anglian Agrarian Riots of 1822', *Agricultural History Review*, Vol. 32.

Neale, K. (ed.), 1975, *Victorian Horsham: the Diary of Henry Michell 1809–74*, Chichester: Phillimore.

Neeson, J.M., 1984, 'The Opponents of Enclosure in Eighteenth-Century Northamptonshire', *Past and Present*, No. 105.

Neeson, J.M., 1977, 'Common Right and Enclosure in Eighteenth-Century Northamptonshire' (unpublished Ph.D. thesis, University of Warwick).

Neuman, M., 1969, 'A Suggestion Respecting the Origins of the Speenhamland Plan', *English Historical Review*, Vol. 86.

Neuman, M., 1972, 'Speenhamland in Berkshire', in E.W. Martin (ed.), *Comparative Development in Social Welfare*, London: George Allen & Unwin.

Neuman, M., 1982, *The Speenhamland County; Poverty and the Poor Laws in Berkshire 1782–1834*, London: Garland.

Norman, P., 1900, 'Notes on Bromley and the Neighbourhood', *Archaeologia Cantiana*, Vol. 24.

Northbrook, Earl of (ed.), 1905, *Journals and Correspondence of Francis Thornhill Baring, Lord Northbrook*, 2 vols., Winchester: privately printed.

Obelkevitch, James, 1976, *Religion and Rural Society: South Lindsey 1825–1875*, Oxford: Clarendon Press.

Olney, R.J. (ed.), 1975, *Labouring Life in the Lincolnshire Wolds: A Study of Binbrook in the Mid-Nineteenth Century*, Society for Lincolnshire History and Archaeology, Occasional Paper, No. 2.

Oxley, G.W., 1974, *Poor Relief in England and Wales 1601–1834*, London: David & Charles.

Patmore, C., 1885, *How I Managed and Improved My Estate*, London.

Peacock, A.J., 1965, *Bread or Blood: the Agrarian Riots in East Anglia: 1816*, London: Gollancz.

Perkin, H., 1969, *The Origins of Modern English Society, 1780–1880*, London: Routledge & Kegan Paul.

Perkins, J.A., 1976–7, 'Harvest Technology and Labour Supply in Lincolnshire in the Mid-Nineteenth Century', *Tools and Tillage*, Vol. 3.

Phythian-Adams, Charles, 1987, *Re-thinking English Local History*, Leicester: Leicester University Press.

Poulantzas, Nicos, 1978, *Classes in Contemporary Capitalism*, London: Verso.

Poynter, J.R., 1969, *Society and Pauperism; English Ideas on Poor Relief, 1795–1834*, London: Routledge & Kegan Paul.

Pruitt, Bettye Hobbs, 1984, 'Self-sufficency and the Agricultural Economy of Eighteenth-century Massachussetts', *The William and Mary Quarterly*, Third Series, Vol. 41.

Radzinowicz, L., 1948–85, *A History of the English Criminal Law and its Administration from 1750*, 5 Vols., London: Stephens.

Razzell, P., 1978, *The Conquest of Smallpox*, Hassocks: Harvester Press.

Reay, Barry, forthcoming, Review of Alan Armstrong, Farmworkers: A Social and Economic History 1770–1980, *Journal of Peasant Studies*.

Reed, Mick, 1982, and Economic Relations in a Wealden Community: Lodsworth 1780–1860' (unpublished M.A. thesis, University of Sussex).

Reed, Mick, 1984a, 'Social Change and Social Conflict in Nineteenth-century England: A Comment', *Journal of Peasant Studies*, Vol. 12, No. 1.

Reed, Mick, 1984b, 'The Peasantry of Nineteenth-Century Rural England: A Neglected Class?', *History Workshop*, 18.

Reed, Mick 1985, 'Indoor Farm Service in 19th-Century Sussex: Some Criticisms of a Critique', *Sussex Archaeological Collections*, Vol. 123.

Reed, Mick, 1986, 'Nineteenth-Century Rural England: A case for "Peasant Studies"?', *Journal of Peasant Studies*, Vol 14, No. 1.

Reed, Mick, 1987, ' "Gnawing it Out": Neighbourhood Exchange in Nineteenth-century Rural England' (unpublished paper presented to The Southern History Society Conference, University of Sussex).

Richardson, J.L., 1977, 'The Standard of Living Controversy, 1790–1850, with Specific Reference to Agricultural Labourers in Seven English Counties' (unpublished Ph.D. thesis, University of Hull).

Roberts, B., 1986, 'Rural Settlements' in J. Langton and R.J. Morris [eds.], *Atlas of Industrializing Britain, 1780–1914*, London: Methuen.

Roberts, D., 1979. *Paternalism in Early Victorian England*, London: Routledge & Kegan Paul.

Rose, G., 1805, *Observations on the Poor Laws and the Management of the Poor in Great Britain*, London.

Rose, M. (ed.), 1970, *The English Poor Law, 1780–1930*, London: David & Charles.

Rose, M., 1972, *The Relief of Poverty 1834–1914*, London: Macmillan.

Rose, M. (ed.), 1985, *The Poor and the City: the English Poor Law in its Urban Context*, Leicester: Leicester University Press.

Rose, Walter, 1942, *Good Neighbours*, Cambridge: Cambridge University Press.

Rotenberg, Winifred J., 1981, 'The Market and Massachussetts Farmers 1750–1855', *Journal of Economic History*, Vol. 45.

Rudé, G. 1978, *Protest and Punishment; the Story of the Social and Political Protesters Transported to Australia, 1788–1868*, Oxford: Oxford University Press.

Rudé, G., 1981, Review of Charlesworth [1979], *Journal of Historical Geography*, Vol. 7.

Rudé, G. 1985, *Criminal and Victim; Crime and Society in early Nineteenth-Century England*, Oxford: Oxford University Press.

Rudge, T., 1805, *A General View of the Agriculture of the County of Gloucester*, London: Board of Agriculture.

Rule, J.G., 1979, 'Social Crime in the Rural South in the Eighteenth and Nineteenth Centuries', *Southern History*, Vol. 1.

Rule, J.G., 1982, 'The Manifold Causes of Rural Crime: Sheep-Stealing in England c. 1740–1840', in Rule (ed.), *Outside the Law: Studies in Crime and Order 1650–1850*, Exeter: University of Exeter Press.

Rule, J.G., 1986, *The Labouring Classes in Early Industrial England, 1750–1850*, London: Longmans.

Samuel, R., 1975, 'Village Labour', in R. Samuel (ed.), *Village Life and Labour*, London: Routledge & Kegan Paul.

Samuel, Raphael, (ed.), 1975, *Village Life and Labour*, London: Routledge & Kegan Paul.

Samuel, R., 1977, 'Mineral Workers', in R. Samuel (ed.), *Miners, Quarrymen and Saltworkers*, London: Routledge & Kegan Paul.

Saville, J., 1952, *Ernest Jones, Chartist*, London: Lawrence & Wishart.

Saville, John, 1969, 'Primitive Accumulation and Early Industrialisation in Britain',

Socialist Register.

Scott, Alison MacEwen, 1986, 'Rethinking Petty Commodity Production', *Social Analysis* Special Issues Series, No. 20.

Scott, James, 1985, *Weapons of the Weak*, New Haven, CT: Yale University Press.

Searle, Charles, 1983, ' "The Odd Corner of England": A Study of a Rural Social Formation in Transition, Cumbria c. 1700 to c. 1914' (unpublished Ph.D. thesis, University of Essex).

Shammas, Carole, 1982, 'How Self-Sufficent was Early America', *Journal of Interdisciplinary History*, Vol. 13.

Shanin, Teodor, 1979, 'Defining Peasants: Conceptulizations and De-conceptualizations Old and New in a Marxist Debate', *Peasant Studies*, Vol. 8, No. 4.

Shelton, W.J., 1973, *English Hunger and Industrial Disorders*, London: Macmillan.

Short, B.M., 1976, 'The Turnover of Tenants on the Ashburnham Estate, 1830–1850', *Sussex Archaeological Collections*, Vol. 113.

Short, B.M., 1979, 'Landownership in Relation to Demographic and Agricultural Change in the Eighteenth and Nineteenth Century Weald', in M.D.G. Wanklyn (ed.), *Landownership and Power in the Regions*, Wolverhampton.

Short, B.M., 1982, ' "The Art and Craft of Chicken Cramming": Poultry in the Weald of Sussex 1850–1950', *Agricultural History Review*, Vol. 30.

Short, B.M., 1983, 'The Changing Rural Society and Economy of Sussex 1750–1945', in Geography Editorial Committee, *Sussex: Environment, Landscape and Society*, Gloucester: Alan Sutton.

Short, B.M., 1984, 'The Decline of Living-in Servants in the Transition to Capitalist Farming: A Critique of the Sussex Evidence', *Sussex Archaeological Collections*, Vol. 122.

Short, B.M., 1984, 'The South-East: Kent, Surrey, and Sussex', in J. Thirsk (ed.), *The Agrarian History of England and Wales, V*, 2 vols., Cambridge: Cambridge University Press.

Short, Brian, and Reed, Mick, 1987, *Landownership and Society in Edwardian England and Wales: The Finance (1909–10) Act 1910 Records*, Falmer: University of Sussex.

Sider, Gerald M., 1986, *Culture and Class in Anthropology and Hisstory: A Newfoundland Illustration*, Cambridge: Cambridge University Press.

Smith, Carl A., 1984a, 'Does a Commodity Economy Enrich the Few while Ruining the Masses? Differentiation among Petty Commodity Producers in Guatamala', *Journal of Peasant Studies*, Vol. 11, No. 3.

Smith, Carol A., 1983, 'Regional Analysis in World-System Perspective: A Critique of Three structural Theories of Uneven development', in S. Ortiz (ed.), *Economic Anthropology: Topics and Theories*, New York: University Press of America.

Smith, Carol A., 1984b, 'Forms of Production in Practice: Fresh Approaches to Simple Commodity Production', *Journal of Peasant Studies*, Vol. 11, No. 4.

Smith, Carol A., 1984c, 'Labour and International Capital in the Making of a Peripheral Social Formation: Economic Transformations in Guatamala 1850–1980', in C. Bergquist (ed.), *Labor in the Capitalist World Economy*, Beverley Hills: Sage.

Smith, E., 1971, *Victorian Farnham: the Story of a Surrey Town 1837–1901*, Chichester: Phillimore.

Snell, K.D.M. 1985, *Annals of the Labouring Poor: Social Change and Agrarian England 1660–1900*, Cambridge: Cambridge University Press.

Spater, G. 1982, *William Cobbett; the Poor Man's Friend*, 2 vols., Cambridge: Cambridge University Press.

Spring, David, 1963, *The English Landed Estate in the Nineteenth Century: Its Administration*, Baltimore, MD : John Hopkins Press.

Steedman, C., 1984, *Policing the Victorian Community; the Formation of English Provincial Police Forces 1856–80*, London: Routledge & Kegan Paul.

Stevenson, J., 1974, 'Food Riots in England, 1792–1818, in J. Stevenson and R. Quinault (eds.), *Popular Protest and Public Order*, London: George Allen & Unwin.

Stevenson, William, 1813, *General View of the Agriculture of the County of Surrey*,

London: Board of Agriculture.

Tate, W.E., 1946, *The Parish Chest*, Cambridge: Cambridge University Press.

Tate, W.E., 1952, 'The Cost of Parliamentary Enclosure in England', *Economic History Review*, 2nd ser. Vol. 5.

Te Brake, N., 1981, 'Revolution and the Rural Community in the Eastern Netherlands', in C. and L.Tilly (eds.), *Class Conflict and Collective Action*, New York: Sage.

Thirsk, Joan, 1975, 'The Peasant Economy of England in the Seventeenth Century', *Studia Oeconomicae*, Vol. 10.

Thompson, E.P., 1967, 'Land of our Fathers', *Times Literary Supplement*, 16 Feb.

Thompson, E.P., 1968, *The Making of the English Working Class*, Harmondsworth: Penguin.

Thompson, E.P., 1971, 'The "Moral Economy" of the English Crowd in the Eighteenth Century', *Past and Present*, No. 50.

Thompson, E.P., 1974, 'Patrician Society, Plebeian Culture', *Journal of Social History*, I.

Thompson, E.P., 1974, Review of Shelton (1973), in *Economic History Review*, 2nd ser. Vol. 27.

Thompson, E.P., 1975, 'The Crime of Anonymity', in D. Hay, P. Linebaugh and E.P. Thompson (eds.), *Albion's Fatal Tree*, London: Allen Lane.

Thompson, E.P., 1978a, 'Eighteenth-Century English Society: Class Struggle without Class', *Social History*, Vol. 3.

Thompson, E.P., 1978b, Review of Rudé, 1978, *New Society*, 14 Dec.

Thompson, E.P., 1978c, 'The Peculiarities of the English', in E.P. Thompson, *The Poverty of Theory and Other Essays*, London: Merlin.

Thompson, F.M.L., 1976, 'A Terminological Confusion Confounded', *Economic History Review*, 2nd Ser., Vol. 24.

Thompson, Flora, 1945, *Lark Rise to Candleford*, Oxford: Oxford University Press.

Tomlinson, H.C., 1976, 'Wealden Gunfounding: An Analysis of its Demise in the Eighteenth Century', *Economic History Review*, 2nd Ser., Vol. 29.

Torr, Cecil, 1979, *Small Talk in Wreyland*, Oxford: Oxford University Press..

Tufnell, E.C., 1842, *On the Dwellings and General Economy of the Labouring Classes in Kent and Sussex*, London.

Turner, M.E., 1973, 'The Cost of Parliamentary Enclosure in Buckinghamshire', *Agricultural History Review*, 21.

Turner, M.E., 1975, 'Parliamentary Enclosure and Landownership Change in Buckinghamshire', *Economic History Review*, 2nd ser. XXVIII.

Turner, M.E., 1988, 'Economic Protest in Rural Society: Opposition to Parliamentary Enclosure in Buckinghamshire', *Southern History*, Vol. 11.

Turner M.E. and D. Mills (eds.), 1986, *Land and Property: The English Land Tax 1692–1832*, Gloucester: Alan Sutton.

Turner, R., 1862, 'Petworth', *Sussex Archaeological Collections*, Vol. 14.

Vaisey, D. (ed.), 1984, *The Diary of Thomas Turner, 1754–1765*, Oxford: Clarendon Press.

Vancouver, Charles, 1813, *General View of the Agriculture of the County of Hampshire*, London: Board of Agriculture.

Victoria County History, 1948, *Cambridgeshire*, Vol. II.

Walker, D., 1795, *A General View of the Agriculture of the County of Hertford*, London: Board of Agriculture.

Walter, J.R., 1976, 'Aspects of Agrarian Change. Oxfordshire 1750–1880' (unpublished D.Phil. thesis, University of Oxford).

Wearmouth, R.F., 1945, *Methodism and the Common People of the Eighteenth Century*, London: Epworth Press.

Wells, R.A.E., 1977a, 'The Revolt of the South-west, 1800–1: A Study in English Popular Protest', *Social History*, Vol. 6.

Wells, R.A.E., 1977b, *Dearth and Distress in Yorkshire, 1793–1802*, Borthwick Papers, No. 52, University of York.

Wells, R.A.E., 1978, 'The Grain Crises in England, 1794–96, 1799–1801' (unpublished D.Phil. thesis, University of York).

Wells, R., 1978, 'Counting Riots in Eighteenth-Century England', *Bulletin of the Society for the Study of Labour History*, No. 37.

Wells, Roger A.E., 1979, 'The Development of the English Rural Proletariat and Social Protest 1700–1850', *Journal of Peasant Studies*, Vol. 6, No. 2.

Wells, Roger A.E., 1981, 'Social Conflict and Protest in the English Countryside in the Early-Nineteenth Century: A Rejoinder', *Journal of Peasant Studies*, Vol. 8, No. 4.

Wells, R., 1982, 'The Militia Mutinies of 1795', in J.G. Rule (ed.), *Outside the Law: Studies in Crime and Order 1650–1850*, Exeter: University of Exeter Press.

Wells, R.A.E., 1984, 'Sheep-Stealing in Yorkshire in the Age of the Industrial and Agricultural Revolutions', *Northern History*, Vol. 20.

Wells, R., 1985a, 'Resistance to the New Poor Law in Southern England', in M. Chase (ed.), *The New Poor Law*, Middlesborough: University of Leeds.

Wells, R., 1985b, 'Rural Rebels in Southern England in the 1830s', in C. Emsley and J. Walvin (eds.), *Artisans, Peasants and Proletarians 1760–1860*, London: Croom Helm.

Wells, R., 1985c, Review of Howkins [1985], in *Agricultural History Review*, Vol. 33.

Wells, R., 1988a, 'Tolpuddle in the Context of English Agrarian Labour History 1780–1850', in J.G. Rule (ed.), *British Trade Unionism; the Formative Years 1750–1850*, London: Longmans.

Wells, R., 1988b, *Wretched Faces; Famine in Wartime England 1793–1801*, Gloucester: Alan Sutton.

Wells, R., forthcoming, 'Popular Protest and Social Crime: the Evidence of Criminal Gangs in Southern England 1790–1860', in B. Stapleton (ed.), *Conflict and Community in Southern England*, Gloucester: Alan Sutton.

Wells, Roger, 1989, 'Social Protest, Class, Conflict and Consciousness in the English Countryside, 1700–1880', in M. Reed and R. Wells (eds.), *Class, Conflict and Protest in the English Countryside, 1700–1880*, London: Frank Cass.

Wessman, James W., 1979–80, 'A Household Mode of Production: Another Comment', *Radical History Review*, No. 22.

Western, J.R., 1956, 'The Volunteer Movement as an Anti-Revolutionary Force, 1793–1801', *English Historical Review*, Vol. 71.

Western, J.R., 1965, *The English Militia in the Eighteenth Century*, London: Routledge & Kegan Paul.

White, A. (ed.), 1891, *The Letters of S.G.O.*, London.

Wilks, A.R., 1980, 'Adjustments in Arable Farming after the Napoleonic Wars', *Agricultural History Review*, Vol. 28.

Williams, D.E., 1976, 'Were "Hunger" Rioters Really Hungry? Some Demographic Evidence', *Past and Present*, No. 71.

Williams, D.E., 1984, 'Morals, Markets and the English Crowd in 1766', *Past and Present*, No. 104.

Wilmshurst, I., 1985, 'A Microstudy of the "Captain Swing" Revolt in the Villages of Bosham and Funtington' (unpublished B.A. finals dissertation, CNAA, Humanities Department, Brighton Polytechnic).

Wilson, J.M., 1870 and 1875, *The Imperial Gazetteer of England and Wales*, London.

Winstanley, Michael, 1978, *Life in Kent at the Turn of the Century*, Folkestone: Dawson.

Winter, Michael, 1984, 'Agrarian Class Structure and Family Farming', in Tony Bradley and Phillip Lowe (eds.), *Locality and Rurality: Economy and Society in Rural Regions*, Norwich: Geo Books.

Winter, Michael, 1986, 'The Development of Family Farming in West Devon in the Nineteenth Century', in G. Cox, P. Lowe, and M. Winter (eds.), *Agriculture: People and Policies*, London: Allen and Unwin.

Wordie, J.R., 1974, 'Social Change on the Leveson-Gower Estates, 1714–1832', *Economic History Review*, 2nd ser. Vol. 27.

Wrigley, E.A., 1967, 'A Simple Model of London's Importance in Changing English Society and Economy, 1650–1750', *Past and Present*, Vol. 37.

Wrigley, E.A., 1986, 'Men on the Land and Men in the Countryside: Employment in Agriculture in Early-Nineteenth-Century England', in L. Bonfield. R.M. Smith and K.

Wrightson (eds.),*The World We Have Gained: Histories of Population and Social Structure*, Oxford: Blackwell.

Young, A., 1812, *An Enquiry into the Progressive Value of Money in England*, London.

Young, A., 1815, *An Enquiry into the Rise of Prices in Europe*, London.